Practical Corporate Planning

Practical
Corporate Planning

JOHN ARGENTI

UNWIN
PAPERBACKS

LONDON SYDNEY WELLINGTON

First published in Great Britain by
George Allen & Unwin 1980, sixth impression 1987

Revised edition published in paperback by
Unwin® Paperbacks, an imprint of Unwin Hyman Limited, in 1989

UNWIN HYMAN LIMITED
15/17 Broadwick Street, London W1V 1FP

Allen & Unwin Australia Pty Ltd
8 Napier Street, North Sydney, NSW 2060,
Australia

Allen & Unwin New Zealand Ltd with the Port Nicholson Press,
60 Cambridge Terrace, Wellington, New Zealand

British Library Cataloguing in Publication Data

Argenti, John
  Practical corporate planning.—Rev. ed.
  1. Corporate planning
  I. Title
  658.4'012   HD30.28
  ISBN 0–04–658231–2

Typeset in 10 on 11 point Times by Computape (Pickering) Limited
North Yorkshire
and printed in Finland by Werner Söderström Oy.

To my wife

Contents

Introduction

This book is written for chief executives, managing directors, general managers, and all senior managers who would like to introduce corporate planning into their organizations.

It is a practical guide – no jargon, no mathematics, no advanced techniques. After an introductory chapter, to explain what corporate planning is, the book takes the reader straight through the corporate planning process, starting at the beginning and going on till it reaches the end, pointing out the pitfalls on the way. It is a cookbook: you are supposed to hold the book in one hand, so to speak, while you go through the process with the other.

Some academics and students of management evidently still believe that corporate planning is a very advanced concept requiring the setting up of full-blown departments complete with economists, computer specialists and other assorted acolytes all wielding fiendishly sophisticated management techniques. I hope this book will open their eyes to the practical realities of corporate planning.

A simple system

My approach is criticized for being naïve and simplistic. I take that as a compliment. What I have devised is a rough and ready, but highly systematic, process for looking at organizations in the round, as corporate entities. I am concerned with the overall shape of the forest, I am not in the least interested in cataloguing thousands of details about thousands of trees. Yes, it is naïve, it is simple, and it is consequently very powerful. The reason that it is naïve – that it has to be naïve – is as follows: strategic decisions are not difficult because they are complex, they are not difficult because of the vagaries of the long-term future (although these certainly do not help), the reason they are difficult is because of *feelings*. When one is talking about changing whole chunks of organizations, casting people out of work, shifting power from one department to another, cancelling much admired research programmes, launching risky projects, altering the articles of association, acquiring and disposing of companies, what one is up against is people's feelings, emotions, desires, obsessions, even passions.

To overcome this obstacle, this essentially and typically human obstacle, the conclusions emerging from a corporate planning process have to be irrefutable. They have to be seen to be correct and seemly, appropriate and right. If there is the slightest doubt about them in the minds of the executives who are going to put them into action, the plans will quite simply never see the light of day. When authors say that implementation is a major roadblock to strategic planning they are quite wrong; it is only so if the executives have not wholeheartedly embraced the strategies.

It therefore has to be plain beyond any doubt what their organization needs to do – plain, distinct, pellucid, sharp, clear and focused. There has to be a full acceptance among the top staff. The planning process has to come to conclusions of such devastating clarity that it breaks through these emotional barriers.

An integral process

I do not believe that directional policy matrices, computer models, assignment charts, or any of the dozens of other modern planning techniques, can inject the necessary level of belief and conviction into the average senior executive to be worth more than a passing mention in my book. No. It has to be something more convincing than mere technology.

This is not a textbook: I do not carry out a wide-ranging review of other authors' works and my pages are not festooned with learned footnotes. Instead, the book contains the practical lessons snatched by one specialist from a fairly long period of experience. As will be seen, I disagree with other authorities quite strongly. I think many of them went off the rails years ago and are still off them.

On the other hand, I have slotted some of their more useful techniques into certain parts of my system. This leads to my chief objection to them. What most of them have done, it seems to me, is to devise planning *techniques*; they have not developed what I hope this book describes – an entire, complete, planning *system*. This is what I mean by 'slotting in'; I have slotted some of their techniques into appropriate points in my overall system. Most of these techniques have limited, specialist application, whereas my system is a complete whole and works for organizations of virtually every type and size.

Its history and development

Two decades ago in the Introduction to my first book, *Corporate Planning – A Practical Guide*, I wrote: 'corporate planning can now be lifted out of the hands of its few high priests and placed in those of the average senior executive.' That was in 1968. The world has, admittedly, become more hostile and competitive since then, but managers today are far better trained and informed than they were then. I feel that my conclusion is even more valid now.

After that book was published I spent several years assisting companies with their corporate planning before writing another book, in 1974, and I then had several more years' experience with many more companies before publishing the first edition of *Practical Corporate Planning* in 1980. Each time I learnt a little more, made fewer mistakes and became increasingly confident that my approach did actually work. Although this second edition has been completely rewritten and greatly expanded, the method described here is essentially the same as the one in the 1980 edition – but I now see it far more clearly and positively.

I feel entirely confident, therefore, in recommending this approach to senior executives. The system of planning described here – it has come to be called the Argenti System of Corporate Planning – has now been used in hundreds of companies around the world (including everything from a Paris fashion house to a Latin American steel company) and, time after time, it yields the desired output: a set of practical corporate strategies which gains the enthusiastic agreement of the top management so that they set about the task of redirecting and rejuvenating their company with confidence and vigour.

Non-profit-making organizations

While the vast majority of organizations that use corporate planning are profit-making organizations – companies, in other words – a great many non-profit-making organizations are trying to use it.

Alas, they often fall at the first fence, where they try to decide their 'corporate objectives', and so they quickly become discouraged. Deciding corporate objectives for non-profit-making organizations is the last unconquered peak in the study of management.

It is a matter of great regret to me that this should be so. So much of the world's resources are devoted to these organizations (I imagine that well over half of the working population of the world works for non-profit-making organizations, far more than for companies) and so important are they in our society that I have, in this new edition, greatly extended the section on corporate objectives for non-profit-making organizations in the hope of saying something useful.

It would be a source of great personal satisfaction to me if this assists a few more of these valuable organiations to achieve the same standard of strategy formulation that is already available to companies. If it does, they will find they can use the remainder of the corporate planning process described here with much the same facility as companies.

The aim of the book

What I hope is that, having read this book, the top management of any company, of any size, in any sector of business – manufacturing, services, quasi-profit-making such as building societies and mutuals, and non-profit-making organizations as well – will be able to move through the corporate planning process and come out at the end with a strong, enthusiastic consensus as to the best new direction in which to take their organization.

Conventions and abbreviations

I shall use the following conventions and abbreviations throughout the book:

Cases. The examples in the book are based on real-life cases. However, in the interests of brevity I always simplify to such an extent that some distortion is inevitable and so I use pseudonyms rather than real names. As an added precaution, I always disguise the real company by changing the product, location, figures or whatever.

This is so even in the three major, detailed cases in the book. One of these, a national life assurance company, appears in sections at the end of chapters to illustrate the subject of each chapter, another in Appendix E to test the student, while the other, the most detailed of all, takes up the whole of Chapter 12. I hope these three complete examples will convey some of the flavour – and the frustrations – of real-life corporate planning.

Inflation. Except where specifically stated, all figures in the text and in the examples will be stated in real terms, that is, in constant prices, with inflation stripped out. So when I say of a company that they 'hoped to achieve £20m profit by Year 5' that means £20m in the currency value of the base year, Year 0.

Titles. I shall use the words 'chief executive' and 'managing director' to mean the most senior executive in an organization. Sometimes they are called General Manager, Senior Partner, Executive Chairman, Director General, General Secretary, Chief Executive Officer, Chief Manager or Executive President – there are dozens of variations. In all cases I mean the person at the top of the management hierarchy who reports to someone who is not another executive but is a beneficiary of the organization or a representative of the beneficiaries such as the chairman of a board or the president of a governing body.

Years. I shall frequently refer to past years, future years and base years. I shall use 'Year 0' to mean the base year (usually the current financial year, but not always). So 'Year 7' means seven years into the future from the base year and 'Year −4' means four years ago.

CHAPTER 1

What Is Corporate Planning?

For over three decades corporate planning has been in use in organizations of all shapes and sizes all over the world, and yet it is still the subject of a number of absurd misconceptions.

There was some excuse for these in the early days when, for example, its exponents liked to boast that all you had to do to make a company grow was to apply corporate planning to it like a magic fertilizer. Another, very contrary, notion put about by its detractors was that corporate planning was just an elaborate version of budgeting or business planning, a belief that is still widely held today. Another school of thought asserted that it is necessary to be very clever indeed to do corporate planning and to have degrees from at least two universities; some of its current practitioners uphold this claim with understandable loyalty.

These fantasies are so unhelpful and damaging to its reputation that I am going to take the whole of this chapter to explain what I think corporate planning really is and is not.

What it is not

As its name suggests, corporate planning involves planning for an organization as a whole – as a *corporate* whole. So corporate planning is *not* the same as product planning, production planning, cash flow planning, manpower planning or any of the dozens of other sorts of planning conducted in organizations today. All these are designed to plan *parts* or *sections* or *departments* of organizations. Most companies, even quite small ones, already employ product managers, marketing directors, production planners and finance controllers to look after the planning of these various parts, and when you do corporate planning you certainly do not want to do all these again under a fancy new name.

As soon as a corporate plan starts to spell out detailed production plans, manpower plans, finance plans, and so on, it is in grave danger of overreaching itself and becoming a busybody. Corporate planning is *corporate* planning. You can only have a corporate plan for an autonomous or quasi-autonomous organization; you cannot have one for any section, part or fragment of an organization unless it is quasi-autonomous, like a profit centre.

Some planners seem to think that corporate planning means planning the whole company and so they produce vast schedules showing what is going to happen to every tiny corner of the organization for years ahead in solemn detail. What a ridiculous thing to do! It is possible to plan ahead in great detail for short periods of time; it is also possible to plan ahead for very long periods, although only in outline. To try to plan in meticulous detail over long periods, however, is quite impossible. No wonder they claimed you needed to be academically brilliant to do corporate planning. No wonder top executives in companies with corporate planning departments became increasingly irritated by 'academics' in their ivory towers, striving for perfection in an uncertain world. No wonder the Russian economy is such a snail.

So that is another misconception out of the way: corporate planning is planning for the corporate whole, not planning the whole corporation.

Corporate planning and marketing

Here is another fallacy. Everyone seems to think that a corporate plan is the same as a marketing plan, that a corporate planning exercise results – indeed that it *should* result – in the repositioning of a company in its market-place, or the introduction of a range of new products, or a shift into a new market. Virtually all the best-known writers in this field have fallen into this trap from Ansoff (1964) to Porter (1985). It would be ridiculous for me to suggest that most corporate plans do *not* contain marketing decisions; most of them *do* call for a major new marketing strategy, but not all of them.

Corporate planning is not marketing. Distinguished entrepreneurs are frequently reported as saying: 'Successful products do *not* come from corporate planning.' Of course they do not; that is not what it is for. That is what marketing is for. I said above that as soon as a corporate plan starts to spell out partial or sectional plans it becomes a busybody and ought to be put in its place. That holds for product plans. This is not its job.

Yet this myth is all-pervading. Look at any so-called 'corporate plan'; it will be a market plan. Look at any case study in a business school; it will relate to a market plan. Inspect the data they give the student; it is all to do with products and market growth and agents and selling prices; it is nothing to do with the factory, the employees, the finances or the tax situation. When someone says the word 'strategy' what they invariably mean is marketing strategy. (You have to hand it to them, those marketing men have done a splendid marketing job on 'marketing'.)

I see this bias towards marketing as nothing less than a disaster. Companies always seem to do corporate planning in order to develop a new marketing stance. They go through the process and out comes a new marketing strategy. Fine, but some companies do not need a new marketing strategy; what they need is to smarten up their factory, or install new computer systems, or move to a tax haven, or sack the chief executive, or dispose of their subsidiary in Brazil.

Even companies who do need a new marketing strategy also need these other strategies, but, because they think marketing is everything – because the marketing experts have told them that this is so, and have gone on saying so for four decades now – they completely fail to address these other issues. For some companies marketing *is* more important than anything else, but for others it is not, something else is. Such as what? Lots of other things. I mentioned a few above but the variety has to be experienced to be believed. I hope it will be reflected in this book.

A further, minor, misconception is the belief that strategies relate to physical things only, that they have to do with information technology, products, factories, distribution networks, or whatever. Of course, this is not so. Many strategies are about attitudes and emotions. I shall give a number of examples later of strategies to improve morale, to strengthen customer confidence, to raise the level of innovation and to change the attitude of a parent company. Psychology is an important element in management and so it frequently features in strategies.

The technology of planning

Another of those damaging misapprehensions I mentioned above was the assertion that corporate planning is enormously sophisticated and advanced, calling for such techniques as computer models, experience curves, cross-impact analysis and directional policy matrices. My strong impression is that none of these are much use and that very few top decision-makers think they are either. I am not merely doubting whether they work: some do, some do not. I am going much further than that. I hold the view that if you are using these techniques then you are not doing corporate planning at all, you are doing business planning or marketing or manpower planning or one of those other types of planning with which, as I suggested above, corporate planning is so often confused. Most of these are partial planning techniques, planning for parts of an organization, as opposed to corporate planning, planning for the whole. They are very important and very useful, you cannot run a modern organization without them – but they are not corporate planning.

If a planner is using these techniques, which are designed to help him sort out complex problems, then he is standing too close to his company to be able to do corporate planning. To do this properly you have to stand much further back so you see only the half-dozen things that really matter. The whole idea in corporate planning is to study the wood, not the trees. This is an extraordinarily difficult thing for executives to do at the best of times and the more they use advanced techniques the more difficult it will be for them. It is like using a microscope instead of a telescope: it will focus your eyes on the wrong things entirely.

Corporate plans and strategic plans

Some people think that corporate planning and long-range planning are synonymous. Not quite. You can make a long-range plan for almost anything. It takes many years to sink a new coal mine, for example, or to design a new aircraft, and the plans by which these projects are scheduled and regulated would rightly be called 'long-range plans', but they are plainly not *corporate* plans. Not all long-range plans are corporate. On the other hand, corporate plans are about major changes to be made to an organization; major changes take time, so most corporate plans are long-range.

There is a similar differentiation between a corporate plan and a strategic plan. You can have a strategic plan for any major part of an organization. You can have a production strategy, a marketing strategy, a finance strategy – any plan that calls for a major change in a major part of a company could be termed 'strategic'.

A typical corporate strategy would be: 'We will go public.' I suggest that this statement, because it concerns a massive change to the company as a corporate whole, is an order of magnitude different from such strategies as, 'We will launch a new product in the European market', or 'We require additional loan capacity' because these, although undoubtedly important enough to be termed 'strategic', each relate only to a part of the company. In corporate plans the whole company is changed, in the others only parts of it are.

What does a corporate strategy look like in a non-profit-making organization? The same principle applies. A corporate strategy for a town would be to privatize large segments of its activities – cleaning, parks, sheltered homes, and so on. It would assuredly be a *corporate* strategy to privatize the whole town.[1] Would the designation of a road as One Way be a corporate strategy? I think not – unless it was the High Street. The decision to move 60 per cent of all handicapped children out of institutions into the community would probably not be corporate; closing down the town's only hospital presumably would.

As will be noted by now, this book is solely concerned with methods of devising *corporate* strategies and is interested in other strategies only as second-level products of the corporate planning process. The reader will also have picked up that the author believes that the attempt to develop these other strategies without developing a corporate plan first is an absurd aberration. I see these other strategies as the intended by-products of a properly constituted corporate plan. I do not believe it is possible to devise these properly without first going through the corporate planning process.

While on definitions, I am quite happy about the word 'corporate' in the title 'corporate planning' and I feel no urge to use 'strategic' instead, as others seem to do – I explained the distinction above. But I do regret the word 'planning'. A plan is rightly seen as something drawn up in considerable detail; a proficient plan is one that is comprehensive, where little is left to chance; a shoddy plan is one where some bungling planner has left great gaps in his schedules indicating a lack of clear, accurate foresight. But that would be a good corporate plan! A corporate plan – indeed any long-range plan – complete in every meticulous detail would be the work of an idiot.

Planning and co-ordinating

That leads me to forecasting. People still confuse 'planning' with 'forecasting'. A forecast is what someone thinks is going to happen. A plan is what someone is going to do. Quite different. They are connected because you often cannot plan until you have made a forecast, you cannot rationally decide what to do about the future until you have had a look at what might happen there. You forecast first, then you plan. Certainly they form a sequence, but that hardly makes them synonymous.

Here is another thing corporate planning is not. It is not 'co-ordinating'. Some organizations prepare their so-called 'corporate plans' by first inviting the various parts – departments, sections, areas – to make their plans and then, having collected these together they 'co-ordinate' them; that is, they make sure that all the plans add up correctly, that no two departments are going to use a scarce resource at the same time, and so forth. This then becomes the 'corporate plan'. What a lazy way to run an organization! All that will happen, if they do it this way, is that the organization will gradually become what the parts or sections want it to become – the tail wags the dog.

This phenomenon can most clearly be seen in groups of companies. The group chief executive tells his managing directors to prepare plans for their divisions. Let us say there are ten of them. They duly send their plans to head office where they are all added together and there you are – a group corporate plan. But all it will do is to move the group in the direction that these divisional managing directors want it to go – probably in the direction that the largest of them wants. There will be no *group* content in the plans; the group chief executive will not have addressed such questions as 'Why have we got ten divisions?' and 'Why have we got *these* ten?' and dozens more issues that may face his group as a *corporate* entity, such as its riskiness, its geographical spread, the management structure and so on.

This is the famous 'top down or bottom up?' controversy. My answer is quite clear: *not* bottom up. (And later I shall say not top down either!)

Why does all this matter? Who cares if some organization has misunderstood what corporate planning is? Well, the answer is simple: if they do what they call 'corporate planning' and instead they merely 'co-ordinate', or 'forecast', or plan a new product, or modify their market posture – or indulge in any of the misconceptions listed above – they will merely tackle those specific problems that are addressed by the specific technique they are using and will not tackle their *corporate* problems at all.

Budgeting and business planning

These misconceptions are nowhere more serious than in the case I have left to last, the confusion between corporate planning and business planning. The reason why this matters so much is that virtually every organization today does business planning and, having done it, solemnly announces: 'We've done corporate planning.' Alas, they most certainly have not. They will have made a careful and highly professional study of the trees and will have missed the forest completely.

Historically, the 'business plan' arose from the 'budget'. A 'budget' is a set of figures, usually prepared just before the end of one financial year, showing, for the coming year, how all the company's revenues and costs add up and hence what the surplus, or profit, is likely to be. It shows what every section and department proposes to earn and to spend each month (or four-week period). When the new year begins, each manager, and his boss, can see month by month if he is sticking to his budget. As well as being the most successful and most effective management tool ever invented, budgetary control must also have been the first example of really participative management: anyone who is anyone in an organization is invited to contribute to the budget discussion.

This technique came into use a few decades ago and is now employed rigorously in virtually every organization in the developed world (at least I thought so but, believe it or not, just after writing this I was introduced to a non-profit-making organization with nearly a thousand employees which did not have a budgetary control system). No one confuses budgeting with corporate planning, so that is not the problem.[2] The problem arose later.

As the rate of change accelerated companies started looking further ahead – one year was not enough. The budget process was accordingly stretched to two, three, five years and so became what is now called 'the business plan'. It was, I believe, a bad day when this superb short-term planning tool was stretched to become a long-term one. Here are some of the reasons:

- Companies prepare their business plans in virtually the same way they prepare the one-year budget – they often do them together and even use the same forms. This springs from the belief that a business plan is just like a budget except that it is for more years – but the differences are numerous and crucial.
- One major difference between short- and long-term planning is the accuracy of the forecasts on which plans are based. It is not too dangerous to base a one-year plan on a one-year forecast; it is dangerous to base any plan on a three- or five-year forecast. The errors in one year will (usually) not be so great as to wreck the company; in a long-range forecast the errors could do exactly that. Very special precautions have to be taken to protect a company from errors in a long-term plan. Alas, if the management has failed to grasp the distinction between short- and long-range forecasts these precautions will not be taken. Because the design of the business planning system stems from the budget system, there will be no space on the forms in which to declare the errors in the forecasts and these will then conveniently be forgotten thus placing the plans, and even the company, at risk when the forecast turns out to be wrong.
- When a sales manager is asked in the budget exercise, 'How many units will you sell next year?' he will give a forecast – that is, he will say what he *expects* to sell next year. But ask him, 'How many will you sell in Year 3?', and not only will his answer be far more inaccurate, because of the greater uncertainty the further ahead he tries to look, but it will no longer be a forecast, it will be a target. A *forecast* is what someone *expects* will happen in the future; a *target* is what someone *wants* to happen. By lengthening the horizon, as you do when moving from the one-year budget to the multi-year business plan, you have unintentionally invited the salesman to dream a little; that is why long-term forecasts are almost always too optimistic – so optimistic at times that they may 'hazard the ship'. They are not forecasts, they are targets – a forecast is what you expect, a target is what you want. The salesman, if he is any good, will want more than he expects, but that is not what you thought you asked.

- The one-year budget is a planning *and* control system; the business plan is a planning document only – you cannot control something that is still three years in the future. So there is no reason at all why the budget and the business plan should both be prepared by the same people, on the same forms, at the same time – usually in a mad rush at the end of the year. Such conditions may be right for the brutal, down-to-earth decisions required to sharpen up a company for the following year, but they may well be wrong for the deeper consideration required for long-term decisions.
- The budget, because it is a short-term tool, will be designed to address such short-term issues as improving the productivity of the compay's *existing* assets. It will not have been designed to address the long-term issues, such as what *future* assets ought to be employed. Any business planning system which is based on the budget system – and virtually all of them are – will not be specifically designed to address long-term issues; it will merely be a short-term planning system modified for the long term.
- Many business plans are still devised for three years, but even this is becoming inadequate. Many companies now need to look five years ahead, occasionally as many as ten. But a ten-year, and even a five-year, business plan would be absurd because the later figures become mere guesses. This means that most organizations do not attempt to plan further ahead than they can trust the figures in the business plan – a couple of years if they are lucky. So, because they do not trust the figures they do no planning beyond a couple of years.
- The budget and the business plan both consist almost entirely of figures. What about such non-quantifiable issues as management development, product quality, proposed government legislation, relations with a parent body, altering the articles of association, the problem of one over-large customer or supplier, and so on, almost to infinity. Where are these issues to be determined? More to the point, where are they to be determined in the same rigorous manner as all the quantifiable issues that are handled so professionally in the budget and the business plan?

The managers may say that they intend tackling these non-quantifiable issues in a separate exercise later. First, I do not believe it: they will not have time, something urgent will intervene. Anyhow, they have already done their 'planning' and will not be keen to do any more. Secondly, even if they do, it will not be a very systematic exercise, certainly not up to the standard of the business plan. Thirdly, there are to be *two* strategic exercises are there? One to handle the quantifiable issues in the business planning exercise and then another, separate, exercise to attend to the others? It is hard to think of a better way to miss the Big Picture than to tackle it in two parts.

Corporate planning and business planning

The point I am making here is that most companies, having carefully prepared their one-year budget and their business plans, believe they have carried out all the systematic company planning they need to do. But they will have done some of it wrong – the failure to provide a statement of forecast errors, the over-optimism invidiously built into the 'forecasts', the absence of error-handling in the design of the forms, the artificially short horizon because of the reliance on figures, the preparation of massive strategic decisions in a mad rush just because it is the end of the financial year, the failure to attend to non-quantifiable issues – many of which are of even greater moment than those that can be quantified – all these will result in the business plan being defective.

In sum, they will have employed a second-hand planning system, a stretched short-term planning mechanism, which is wholly unsuitable for addressing the long-term, corporate, issues. Would it not make more sense to design a long-term planning system, specially formulated to address *corporate* strategic issues, completely from scratch? Without this an organization is in danger of either making major strategic decisions incorrectly, or not systematically, or even not at all. Anyhow, that is what I am trying to do in this book.

I have listed many of the misconceptions about corporate planning in Figure 1.1. Regrettably, I have to say this: I believe that many of these are due to a deliberate tactic by academics, writers and consultants in this field – people like me, in other words. Our problem is that, correctly defined and properly practised, corporate planning is an embarrassingly small subject area. In practice, a corporate plan, crucially important though it is, is a tiny document of just a few pages. It is easy to see why academics and consultants need to expand the definition of corporate planning in their books and assignments. They need to throw in anything remotely rele-

Figure 1.1   What it is not

It is not marketing, product planning, market research, marketing strategy, IT strategy.

It is not long-range planning, strategic planning, business planning or budgeting.

It is not forecasting.

It is not finance planning, cash flow planning, manpower planning, production planning, project planning

It is not co-ordinating nor operational planning.

It is neither sophisticated nor advanced.

---

vant, such as business planning, marketing and product development, strategic management, portfolio analysis, research into new markets, financial planning and raising capital, acquisitions and mergers planning, action plans, restructuring the management, managing the research function. All these do need to be done at the end of the corporate planning process, but to include them in the definition of corporate planning is most misleading.[3]

This is not a trivial academic point. I suspect that a lot of damage has been caused by the confusion this has sown in the minds of executives. Figure 1.2 may help to clarify it a little. This suggests the following planning hierarchy: corporate, strategic, business and operational.

What it is

In one respect corporate planning is like all other types of planning: it is an attempt to decide how best to respond to, or to anticipate, change. Just as the computer manager will have a three-year plan to deal with the obsolescence of his equipment, knowing what he knows about the emerging technology, and the marketing director will be planning changes in the product range for some years ahead, knowing what he knows about product life-cycles and changes in

Figure 1.2   The hierarchy of plans

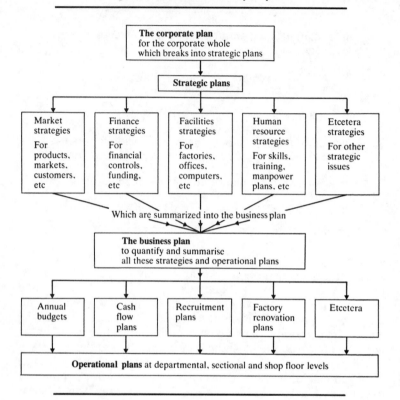

the market place, so it is with corporate planning. There is nothing mysterious about it, it is just someone planning changes to the corporate body, knowing what he knows about the organization and its possible future.

The chief distinguishing feature is that it is concerned with plans that lie one step up the hierarchy from all the others, that is, not plans for parts of an organization, but plans for the organization itself – for the forest, not for the trees.

At this level, however, various unusual phenomena appear. For one thing, there seem to be very few issues that need to be planned, or indeed that *can* be planned. The long-term destiny of organizations seems to depend on a few huge decisions. This is the hallmark of a corporate plan, the small number of decisions and their great impact. Get these decisions wrong and the organization will quite simply be in the wrong ball park. No amount of brilliant advertising, no stupendous effort by the employees, no attention to detail, however meticulous, can rescue the organization from its strategic error. Get them right and it can thrive.

Corporate planning consists of identifying what these few decisions are and then finding strategic answers for them. Many, perhaps most, of these top issues are non-numerical – that is why corporate planning does not involve a lot of figures, it is why business planning fails to address these questions, it is why this area of enquiry is not suitable for computers or for advanced management techniques or for geniuses in planning methodology.

Most corporate plans are not complex, they are simple. This does not mean they are easy – far from it; strategic decisions demand careful, experienced judgments because they are bedevilled by the huge uncertainties inherent in the future and because they are intended to affect the destiny of the company deeply and permanently. This is the wrong field for the clever academic, but it is absolutely right for the experienced senior executive.

A few major decisions

A corporate plan, then, consists of a very few but momentous statements about the long-term future of the company as a whole. 'We will merge with a competitor' is a message of the utmost simplicity but of huge importance for any business – if they do merge life will never be the same again. Notice the stark simplicity of this statement; contrast its half-dozen words with, say, a hundred-page report on a new product.

Contrast it, too, with the alternative: 'We will not merge.' Surprisingly often the issue in corporate planning seems to boil down to deciding between diametrically opposite strategic directions: a parting of the ways; the company at a crossroads; the horns of a dilemma; reassessment of its roots; diversify or, on the contrary, trim back to the core; cut manufacturing costs or, on the contrary, increase them to add value; gain share in the home market or, on the contrary, go for exports; go public or stay private.

Of course, not all companies have to choose between opposites. Later on I describe a company whose strategy was to go headlong for exports. It set itself massive exporting targets and began to change the very structure of the company to this end. As they then discovered, what they should have been doing was to plunge all available resources into something completely different – catching up with the changing technology in which they had begun to lose the lead to other competitors. It had nothing to do with exports at all, a different road altogether.

I am surprised how bluntly these choices are often presented to managements when they really get down to fundamentals. Issues that executives used to fight over, sometimes for years, problems that have been examined by committee after committee, pale into insignificance when the real strategic problems – the corporate ones – are finally identified, stark and simple. The focus of the top managers' thinking switches abruptly into the true area of concern.

Every company of every size and type occasionally has to make a really big decision, the sort of decision that affects its entire destiny for years or even decades into the future, decisions which change not just parts or departments or sections of the company but which alter its whole structure and the very nature of the company itself. They are the sort of decisions which the company and its employees will look back on in years to come and say: 'That was the year when . . .'

Sometimes these major decisions are forced upon a company because of some momentous change that occurs *outside* it in its business environment, such as a shift in the market, the appearance of a new technology or a change of government. Sometimes it is something *inside* the company which demands a major reappraisal to be made, such as when the company is on a profits plateau and cannot move off it without a fundamental reorganization. Or the opposite case, when a company has to regroup after a period of rapid expansion. Or, sometimes, there is an unresolved difference of opinion among the owners or the senior managers about its long-term future, or maybe there is no consensus at all and the company is just drifting.

Consider a company manufacturing agricultural pesticides whose national market share is moving towards 20 per cent. Imagine that, looming above them, is a competitor with 30 per cent. The company decides to use its strongly positive cash flow to acquire companies outside its traditional field, in fertilizers, foodstuffs and pharmaceuticals. This is its corporate plan. Its rationale may be stated in the four extremely simple sentences contained in Figure 1.3 and, once action has been taken, its destiny will be sealed for decades. The company will never be the same again.

Figure 1.3 Pesticide company's corporate plan

1 Our market share is rising towards 20 per cent.

2 Our major competitor may feel threatened by our continued success and may act against our interests.

3 Therefore we shall use our cash flow to diversify away from pesticides whose share will be held below 20 per cent.

4 Accordingly we shall acquire companies in fertilizers, foodstuffs and pharmaceuticals.

You may feel that this is far too brief even for a corporate plan as defined in this book. Surely there should be further levels of decisions such as the names of some of the proposed acquisition targets, the amount of cash available in each year, and so on? Certainly there should; without doubt these decisions will have to be made eventually. The point being made here, however, is that, before one moves on down the decision-making chain to levels below these four sentences, we should be perfectly sure that these sentences themselves are correct. I believe this company – based on a real-life one, as all my examples are – had already made two strategic blunders.

First, Statement 3 does not follow from 1 and 2. The mere fact that the company may face some hostility if its market share rises above 20 per cent does not *per se* mean that it must diversify. There are alternatives, including not diversifying and meeting the problem head on; or using other strategies to keep its market share below 20 per cent (they could put their prices up to stop it rising); or turn to exporting so that volume goes on rising while suppressing their share at home; or use all that cash to acquire a competitor in Europe. That is four alternatives they did not consider before going on to the next level, and there must be many more, including some sort of deal with the big competitor.

Even if 'diversification' is right, and we accept Statement 3 and go to the next level of decision at Statement 4, why diversify into three different areas? Why not one – or seven? Why those three?

Why not go for veterinary products? Or farming? The number of alternatives they did not consider at this second level is quite stunning.[4]

Corporate planning is studying the big decisions. When you have got these right you then need detailed strategies; that is when you pass out of the realm of corporate planning into the other types of planning. Before you go, make sure you have got these top ones right. If you get them right then, not only will these be valid but a whole cascade of second- and third-level decisions will be made abundantly plain. *This* is what corporate planning is for.

First- and second-order decisions

I believe most companies take these vast decisions with hardly any systematic discussion at all. One only has to look at the way internationally renowned companies make acquisitions, and then, desperately trying to hide their embarrassment, have to dispose of them again a few years later. Evidently, even among the world's finest companies, there is a puerile lack of understanding about strategy formulation. Many of these errors are due to jumping straight to the details without first looking at the Big Picture.

Most executives just do not know how to take destiny-changing decisions. They leap past these and gratefully move as quickly as possible on to the lower levels where they feel more at home, especially with decisions that can be quantified. That is why so many corporate planning textbooks recommend that one starts with 'mission statements'. They advise you first to decide the 'mission' of the company so you can then get down to 'corporate planning' and make such decisions as which new products, and which new acquisitions, within the mission statement, you propose to launch.

The pesticide company above did much the same thing. It would probably have declared its mission statement as: 'We shall become a diversified agricultural chemical conglomerate.' These textbooks do not tell the reader how to determine a mission statement; one simply makes one. In doing so, however, one ducks all the difficult questions which the corporate planning process described here is designed to address. These textbooks tell you to do what the pesticide company did. I find this ridiculous. In any meaningful corporate planning system the mission is not the input, it is the output.

Here is another simple example. Imagine a company with one dominant customer. In that situation many managers would start the planning process by saying: 'We must reduce our dependence on Mallard & Co. Now, which are the other potential customers whom we might supply?' They then go on to a massive market review to select possible alternatives and this becomes the guts of their 'corporate plan'. In my view, however, they have just shot straight past the real guts – whether to look for other customers at all or, on the contrary, to stay with the one they have. Just imagine the value of having one customer; consider what powerful links one might make with him all the way up and down the management hierarchies of both companies. Our managing director would discuss major problems with Mr Mallard himself almost every day, our despatch clerk would chat with their invoice supervisor, and so on. We could become Mallard's most valuable asset. Our profits would soar.[5]

Most managers, when considering a major project, ask themselves whether it is a sensible step for the company. Faced with a suggestion that they acquire Eagle Engineering for £635m they might well ask themselves if Eagle is really worth it. They seldom ask the much wider questions: 'Is acquisition the right route for us?' 'Is this the right way to spend £635m?' Why do they not ask these questions? Because they take decisions piecemeal instead of seeing them set against a backcloth of their company's overall strategic situation. If they only have one project in mind – 'acquire Eagle Engineering' – they cannot compare it with other ideas they do not currently have.

I have seen this strategic sub-optimizing repeatedly, where the big decision is made ad hoc in about three minutes and then the remaining solutions in the decision hierarchy are determined, usually with an impressive show of logic and technology including, of course, portfolio analysis, computer studies and masses of graphs showing where we are on the experience curve.

An elephant hunt

Corporate planning, as seen in this book, is a *systematic* procedure for identifying these top key issues – the half-dozen that every organization *must* get right if it is to prosper over the next few years. A formal definition of corporate planning would probably include the phrase 'identifying and addressing the Unresolved Key Issues'.

I refer to corporate planning as an 'elephant hunt'. It is a process for looking for strategic elephants in the organization's undergrowth, identifying them, then corralling them in one place so everyone can see all of them together and can note the sum total of the organization's strategic situation. It is very important to see these elephants against a very broad, panoramic, background and then to deal with all of them at once in one major, holistic, strategic review.

Every company I have ever seen has one or more of these 'strategic elephants'. Let me give a few examples of some I have seen in recent years:

- A company with two products, one with a turnover of £6m, the other with a turnover of £12m. Both make about 20 per cent contribution to overheads and profit. The larger product, with £12m turnover, is made under licence. The licence is renewable *annually*.

- A company with five products. To modernize the production facilities, and to ensure they keep pace with the customer's increasingly strict requirements of service and quality, will demand the expenditure of £50m over the next five years. This company's parent has told them they may spend only £20m.

- A company operating in a backward nation has for years produced a range of low technology products. Now their customers are demanding increasingly sophisticated technology. The company is quite simply unable to attract, at any price, the necessary highly skilled design engineers, or even production workers, to its rather unpleasant part of the world. It is in the wrong nation!

- A diversified group of companies has three divisions. One subsidiary is a manufacturer of moderate repute. It makes a fair return on capital although nothing like as high as the other two subsidiaries. These are both service companies which have expanded rapidly for several years and are now seen as leaders in their respective fields (which are in no way related to the manufactured product). They both require substantial additional capital for expansion. The company's gearing is above average. Should they sell the manufacturing division?

- The elderly directors of a family firm have not developed any of their sons to board level standard.

- 'Mad Aunt Maud' has just sold her 25 per cent share of the family business to a 'merchant investor'. Everyone (except Aunt Maud) knows that he is a scoundrel. He is now demanding a seat on the board.
- This company is renowned in Europe and the US, but is not yet established in the Pacific. Three of its executive directors are members of the owning family, three are highly qualified professional executives. These latter have just told the three former that they do not consider them to be capable of making an adequate contribution to the management of such a large company in the modern world.
- A multinational whose matrix organization structure has plainly not been working for many years.
- A non-profit-making organization which may have to alter its articles of association. This requires an Act of Parliament.
- A non-profit-making organization which may lose 50 per cent of its funding in the next five years. This is bad enough, but this is a warning sign that its original purpose, set 60 years ago, is no longer valid in the modern world.

Strategic elephants

I have now seen so many of these 'elephants' that I feel able to generalize about them as follows:

- Virtually every company in the world faces at least one major strategic issue which they have not yet addressed. In a few cases there will be only one elephant; more often there is a small herd of them, although I have never seen more than six. These key themes will be seen to stand head and shoulders above all other issues in the company and will be recognized by the management as the items which will shape the company's destiny for many years ahead. Contrary to common sense, experience suggests that there is no smooth gradation in ranking by importance. Either something is seen as plainly worthy of classification as a major strategic issue – an elephant – or it is plainly not.
- Companies which have recently been through a business planning exercise will often be found *not* to have identified some of their 'elephants'. The same is true of companies which have recently completed a marketing exercise. Neither of these

exercises is designed to pick up all the various types of issues that are of strategic importance to companies. The same is true of companies having 'corporate planning departments'. They will not have addressed their elephants because the staff in these departments are too junior or too specialist to be able to address them, or sometimes even to identify them.

- Perhaps a third of all the elephants that will be discovered in a corporate planning exercise are good news – such as the company which realized that its market would probably now expand at three times the rate it had previously assumed. Alas, most elephants are bad news – the product is obsolescent, the board is elderly, the office is in the wrong place and so on to infinity.

- Because these top issues have not been tackled there will be a cascade of other problems in the company that have not been solved, like the newspaper companies in London's Fleet Street who were not able to introduce the new printing technology until they had addressed their scandalous Industrial Relations elephant.

- Some of these elephants will have been present, untamed, in the company for years (or even, as in the case of Fleet Street, for decades). Some of them will be known to virtually everyone in the company but no one will have tackled them, partly because, as explained above, they have no systematic planning system for raising and addressing such major interlocking strategic issues.

- Companies which have such elephants may sometimes be identified by their lack-lustre performance. This is not always so; some elephants are to be found in the future of the company so that, naturally, no ill effects may yet be seen. Even so, the company ought by now to have started to respond to the looming trend and the fact that it has not yet done so is becoming an elephant.

- Half the elephants in any company will be in the marketing area. This means that half of them are *not* in the marketing area and are nothing whatever to do with customers, products and markets, or positioning the company in its market-place, or analyzing competitive advantage.

I feel it necessary to repeat this last one: only about half the elephants are in the marketing area. That is to say, in a completed corporate plan for an average company, in which there will typically be six strategic statements, two or three of them will relate to products or markets and two or three will relate to areas that are in no sense marketing: the employees, the computer, the shareholders, the factory, the management, taxation, or even the corporate objectives themselves.

At a guess, then, the Boston Consulting Group's famous farmyard of cash cows and dogs, Shell's directional policy matrix, Porter's competitive analysis, Ansoff's diversification matrix, and so on, are exceedingly useful and relevant for half the strategies that the average corporate plan will contain – and useless and irrelevant for the other half. The company above in which an expansion in the Far East was an obvious next marketing move would have been crippled had it undertaken such a step without first tackling its problem on the board. It had no marketing elephants – it did have a top people elephant.

Figure 1.4   What it is

Corporate planning is a systematic process for deciding what are the top half-dozen decisions that an organization *must* get right in order to prosper over the next few years.

Herds of elephants

I said above that these elephants seem to come in very small numbers only. One, two or three is common (two surprisingly so), six is virtually unknown. I shall give many examples of this phenomenon in the rest of the book.

When one sees all the elephants together, as a herd, it will be found that no two companies, however similar they appear, ever require the same set of strategies. Every company has a different permutation of elephants, and therefore requires different strategies. I recently saw a group of companies in which one of its elephants was the fact that one of its four profit centres was at risk from several different unpredictable events any of which could, and occasionally did, throw it into losses. None of the other profit centres had made a loss for many years. It was like a table with one wobbly leg. So what? Lots of groups have risky subsidiaries. One

week later I saw another group with exactly the same problem –
sudden unpredictable events which could throw a subsidiary into
losses. In this case, however, all five subsidiaries had made a loss in
one of the past five years. This was like a table with five wobbly
legs. Strategies to deal with the riskiness of the first group will be
wholly unlike the ones required for the second.

Again, some companies are leaders; for them innovation is a key
strategy. Other companies follow; imitation, coupled with niche
marketing or price competitiveness, is the right way for them. Some
companies suffer from supine, sleepy management; others from
overactive autocrats. Each requires a different strategy. I mention
this because, while I believe my *system* of planning will work for a
huge range of different organizations, no *strategy* is ever right for all
companies. Some consultants recommend market share as a
virtually standard cure. Corporate planning is the process for
selecting the right strategy for each individual company. I know of
no panacea.

On the other hand, academics claim that multinationals are in
some way different to say, a Ma and Pa corner shop. I disagree. The
variety of strategies that are available to both are the same, the
rationale for adopting any one of these is the same – both would
deploy the same arguments for diversifying, moving up-market,
improving productivity, and so on. What determines strategy is not
size but the overall strategic situation of the organization.

My experience suggests that strategy formulation is easy. All you
need to do – and this is not so easy – is to identify all the elephants.
Once they are paraded before you, clearly labelled and described,
the strategies to deal with them will become apparent. But because
no two companies will harbour the same *combination* of elephants
no two companies require the same set of strategies. There are no
standard nostrums.

A definition of corporate planning

Corporate planning decisions, then, are decisions that affect the
whole structure of an organization for many years or decades into
the future – huge decisions taken in conditions of uncertainty about
the future. It is the size of these decisions, the fact that there are so
few of them, and the enormous errors in the forecasts on which they
often have to be based, that characterize corporate planning. I
would sum corporate planning up as 'a systematic process for

deciding what are the half-dozen top decisions that an organization *must* get right in order to prosper over the next few years'.

Decisions of this magnitude deserve to be taken in a thoroughly professional manner. Such an exercise cannot be rushed, the company's strategic situation must be seen in its totality and from a bird's-eye view – the forest, remember, not the trees. Rember, too, the extraordinary variety of issues – not just marketing! In one company it may be a major product threatened with extinction by environmental protesters, in another it is lack of capital, in another it is the elderly chairman, or an entire division has gone sour, or a militant union – or, even, all of them at once!

When it is all over, when the corporate plan is completed, what should it look like? It should consist of perhaps a dozen pages of text with a few pages of figures to show the orders of magnitude involved. Most of the pages will consist of background data and the sequence of enquiries and discoveries that were made on the route to the corporate strategies – targets, forecasts, and so on, which will be described in great detail in the following chapters. Probably on just one page will be the corporate plan itself, in just a few simple sentences. These will describe the half-dozen vital strategic steps the company intends to take to ensure its prosperity over the following few years. These will be stated with such clarity and simplicity that the management will wonder what all the fuss was about.[6]

It might be thought that for a company to harbour a herd of elephants, sometimes for years, would simply reflect an exceptionally poor level of management. Sometimes, undoubtedly, it does. However, elephants are far too prevalent to be passed off so easily. Almost every company in the world has, or has had, elephants at one time. However grand it may be every company in the world has at one time got itself into a strategic bind – IBM, ITT, Pan Am, GM, GEC, BL, Woolworths, Dunlop, RR, ICI. No one is immune.

I know two companies, both employing several thousand people, which still have problems with their unions. One has recently (1987) had a strike and in the other the unions still run the catering facilities, including the senior executives' dining room – a source of endless friction. This is nearly a decade after the 'collapse' of union power in Britain. Supine management? In one case, yes. Not in the other.

The fact is that companies do have these problems. They do not know how to tackle them, or they know how to but have not done so. Sometimes, it is impossible to blame them. Some of these elephants are huge. To tackle them requires immense courage.

That brings me to the final comment in this chapter – feelings. Top executives are supposed to be highly trained, analytical, logical (ruthless, too, if we are the believe the popular press), decisive and resolute. Many of them are, but they are also human. There is not the slightest doubt that one reason that elephants exist in any organization is that the top executives have psychological reasons for not tackling them. Some are afraid of them, some are more anxious of the consequences of addressing them than not address-ing them, others are so worried about them that they pretend they cannot see them, others fear that if someone else sees them they will be disgraced. I cannot stress enough the importance of this aspect of corporate planning. To tackle the elephants certainly requires a systematic approach. Finding a way to tackle them methodically is what corporate planning is for. It is useless, however, unless the psychological factors are given full weight in the design of the system.

Summary

Corporate planning is planning for the corporate whole, not for its parts. It is not business planning, production planning, strategic planning or any other type of partial planning, and it certainly is not marketing. It is not co-ordinating, forecasting or budgeting. It is a process designed to yield a corporate plan – a statement of strategies designed to affect the organization as a corporate whole.

Because its output relates to only a few top decisions corporate planning is a relatively modest area for study. The small number and the great impact of the decisions are two of its notable features. Because these are not complex and because they are highly judgemental in character advanced planning techniques are not often helpful and may actually hinder a clear, simple conclusion.

The purpose of the corporate planning process described in this book is to reach an enthusiastic consensus among the top executives in an organization as to the half-dozen actions that they have to take in order to place their organization in a strong position to face the long-term future.

CHAPTER 2

Who Should Do It?

Having established that corporate planning is a systematic process for reaching into the very heart of an organization's long-term concerns, the next question is, who should attempt to carry out this exercise? There cannot be very many possible candidates for this unusual task. Among them must be the chief executive, his senior colleagues, a specialist planner inside the organization, a specialist from outside it, and any combination of these.

I have reached two very firm conclusions over the past twenty-five years. The first is that the sequence of steps is an effective process no matter who carries them out – the same stages have to be taken in the same sequence regardless of the players in the drama. The second is that a team consisting of the chief executive and his closest colleagues is by far the most reliable combination.

Thus the key is that the planning must be performed by a top-level team of executives. Any specialists they wish to employ should merely assist, not the other way round. I thus rule out, for virtually all cases, the corporate planning exercise being performed by a planning specialist.

The planning team

The first thing a chief executive should do, having decided to undertake a corporate planning exercise, is not to call on a specialist to do it for him but to form a planning team. While each type of organization will require a different combination of members, as described below, the leader of the team must always be the chief executive. Without him as the chief hunter some of the elephants will not be addressed or will not even be discussed. No one else, *no one*, has the authority even to mention some of the elephants in some organizations. The idea that the subordinates of the head of a family firm could discuss going public, for example, without him being present is preposterous. The idea that any executive could discuss diversification or an acquisition without the chief executive being there is senseless. But topics of this magnitude is precisely what the exercise is all about. It is only about them.

I have seen two corporate plans prepared without the chief executive in the team. Both were disasters because, when the team informed him of their conclusions, he simply ignored them in one case and contemptuously rejected them in the other.[1] The chief executive must lead the team. Today, however, when the team style of management has largely replaced the autocrat, it is essential that he discusses matters of such moment with his closest colleagues. I cannot imagine a modern system of corporate planning in which their full participation is not a central feature. Of course, if the chief executive is an autocrat he will neither wish to discuss such sensitive affairs with his colleagues, nor will he need to – he is the sole decision-maker, there will be no others. The team leader, however, must do so. He must obtain the approval of his colleagues for almost everything he does. He must, of all things, discuss strategies with them and obtain an enthusiastic consensus.

A corporate planning system that failed to place this participative feature at its heart would be useless in today's managerial milieu, but quite apart from this reason for selecting such a team, there is another of almost equal importance: these top men will know more about their company than anyone else in the world. Anything they do not know they have the authority to find out. A corporate plan based on faulty information will not stand; a plan based on the knowledge of these top men will have firm foundations.

The conclusion is plain: the team must be led by the chief executive and must include his closest colleagues.

Variations on a team

The various types of organization will require different team structures. I describe some of these below, starting with the odd one out.

Organizations run by autocrats   The key distinguishing mark of an autocrat is that he does not seek advice. On the contrary, he gathers around him a team of people, often of the highest competence, whose advice he does not intend to take. They are his aides, attendants, even lackeys. Very few autocrats contemplate adopting a systematic approach to strategy formulation of any sort, and they would certainly not use anything so deliberately participative as the system described in this book.

It is fashionable to denigrate the autocrat, to treat him as an aberrant joke. I believe these people manage their businesses far more effectively by flair and entrepreneurial aptitude than most companies employing more formal management methods. The single-minded vision they have of how they want their organization to develop often far surpasses anything a team can envisage, with its inevitably differing perspectives. Alas, their organizations are far more vulnerable because when the boss does make a mistake it is a big one. Of all the causes of corporate collapse, there is not the smallest doubt that the autocrat is the prime.

On several occasions I have witnessed an autocrat using corporate planning to initiate the difficult process of delegating greater responsibilities to his team. His colleagues are delighted and relieved to be asked their views on this previously taboo subject of overall corporate strategy. Alas, the opinions they express often prove too much for him; he either rejects their views as 'incorrect' or accepts them but fails to take them into account when leading his team to its strategic conclusions. The ingenuity of the tricks and devices some of these autocrats employ to avoid accepting the opinions of their senior colleagues is impressive. Common among these are the selection of too large a planning team to allow a free-ranging discussion, the appointment to the team of those who may be expected to agree with him, the release to the team of previously unpublished data in a form they will not understand, and above all, talking five times as much as all the others put together.

Autocrats and corporate planning do not mix.[2]

The small firm   Some companies are so small that they only have one manager, usually the proprietor. Obviously he cannot form a team, but I would recommend that he makes every effort to find someone else to join him on the corporate planning journey.

Because his view of his company will be so biased, and because two heads are better than one, he should invite someone whom he respects to become his devil's advocate, or his counterbalance, or simply his guide and companion on the hunt: a friend, a relative, a professional adviser – the latter is especially appropriate because he can bring a wider, more objective opinion to the discussion (see Figure 2.1).

Figure 2.1   A planning team for a small firm

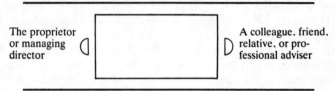

The planning process described in this book is valid even for one-man planning teams so it would be perfectly acceptable to use it in such a small organization.

Larger organizations   In larger companies, employing from dozens to many thousands of people, and in almost all non-profit-making organizations, the chief executive should invite his most senior colleagues, the people who share the reins of power with him, to join him in the corporate planning process. As a guide, a team of three people is probably the practical minimum, while a team of eight people is too many. The ideal numbers are four to six. This allows full discussion but there are not so many voices to be heard that the process is intolerably delayed (see Figure 2.2).

Figure 2.2   The planning team for companies and non-profit-making organizations

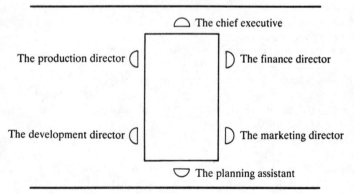

Anomalies should be discouraged. Thus, if the chief executive normally runs the organization with three others then these four should form the planning team – and no one else should join them.

Groups In groups of companies, that is where the company is divided into autonomous profit centres, and in federations, the same principle applies – the team should be formed from those who hold the reins. Thus if the group chief executive normally works with two other group executives (such as the group finance executive and the group vice-president for development, or whatever) and with the managing directors of, say, three profit centres, then these six people should form the planning team and no one else. If, on the other hand, he habitually runs the group with three other group executives only then these four *group* executives should form the team and they should not be joined by anyone from the profit centres (see Figure 2.3).

The basic theme is: those who hold the reins of power are those who do the corporate planning. Their task is quite clear. They are to move through the corporate planning process, as described in the remaining chapters of this book, reaching a consensus at each stage, until they have determined a practical set of strategies. This corporate planning process is a magnificent team builder, a quality that newly appointed chief executives much appreciate.

A considerable commitment

As a general rule they will need to meet as a team for half a day every two or three weeks for several months. In very small, simple companies, it may take only a couple of months to complete the operation; in very large groups, employing thousands of people in several nations, it may take a year. Most organizations take several months. The reason they take so long is because most teams feel it is necessary in order fully to absorb the implications of what they are discussing.

I stress again, this exercise is designed to lift their thinking beyond anything they have considered collectively before. Time after time I have heard executives saying at the beginning of the exercise, 'Of course, the most important question our company faces is "A"', and then, towards the end, this 'A' begins to pale into insignificance and 'Z' – something completely unexpected – is seen

Figure 2.3 Planning teams for groups

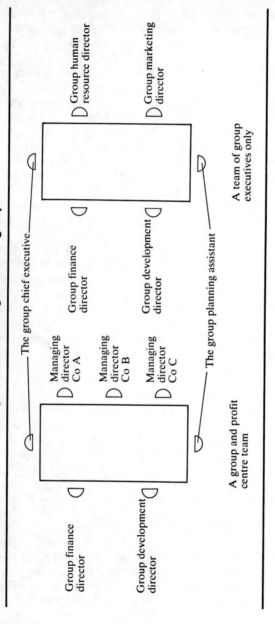

as the most important strategic factor facing the company.[3] Sometimes, on the contrary, the elephants turn out to be old friends, but now, seen in the full glare of consensus, some are much more forbidding and urgent – indeed are about to charge. Others are discovered not to be elephants at all and they melt back into the obscurity of the undergrowth.

Mercifully, the aim is to determine a set of strategies that will be valid for a number of years and so the corporate planning exercise needs only to be carried out every few years. In this respect it is also quite unlike business planning and all the other types of planning found in the modern company which need to be prepared annually. Even so, it may be thought ridiculous to take so long over this task. In fact it certainly can be accomplished in much less than several months – in days even, if really necessary – but there are three reasons why one should not attempt to accelerate this planning process:

- Most companies operate in highly competitive, rapidly changing conditions. To suggest that the senior executives should take their eyes off their immediate business problems for more than a few hours a week could be impractical and, in a small firm, even dangerous.
- It would be most unwise to base long-term decisions on short-term data. It is easy to imagine a management, excited by recent good news, devising a strategy that was so ambitious that it overstretched their company, or vice versa. It would surely be more sensible to allow a lengthy sequence of good and bad news to be assimilated before devising a strategy that might commit a company for many years ahead.
- So fundamental are some of the changes that may be called for by this exercise that the executives may well require a fairly long period in which to make the necessary mental adjustments. Just consider what a major change in attitude would be required from a proprietor, say, if he had to face the fact that his company is no longer viable in its present form. Or, taking the opposite cases, what a shift in mental outlook would be needed if a planning team discovered that their cash flow was going to be *five times* greater than they previously thought. Or imagine the feelings in a non-profit-making organization as it dawns on them that they are soon to be privatized.

Experience suggests that strategies that have been devised in a rush are seen in retrospect to have been less than satisfactory. To take one's thinking about one's company into the longer-term strategic levels required by this exercise, compared with the very short horizons of thought which managing directors normally give to their company's affairs, does require some time.

In my view those who believe that corporate planning is a high-technology, very sophisticated form of business planning have completely failed to grasp that it is the emotions, not the logic, that provide the greatest barrier to decision-making. The reason it takes so long to reach a strategic decision using my system is that it demands that each of the top executives should be personally convinced that the correct decision has been reached. The decision has to be so patently right, so overwhelmingly obvious that their emotional barriers are breached. I would go so far as to say that if an organization has completed its corporate plan in less than a few months they will have failed to address some of their elephants.

One should have excellent reasons for trying to telescope this process.

I should also warn against setting a completion date. The reason for this advice is as follows: a team which is hoping to finish by a certain date presumably wish to do so because they know that something is going to happen soon after – they are going to have to decide whether to extend their offices, perhaps, or recruit more employees, or it will be time to prepare the annual budget. However, if they have any of these deadlines in mind the corporate planning exercise is bound to become a 'shall-we-extend-the-office?' exercise, or a 'how-many-shall-we-recruit?' study, or even worse, a 'must-get-it-done-before-the-budget' race. If the management gear their corporate planning to one factor which they think is important this may prevent some other factor coming to the front of their minds.

The planning assistant

We have seen that this is a rather large commitment of top executive time. It is therefore recommended that someone else should be invited to join the team as what I call the 'planning assistant'.

The planning assistant has up to three roles. First, he may act as secretary to the planning team, feeding them with reports, collecting data, making calculations, carrying out enquiries for them and acting as the clockwork for the team, calling them to meetings, issuing agendas, circulating minutes, and so on. In this role his task is to ensure that these busy people do not waste any of their precious time. He may, secondly, act as their guide through the planning process itself, explaining to them where the technical pitfalls are, suggesting the next steps, and generally ensuring high professional planning standards. Thirdly, he may act as a member of the planning team in his own right in addition to either of these two other roles.

In a small company the planning assistant should, I suggest, act in all three capacities. It will be recalled from above that where a chief executive of a small firm is working on his own he should make every effort to find someone to join him in the exercise. It may be that the most suitable person is a trusted professional adviser – accountant, lawyer, banker or consultant – who could help him with calculations and collecting data, could guide him through the process and, most valuable of all, could become his confidant and adviser in the strategic discussions. The addition of such an experienced outsider's view is invaluable for the small firm and very valuable for any firm.

Such a person could also usefully fill out an otherwise rather slim team – where there are only two or three suitable people in a company. The planning assistant is, of course, a temporary appointment and usually part-time. His job lasts no longer than it takes to form the plan although his services will be required again, very part-time (except in the largest companies), in the monitoring stage.

This leads to the question, would it not be preferable for a professional adviser to carry out the entire corporate planning exercise for an organization? Surely the skilled outsider could do a better job in selecting strategies than the management might do, bearing in mind their inevitable biases and their narrow, irrational commitments to the various parts of the organization? My answer is a categoric no.

The strategy consultant

Corporate plans prepared by consultants too often suffer from these major defects:

- Errors made in the analytical stages. These are errors of fact which no senior executive would ever make about his own company but which the outsider cannot avoid unless he spends a quite inordinate time on his investigations.

- Recommending strategies which are not in accordance with the culture of the organization or with the personal wishes of the top executives or with their skills which the outsider may not have fully fathomed.
- Trying to be clever – consultants are tempted to propose strategic initiatives that appear imaginative, exciting and brilliant when what the company really needs is something that may be dull and boring but which is practical and profitable.
- Probably the most important, a company's executives will feel very little commitment to a set of strategies, however valid they may be, which they themselves have not proposed.

I believe that these defects are so severe as to render this route – handing over to the outsider – too dangerous to contemplate. A dull, limited strategy that has been devised by its executives, and owned by them, will take a company further, faster, and more safely, than any proposal from a consultant.

But what about a management that is unable to see their way out of a difficult strategic situation? Surely a consultant could show them? Well, possibly – certainly the views of an experienced outsider are often invaluable – but if a management cannot find their own route to salvation they may not be capable of following anyone else's. So while one should never hand the strategy formulation over to him, one certainly should consider whether a suitable blend of talents might result from some input from a consultant, either ad hoc when it was felt to be needed or as a full member of the planning team – but, notice, the consultant would then be acting within this team, as a member, along with several executives from the company. Given this clearly defined, limited, relationship the experienced consultant would be most helpful.

Surely, however, as a method of waking up a sleepy organization, the strategic ideas of a lively outsider would be ideal? No, I think not. Better by far to change the chief executive. He will invigorate the organization from inside, not just for the planning exercise but for every aspect of the organization.

My views here are so much at variance with other consultants that I need to expand them a little. First, on three occasions I have read the reports of consultants who have advised clients immediately before I have been invited to do the same. These reports –

from consulting firms of world renown – had failed to carry conviction with the client, and, to be frank I thought they were just plain wrong. I must emphasize that these were strategy consultants – they actually recommended certain specific strategies to these clients. I have already listed the reasons why strategy consultants get it so wrong. My specialism is as a process consultant, showing organizations how to devise their own strategies.

You may object that organizations call in advisers for every other subject under the sun, so why not corporate planning? My answer is that among the ingredients that go into a corporate strategic decision are the feelings, aims, experiences and ambitions of the top executives. As I said above, the views of the top people who run organizations today are becoming progressively more influential, but perhaps it is not fully realized how pivotal these sometimes are. Consider, for example, a group of engineering companies whose operations span a wide range from building power station generators (they make two and a half a year on average and each costs many millions of pounds) to manufacturing silicon chips (millions of them costing pennies each). Imagine that it is headed by a 62-year-old group chief executive whose career took him up the hierarchy via the generator division. He retires. The best man available – and he is very good indeed – is aged 41 and comes from the silicon chip subsidiary. It cannot seriously be said that this man will devise exactly the same strategy for this group as his predecessor.

A percentage of the ingredients that go into these decisions are the personal predilections of the chief executive, of his senior colleagues and, rapidly diminishing in influence, the next few levels in the hierarchy. My case is that too many strategy consultants fail to take these considerations into account.[4] Worse, consultants also have their own personal experiences, aims, ambitions and interests. Some will be perfectly at home in marketing and like a fish out of water in, say, acquisitions in Europe. They will weave all these traits into their recommendations. I have worked with other consultants on strategy assignments and have seen them doing it. They inject their own virus into the corporate body and it is rightly rejected. I do it myself – it is unavoidable when one's opinion is sought – but at least, when acting as a process adviser, one's views are taken as just one more opinion out of many that the team will be considering. When acting as a strategy consultant the consultant's views are paramount.

Planning directors and planning departments

One further alternative exists. This is to employ the services of a professional corporate planner inside the company and to hand the process over to him, as some very large companies do. This, it is argued, has the great advantage that he will understand the company much better than an outside consultant, will be in touch with the executives' opinions and aware of their biases, will appreciate their skills, and so on. True, but it does nothing to overcome the defect noted above – that executives will not feel they 'own' a plan that is not proposed by them. If this objection was of trivial or marginal significance then it might be out-pointed by the advantages of employing one's own corporate planner. Alas, this objection is neither trivial nor marginal, it appears to be central.

There are three possible roles for planning directors or managers. One is to invite them to prepare the plan themselves. It will be their plan, not that of the executives. I reject this.

Another is to act as a member of the planning team itself, providing they are of sufficient stature. I do not reject this because they may then become just one voice among the several on the team. However, as a member of the team *and* as planning director, this man's influence is going to exceed that of any other member. I doubt if it will really be their plan. Furthermore, especially if he has been selected for this post because he is academically well qualified – the myth that corporate planning requires acute intellectual prowess dies hard – he may consequently be lacking in practical operational experience and incapable of appreciating how difficult it is to carry through certain seemingly excellent ideas in the real world.

The third alternative is for him to act as planning assistant. At last I am happy. This is the correct role, I believe.

The above remarks apply not only to individual corporate planners but to whole planning departments, such as those employed in many large organizations. I am convinced that companies with corporate planning departments are, if anything, more liable to harbour neglected elephants than those with no such departments. This is because the top executives will have delegated corporate planning to the corporate planning department. This may lack the clout, the experience and the knowledge to address the elephants – so no one does.

Planning departments most certainly have their uses: to provide unbiased, professional, independent studies for the top executives, make economic and market forecasts, provide position papers, analyze country risks, hunt for new business areas, make strategic suggestions, analyze strategic proposals, wield planning techniques, search for acquisition candidates – all vital and excellent work, which many smaller companies would envy, but this is *not* corporate planning, it is strategic planning, often rather technique-orientated. This in no way detracts from the value of these departments – see the example in Chapter 12, where I describe how a group of companies realized that they stood in urgent need of just such a department.

The conclusion I have reached is that in only very few cases should any company consider inviting any person other than those who hold the reins of power to prepare a corporate plan for them. The very first step any top managers should take, after deciding to go ahead with such an exercise, is to form themselves into a planning team. If they appoint someone to help them he should be firmly informed that it is to be their strategic plan that comes out of the process, not his. That is why I insist on calling him the planning *assistant*.

Early problems

I said that the corporate planning process is an elephant hunt. In some cases the first elephant is found within seconds of the start. This occurs if the chief executive cannot *immediately* name his planning team. If he cannot do this it may imply that there is some defect in his top management structure. Either the structure itself is not appropriate or some of the executives are personally inadequate or at odds with each other. If such defects were found among, say, half a dozen salesmen, this would not cause any great distress to a company, but found among the top five people who run the company these symptoms might well amount to a strategic elephant.

I recounted just a case in Chapter 1 (the family firm with a split board hoping to expand in the Pacific Basin). I could have quoted many others. I know three building societies in which the chairman will not allow the general manager to manage, several family businesses where the executives are on positively poisonous terms with each other, a large electronics group where no less than ten executives report to the managing director, a group where there are 'dotted line' relationships with the senior functional heads (a very old-fashioned concept to find today) and a multinational with an unworkable matrix structure. Trouble at the top is quite a common elephant even in the best run companies. It is common in non-profit-making organizations who, as a rule, have not yet adopted the 'lean team' management philosophy of today (see Chapter 10).

Another early problem arises if the executives do not wish to undertake this planning project at all! There is a considerable body of opinion, whose views are understandably strengthened by the misconceptions I listed in Chapter 1, who quite simply reject the whole idea of corporate planning as useless. It all depends on the chief executive: if he does not wish to lead his team then the whole idea should be abandoned – the elephants will simply not be addressed if he is not the team leader, and corporate planning is worthless if the elephants are not caught. If he does wish to – and newly appointed chief executives virtually always do – then any sceptical colleagues will go along with him and I can almost guarantee that, by the second meeting, there will be no sceptics left.

A third early difficulty is that the constitution of the team will itself condition the nature of the strategies. Thus, if the chief executive has selected two people from the marketing function to serve on the team and no one from the finance function then he will have predetermined that the strategies will be market-biased. It is therefore important for a chief executive to check that his team fairly reflects the major areas of his company.

Group planning teams

This problem becomes acute in the case of groups of companies. Suppose a group has eight subsidiaries ranging in size from, say, £100m turnover down to £8m. It would be impractical to recruit all the eight managing directors (in addition to any group executives) on to the team. So who should be left out? Obviously, the three or four managing directors of the smallest divisions. This, however, invites a corporate plan that favours the largest divisions at the expense of the smaller.

In my view, this factor could be so critical that a group chief executive should either include all his divisional directors or none of them. If a group has three or four divisions then he could include them all. If it has many more than this then he should exclude them all. But he should then take note that his subsidiaries are so numerous that he ought to form a true group management team – a team of executives whose responsibilities relate to the group, not merely to the divisions. Thus he would have found his first elephant in the first five seconds – his group structure is defective!

What if one division is making a loss while the other two are profitable? Should the loss-making managing director be invited to join the planning team? The answer that group chief executives always seem to give today is, yes. But will he not be a nuisance, will he not seek to damage the process if it looks like leading to an unfavourable conclusion? The answer is, no. What often happens is that the managing director under attack gives a good defence of his section and may well help to bring its problems and its benefits into better focus. Whether he persuades his peers is another matter for they are all there, sitting round the table in the planning team with him, listening and judging – see Chapter 12 where the deliberations of a group planning team are described in intimate detail.

I can quote several cases when the presence of a divisional managing director has materially altered a planning team's conclusions. In one the closure of a loss-making division had been repeatedly demanded by other divisional executives – 'the group's life blood ebbing away'. However, during the corporate planning process, this divisional director was at last able to make it clear that this was not the case; his division was showing a loss only if certain accounting assumptions were made, assumptions which the other managing directors did not accept for their own divisions.[5] In another group the presence of a divisional director hastened the decision to sell off his division because he was strongly in favour of that move. He had never felt comfortable in the group and was sure his division would do better in another more suitable one.

However, having said this, there will certainly be occasions when, because this method of corporate planning relies so heavily on the executives themselves, they will fail to come to the right strategic conclusion or even to any conclusion at all. I have seen the latter twice. In one case there was not a majority in the team for the closure of part of the company and so the corporate planning process ended with no significant results. The closure was, however, effected a few months later, so perhaps the failure was more apparent than real. In another case the process came to a halt because of differences of opinion at the top regarding the long-term future.

Might it have been better, in these cases, if the company had invited outside consultants to prepare the plan for them and then persuade the executives to adopt it? Possibly. I cannot tell for sure but I doubt if they would have accepted an outsider's unpalatable opinions any more readily than they were willing to accept those of their colleagues.

One other problem arises where one division is much more profitable than the others. The director of that division will become impatient while his colleagues wrestle with various possible group strategies. It is all right for him, he is obviously going to get the lion's share of the group resources and he cannot understand why they are taking so long to say so. The group chief executive will simply have to exert his usual charm to keep him quiet, perhaps by reminding him that, only a few years ago, it was his division that was letting the side down. (If it never has then perhaps his impatience is justified!)

I have certainly seen members of a number of planning teams shift uncomfortably in their seats when the discussion touches a jagged departmental nerve, but I remain convinced that for the modern organization the planning team is by far the best medium for the corporate planning exercise.

The corporate planning process

Because the whole of the rest of this book is devoted to describing the corporate planning process, I shall be brief here. My aim now is merely to give a bird's eye view of the design of the process, now generally called the Argenti System of Corporate Planning.

Essentially the process consists of, first, collecting the necessary data, then looking at it in one grand picture so that the managers, by standing a long way back, can see their organization set within its total panoramic strategic situation, and then finally they will be able to decide how to steer it to prosperity through the next few years: data – study – decision. The amount of data required to play the game is tiny. You need to collect only three types of data: the corporate objective of the organization, its internal strengths and weaknesses, and the threats and opportunities that may lie ahead of it. That is all (see Figure 2.4). Collect these, lay them out clearly before you, and the strategic conclusions will spell themselves out with quite extraordinary clarity.

Figure 2.4 The data required

- The corporate objectives and targets.
- Strengths and weakness inside the organization.
- Threats and opportunities in its environment.

Just three key areas; leave out any of them and the corporate plan will be defective. One would think that it was a fairly obvious list of essential desiderata, yet companies prepare their corporate plans with one, or even two, of these essential elements missing!

So far as I know, my process is the only one that is complete. Other books on corporate planning deal only with parts of the process or suffer from the confusions considered at length in Chapter 1.

The ten stages

The actual process is broken down into ten stages (see Figure 2.5 and Appendix 4). While it is shown as a straight-through sequence, in practice there are sure to be eddies and whirls. Lessons learnt towards the end will invariably cause the planning team to look back and revise what they had previously decided.

The first stage calls for the formation of a planning team as described above. At their first meeting a number of miscellaneous administrative matters have to be attended to. They will select the planning assistant, discuss such matters as the timing of the next few meetings, make an approximate estimate of the duration of the exercise, select a suitable planning horizon (normally five years, see below) and so on.

The team then moves methodically through the remaining nine stages starting with one called 'corporate objectives'. As will be seen in the next chapter, my system places much emphasis on starting the corporate plan with corporate objectives and utterly disdains all planning systems that leave this step until later. This stage is completed when these objectives have been quantified into targets.

At Stage 3 the team is asked to forecast the likely performance of their company for the following five years (usually) in order to compare the target with the forecast to reveal the Gap.

Figure 2.5   The ten stages shown as a sequence

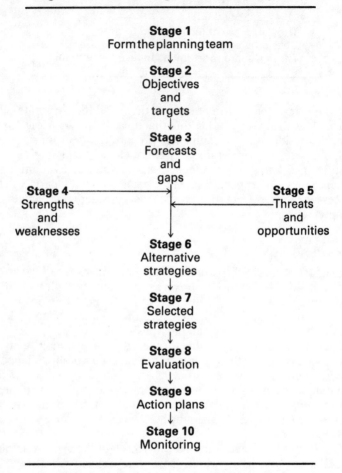

Many corporate planners dispensed with gap analysis after the oil crisis of 1973 because they felt that it had become impossible to make accurate long-term forecasts. In my view, it has never been possible to make an accurate long-term forecast and the correct approach is to admit that you cannot do this and to show explicitly how gross the errors might be. So in my system the team is very strongly recommended to make these forecasts and boldly and deliberately to display the errors. Having thus restored the act of forecasting to its rightful place in any planning process, gap analysis becomes possible again and it reveals a wealth of new knowledge about the strategic situation of the company.

Provided they have a competent planning assistant the team will be able to complete these two stages in two meetings – although not if there is a philosophical problem with the definition of objectives as there frequently is in non-profit-making organizations. If there is, it may take several meetings to resolve. When completed these two stages reveal to the team just what kind of strategy they should be seeking – whether it should be aggressive, defensive, profit-seeking, risk-reducing, or whatever, as well as how urgent and how large the strategic task is. A number of elephants will always be identified in these two stages. It is quite inconceivable that a corporate plan can be properly prepared without a gap analysis being performed; the sizing and phasing of the strategies depend upon it quite apart from the elephants invariably found here.

More will be found in the 'appraisals', beginning with the one in Stage 4, the Internal Appraisal. This is also called the strengths and weaknesses analysis, and I consider it to be the most important stage in the entire process – a view not shared by most corporate planners who seem to see the External Appraisal, especially the study of the market, as the most important.

One of the (deliberate) consequences of the design of this process is that strategies arising from it are biased against diversification unless it is related to a particular strength. Some strategists would see this as being unnecessarily risk-averse; I do not: I see diversification not based on a strength as irresponsible – but, of course, it is up to each organization to decide how much notice to take of these protective features in my design.

In the past twenty-five years I have tested a number of devices intended to identify strengths and weaknesses and have now stabilized on just one procedure which, because it is highly participative, seems to achieve excellent results in the democratic atmosphere that obtains in many companies today.

One of the most powerful roadblocks to the truthful identification of an organization's strengths and weaknesses is the emotional biases and prejudices that every executive harbours in his breast. Certain details in the process have been designed to reduce these obstructions.

This Internal Appraisal flushes out perhaps a dozen possible elephants relating to the company itself. Several others come out of the External Appraisal, or threats and opportunities analysis, in which the team searches for trends and events outside itself, and usually beyond its control, in its environment.

The strategies emerge

When these two appraisals are put together the team will begin to see in which general direction their strategies should lie. Thus while the size and urgency of the strategies will be shown by the gap analysis, the thrust of the strategies will be suggested by the appraisals. The gap and the appraisals together define all the corporate strategies that the organization requires.

The next two stages will see the strategies emerging. Stage 6 encourages a full range of alternative strategies to be considered and then the final list – the list of major actions that will ensure the company's longer term prosperity – is determined. As mentioned before, these strategic statements are usually very brief and they emerge from the process with extraordinary clarity. Here, for example, is the complete strategic statement for an insurance company:

- The most important strategic fact we identified was the relationship we have with our parent company. It is quite clear that even after seven years of association with them they have still not understood us. They have no idea how to set targets for us, do not know what we mean by 'appraised value', have no idea how an insurance company operates. Our first step in this strategy must be for the managing director to make a thoroughly professional, fully illustrated presentation to their entire top management team. It is ridiculous that it should be so, but this – our relations with our parent – is now seen as by far our largest elephant. It stands in the way of everything we want to do.
- Our expansion has been rapid. We see the market remaining buoyant for perhaps two more years. We should move into all areas adjacent to our existing business especially householder-related insurance, particularly contents, motor and personal householder needs. We will not enter aviation, marine or life in the foreseeable future. All suggestions in this direction are now seen as irrelevant to our needs.

- We have far too many branches in high streets. We should halve these but treble our direct selling staff in the next three years and switch emphasis in two ways: first, seek the AB socio-economic groups more vigorously (whom we cannot reach at present because our branches are generally in down-market areas) and greatly increase cross-selling – especially to the customers of our parent company and its other subsidiaries.
- We should double planned expenditure on the computer systems. These have very clearly been a major element in our past success. The systems cannot at present handle cross-selling and this is a major requirement of the new systems.
- We shall run out of office capacity in this town late next year. We already employ 12 per cent of local part-time female office workers and we should at once seek new premises and staff in a town not too distant from here (Northtown is an obvious choice).
- No change in personnel strategy is needed but, at the current rate of expansion, we must very carefully ensure that recruitment, training, salaries, promotion, etc., are commensurate with our future needs, while constantly bearing in mind that the current rate of expansion might stop dead at any time in the next two years.

In Stage 8 the planning team should undertake a very thorough evaluation of the strategies selected. As emphasized above, the Argenti System relies for its success on eliminating all details from the early stages, so that the elephants may be more clearly seen, but this means that, after the strategies have been provisionally agreed, a *detailed* analysis of their feasibility must be made.

Finally, someone must draw up a set of action plans designed to give effect to the strategies. Whether this is a legitimate task for a planning team is a moot point. I believe that it is not and that this is better done by the company's executives working in their normal executive capacities rather than as a planning team. The action plan stage, then, is often only supervised, not executed, by the planning team.

When the strategies have been put into action the team should meet again every few months for a monitoring session. This is intended to keep the strategies under review for their duration – a great many years in some cases. As the world changes, however, as trends and events that were not foreseen unfold, as targets are met and strategies successfully completed, as mistakes are made, so gradually the team will lose confidence in their original strategies. At last a monitoring meeting will inevitably take place at which it is agreed that the original strategies need to be revised and so the whole corporate planning process starts again with the setting of objectives, and so on through the process again, in the search for fresh strategic directions.

It would be most disappointing if any team had to start the corporate planning process again in less than a few years. After all, the whole idea is to review the company's long-term future and to devise a set of strategies that 'will attend to all the matters that it must get right in order to prosper over the next few years'. Most corporate plans should therefore be expected to endure for several years, occasionally even as long as a decade.[6]

Top-down

The philosophy of this method of corporate planning is essentially top-down, that is, a corporate plan should never be built up by adding together the plans of the company's constituent parts. This does not mean that the corporate plan should be prepared with no regard to the parts – that would be absurd – but it does mean that any part that does not fit may be discarded, rather than the corporate entity having to accommodate all the parts whether they fit or not. Top-down means the strategy is right for the whole; the dog wags the tails.

In practice, this has particularly important implications for groups of companies (see Figure 2.6). It is essential to start a corporate plan for a group with a group corporate plan. This will answer such questions about the group as whether the number, size and activities of each subsidiary is appropriate, whether the group's geographical spread is sensible, whether it is effectively structured – all matters that relate to the group as a corporate whole. Only when these group issues have been addressed should the divisions, and then the profit centres, start to prepare their plans.

Their plans will, needless to say, be made with the result of the group plan firmly in mind. Part of the result of the group plan will be a statement of the intended role for each division or profit centre in the group, and so the output of the senior plan becomes part of the input of the junior one – not the other way round. Top-down, not bottom-up; the tails do not wag the dog.

Figure 2.6   Top-down means starting the process for a group before starting for a division

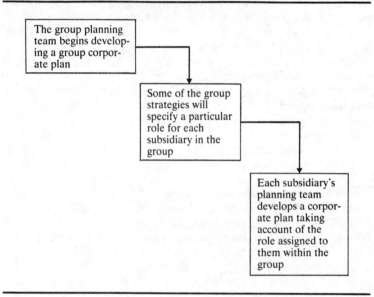

The group planning team begins developing a group corporate plan

Some of the group strategies will specify a particular role for each subsidiary in the group

Each subsidiary's planning team develops a corporate plan taking account of the role assigned to them within the group

All these matters will be described in great detail in the succeeding chapters. I end this section on a note of uncertainty. I suspect that corporate planning can only be performed in a profit centre, not in a cost centre. I am quite sure it cannot be carried out in a single department because that would become production planning, or manpower planning, or whatever, not corporate planning. In a profit centre, where a general manager is responsible for incomes as well as costs and expenses, an infinity of strategies is available to develop the business in limitless different ways. In a cost centre it may only be possible to cut costs, and where that is so then I doubt if corporate planning can usefully be employed. Where the brief is wider than that then presumably it can.

The currency of a plan

The intention is that the corporate plan resulting from this process should remain valid and viable for a considerable number of years.

Of course, the details of any plan will need to be changed as the world changes but the strategies themselves should remain current for years. My vision of corporate planning is that it is a batch process, not a continuous one like budgeting, production planning and so on. You do not have to keep doing corporate planning, you do it from time to time when something warns you to do it, just as in one's own private life one does not continually ask oneself whether one is in the right job, the right house, the right nation, married to the right spouse with the right number of children – one asks oneself such strategic questions only at rare intervals, prompted by major trends and events in one's life. It is the same with companies.

As time passes certain trends and events will occur and, eventually, the original strategies will be completed, will run out of steam or be rendered invalid by the changing world. The monitoring stage is intended to pick up such trends and to alert the management when a new change in strategies is required. My monitoring stage is equivalent to the 'Strategic Management' that one sees in textbooks. After a top management team has been through the corporate planning process described here they will never again allow their company to slip behind the times. They will constantly be watching their company's strengths and weaknesses and the threats and opportunities that will be developing in the world outside, constantly monitoring their strategic stance. They will then be managing strategically.

A major feature in the design of the Argenti System is the principle that no strategy that might become invalid within a few years should be adopted. The aim is to design strategies that take account of the fact that certain important changes *cannot* be predicted. The aim must be to look beyond and above such unpredictable trends and events and to design strategies to take account of them. For example, since one cannot predict the price of oil – not even whether it will go up or down over the next few years, let alone trying to pick a figure, as the experts pretend they can – a company may need to develop a strategy that begins: 'In order to protect ourselves from fluctuations in the price of oil, we will . . .' and they alter the whole strategic shape of the company for that precise reason.

This is what *strategic* means. Operational planning is planning what you have got as best you can; strategic is changing what you have got. Operational planning is handling a rowing boat in a storm; strategic planning is building a bigger boat. The trouble is it all takes time.

Of course, major events do occur unpredictably, and then even one's *strategic* plans may have to be scrapped and rebuilt entirely. As a general rule, however it is the aim of the Argenti System to develop strategies that will be valid for a number of years. There are a number of specific devices in the system designed to deter managements from basing a strategy on a forecast that may turn out to be unexpectedly wrong (these are listed in Appendix 4). Facing up to errors in forecasts is a major feature in the system.

The planning horizon

This leads to one further technical question to be discussed in this chapter, how far ahead should you try to plan and what should be the 'horizon' of the plan?

I recommend that most companies should start with a five-year horizon. Some may need to lengthen this later in the process or, occasionally, companies find that it is practical to reduce it. Five years may seem a very long way ahead to look in the uncertain world of today but the following should be borne in mind:

- Corporate planning is concerned with major structural changes to the very nature and character of a company. Some of these may take several years to bring about and one needs to think ahead to the time when these changes will have taken effect.
- Many changes in the outside world take four or five years to occur. Political change, for example, is closely geared to general elections which, in many democracies, take place at four- or five-year intervals. Economic cycles often come to their peaks or troughs over a four- or five-year period. Many new technologies take several years to affect any given business area after they have first appeared.
- If one focuses on a much shorter period – two or three years, say – the planners will merely revisit their current problems. It is an essential function of the corporate planning process to look *beyond* these. By not looking far enough ahead they could miss the whole point of doing corporate planning and they would just go over all the same problems with the same short-range view as they normally use, when what is really needed is to step well back from everyday affairs and take a

more distant view of their company. For a fashion company, for example, not to look five years ahead, because its business is geared to the Collections, is to miss the point of corporate planning completely.

So one should start with a minimum of five years and expect to have to increase this span rather than reduce it. There are occasions when five years is excessive. For example, for a small company that is growing very fast – 30 per cent per annum or more – in a rapidly moving industry it may not make sense to look further than, say, three years. On the other hand, a company in which any strategic act might take more than five years to complete should look ahead to the completion of that project. For example, it takes several years for a government to draw up a specification for a new military aircraft, it then takes several years to develop it, and it is in service for decades. Plainly, aircraft companies need to look ahead at least one decade. Some very large companies look ahead two or even three.

The general rule is, look further ahead in corporate planning than the company has ever looked before. This exercise is intended to change the future course of the organization. Organizations tend to endure for several decades before they finally shrink to insignificance – 'rags to riches in three generations' is rather more than just a joke – and this exercise is intended to span quite a significant fraction of any organization's entire life-cycle.

When it should not be used

There are a few occasions when it would be best not to attempt to introduce corporate planning into an organization at all (see Figure 2.7).

If a company is in serious financial difficulties – in other words, if it is in danger of going bust – then it should not attempt this exercise. If a company is going bust it simply does not have the time to do corporate planning. What is needed in such circumstances is a vigorous turn-round or a liquidation. It is very understandable for a chief executive, whose company is in dire difficulties, to seek refuge in dreams of a distant future, but it will waste time – an essential commodity when the writs are flying.

Careful timing is also required if a company is about to experience some major internal or external upheaval. Experience warns me that if, for instance, two out of the six most senior managers are about to retire it might be wise to wait until their replacements have been appointed; or if the government has announced that it proposes to legislate major changes in the company's industry it may be better to wait until some of the details are announced; or if the company is expecting to be taken over; or if it is about to be listed on a stock market – a process with a notoriously ravenous appetite for top management time.

Figure 2.7   When not to use corporate planning

- When a company is going bust.
- When an organization is very young and still knows exactly what it is doing for whom and is patently on course for doing it.
- In any organization run by an autocrat.
- When a brief major upheaval is in prospect.

As I have said before, I doubt if corporate planning should be attempted where an autocrat rules. Such people prefer to develop their own plans in their own heads without reference to anyone else and then, when their plans are ready they do not often bother to explain them but simply give instructions. Such people neither need nor will want to use a participative process such as this one.

Summary

This is what corporate planning is for: to identify what are the half-dozen things that an organization *must* get right if it is to prosper over the following few years. Normally, indeed usually, it achieves not only this task but it does so to the sound of acclamation from the participants with a consequent lift in morale and motivation.

Corporate planning is not business planning; nor is it forecasting, manpower planning, merger planning, financial planning or co-ordinating. It is unique in that it is designed to look at the forest, not the trees. It demands very little data. It is simple, not complex. It is judgmental, not technical. Above all, it is nothing to do with marketing – it is to do with whatever is strategically important (which often is marketing, of course).

The process itself is quite simple, consisting of setting objectives, then a data-gathering stage (data is required both from inside and outside the company) and a strategy-formulating stage. It is rare for a corporate plan to contain more than half a dozen strategies. These must then be developed into detailed action plans and business plans – but these are executive tasks, not part of the corporate planning process. Finally, there is the monitoring.

It is a process that should be carried out *only* by those who hold the reins of power, assisted by a 'planning assistant', and perhaps an experienced outsider.

CHAPTER 3

Corporate Objectives and Corporate Conduct

As I explained in the previous chapter, a most important feature of my system of corporate planning is the sequence of meetings to be held by the planning team, each meeting being dedicated to one of the major stages in my process. This sequence is the backbone of the system, each meeting is a vertebra.

I also explained that, apart from the first meeting, in which the team would make a number of administrative decisions, their first working session should be devoted to deciding corporate objectives and corporate conduct, and setting targets for these. Although this stage will normally take only one meeting, some of the issues raised here are so important and controversial, especially for non-profit-making organizations, that several meetings may be needed to do them justice. In this chapter I will discuss corporate objectives and corporate conduct in general and for companies in particular, leaving objectives for non-profit-making organizations to the next chapter and setting targets in Chapter 5.

Corporate objectives

In my view, the confusion over the meaning of the words 'corporate objective' is responsible for more planning disasters than almost anything else. Some corporate planners seem to think that corporate objectives are so philosophical as to be not worth discussion and they leave them out entirely. Some set objectives of such unctious saintliness as to be unattainable. Some decide objectives at the end of the corporate planning process, some in the middle, and some review them only after deciding the strategies. The whole debilitating muddle is due to a failure to understand just how fundamental the words 'corporate objective' really are.

Three meanings of the words

The words 'corporate objective' are commonly used with at least three entirely different meanings. Consider this typical statement of objectives that one might find in any textbook or in the corporate plan of any company:

'Statement of Corporate Objectives for The Eagle Engine Company

(1)   We propose to increase our share of the market.
(2)   We aim to be excellent employers.
(3)   We intend to make satisfactory profits.
(4)   We wish to lead the engine industry in technology.
(5)   Our objective is to remain independent.'

The five statements above may all appear to be 'objectives', but in fact they fall into three entirely different logical categories. In my view, only statement 3 represents the genuine 'corporate objective'. For a company to aim to make a profit is, I believe, its only true purpose. Every company that was ever formed was formed to do that; every company that ever failed did so because it did not make a profit. Profit is the *raison d'être* of every company; a company which is not aiming to make a profit is simply not a company.

What about the other items? The Eagle Engine Company was not formed to increase its market share and it will not fail even if its market share declines. It will not fail if it does not lead the industry. It will not fail if it stops making engines and switches to crankshafts instead. It will not fail if it is not independent and so on through all the other items, and indeed, *for any other item anyone can think of, with the sole exception of profit.* In other words, you cannot think of *any* reason for forming a company except to make a profit. If you are thinking of forming an organization in order to make a profit then what you are thinking of is forming a company.

If that is so, what is the standing of the other four 'corporate objectives' in the list? Two of them turn out to be possible corporate strategies; two of them are statements about corporate conduct.

A corporate *strategy* is any line of action which a management believes will help to achieve the corporate objective – increasing market share, for example, and becoming a leader in technology. Making engines is a strategy – all these are strategies that may contribute to profits. A corporate *conduct* statement is any general rule that regulates one's actions on ethical grounds, such as being an excellent employer.

Let me summarize these three entirely different uses of the phrase 'corporate objective' and then I shall use it only with one particular meaning, as 'the Corporate Purpose'.

Corporate Purpose Corporate purpose is the reason why any organization was formed and why it continues to exist. Corporate purpose is the vindication for all its strategies, all its actions, indeed, everything it ever does in its entire life history. It is the justification for its very existence, its *raison d'être*. It is the sole criterion by which one may judge whether an organization is a success or a failure. It is the ends as opposed to the means. An organization's corporate purpose is unalterable. If it is changed, the organization itself would have to be reconstituted as a new legal entity.

Corporate Conduct Any action taken (or deliberately *not* taken) because it is felt to be morally, aesthetically, socially or personally desirable (or repugnant). Actions taken for this reason would be taken *regardless* of whether they increased or decreased the organization's ability to achieve its corporate purpose, or even if they made it impossible; they are taken because they are the right thing to do. Conduct is largely independent of purpose. (Corporate conduct is also referred to as ethos, values, culture, code of ethics, standards of behaviour, social responsibilities, etc.)

Corporate Strategies These are actions taken because, and *only* because, the management believe they will improve the organization's ability to achieve its purpose or its standards of conduct. If they believed such actions would not help to achieve these they would not take them. Strategies are means, not ends. Their *sole* justification is their effect on achieving the purpose or conduct.

These are the only three legitimate corporate decisions any organization can make; either it is deciding its corporate purpose, or its

conduct, or it is selecting a strategy. No other decisions are
legitimate or required, nor even logically possible. Objectives,
conduct, strategy: see Figure 3.1.

Figure 3.1   The three decisions

There are only three types of decision that any corporate body can
take:

- Deciding the **corporate objective** – i.e. describing what is its
  purpose or *raison d'être*.
- Defining its **corporate conduct** – i.e., describing how it proposes
  to behave while achieving its objective or purpose.
- Determining its **corporate strategies** – i.e. resolving how it is going
  to achieve its objective while adhering to its code of conduct.

Once these have been recognized there is seldom any doubt as to
which is which. For example, does the Eagle Engine Company wish
to treat its employees well because this is the right thing to do, or
because this will improve their profits – is it part of its culture or a
strategy? There is a simple test. You ask the organization, 'Are you
doing this to increase your profits?' If they are, it is a strategy. If
not, it is part of their culture.

So far as I know this analysis is not clearly stated anywhere else
and so I would like to disentangle the interaction between these
three elements as follows: an objective is *what* it is trying to do,
strategies are *how* it is going to do it and conduct is how it is going to
behave while doing it. An organization can set itself such a rigorous
set of moral rules that it fails to find any strategies powerful enough
to achieve its aims.

Corporate perversion

While these three are the only legitimate decisions, there is a
category of illegitimate ones. For example, what is behind Eagle's
objective to 'remain independent'? If Eagle is a privately owned
company, and if this statement reflects the aims of the owners, then
this is a perfectly legitimate 'culture' statement which reflects the
owners' personal pleasure in running their own company.
However, suppose Eagle is a public company, or suppose this

statement comes not from the owners but from the management, then this may be a case of 'corporate perversion' – that is, where the management (in this instance) turns an organization to their own advantage. Obviously, if Eagle was sold off the owners would benefit but the managers might lose their jobs.

As a general rule the more accurately an organization's objectives are stated the more difficult must it be for anyone to pervert it.[1]

Because of this phenomenon perhaps we need a fourth category for the meaning of the word 'corporate objective' – 'corporate perversion', which could be defined as: 'Any corporate objective, conduct or strategy declared by any interest group or pressure group (often the managers themselves) which has the effect of perverting the resources of the organization for their own ends.' Any action taken on behalf of an organization that contributes neither to its purpose nor to its ethos is probably perverted.[2]

I do not believe this analysis is of merely academic interest. I believe it goes to the very heart of the massive range of misunderstandings that swarm around the 'set objectives' stages in the various rival corporate planning systems and, indeed, in the art and science of management itself. Setting the wrong corporate objectives, whether out of ignorance or due to deliberate perversion, is, I believe a *far* greater cause of poor corporate performance than inadequate management.

At the technical level, where one is concerned with the design of planning systems, the above discussion shows that 'corporate purpose' and 'conduct' are *inputs* to the corporate planning process while strategies are the *output*. Failure to understand this vitiates the design of many other planning systems, but I will come back to this later.

The above also shows how vital it is to 'set objectives' *before* one attempts to design a strategy – strategies are supposed to achieve the objectives, that is what they are for. To decide strategies first and then to set objectives makes no sense whatever. Only in a world of madmen would one tailor an organization's ultimate purpose to fit its strategies rather than the other way round.

It is absurd, therefore, to show strategies and objectives as part of a cycle – see Figure 3.2, which one finds in many forms in almost every textbook on management. The last thing anyone wants a management to do is to select a strategy and then, as in the left-hand loop of this figure, alter the objectives so the strategy will achieve them – that would render the task of management a little too easy!

Figure 3.2   A false picture

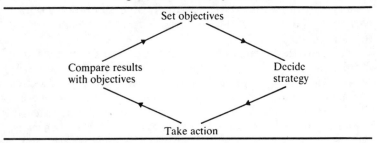

There is something else that these illiterate writers on management have failed to grasp: a *corporate* objective is not merely the top objective in the hierarchy of objectives that one finds in every organization. It is not only different in degree, but, because it is the top one, it is different in kind. This is because at the very top of any organization there is a supreme objective which is not set by a manager at all. It is set by the nature of the organization itself. It is different in kind to managerial objectives – just as, in a chain, the links at each end are logically different to those in the middle. This top one cannot be altered at all because it is determined by certain people who sit *above* the most senior executive of all (i.e. above the 'chief executive'). Who can these people be, who are more senior than the most senior manager?

Cui bono?

This Latin phrase, 'For whose benefit?', seems to be forgotten in discussions on corporate objectives. But organizations are formed by people for people. Normally the intention of the founders, at the time of formation, is absolutely clear and stunningly simple: 'to make us a profit', 'to educate the children of Eastville', 'to help the handicapped of Northtown', 'to protect the environment of Northern Europe', and so on – the variety of the aims and objectives of human organizations are a spectacular tribute to man's ingenuity! All organizations, remember, are formed by one group of people for the benefit of another group – or sometimes for their own benefit.

Some organizations are more successful than others and part of the explanation of their success rests in the selection of the corporate purpose itself. Thus, as a general rule, success is related to the homogeneity of the beneficiaries, the simplicity and verifiability of the objective, its appeal to the beneficiaries and its social acceptability.[3]

Management textbooks are full of prescriptions for success, but these invariably relate to the actions that the *managers* can take to influence the performance of their organizations – how to motivate employees, design new products, evaluate projects and a thousand others. Alas, we are seldom told of the importance of setting the organization's objective correctly in first place (see Figure 3.3 for the five factors relating to the objectives on which the success of all organizations so much depend).

Figure 3.3 The five criteria for corporate objectives

---

(1) The homogeneity of the beneficiaries.
(2) The appeal of the objective to them.
(3) The simplicity of the objective.
(4) The objective's verifiability.
(5) The social acceptability of the objective.

I shall be referring to all these factors later but I want to highlight one of them now. One of the reasons why profit-making organizations have been such a remarkably effective form of human organization – in terms of their impact on mankind they must rival even those great religions and the mighty military organizations of the past – is the unusual ease with which their objectives may be verified. There is really not much doubt about whether a given company is making a satisfactory profit or not.

To determine the corporate objective of any organization correctly we need to know three things with some precision: (1) who are the intended beneficiaries, (2) what is the benefit they are entitled to expect from their organization, and (3) what is a 'satisfactory' level of this benefit (see Figure 3.4).

Figure 3.4   The three essential elements of the corporate purpose

- The **intended beneficiaries** – i.e. the people for whom the organization exists.
- The **intended benefit** – i.e. what the organization is to do for them.
- The **corporate performance** – i.e. what level of benefit is satisfactory.

The Intended Beneficiary

Let us start with the Intended Beneficiaries. Notice the word *intended* beneficiaries. I insist on this because most organizations yield benefits to a wide range of people. A school, for example, benefits the teachers because they derive satisfaction and employment from it, it benefits the local community, the nation benefits, the school's builders and maintenance workers benefit, and so on. That is not what the school is for, however; no one founds a school saying to himself, 'This will be good for the teachers, the nation, the builders', although the fact all these other people do benefit would certainly be a positive factor in his mind. He would found the school even if this were not the case; he would found it just as enthusiastically even if it was to be built and operated entirely by robots. All these are incidental beneficiaries. The intended beneficiaries are quite obviously the children. The intended beneficiaries of any organization are the people for whose benefit it exists. That is what it is for. The Northtown Golf Club is for the golfers of Northtown. The Union of Boilermakers is for the benefit of boilermakers, and so on. Normally the intended beneficiaries are easily identifiable.

Then we come to the second feature in the definition of corporate purpose, the intended benefit; that is, what the organization is going to do for its beneficiaries. A school is going to educate them, a hospital will restore them to health, a golf club will provide facilities for playing golf, and so on. No need to bore the reader with the obvious. The trouble comes, as we will see later, when it is not so obvious.

I suggested above that one of the most successful types of organization yet devised by man is the company. Because its purpose is so simple, so verifiable, so powerfully attractive to the beneficiaries, it is remarkably easy to set its corporate objectives – it is far easier to do this for a company than for almost any other type of organization. I propose to spend some time, therefore, describing the process of setting objectives for companies before going on to the more difficult case of non-profit-making organizations in the next chapter and then setting targets in Chapter 5.

Defective corporate objectives

First, I want to spend some time discussing a number of highly popular, but completely erroneous, objectives for companies that one frequently finds in management textbooks. Managers in non-profit-making organizations please note, they are as wrong for you as they are for companies.

Survival

It is said that the prime aim of all organizations is survival. I would respectfully suggest, however, that no organization in the history of mankind has ever been formed in order to survive. All organizations that have ever been formed are founded to do something useful for someone, like make a profit, feed the starving or succour the poor.

If you want to argue that an organization would not survive if it failed to achieve its aims and therefore its first aim was to survive, fine, but do not waste the time of a busy chief executive with such a trivial tautology.

Survival may well be the aim of a company in trouble – it will aim to survive for another year or so in the hope that it can then turn the corner – but this is a short-term minnow of an objective: it is hardly what we mean by 'the corporate purpose'.

I imagine the idea that 'survival' is the aim of organizations is due to a silly mix-up with the word 'organism'. The aim of most organisms does indeed appear to be the survival of their species but to make the mental leap from the aims of a creature to those of an organization is to stretch our language a little far.

Maximize

There are two problems with such objectives as, 'We aim to maximize profits' or, 'We aim to optimise return on capital', or, 'Our objective is to minimize costs' or, 'As much as possible'. First, you cannot verify whether you have done it. How do you verify that the profits made last year were 'maximized? How do you check that they could not conceivably have been higher? Do you call in a firm of accountants to sign a certificate: 'I certify this company maximized its profits last year'? Or that costs were truly minimized, that not one more penny could have been squeezed? If you cannot tell whether you have achieved a certain objective or not there is no point whatever in setting it. Secondly, I am not sure that many companies really do want to maximize their profits. Do many companies wish to strain every whisker to earn more profits even though they know that these are already munificent? Would they really ignore all risks, cast aside all humanity, deny all morality just to extract the last penny?

Strategies

I have already suggested that, 'Our objective is to increase our market share', cannot be a corporate objective. It might be the objective of a marketing or a sales department in a company, but it cannot be the *corporate* objective for the company itself, as a corporate whole. If this is not a corporate objective, what is it? Answer: it is a strategy. A company will attempt to increase its market share if, but only if, the management believe that increasing market share will increase its profits. But surely companies always want to increase their market share?

Contrary to the impression given by some academics and consultants, there are without doubt occasions when increasing market share has a wholly damaging effect on a company's profits: when it has stretched its market so far that it is now serving uneconomic customers, when its battle to retain its share against a competitor costs it more than its margins, when it should be developing an entirely new market, and so on. To state baldly that 'increase market share' is an objective, before even considering whether it is valid for one's company in its current strategic situation, does not seem to me to be very bright.

'Market share' is, alas, only one example of countless other strategies which have found their way into textbooks masquerading as corporate objectives. Others are: 'Our function is to make widgets' or, 'We aim to be the leading company in this field' or, 'We wish to become the technology leader' or, 'We must increase turnover'. Certainly, any of these *may* be the route to greater profit, but they may not. How do we find out? Answer: by going through the corporate planning process! This is what it is for. It is a process for deciding which are the key strategies that the company should adopt to ensure the attainment of a satisfactory profit over the next few years. One of these strategies might be to increase market share, another might be to gain the leadership of the industry; or, on the contrary, it may be better to *reduce* market share, *not* to gain the leadership.

All these strategies, therefore, should be *outputs* of the corporate planning process; the only legitimate inputs are the corporate objectives and the conduct statements. One may – indeed one must – tell the corporate planning process what the objectives are and what the ethical parameters are to be. The process is supposed to generate the strategies for you, so to start the process by telling it the answers is a very silly thing to do.

Trojan Horse objectives

Let me give some more examples to make sure that there is no misunderstanding. What I am discussing here are all 'Trojan Horse objectives' where the management thinks it is deciding the corporate objectives but, hiding inside them, so to speak, is a strategy.

One 'corporate objective' I have often seen stated at the start of the planning process is, 'We must improve our profit margins'. It is very tempting, when margins have fallen recently, to wish to reverse this painful, even frightening, trend. However, making this statement right at the start, as an input, automatically rules out all strategies that might have the effect of reducing margins. You may ask why a company should ever want to *reduce* its margins, but this is quite often the case.

For example, if a company wishes to make a strategic move down-market it might have to cut its margins – providing that volume increases at least pro rata, or providing that it cuts costs pro rata, this move could enhance its long-term profits. By stating at the start, 'We must increase margins', the management arbitrarily eliminates all strategies based on decreasing them.

Another occasion is when an industry has reached maturity and competition is so strong and persistent that there is no hope of increasing margins. All sorts of other strategies may be called for in this condition, including getting out of that sector. Then there is 'de-skilling' – that is, reducing the value-added content of a product perhaps because one cannot obtain sufficient skilled labour.

'Increase margins' is not an infallible strategy, therefore. You cannot take it for granted. You surely ought not to rule out a whole raft of alternatives before even thinking about their effects?

Here is another example of confusing objectives with strategies. This one warped the whole of the subsequent corporate planning exercise. A company, whose chairman was the head of a government agency for promoting exports, decided that its corporate objective statement should include the words, 'We aim to double exports in the next five years'. Now, this company had, over the past many years, been the industry's technological leader and had lavishly exported all over the world, but, quite recently, it had lost this lead. It was no longer number one, it was now fourth; its foreign competitors were demolishing it at home and abroad. What the company plainly needed to do was to modernize the processes by which its products were manufactured – then, with any luck, it could regain a little of its former glory. As for doubling exports, that was a completely irrelevant dream; the company would be lucky not to have them halved. It was some time before any of his executives had the courage to point out that the chairman's Trojan Horse had saddled them with a red herring.

Perhaps the most popular of all these Trojan Horse objectives is turnover. *Everyone* goes for that. There is a multinational group whose current turnover is $2,600m. The group headquarters has publicized a wonderful new corporate objective called 'Target Five Billion' – they are aiming to double turnover to $5,000m in five years. The UK subsidiary earns 18 per cent margins on sales and the Italian subsidiary earns 7 per cent in a good year. Who cares about such trivia – everyone must double turnover – even though the UK company could quadruple it and Italy should halve it!

It is exceedingly difficult to wean executives off turnover. It is the one figure the entire top team will know by heart for the past several years. Few of them will remember the profit figures for even last year, let alone for several years ago.

The lesson seems to me to be this: *never* pre-empt the corporate planning process by stating what the strategies are to be before you start. Objectives and conduct are the input: strategies are the output. I like the phrase 'strategy-neutral' corporate objectives. The corporate objective should tell everyone very clearly what the purpose of the organization is; it should never tell the managers how to achieve it. Aims, not means.

In the past year I have seen three parent companies set what they thought were objectives to their subsidiaries, but which in my opinion were actually strategies. One was Target Five Billion, above. Another told one of its subsidiaries to increase its national market share from 6 per cent to 15 per cent by Year 5 – an instruction we found rather odd since this subsidiary had 25 per cent market share in one area of the country and nil in the rest. Where was it supposed to aim for 15 per cent we asked head office? 'Oh, um, er' came the crisp reply. The third told its subsidiary to cut its staff by 10 per cent across the board; it was not given the chance to cut the over-staffed sales department nor to preserve intact the highly respected research team. 'Cuts' is a very common measure for which there is some excuse since it is plainly born of panic at head office.

It is perfectly legitimate for a parent to tell a subsidiary what its strategies should be, especially if there are in the form of a carefully considered role for the subsidiary within the group's corporate plan. 'Due to the balance of risk in the group we are asking the subsidiary in India to reduce its activities' – that approach seems entirely legitimate. But none of the groups above had a group corporate plan! (The example in Appendix E describes how to, and how not to, develop a strategy for a subsidiary within a group.)

I am amazed at the casual way some highly professional managements treat the setting of objectives. The amount of damage one can do to an organization by setting it the wrong corporate objective is quite startling!

Service to society

'We provide a service to the community.' All organizations do this (all legal ones, anyway) and so it tells you nothing new about any organization. My own view is that no entrepreneur ever forms a company saying to himself, 'I will form a company to provide a service to the community.' What he may say is, 'If I form this company I might make a satisfactory profit out of providing this (specific) service to (specific) customers.'

Surely no person in his right mind would ever form an organization 'to benefit society'. To benefit the homeless of Southtown, yes; the golfers of Eastville, yes; even, in the case of the British Government, to benefit the British, and the European Community, to benefit Europeans. But no organization, however wide its remit, can aim to benefit 'society'.

Management ratios

The planning team should avoid corporate objectives that are really just *management* objectives. 'We must improve output per hour', is a suitable objective for a factory manager. 'We must aim for zero defects' is fine as a target for the computer department or the despatch section. Miles per gallon, defects per thousand, profit per employee, sales per call – all excellent targets for employees throughout the organization but absolutely irrelevant at the corporate level.

If you set these as the top, corporate, objective, you simply pre-empt all strategies that might be based on reducing some of the ratios you thought you should increase. But why should a company ever want to *reduce* output per man-hour? 'Reduce output per man-hour?' I hear you snort. 'Must be mad!' However, there are a dozen possible strategic reasons for doing so: going for higher quality, going for higher added value, buying in less of the product – all these are perfectly reasonable strategies which would have been arbitrarily ruled out if this objective had been adopted. But surely you never want to *increase* the amount owed to you by customers? Yes you might; in some situations this is a splendid device for securing customer loyalty.

I know of no ratio which is intrinsically 'better' just because it is bigger.

Mission

A mission statement often reads as follows: 'We aim to become the leading concrete mixer company on the West Coast.' Or, 'Our mission is to serve the shipbuilding industry of the United Kingdom.' Or, 'By 1995 we will become the pre-eminent group selling financial and related services to the UK mass market.' Or, 'We aim to develop as a Centre of Excellence.'

While I do not object to mission statements that *come out* of the corporate planning process – they are, after all, very like my strategy statements – I am alarmed and astounded when textbooks suggest that they should *precede* the corporate planning process, that companies should make their mission statements before they start their corporate plan. The mission is thus an input, it is given the status of the corporate objective. However, except by means of a careful, logical discussion, similar to the corporate planning process, I know of no way of deciding what any given company's mission statement should be.

Suppose a company decides to 'be the leading paint supplier to the marine repair industry in the UK'. It presumably chose this mission because this is actually what the company already is. Now, this does not seem a very clever thing to do; mission statements are surely like strategy statements, they are supposed to guide a company's strategic decisions over the next few years. The above statement suggests that this company should remain just what it is. Not very adventurous. Or maybe this is *not* what it already is, but in that case how did they select this mission? Either they just selected it, off the tops of their heads, or they went through a corporate planning-like exercise.

I believe that mission statements are nothing to do with corporate planning, they are public relations statements. Mission statements usually dwell on the moral aspects of a company. One would happily adopt the statement, 'We will enhance the quality of our products.' That is fine, you can say this in public. But what do you say in public when your strategy is, 'We will move down-market, cut the price and the quality, and deskill the labour force'? You cannot put it like that out loud, certainly not to the employees. Mission statements are useful for non-profit-making organizations, too, and several local governments have adopted slogans like 'Serving Our Community' which they display on their vehicles.

Mission statements should either be outputs of the corporate planning process, not the inputs; or they should be seen for what they are: PR. They have to sound good. They are very useful, too, for inspiring the troops, for summing up in one pithy, positive, phrase the outline of the company's strategies. One multinational is even thinking of making 'strategic vision statements' within which a mission statement will be used to describe its moral code.

I have said that 'profit' is the sole purpose of a company. Some people are highly motivated by this aim: ambitious managers, shareholders, pension funds, and so on. Others, however, find it boring or even immoral. Very well, let us make use of a rallying cry to motivate the troops, something like, 'We aim to be one of the nation's top wealth creators.'

I have a further objection to mission statements: they seldom include a reference to the beneficiaries of the organization. It is somewhat sterile to do something, however grand the design, unless it is clear for whose benefit you are doing it. Mission statements invariably lack this key element. 'We aim to become the world's leading left handed widget maker.' Cui bono?

What business?

Some textbooks tell us to start the process by asking, 'What business are we in?' The answers often look rather like a mission statement. 'We are in the business of illumination', says a company making light bulbs. Or, 'We are in the business of pest control' – that was from a company making rat-poison.

I have the same objection to starting from this point as for the mission statements; I know of no rationale for such decisions (other than via a corporate planning-like process). The company making light bulbs, for example, could equally well say that it was 'in the business of glass-blowing' or '. . . of electronics'. The rat-poison company could have selected, 'We are in the business of chemical manufacture.' Each definition points these companies in different directions. Which direction is correct – chemicals or pest control, drinking glasses or lasers? How on earth are we to know until we have made our study in the corporate planning process? The simple announcement that one is a chemical company does not make it so.

I am making the same point again: never start the corporate planning exercise with a statement of anything except that the company wishes to make a satisfactory profit and that it is going to observe a certain code of behaviour in achieving this. If you say anything else at all, you simple pre-empt all the rational decisions that are supposed to come out of the corporate planning process.

Excellence

One result of that remarkable book *In Search of Excellence* is that many companies now aim for excellence. In my view this is not a corporate objective, it is a possible strategy. But excellence is not so universally desirable as a strategy that it can be assumed to be appropriate for every company.

Decades ago there was a hotel that catered for the crowned heads of Europe – it was beyond compare, it exuded excellence from every crevice. Alas, the crowned heads lost their crowns (some of them lost their heads, too) and the hotel is no more. There used to be a company that made the world's most luxurious blankets; it has gone bust because so many people turned to duvets. Where today is that glove manufacturer who led the world? Excellence is an ideal strategy for some companies; it is a disaster for others who ought, for example, to be moving down-market, into another market, taking over a competitor, increasing exports or whatever.

I doubt if many companies, on the other hand, should come out with a mission statement that reads, 'The company is determined to develop into a Centre of Awfulness.' No. The truth is that we can not all be Rolls-Royce – oops! (They went bust in 1971; obviously not sufficiently excellent!)

All such prescriptions are false, in fact. Peter Drucker is only one among many management gurus who proclaim that 'innovation' is a key strategy for companies. One would think that this, at least, could be accepted as a strategy without going through the corporate planning process. Alas, even this is suspect. Do we look for innovation in a French restaurant, in an antiques shop, a country hotel, a company making hand-printed wallpaper?

I despair of ever making the point strongly enough: there is no strategy that is right for every company, not even for two companies that seem to be identical. The only correct strategy is the one that comes out of an analysis of the company's total strategic situation – a situation that will be different for every company, however similar it may appear to be.

No. At this stage I want the planning team to cast out of its mind everything that is not the 'corporate purpose'.

Corporate conduct statements

Many companies include 'We wish to remain independent', or 'We intend to treat our employees with respect', or 'We will not pollute the atmosphere' among their corporate objectives. I see these as statements defining an intended code of corporate conduct, or culture, not as corporate objectives. They are very important indeed, but they describe how the company intends to behave itself in society rather than what it is for. I shall discuss them at length later in this chapter.

Now I have at last reached the end of the long list of corporate objectives that are not. Here is the one that is.

Corporate objectives for companies

I believe the corporate purpose of all companies is 'To make a satisfactory return on the owners' investment', or words to that effect. There are three elements here: the intended beneficiaries are the owners, the intended benefit is return on their investment, and the criterion by which they will judge the management is whether their return is 'satisfactory'.

John Finch, for example, who founded his company three years ago, might select the corporate objectives statement contained in Figure 3.5.

Figure 3.5   Corporate objectives for John Finch Limited

The Intended Beneficiaries	Mr & Mrs John Finch
The Intended Benefit	Return on money and effort invested in forming the company.
Performance Targets	See Chapter 5.

In other words, John Finch will be content if the management (in this simple case it is probably himself) achieves a certain return on his capital. Now, because John Finch is the sole beneficiary, he can alter any of these statements whenever he likes; he is the sole arbiter. He could, if he wishes, add his daughter to the beneficiaries and then he might add to the benefit, 'and a job for Jane if she wants one'.

Let us now move to the other end of the scale. Imagine a major public company with millions of shareholders. Its corporate objectives will be those outlined in Figure 3.6.

Figure 3.6   Corporate objectives for Mallard Universal plc

The intended beneficiaries	All current shareholders
The intended benefit	Return on their capital.
Performance targets	See Chapter 5.

In my view there is very little more to be said about a public company – return on shareholder's capital is 'it'! I very much doubt if a public company can ever legitimately add any of the personal aims that private companies may add, such as 'remain independent', 'provide jobs for our relatives' and so on, without incurring corporate perversion.

This idea, that the sole corporate purpose of a company is to make a profit is not accepted by everyone. Twenty years ago few would dare to suggest it at all. When I was reported in the *Financial Times* as saying this at a conference, not only was it emblazoned in a headline but they published an irate letter a few days later (4 December 1967) saying that such remarks were not only wrong but played into the hands of the Marxists!

I confess that I find it disheartening when people deny that profit is the aim of companies. I am quite prepared to call companies 'wealth creators' in polite society, but it all seems rather puerile to me.

Before moving on to objectives for the non-profit-making organizations we must pause to consider the quasi-profit-making ones. These include nationalized corporations and mutual organizations such as building societies, co-operatives and insurance companies.

State enterprise

The 'state enterprises' have a particular problem. This is not so much the definition of their corporate objectives as the fact that each successive government of different political hue keeps changing them. The right-wing political view is that they should act exactly like any other independent company and make a satisfactory return on capital. In this case the shareholder is the government and dividends go to the state. (There are some severe accounting problems here due, for example, to the habit governments have of 'writing off' chunks of capital from time to time so no one knows how much capital the return is on.) I am not quite sure why any government would wish to be a shareholder in these industries if it is not going to regulate them in some way, but at least the arrangement is perfectly clear and simple.

The left-wing view is quite different. It is that these industries should be used as an arm of social policy. If there is severe unemployment in Northtown then any nationalized industry operating there should refrain from dismissing workers, and should even recruit some they do not need. Any nationalized company not operating in Northtown should start operations there, regardless of profitability. This approach probably reached its peak in the 1970s when British Leyland was asked (the Ryder Report) to protect the jobs of its 100,000 employees, to maintain exports at £1bn and also to be profitable. Not surprisingly, it failed at all three. I trust that even in Britain we have for ever moved beyond such ruinous beliefs.

A third view points out that, even in the above case, it is still possible to set a realistic target return because the cost of these social acts can be calculated and a subvention made to the company for carrying them out. Many nations still employ this device. A railway company, for example, instructed by its government not to close a branch line, would receive a subsidy equal to the opportunity costs of not closing it. Its return on capital may still then be calculated.

Each of these attitudes is fairly clear. A major problem arises, however, as it did in the UK for many of the post-war decades, when state enterprise managements were asked to go to Northtown by one government and not to go by the next. It proved a grotesquely debilitating regimen. The current, Thatcherite, view is that governments should not own or manage companies at all.

The history of the nationalized state enterprise over the past few decades provides us with a vicious warning to take some care over corporate objectives. There was, I suggest, very little wrong with the managements of many of our great nationalized companies – in spite of all the criticism levelled at them by governments and the press. What was wrong was that their corporate objectives were intermittently senseless, or unobtainable, or both. Many of the rules I am suggesting here for the setting of objectives were broken. For a start, I am not sure for whose benefit they were being run. If an organization does not know who are its intended beneficiaries then it has indeed lost its way.

I repeat, the amount of damage one can do to an organization by setting it the wrong corporate objective is quite startling.

Co-operatives

The history of co-operative organizations repeats the warning. One would have thought that an organization owned by its employees would beat any similar company owned by outside shareholders. The double motivation of advancing one's career and of earning a shared dividend, should, one would have thought, generate considerable enthusiasm amongst its employees.

While a few do succeed, most worker co-operatives are relative failures. One of the reasons is, I believe, that the rewards to the employees as shareholders are normally not sufficient to motivate them – thus breaching one of my rules above (Figure 3.3) that objectives have to appeal to the intended beneficiaries.

The following calculation, taking fairly average ratios, illustrates this. Suppose a co-operative employs 100 people whose remuneration totals £1,000,000. Turnover is £3,000,000 – or £3 per £ of remuneration. Profits are 10 per cent of turnover, or £300,000. Corporation tax, however, takes, say, £100,000 and so a suitable dividend, covered three times, would be £66,000 or 6.6 per cent of any employee's annual pay – not a huge incentive. Of course, they would also get any capital gains in the share value but if they realize these by selling their shares it ceases to be a co-operative. Not to mention the possibility of a loss.

What has been successful, however, is the management buy-out. Here only a few of the employees own the company – the ones on whom its performance mainly rests – and their individual shareholding is therefore sufficient to offer a major incentive both in terms of dividend and capital appreciation when they eventually go public.

Perhaps the above also explains why customer co-operatives are not as successful as one would expect. Because there are so many of them each individual customer receives such a small refund on his purchases that it is lost in his overall expenditure. Again, in the case of the mutual insurance company it is seldom possible for a policy-holder to distinguish the difference in the rewards from a policy he holds in a mutual versus a proprietary insurance company.

On the other hand, some supplier co-operatives are very successful. A dozen farmers setting up a co-operative dairy for their milk output, for example, may each receive sufficient benefit to give them an incentive to sell their milk through their co-operative, rather than elsewhere. My rule is thus further illustrated: the more attractive the benefit is to the intended beneficiaries, the more likely is an organization to flourish. If it is insignificant in volume or in importance to the beneficiary then, however well managed the organization might be, it will not flourish. I thus come back to this neglected issue: management is one element in success and failure;

what the organization is for is another. Everyone discusses the former *ad nauseam*, it spawns an infinity of books and articles. What about the latter?

Mutuals

One mutual insurance company I know spent many weeks wondering what its aims were. They accepted at once that 'doing our best for the with-profits policy-holders' was the central aim of a mutual, but the problem was to find a verifiable measure of this. At first they selected 'surplus' but the problem with this criterion is that it has to be calculated by the 'appointed actuary' using methods which allow him very wide discretion (remember, he has to make some of his estimates over the life-span of the insured – decades) and that, if 'surplus' became the leading indicator of success, great pressure could be placed on him to dress it up, or down.

Next they tried 'growth of assets', but this can be 'dressed' by taking on poor quality business or cutting rates. My own view was that they were overstating all these technical problems (many top managers in most insurance companies are still actuaries) and that measurement was not really the problem.

Another mutual toyed with the following corporate performance indicators: distribution of assets, return on investment (over three and five years); free reserves, expense ratios, new annual premiums per employee, annual premium growth, renewal retentions, surrenders, solvency margins and market share.

I have discussed this problem in some detail to remind managers in ordinary profit-making organizations that life for other people is not so simple; the act of selecting a verifiable objective is not always so easy as it is for them. It may become worse than just difficult; it may be impossible. Then what do you do? One answer for a mutual is 'de-mutualization', to which there is a slow trend.

I was intrigued to discover, while advising on their corporate planning some years ago, how certain Spanish savings banks operated. They took in savings from the public and paid, say, 6 per cent interest. They lent to various organizations at the going rate of say, 14 per cent. The result is huge profits. However, these banks are non-profit-making so what happens to the profits? The answer (apart from the magnificent boardrooms and art collections) is that they do good works such as building roads, low-cost housing and public utilities.

Isn't that rather marvellous, I hear you asking? What is wrong with it? Well, the decisions are made by the bank boards, the boards are composed of local government members and such local worthies as construction company owners and shop owners. It sounds to me an ideal set-up for the perversion of the interest on the funds entrusted to the banks by the small saver. I can certainly vouch for the fact that this system produces better roads than most democratic governments!

The point I am making in this section is that some mutuals and co-operatives do not work as well as one would expect. Their effectiveness seems to be less dependent on the quality of their management than on the level of the benefit they yield to their beneficiaries. Thus it is possible, simply by the design of the corporate objectives, to hamstring one organization or to release the fiery energies of the management in another.

Building societies

Building societies are another form of quasi-profit-making mutual organization in which the determination of the objective is difficult.

Traditionally a building society benefits the small saver by offering him a convenient vehicle for his savings and, at the same time, it offers mortgages to house-buyers. So it has two sets of beneficiaries and is thus in breach of one of my rules: that the more homogeneous the beneficiaries are the more successful will be the organization (Figure 3.3). But here we have an organization in which the beneficiaries are not merely heterogeneous, they are incompatible – in giving a better deal to the savers the building society, by definition, damages the interests of the house-buyer and vice versa.

In recent years the building societies have been operating largely for the benefit of the house-buyer and contrary to the interests of the saver. This arose by default, not intentionally, when the rapid inflation of the 1970s resulted in a negative real interest rate for the saver while the house-owner's equity value increased enormously. It was, I presume, lack of sophistication on the part of the small saver that permitted this situation to prevail for so long.

Currently, in 1988, many UK building societies are still reviewing their objectives following the Building Society Act and the Financial Services Acts of recent years. The tribulations this brings has to be witnessed to be believed. One society decided, in the 1970s, that 'get bigger' was its corporate objective. Then, in 1982, this became 'increase market share'. In 1985 'profitability' became its top aim. In another society, 'growth of assets' was the prime objective and 'growing faster than our direct competitors' became the target. They rejected profit because it did not appear to sit comfortably with mutuality – in other words, they could not decide to whom any profit would be due. I agree that this is a major defect – we must know both the benefit *and* the beneficiary. To make a profit but not to know who is entitled to it seems a sterile and empty task; it could also be dangerous.

This danger became very real to me when I heard several building society planning teams flirting with the idea that, in reality, it was the managers of the society – themselves, in other words – who were the true beneficiaries. After all, they reasoned, both the savers and the mortgagees behave like customers, not like owners. They began wondering about profit-sharing incentive schemes for the senior managers. The words 'corporate perversion' slipped into my mind at these times but, mercifully, slipped out again as the implications of this conclusion became clear to the planning teams themselves. But pause for a moment to recall my warning earlier: if it is not absolutely clear who the beneficiaries are, and what benefit they expect, any organization is liable to be hijacked by someone else for their own ends. The people best placed to do this are the management.

Eventually many building society teams seem to have identified the house-buyer as the intended beneficiary and that the benefit they are offering him is cheaper and more abundant finance for his house purchase and for assets associated with it (furniture, contents, etc.) or associated with him (pensions, insurance, etc.). One team, however, did not identify the mortgagee as the intended beneficiary but, on the contrary, decided it was the saver – because there were more of them than mortgagees (it takes about seven savers to provide one average mortgage).

I do not find these conclusions inspiring and I cannot score them very highly judged by the five criteria in Figure 3.3, although I do welcome the trend towards accepting just the one beneficiary in place of the two they recognized in previous times. In other words, out of the various possible alternative corporate objectives that could have been selected these societies chose virtually all of them. Not all at the same time, though, thank goodness!

If these organizations do ever adopt 'profits for shareholders' as their philosophy a serious legal problem will be exposed, namely, that for decades – indeed for a century – their supposed 'beneficiaries', the small savers and the mortgagees, have not received the surpluses that these societies have been building up in their name (as, indeed, have all mutual organizations, as well as learned societies, institutions, charities, and so on) but which they will not now receive – most of them are long dead. Individually the sums are puny; collectively they amount to billions. My immediate concern, however, is not these sums of money; it is that some of these organizations do not appear to know what they are doing for whom and have not known this for a very long time indeed.

Corporate conduct

I shall use the words 'corporate conduct' to refer to how an organization behaves in society, how it discharges its responsibilities towards its employees and third parties; in other words its moral code, its values, its ethos, its culture, its principles, its scruples.

I prefer 'corporate conduct' to 'corporate culture' for three reasons. The most important is that conduct is more concrete and verifiable than culture. You can actually see how an organization conducts itself whereas it is possible to get away with such vapid generalizations as 'we have a very positive culture'. It is so much easier to judge what an organization does than how it thinks.

The second is that 'culture' has come to refer to the attitude of the employees to their work; it started out with a much wider connotation but it seems to have shrunk so that now, when a company talks of its culture, it usually means its employees' work ethic – very important, but not everything. Culture does not really cover the organization's attitude to polluting a river, for example, or the employment of disabled.

The third is that culture is a slightly precious word. I want to be able to talk about such evils as Rachmanism (after a notorious property developer who employed thugs to drive out unwanted tenants) and I feel uncomfortable using the word 'culture' in that context. Conduct is more robust and covers a wider spectrum of how organizations actually behave – and misbehave – themselves.

Corporate objective and corporate conduct

I hope the relationship between corporate objective and corporate conduct is clear: the objective describes what the organization is doing for whom; conduct describes how, while achieving this, the organization proposes to behave within society.

An organization which sets itself a strict code of ethics will have to strive that much harder to achieve its corporate objective. That was one of the reasons that Marks & Spencer earned such high praise – it achieved dramatic annual increases in its earnings per share for the shareholders while at the same time treating its employees, suppliers and customers with much excellent care and consideration. Normally, when one observes a person or organization achieving outstanding success, one wonders by what tortured paths he has attained such pinnacles, but here was a genuine case of getting everything right. Most would recognize that profit is a reward for getting them right.

It is perfectly possible to impose such ethical burdens on an organization that the objective becomes unattainable. Managers of organizations frequently take such decisions at the operational level – where they may judge conditions in the factory too dangerous to continue work, for example, or when the efficacy of a drug is in doubt and the company decides to withdraw it from the market.[4]

Such decisions are also taken at the corporate level, and so certain actions taken by organizations are taken regardless of whether they improve the chances of attaining the objective. They will be taken (or not taken) because they are the right thing to do.

Just because I place corporate conduct below corporate objective in the order of decision-making does not imply that one is more or less important. I do not think it is logically possible to place 'objectives' and 'conduct' in order of importance. They are logically in different categories and do not belong in the same list at all. Just as one can place apples and oranges in order of preference but not apples and windows.

Corporate conduct guide-lines

In my opinion, it is seldom necessary for an organization to spend much time on this aspect of strategy. This is not because the issues are not important – I have explained that they are – but because they are usually fairly uncontroversial. Most organizations in most

Western nations behave in much the same way. There is a broad consensus as to how one should behave in civilized society towards employees, customers, the community, and so on. Common sense, custom and practice are often sufficient guide-lines for most organizations.

Every day the media, the business schools, the man in the street, protest movements, and above all government legislation and statutory regulatory bodies, tell us how organizations should respond to this or that moral issue. There are even standard codes of behavior such as the Sullivan Rules which regulate corporate policy towards colour and which many foreign companies in South Africa subscribe to. There is the Business in the Community Club, Christian Business Executives and the One Per Cent Club – whose members subscribe up to 1 per cent of their profits to worthy causes – and so on. There is legislation in many nations to prevent companies applying more than a certain percentage of shareholders' profits in this way. There is also the 'No Harm Principle', described below.

In most organizations, however, there is one sensitive area, occasionally several, which are excruciatingly difficult to resolve and which, plainly, should be discussed by the planning team to make quite sure that no strategies are developed which may infringe any of these susceptible areas of behaviour. For example, if a company's products can damage the environment, are of political sensitivity, or may be deemed immoral by sections of society, then a clear statement of the company's attitude to these problems ought to be devised and included in the corporate conduct statement. Obvious examples include tobacco, drugs, arms, pornography and pesticides. I review a list of other possible topics below and in Chapter 5 I will suggest that targets are set for some of these issues as well as for the corporate objectives.

Even companies occasionally do things out of the kindness of their hearts – a cynic would call it merely enlightened self-interest. I particularly like the small horticultural company which maintains one heated greenhouse full of rare plants (which have no commercial value), and the company I know in South America which built a new cathedral when their home town was struck by an earthquake.

Some examples

Figure 3.7 contains a list of the areas in which organizations may wish to make conduct statements, together with one or two actual examples. In practice, very few organization will need to make statements in more than a few of these areas.

Figure 3.7 Corporate conduct statements

Interest groups, etc.	Examples
Management	We aim to provide attractive job satisfaction and career openings. We like to see managers' remunerations rising in real terms, but we do not propose to encourage share options.
Employees	We wish to enhance the careers of all our employees. We like to think this is a satisfying company to work for where conditions are above average for the area.
Products	We shall undertake rigorous testing, beyond that required by law, to ensure our product is not harmful.
Customers	The customer is why we are here. We shall not only give good value for money, we must satisfy his every demand. Certainly no misleading advertising.
Competitors	We will compete vigorously but not illegally.
Suppliers	No bribery. No excessive 'commissions' will be given.
Local community	We will contribute generously to relevant local charities. No pollution. No noisy activities at night.
Government	We will resist interference from local government. We will take every possible step to avoid, but not evade, taxation in all its forms. No donations to political parties.
Pressure groups	We will politely respond to all these and will accede to their minimum demands wherever necessary.

The stakeholder theory

The last entry in Figure 3.7 is interesting. Many organizations are challenged by protest groups today. Trading with South Africa, disposing of radioactive wastes, building bypasses, using farm chemicals, and dozens more such activities are under attack. In some cases the threat is so severe – regardless of the rights and wrongs – that some organizations have to treat the protests as elephants. (Of course not all protest movements are threats to companies: those food, clothing and cosmetics companies who acknowledged the strength of feeling against the use of artificial ingredients and inhumane methods in their industries have prospered exceedingly by recognizing these as opportunities.)

The problem for most organizations is how far to concede to the demands of such groups. In this respect there is one theory which gained considerable currency in recent years which I find most unhelpful. It does not specifically relate to protest groups, more to interest groups, but it also has implications throughout the whole area of conduct, ethos and behaviour. This is the Stakeholder Theory.

I have suggested that organizations should not aim to satisfy large numbers of disparate beneficiaries. On the contrary, I advise that an organization should aim to benefit one quite specific set of people but that, in achieving this aim, it should recognize the needs of others. The Stakeholder Theory says that, on the contrary, organizations do, and should, benefit a wide range of people. Indeed, everyone who comes into contact with an organization may be deemed to be a stakeholder – to have a stake in its future. (Similar views are put forward in the Consensus Theory.) Thus, in addition to the intended beneficiaries, who, in this theory, are deemed to stand in no special relationship to it, an organization should benefit its employees, the local community, customers, competitors, suppliers, the state, interest groups, pressure groups – anyone who may be affected by it.

The reasons why I reject this theory are as follows:

- Organizations do not behave like this in real life. On the contrary, most organizations would find themselves in hot water from their intended beneficiaries, and even from the law, if they acceded to significant demands from third parties.
- There are no rules to determine who is a legitimate stakeholder and who is not. Employees obviously are, but what about competitors, suppliers, passers-by, pressure groups? On what grounds could any organization approve or reject any given claim by any party to be treated as a stakeholder?
- There are no rules by which a company can approve or reject

any demand from any of these people. If the local community asks a company to build it a swimming pool, must it do so? The Stakeholder Theory provides no grounds on which any request by anyone may be rejected.

I have become profoundly suspicious of claims such as those made by stakeholder theorists. I find it hard to distinguish between the idea that all and sundry should benefit from an organization and the concept of 'corporate perversion' I mentioned earlier. Both seem to grant any person capable of doing so a licence to pervert the assets of the organization to their advantage. The management becomes a Father Christmas, dishing out goodies to all concerned in accordance with a set of rules that the recipients themselves have concocted. I hope Save The Children, for example, or Help The Aged, do not subscribe to this theory.

Of course, no organization can aim to satisfy its beneficiaries *at the expense of* society, employees and other third parties, but there is a wealth of difference between that and granting their every wish. In my view, as good a guide as any for corporate conduct is the No Harm Principle. This states that, in pursuing its aims, no organization should cause significant harm to any third party. If it does, full compensation should be made.

The governing body

I have emphasized how important I think corporate objectives are to each organization. I have warned that, if they do not define the corporate objective very accurately, and if they do not monitor their organization's performance very closely, then it may go into a long slow decline and perhaps fall prey to perversion. Much the same is true of its conduct; it must be monitored. But how? How should beneficiaries monitor their organization?

I maintain that all organizations, certainly all those of any social significance, *must* equip themselves with a board of governors whose task would be to ensure that the organization continued to meet its corporate objectives satisfactorily. This body should also approve the conduct statements and monitor adherence to them. It should be composed entirely of the beneficiaries or their representatives. It should be held remote and aloof from the management. Its members should be paid by a trust fund, not by the organization direct.

I believe that an organization cannot be said to be properly equipped to do its job – any organization, any job – unless it has two clear hierarchies: a beneficiaries' hierarchy and a management hierarchy (see Figure 3.8). Of course, the smaller and the more introvert the organization, the more informal can this be.

Figure 3.8   The essential double hierarchy structure

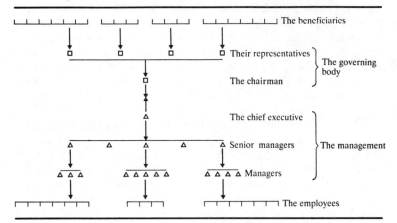

At the apex of the beneficiaries' hierarchy are the governors (non-executive, of course) headed by a non-executive chairman. Their duties are listed in Figure 3.9 below.

Figure 3.9   The duties of the governors

(1) Specify exactly who the intended beneficiaries are.
(2) Define what benefits the organization is to yield to them.
(3) Set performance targets (see Chapter 5).
(4) Delineate the conduct of the organization.
(5) Monitor that the organization is conforming to the above.
(6) Appoint and supervise the chief executive.

At the apex of the management hierarchy is the chief executive with his hierarchy of managers and other employees. Their task is to devise and carry out strategies to achieve the targets while conforming to the culture. An organization not set up in this form stands little chance of meeting the standards of performance and behaviour that we ought to be demanding of it in the modern world. Without it, perversion becomes effortless, especially for the managers. The design of the top hierarchy is every bit as important as the managers' hierarchy.

Such a concept will not function if elementary common-sense rules are broken, which, alas, they often are. One rule must surely be that the governors must be independent of the management but must have an interest in and knowledge of the beneficiaries. Thus while parents are no doubt the right people to sit as school governors, it would be wrong if any of their own children were currently at the school. It would plainly be wrong for teachers of a school also to be its governors. The phenomenon of conflict of interest is too well known to dwell on here.

I find the German supervisory board concept wholly absurd. There, half the board are worker representatives and half are shareholder representatives. What are the workers there for? If to protect the interest of the workers, why not also appoint representatives to protect the customers, suppliers, the local community, the State and environmental groups? It is a crazy lopsided physical manifestation of the Stakeholder Theory. (I gather the Germans are not too sure of it either. One director said that the workers on his board hold everything up for so long, he would rather have a strike!)

Many governing bodies are composed of many dozens of governors. What are they all doing there? It does not take more than half a dozen sensible people to supervise any organization, however large. Look at government agencies, institutions and building societies – all are cursed by hordes of worthy directors who have no idea what they are supposed to be doing. They are not alone in this folly. General Motors' own bye-law states that the board shall have more than fifteen members (but not more than thirty-five). Nissan has forty-eight. By law, large German companies have to have twenty people on the supervisory board.

I would enjoy saying what I think about executive chairmen in large companies who think so highly of their own abilities that they tackle the job of running the company *and* safeguarding the interests of the shareholders, but there is no room here to pursue this matter any further. Suffice it to say that, without a properly constituted board of governors, sitting above the hierarchy of managers, any large organization is in danger of long-term decline and perversion. Which indeed is often the case.

Finally under the heading of corporate conduct, I appreciate that the ethical system I am describing here – that organizations should, indeed have a duty to, pursue only the interests of their intended beneficiaries, so long as they do no significant harm to others – is at least one notch down the scale of morality from the Stakeholder Theory (and the Christian ethic itself) which demands that an organization has a duty to benefit all its stakeholders. I simply believe that the former is how we really live as human beings in organizations and that the latter is a practical way of life only for the saints among us.

Summary

I think corporate objectives *matter*. I am constantly embarrassed by the casual attitude to them by august and worthy organizations who pay them so little regard. I remain profoundly convinced that corporate objectives are crucial not just to the corporate planning process, but, vastly more important, to the performance of every organization.

Management today is a finely developed art. Managers of all sorts of organizations have fully absorbed the modern technicalities: 'niche marketing', 'benchmarking', 'brand name', 'sensitivity analysis' and a thousand other tricks of their trade. Alas, many of them are running these organizations, probably very efficiently, but without really knowing exactly what they are doing for whom. It is only when they pause in their headlong hurry to meet their short-term objectives that they realize that they do not know what the long-term ones are.

I see a perfectly straight path down which all organizations should travel in their hunt for their corporate objective. First they must rid their minds of everything that is not a corporate objective such as statements about conduct and strategies. Then they must define three elements of their objective: the beneficiaries, the benefits and the level of benefit considered satisfactory by the beneficiaries. For a company this is easy. The answers are, respectively: shareholders, profits, satisfactory. That's it. (See the next two chapters.) It is much less easy as we move away from the profit motive. As we pass the quasi-profit-making organizations we already sense the mists gathering around us. In the next chapter we enter the fog.

As for corporate conduct, or how organizations should behave themselves as they search for ways to achieve their corporate objectives, I do not think it is normally very difficult. Society, the law, one's own common sense, the way other similar organizations are behaving, are pretty reliable guides to 90 per cent of requirements. Some organizations have a particular sensitivity to which they must pay especial attention, however, and occasionally one hits a really difficult moral problem. Each organization will doubtless have their own views but I personally feel anxious that the tenets of the Stakeholder Theory might slide imperceptibly into perversion. On the other hand, the No Harm Principle, for me, strikes the right chord.

Finally, I believe that all organizations of social significance should have a small independent governing body representing the interests of the beneficiaries, the design of which is every bit as important as the management hierarchy.

CHAPTER 4

Objectives for Non-profit-making Organizations

General

We now turn to deciding the corporate objectives for such non-profit-making organizations as foundations, charities, societies, clubs, associations, colleges, leagues, orders, institutions, sects, local, national and international governments and their agencies, state corporations, parties, academies, schools, hospitals, universities and commissions.

Most of these organizations do not do corporate planning as I define it; most do not do it as anyone would define it. Why not? Chiefly because they cannot determine their corporate objectives to the same standard as companies can and, consequently, cannot use corporate planning as portrayed in this book. Alas, they fall at the first fence.

My aim in this chapter

The goal I want to reach here is to draw up a set of rules which will enable non-profit-making organization (NPOs) to define their corporate objectives as precisely as one can in profit-making organizations. I do not know if this can be done, I only know that it ought to be. I have spoken to dozens of managers from a wide range of NPOs – or, rather, they have spoken to me – who tell me that what they lack is a set of rules to guide them in defining objectives for their organizations. It is the most difficult thing they are called upon to do.

I also know many have attempted this task before and failed; my own venture is therefore offered here with much diffidence and humility. I would not dream of such presumption had not the prescriptions proposed in the previous chapter apparently proved so helpful for so many companies. I do not think I am saying anything original, either, but I hope I have put it all together in a logical, practical sequence.

There are some huge problems, however. We glimpsed some of these towards the end of the previous chapter where I discussed state enterprises, co-operatives and building societies. There, however, we had only reached the fringes of the area we are now entering; those were quasi-profit-making organizations and close enough to being a sort of company to be able to borrow some of their answers. Now we are venturing into an area where profit is not only not the aim, but is often wholly incompatible with it.

In essence, this chapter is an attempt to lay down guide-lines by which organizations may answer such questions as: 'What are you doing? Are you doing what you set out to do? How well are you doing it?' We want the answers to the same level of accuracy and verifiability that we can obtain when we ask the questions of a company.

I am asking for the equivalent of 'profits' – an unambiguous, overall indicator of the success or failure of the organization as a corporate whole – a criterion for the whole organization, not just its constituent parts. I am *not* asking for everything in sight to be privatized; profit is *not* the aim of most NPOs and never can be. I am, however, asking for a Corporate Performance Indicator (CPI) that is as powerful as profits. Many NPOs do not even use ordinary performance indicators yet, let alone a *corporate* performance indicator and few of them set numerical targets at all, but this is precisely what they want to be able to do.

In case it is feared that this is too strict an aim, please recall that, in fact, profit is not as precise a measure as is often believed. We had considerable trouble hacking through the undergrowth to reach a suitable definition for the corporate objective for comp-anies in Chapter 3 and we will have a lot more fuss when we try to set the numerical targets for them in Chapter 5. We must remem-ber this: we are not looking for perfection, only for something approaching the same level of utility as 'profits'. Many NPOs do already achieve this enviable standard.

What we should ask of an organization, then, is: 'Who is it for, what is it meant to be doing for them and is it actually doing it?' This seems to me a critically important trio. We are entitled to be given a reasonably reliable and verifiable answer from organizations of such social significance as the Red Cross, the Freemasons, the TUC, the Football Association, the National Gallery, UNESCO, the Institute of Chartered Accountants, and a couple of thousand more.

The exceptional importance of this topic

I have already explained that the corporate objective describes the very *raison d'être* of an organization. It is the sole criterion by which it may be judged; it reflects what it intends to do for whom; it justifies everything it does in its entire life history; it is the only means by which the managers can decide what strategies to adopt; it acts as a bulwark against corporate perversion; and, if it is skilfully set, it may turn a dotard organization into a champion. It really would be hard to think of a concept of greater force for good or ill. The role of the corporate objective in determining the performance of organizations is without parallel – not even the quality of management can surpass it.[1] The planning team must, simply must, get it right for their organization. Get this wrong and, I believe, the strategies will be deformed at birth.

I imagine most people would judge that, as the wealth creators, the private sector is of high importance to us in our society. But now consider NPOs, how important are they to us? Government expenditure in many Western nations amounts to over 40 per cent of the Gross National Product. In the less developed world it is often much more. Add to these all the non-government non-profit-making organizations and they must, together, account for well over half of all the activities of mankind.

It is not just the size and volume of these organizations, however, it is also their social significance. It could be argued that a children's charity employing a thousand people is of far greater social significance than any thousand-employee widget company: make a mistake in the latter and the result is a few broken widgets, make a mistake in the former and you could wreck someone's life.

Taking the number, the size, and the importance of non-profit-making organizations into account, together with the role of the corporate objectives in influencing their performance, I feel justified in saying that this topic is of critical importance.

The allocation of society's resources

I find it quite remarkable that anyone who wishes to do so can compare the performance of, say, an English pesticide company with a Japanese health insurance company. There are some difficult technical snags in doing so, but it can be done, and indeed is being done every day of the week. As a result, anyone with capital to spare can decide to invest in one rather than the other and, by making this resource-shifting decision, he encourages the one to expand and the other to decline.

In this way, if Japanese workers want more health insurance and if the English farmer turns against pesticides, if the Greeks decide they want more turtle soup and the Americans lose interest in football – or anyone wants anything, anywhere in the world, or ceases to want it – then, thanks to the comparability of the return on capital earned by the companies that provide it, they may have it. Up goes the return on insurance in Japan, down it goes on football stadiums in America. A high return brings capital for expansion, a low return repels it. Never has there been a more effective mechanism for change in the history of man. A billion little ballcocks, regulating the flow of our desires around the world!

Now try comparing a government-run dockyard in Italy with Northtown Secondary School in England, or the Workfare Scheme in America with the National Gallery. It is impossible. Not only can you not compare these unlikes, you cannot even compare like with like. Try the National Gallery with the British Museum, or even Northtown Secondary School with Northtown Primary School.

If we cannot make these comparisons, how can society allocate resources between them? Do we want to double the size of the National Gallery and halve the British Museum? Or the other way round? We do not know. Of course, we rely on our politicians to make these value choices for us. They love to pretend that they have some secret mystical wisdom that cuts through all this corporate objectives nonsense. But I know no way that they can do it either. There is no evidence that they can. No one goes to a politician to ask him his views on how a particular company has performed. We can see for ourselves by looking at the figures. Why should we have to ask him about the British Museum?

I find this contrast between profit and non-profit stunning and profoundly troubling. So far as I can see, it is solely because we do not know what are the corporate objectives of these NPOs and so we have no way to judge whether they are performing well or badly, whether they are useful or useless, whether we want more of them or less.

Why it is even more important today

It has always been important to know what any given organization is supposed to be doing and how well it is doing it, but recent events seem to me to make it very much more so.

First, the art of management, having been systematically studied for five decades or more, is capable of extraordinary feats of operational efficiency, aided as it now is by the computer and information technology and by the almost universal use of such systems as budgetary control. Management today has the potential to guide and control organizations to new levels of performance.

Secondly, Thatcherism has provoked a wave of interest in efficiency and effectiveness. Even the man in the street is today aware of the difference between a hit and a miss in the management of organizations. He now wishes to discuss the corporate objectives of NPOs in public, he wishes to see higher standards of perform-ance and increasingly demands keener monitoring of results. This heightened public interest in NPOs is something that their planning teams must recognize as an elephant.

Thirdly, Thatcherism has drawn the private sector increasingly into the running of public sector organizations. The businessmen who now help to run and to finance NPOs will not be satisfied with vague objectives, they will want to see them clarified so that more convincing managerial judgments may be made. Moreover, while 'privatization' has worked wonders for some NPOs, not everyone is entirely enamoured of it and, as will be readily admitted even by its enthusiasts, it is not an appropriate solution for a vast swathe of non-profit-making organizations. The escape route to privatization is firmly barred to many NPOs.

Fourthly – and this partly accounts for the Thatcher revolution itself – we have in recent decades experienced a number of very public and extremely damaging failures in the non-profit-making sector. I mentioned the nationalized industries in the previous chapter, a clear case of failure due to defective corporate objec-tives. The behaviour of the unions during the past few decades, where they seem to have lost sight of their objective – to benefit their members – and rampaged off into national politics for the vainglory of their leaders, was a similar debacle. Together with the state industries, many people believe they hogtied the economic development of this nation for twenty years.

The majority of British people view the Common Agricultural Policy as a massive government-sponsored perversion; they see the United Nations as having been hijacked by the Third World; and so on – there is no shortage of important organizations which are felt to have gone astray. Indeed, so many of our modern organizations are so large that when they do let us down, they do so with a bump.

Everyone has their own pet list of organizations which have lost their way. My own would include the Church of England, the entire British legal system of police–justice–prison, the various societies for prevention of cruelty to children, our state schools, virtually the complete local government system, certainly in towns. What distresses me most is that I cannot justify these opinions by comparing the performance of these organizations with their corporate objectives to prove that they have failed. We do not know what their objectives are. We fall at the first fence. Either we should be able to prove the case or they should be able to disprove it. We can do neither. So they carry on, year after year, assuring us that everything is fine, and no action is taken – sometimes for decades.

There is no such uncertainty about even the tiniest company. Challenge a managing director over the performance of his tin-pot, five-man, back-street business and he can show you the past five-year figures. These will clinch the case with little room for error either way. But what about the BBC, NASA, the Samaritans, the Eastville Ladies Club, the British Commonwealth, Amnesty International? Does anyone know if Greenpeace is better at its job than Friends of the Earth, the Nature Conservancy Council, the World Wildlife Fund or the International Union for the Conservation of Nature and Natural Resources? Should you send your money to Save the Children, Band Aid or Oxfam? We have little idea.

That, then, is a fourth reason why this topic is becoming critical: some notable NPOs appear to have gone downhill in recent decades but there is no way of telling whether they really have or not, nor whether someone ought to have done something about them before now. We have also seen the spawning of a huge number of new organizations, some with very remarkable marketing skills and massive financial resources, but whose real performance is unknown and perhaps unknowable.

As the world grows in wealth so we shall see an increasingly lively and diverse public sector. Marvellous. As our standard of living rises as a result of the efforts of the company sector, so will our quality of life due to the exertions of non-profit-making organizations. Wonderful. But it places an urgent onus on planning teams in this sector to define the corporate objective with greater precision.

Some examples

Most NPOs already make strenuous efforts to tighten up their definitions of corporate objectives. Figure 4.1 contains the statement of one well-known charity for children which was laboriously carved out of a two-day conference of senior executives, together with a number of conduct and strategy statements (not shown).

Figure 4.1 Corporate objectives for a charity for children

- To help children and young people grow in their families and communities.
- To help them take charge of their own lives.
- To help change the conditions that stand in their way.

I know this is one of the most difficult areas of all in which to set clear sharp objectives but I am not sure I understand exactly what they are trying to do, nor would I know how to judge if they are doing it. 'Exactly'? Do we need to know *exactly*? Yes, we do. The managers do, the children and their parents do, the other social services who work with this charity do. Moreover, I even want to put a figure on this aim, so a target can be set, and I do not know how to do that from these statements.

Again, consider the corporate objective of a typical institution or government agency. Take the Royal Society for the Advancement of Science. Their 1986 corporate plan says the objectives are: '(1) To promote the exchange and development of scientific ideas and knowledge.(2) To recognize excellence in scientific scholarship and research. (3) To encourage scientific research . . .' There are no less than eight 'objectives', all in similar vein to the above. It would be mighty hard to prove or disprove whether they are doing any of these – and they have eight objectives. What are we to say if they hit three and miss five? Is that OK? And does it matter which five – do we have to introduce a weighting system? How did they get on with these eight aims last year – what does it say in the annual corporate plan? I could not find anything.

I will not bore the reader with the corporate objectives of the Natural Environment Research Council, the Science and Engineering Research Council or the Medical Research Council – their 'corporate plans' show either no stated corporate objective at all or so many of them, all in similar vein to the ones above, that one becomes quite bewildered. Few are verifiable, quantified or dynamic (see later) and none of the figures included in the corporate plans go anywhere to show whether the objectives are being met. Alas, what travesties of corporate plans these documents appear to be to a private sector corporate planner.[2]

How about the Arts Council. Is it doing a good job distributing subsidies to 'the arts' in Britain? (In my view it is not difficult to answer this, it is quite simply impossible!) What is Dr Barnardo's doing now? What is the YMCA doing, for whom?

This is why this chapter is so long and why I attach so much importance to it: the non-profit-making sector is growing, fast, it is consuming a huge percentage of Western society's resources, and I hope it always will; but it has, in my view, had a number of momentous public failures in Britain in recent decades. From now on increased interest in it suggests that it is going to have to pay more attention to the definition of corporate objectives. Corporate objectives are far too important to be treated as lightly as most NPOs seem to do.

Defective objectives

Before attempting to discover the guide-lines which I hope will prove helpful, I must review the reasons why planning teams in NPOs find it so difficult to determine their corporate objectives. As will be seen, the list is daunting. I sometimes wonder if it will ever be possible to make much progress in this area.

In no particular order I see the barriers as follows.

The three meanings

I explained in the previous chapter that 'corporate objectives' may be used with three quite different meanings: corporate purpose, corporate conduct and corporate strategies. In this chapter, as in the last, I am using it to mean purpose.

Unfortunately, senior executives in NPOs have not sorted out the various meanings any better than their counterparts in companies and so we find all the problems here that we found before, including Trojan Horse objectives – where the management thinks it is deciding objectives but is actually selecting strategies. Or they select 'we aim to become a leading charity in this field', or increase their share of the market, or reduce their costs, or they use 'survival' or 'maximize'.

I also warned against statements such as: 'We provide a service to the community.' All organizations do this and so it tells you nothing new about any organization. My own view is that no one ever forms an organization saying to himself: 'I will form an organization to provide a service to the community.' What he may say is: 'I will form this organization to provide this (specific) service to these (specific) people' – Meals on Wheels for the house-bound, gymnasia for the disabled, or whatever. Never for 'society'. Not even governments do that: the British Government acts only for the British, not for 'society'.

One of the most common errors I mentioned in the previous chapter is to confuse objective with strategy. Thus, a fund-raising charity may state its objectives as 'raise funds by house-to-house collection'. Surely its objective is simply to 'raise funds'? One strategy is to do this by house-to-house collection, but that is only one, there must be many more. Or again, a professional institute may conceive its objectives as to draw up a code of conduct for its members. Yet its real objective, I assume, would be to 'enhance the profession' (or words to that effect). One strategy for doing this would be to draw up this code, but another would be to carry out some public relations work to lift its image in the public eye; another might be to become a certificate-granting institution – and so on. By setting one strategy as 'the objective' the managers may not look for others.

Again, have a look at the eight 'objectives' of the Royal Society. They are all strategies, aren't they? I am not suggesting that any of these are wrong, but I am suggesting, as I did in the previous chapter, that none of them reflect the 'purpose' of the organization. The true corporate objective – whatever it is – will be strategy-neutral; it would allow, indeed it should demand, that the management hurries round searching for the best way to achieve it. It does not tell them, it asks them. You never know, if the Royal Society told its managers what the overall corporate objective is they might find a ninth strategy!

Did the charity for children in Figure 4.1. do the same thing? Was their third objective really a strategy?

Again, note the limitation in giving an organization the aim of 'research into cures for cancer' because this overlooks research into preventing it. But a charity to 'reduce the incidence of cancer' while including both prevention and cure, omits alleviating the symptoms – to include this as well the charity would have to be for 'reducing the effects of cancer'. And so on. All these aims are perfectly legitimate. All I am saying is that by laying down strategies you hamstring the managers; by setting them objectives you inspire them.

Corporate and partial objectives

This is our old friend corporate planning versus departmental, sectional and operational planning which bedevils executives in companies and NPOs alike.

It is very difficult for any planning team to concentrate solely on the corporate issues rather than partial ones; most managers will spend most of their working day immersed in operational detail. Alas, as soon as they introduce these departmental minutiae into their corporate planning exercise, they are lost beyond recall. They will no longer see the wood for the trees. While festooned with detailed technicalities it is simply not possible to achieve a holistic view, a Gestalt, a Weltanschauung. One of the roles I frequently have to play when serving on the planning teams of companies is to ask the question, 'Is that really an elephant?' and 'Wait a minute, is that a *corporate* issue?'

We must remember that we are discussing *corporate* objectives here, objectives for a whole corporate body, not for a part of a body. This means we cannot expect to determine the corporate objective of, say, the computer department in the Ministry of Industry, because this is a part of an organization; nor for the eastern region of the Institute for the Blind. If something is a part of an organization then it will not have a *corporate* objective at all, so it is no good trying to determine it. We can only hope to decide what the corporate objectives are for such corporate entities as the Samaritans, the Northtown Ladies League, the Law Society, the European Community, the Southtown Golf Club, the Royal National Lifeboat Institution, the Citizen's Advice Bureau, the Salvation Army, the Rotary Club, and so on. These are autonomous or quasi-autonomous organizations with their own corporate identity.

The long-term view

One reason why planning teams in some NPOs shy away from setting proper corporate objectives is that it takes so long to verify whether these are being achieved or not. So they go for objectives that can be verified more quickly; in other words, operational objectives.

I suspect there is a misapprehension about companies here. Company executives like to give the impression that they know to the nearest penny what their profits are each month – and, indeed, they do. But no one judges a whole company from its monthly results. No one expands or shuts down even the smallest limb of an operation in that time-scale. The decision to close down an entire company takes years.

It is most unlikely that a school, for example, can be judged as a school in less than a number of years, regardless of the exact definition of its objective. We just have to accept this as one of the normal features of corporate objectives for corporate wholes. How long would one give a new chief constable, for example, before one expects to see a significant change in the performance of a metropolitan police force? If anyone thinks the answer is weeks or months they must be thinking of operational or departmental changes, not corporate; they are still in the wrong mental gear.

It is possible to judge most organizations at a glance – the seasoned traveller, for example, can tell at once when he walks into a hotel whether it is well run, the experienced consultant can see how well a company is doing. One may lay down and monitor adherence to codes of best practice, one may use opinion surveys, and in Chapter 11, I describe a highly systematic monitoring system which cuts down the delay in judging the performance of organizations. All these are only snapshots, however, some in better focus than others, which tell us about today's performance. You can judge the progress towards their *corporate* objective in only very few organizations in under a few years, companies included. I would go as far as this: if an objective can be seen to be achieved in less than a few years it is not a *corporate* objective.

Is it essential to measure these objectives numerically or will some form of 'assessment' do? Presumably the more accurately you can measure an organization's performance the sooner you will know whether it is successful or not. For some we will never know, however we measure it; we will hopefully never know, for example, whether the Ministry of Defence has done enough to defend the realm against a Russian attack. For most organizations I believe assessment is not good enough because judgement is subjective and over time subjective standards can gradually slip. No one suggests we should 'assess' a company – you simply turn to the five-year record and look at the figures. That was, you will remember, the touchstone I want to aim at here for NPOs. But, above all, if we allow 'judgement' or 'assessment' then organizations need not bother to set targets at all. 'Assessment' is a slippery slope; the targets have to be quantified if we are to keep up with companies.

There is another reason for not relying on short-term criteria – companies call it 'creative accounting'. It is possible (indeed, it is easy) to fiddle the accounts of a company to inflate or deflate its reported profits, but only for a short period. Most auditors can pick up most fiddles by the second year and certainly by the third. No doubt any CPI adopted by any organization would be open to creative accounting but, assuming we insist on also auditing CPIs for NPOs, it should be possible to relegate this problem to the sidelines.

Ignorance of the damage

I believe many senior executives are quite simply unaware of the damage that can be done by setting an organization the wrong objective or not setting one at all. I have mentioned the nation-alized industries during the 1960s and 1970s. The damage they did to the nation was not due to the incompetence of the managers, it was due to defective corporate objectives. Even now, the best that most nationalized companies can come up with for a strategy is 'cut costs'. As soon as they are denationalized you see them 'developing the business'. That is an order of magnitude change in attitude. Just this one act – changing the top objective – turns frogs into princes.

Or take, 'Put a man on the Moon and bring him safely back within a decade' – an objective which, by its precision and audacity, inspired NASA to become one of the most impressive organizations any of us has ever seen. Alas, having achieved this aim, NASA went into a decline because it was not then given a new objective of the same stature. An organization which has achieved its corporate objectives is dead from the neck up; it just goes running on, sometimes for decades, as aimless as a headless chicken.

Organizations are aims addicts – they must have their fix. If their aims are not clear, attractive, challenging, simple and dynamic then they wilt. Setting such goals is the most potent factor in determining their performance – all great managers down the ages have known this. But we do not just want inspiration and vision; we do not want mission statements such as, 'We aim to be the most influential charity in this field', which I saw recently. That tells us what the *management* wants. It does not tell us what the *beneficiaries* want.

Few people have truly understood what immense damage it can do to an organization to be given spurious corporate objects – or none at all. So intense is the study of 'management' – the *running* of organizations – that the study of setting their corporate objectives has been ignored. Its treatment in management textbooks is appalling.

Efficiency

The planning team should be wary of the word 'efficiency' in the corporate objective statement. Virtually all organizations rightly wish to be efficient, so it would not be wrong to say so; on the other hand, it is, on its own, completely inadequate as a corporate objective. No one ever forms an organization 'to be efficient'.

What we really want to know in the first part of any corporate objective statement is what the organization is trying to do for whom. Only when we are sure of that are we interested in whether it is meeting this aim efficiently. For example, in the case of a famine we really do not care *how* a charity gets the food to the starving, so long as it is fast. Only later does efficiency begin to matter.

Yet, all too often, NPOs chose 'expense ratios' or some other efficiency measure as their corporate objective. One of the measures which the Charity Commission monitors is the percentage of funds raised by each charity that is spent on management. The building societies' regulatory body watches a similar ratio. Quite right, this is an important safeguard, but it tells us nothing about the purpose of the organization and my anxiety is that, having identified this figure as important, the planning team will devote their time to amplifying its precision rather than identifying and measuring the benefit to beneficiaries. Another example is the 'teacher/pupil ratio' so beloved of the various institutes who collect and compare public sector statistics, which tell us nothing whatever about the effectiveness of a school. It just tells us how many teachers and pupils it has.[3]

There is yet another problem here. Management expense ratios are only one out of dozens of ratios that can, and should, be used to measure efficiencies. However, as noted above, these will be operational efficiencies, nothing to do with the provision of benefits to the beneficiaries. Now, many organizations seem to think that they should select a dozen efficiency ratios, add them up, and that is the CPI.

The National Health Service in Britain appears to use this method. They measure the efficiencies of all the various activities in a hospital, weight them, add them up and then compare this with other hospitals. As many as 400 performance indicators make up each hospital's 'overall performance indicator'. But, I say again, this merely measures departmental efficiencies and says nothing about whether the hospital, let alone the NHS itself, is doing what it is supposed to be doing. We do not know what that is; is it 'to provide the population with easy access to medical facilities', to 'heal the sick' or 'to improve our health'? All these have been claimed as objectives for the NHS at one time or another, but they are all different and each demands a different CPI. Not one of these are measured by any amalgamated efficiency index.

It is said that companies are more efficient than NPOs. Apparently it can be shown that output per employee in many State-run industries is lower than in a comparable company. Private hospitals are said to show a better cost per patient than State hospitals. It is also said that when an executive moves from the public to the private sector he suffers a culture shock due to the more focused professional demands upon him; conversely, those who move in the opposite direction say they find it difficult to rationalize strategic decisions because there is no clear-cut overall objective against which to evaluate them. There is some evidence, therefore, that efficiency is higher in the private sector.

This heightens two further major complications in using 'efficiency' as objectives. First, the word is usually interpreted to mean 'providing a service at lower costs'. In recent years, though, companies have learnt that what a lot of us want today is a better service even if it is at a higher cost. You only have to dine at an expensive restaurant, or enjoy any luxury in this sybaritic world, to know that some companies are not efficient at all – they are positively wasteful. Marketing men use the cliché, 'do it cheaper, do it better or do it different'. To aim at 'efficiency' almost automatically steers managers to the first strategy and away from the latter two – precisely the ones that are in the ascendant. Some NPOs risk being left on the beach after the tide has turned if they take cost-cutting as their overall aim. See my comments on 'The Woolworths Effect' in Chapter 10.

Secondly, as we have just seen, efficiency is not the prime advantage that companies have over NPOs; of far greater significance is their responsiveness. I explained above that a company either provides its customers with their continually changing needs, and so makes a profit, or it dies. No matter how efficient a company is – its costs may be unrivalled in all the universe – yet it will die a lingering death if no one wants its product any more. The key justification for the private sector is not efficiency but that it is such a dependable agent for change – all those little ballcocks, remember.

To summarize, while it is important that organizations carry out their corporate purpose efficiently, and while it is generally quite easy to devise effective performance indicators to measure this, unfortunately efficiency is *not* itself the corporate purpose and may even divert attention from what is. We are surely on the wrong track here.

So far I have described a number of rather technical reasons why planning teams find it difficult to set corporate objectives for NPOs. They closely resemble those I listed in the previous chapter for companies. I move on now to a number of impediments that are more particular to NPOs.

Comparability

There is undoubtedly a cachet in being able to claim that one's organization is 'different'. Everyone likes to believe it. Even perfectly ordinary widget companies like to assert that their company, or their widgets, are unique. This is a routine hurdle that I normally expect to meet when companies are attempting to set targets for themselves. I mention it in Chapter 5.

I have recently seen a non-profit-making organization which suddenly introduced corporate planning after 50 years of successful existence without it. Why? Because the government decided that its monopoly should be broken and, as a result, a private sector competitor has appeared. Suddenly people will start making comparisons. Suddenly the non-profit-making organization needs to define very accurately what benefit they are supposed to be generating and for whom.

No organization is an island, all of them have competitors. Indeed, there is no way of judging the performance of any organization on its own, it can only be assessed by comparing it with other, similar organizations. So this claim of singularity has to be rejected, otherwise the management will be able to escape evaluation. Perhaps that is one of the motives behind the protestation, 'We are so remarkable, unusual, peculiar, rare, unique even, that there is no way to evaluate our performance.'

I was recently told by a senior civil servant that crime rates would be a very useful indicator for judging the performance of a police force; alas, he added, each area is unique, it is impossible to compare one with another. I find this surprising. In my ignorance of these things I thought that the crime rate figures in Southtown were indeed comparable with that in Northtown, the rate in Britain with France (Germany, Belgium, Holland, Egypt, Japan . . .).

I suppose the same is true of the clear-up rate, too. That would be unfortunate. I was hoping to be able to find some criterion by which the police could be appraised. I suppose also that the health of one nation cannot be compared with the health of another so there is no way to judge the performance of a health service? And we cannot even compare any one of the regional health authorities with any of the other fourteen in Britain?

But come now! We are not looking for accuracy to the tenth place of decimals; we are looking for a long-term overall indicator of performance for an organization as a corporate entity. I fear this 'we are different' is sometimes a ploy to obfuscate, to obscure, cloak and conceal the true picture from our prying eyes.

In some NPOs there is a non-competitive – and sometimes a downright anti-competitive – culture. Yet the plain fact is that most organizations, whether they like it or not, are in competition with their rivals. When the World Wildlife Fund increased their UK income from £0.6m in 1977 to £6m in 1987 this money did not come from thin air, it came from other charities. Some of it came from the societies protecting birds in Britain. Someone who decides to live in Northtown does not go to live in Southtown. If I go to the British Museum I will not have time to visit the National Gallery.

Let us pass on to the next, rather similar, issue, pausing to note that all organizations have competitors, or at least comparators, which are sufficiently similar to allow us to draw a conclusion as to their relative long-term corporate performances. Senior executives who pretend they are unique may be trying to hide something.

'We are not a profit-making organization'

The full expression, usually stated with an air of righteous indignation and a slightly raised nose, is: 'We are not a profit-making organization; *we* provide a service to the community.' The implication is that profit-making organizations do not provide a service to the community, or, if they do, they only do so to make a profit. I am aware that some of the things done in the name of profit are utterly repulsive and repugnant, yet to condemn everything that any company does on the grounds that it is done for profit goes beyond all reason. Yet we hear it constantly: 'Ah but they will only be doing it for profit.' Those who make these statements seem to believe that the non-profit-making service they provide is in some way more wholesome than the equivalent provided by a company. Do these enthusiasts seek out government-run shops and offices because they find the service there so much better than Marks and Spencer? And I think they forget that a company makes a profit *because* it provides the customer with what he wants – not in spite of it, not in addition to it but because of it.

My suspicious mind sees in this another defensive ploy, a warning: 'Keep away, we are special; we are non-profit-making; we provide a service to the community. Do not attempt to evaluate our performance.' Variations on this theme include: 'We are not like profit-making organizations – we have moral responsibilities.' 'We do not have a single overall corporate objective; we serve the whole community.' 'We are constrained by the vagaries of government decisions.' 'Oh, you mean we should put profit before our patients, do you?'

NPOs *are* different to companies, there is no getting away from that. They do have different cultures; their staff are more caring, are far more motivated by concern for the public good; personal wealth and self-aggrandizement is not their chief desire; they do have to take many of their decisions in the glare of publicity; government does keep changing its mind. And yet, are the differences so great that we have here a wholly distinct form of human endeavour? I think not.

Some executives are fearful of being privatized. And frankly who can blame them? The behaviour of some entrepreneurs and of some profit-making organizations has led many people to conclude that profit-making is a thoroughly unworthy activity. This is the land where managers flaunt their bloated pay-packets, where companies sack loyal employees without notice or compensation, where 'marketing men' deliberately dream up new and more powerful ways to trick their customers, and where everything is reduced to the lowest denominator – money. Who can blame the non-profit-making half of humanity for not wanting any of that?

Some of those who work in NPOs are so disenchanted by the profit motive that they reject the use of money in any of its forms as a relevant indicator for the performance of their organization. While recognizing that 'money is greed', to quote one slogan, it must be remembered that it is also the *only* universal measure of value yet invented by man. When I use money as an indicator later on, which I shall have to do frequently, I hope I shall be recommending it as an indicator of comparative value and not just preaching the creed of greed.

The scientific staff in one well-known government research establishment were utterly dismayed when they were told their organization was to be privatized. The idea of working for *money* was thoroughly repulsive to some. They went round expostulating, 'But we are *scientists*. We are judged by our peers on the excellence of our published papers.' Some of them now revel in earning substantial fees for their organization from their highly specialized advice, and take great pride in the recognition of their worth that their considerable earning power implies.

This route is not for everyone, however, and as will be seen later, I do not advocate privatization for everything in sight; on the contrary, I recognize that it is wholly inappropriate for many organizations. But if not privatization, what?

Multi-purpose organizations

I believe this is the chief stumbling block to clear objectives. Most of our best brains go into NPOs. Bright people enjoy complexity, thrive on intellectual conundrums and are not at home with the curt simplicities of profit and loss. I suspect they like their organizations to have multiple objectives because, for them, this provides an intellectual challenge. They do not want their organization to be judged, nor to be *capable* of being judged, by any simplistic criterion of success: 'This is a university; you must realize it is a very complex and demanding organization.'

Does one really have to be brilliant, however, to determine what, say, the Boy Scouts is for, or Alcoholics Anonymous – or a university? When someone founds an organization does he have some vastly complex aim in mind? Surely it will be simplicity itself – to relieve famine, save the whale, provide a refuge for battered wives or whatever – determined with great clarity and, often, with passion. Therefore if an organization tells me that all this may have been true at one time but is no longer so – 'we live in a modern, complex world' – then I am tempted to wonder whether something has gone seriously wrong. Perhaps the organization has become encrusted with bureaucracy or personal ambition or has become perverted.

I have never really understood the craving people have for forming organizations with multiple objectives. Let us form one now. How about an institute with these objectives: 'To supervise the veterinary profession in Britain and preserve the art of tribal dancing in Nigeria.' No one would be such an idiot as to form, or work for, or subscribe to, an organization like that. For a start, how on earth would the management allocate funds to two such disparate causes? It would not just be difficult, it would be impossible!

Do you think that the YMCA should merge with Help The Aged? No? Well, let us try again. This time we will form a very serious and learned institution: 'To encourage the classification of natural fauna and to entertain the kids.' I have rephrased it slightly, as you see from the official wording below, but these are, in fact, the corporate objectives of the British Museum (Natural History), an organization that has earned the affection of generations of people. The exact wording is:

'1. ... to discover and make available to the scientific community the information contained within its collection of natural objects, and
2. to entertain, interest and educate children and adults in natural history.'

It will come as a surprise to members of the public that half its budget is devoted to the first objective and only 10 per cent to the latter (the rest is administrative and other common service costs). The explanation is that, behind those fascinating public exhibits are nearly 400 scientific staff busily studying the 65 million specimens, writing books and reports, advising governments, and so forth.

One question is, why is it not the other way round – 50 per cent for the public objective and 10 per cent for the scientific one? A second question is, why was its budget (in 1986) £14m? Why not say £28m, or £7m? I do not believe anyone has the slightest idea whether to double the Museum's budget or halve it; close it down entirely as a waste of taxpayers' money or treble it; whether its scientific work is worth £7m per annum or £70m; or its educational work is worth £1 or £100m; whether the management is brilliant or appalling. The trouble here is, first, we have two disparate beneficiaries: 'scientists' and 'the public' (and therefore two different benefits: 'research' and 'education'). Secondly, there is no way to quantify *either* of its aims or to verify whether the Museum is achieving them. The fact that demand for both services has actually doubled in the past two decades certainly tells us that the Museum is not a failure, but it does not tell us how much more demand there might have been had its budget been increased, nor how much less demand there might have been had they charged for their services. There is simply no way to know how much resource society should lavish on this organization.

A prison is another double objective organization. One objective benefits 'society' by locking away the miscreants; the other benefits the prisoners who are supposedly being deterred from crime. Does it work? Is it well managed? Do we want more or less of it? Another is a university where we find research and teaching. Which do we judge by? Does sparkling research make up for dull teaching? The other way round? Again, the Customs and Excise Department collects Value Added Tax *and* it regulates imports and exports. How does HM Government judge this department as a department?

Double objectives are occasionally found in companies, too. I know one in which an American conglomerate owned 50 per cent of the stock and the Spanish Government the other half. Imagine the tension when there was in an economic downturn, the American parent demanding dismissal of surplus workers, the Spanish parent demanding the contrary. Eventually they could not stand it any longer; they did the sensible thing and split it into two so that each had his own organization with its own simple objective.[4]

I cannot understand the urge to form multi-objective organizations, to which the Victorians seem to have been particularly prone, for you can no more drive an organization in two directions at once than you can a bus. Perhaps in the past methods of management were less precise than they are today and so maybe it was less obvious when organizations were on the brink of failure, but really, just consider what we would do with an employer who was still using a Victorian 'safety at work' manual. Yet we allow all these organizations to get away with using a Victorian 'setting objectives' manual.

Peter Drucker says that most modern organizations are multi-purpose now, whether we like it or not. I do not like it. I do not believe it either. In my view, any organization with more than one corporate objective is unmanageable.

This ends this section of the chapter. In it I have been suggesting that, just as the planning teams in companies have to avoid selecting any of the fallacious objectives that I listed in the last chapter, so teams in NPOs have to do the same, but this time the list is longer and more controversial. Some executives simply do not want their NPOs to be given clear corporate objectives and some of the items in the list above may have their roots in this feeling. I am further suggesting that they may have to modify their opposition to setting clear objectives. Society today knows the difference between a hit and a miss and is becoming impatient with standards of corporate management that fall too far below those seen in the private sector.

One way through?

In this section of the chapter I am, very tentatively, because I recognize the depth of the problem, going to propose a system for setting corporate objectives in NPOs. As will be seen, it consists of a brief step-by-step sequence of questions for the planning team to consider, very much as I suggested for companies in the previous chapter except that it must also encompass the additional difficulties listed above.

The corporate description

The first duty of the planning team should be to determine the first two features in their organization's corporate description, just as I suggested for Mr Finch and for Mallard Universal plc in the previous chapter: who are the beneficiaries and what benefit do they expect? (The targets, which will define the term 'satisfactory performance' will be discussed in Chapter 5, where it will be seen that the attempt to set numerical targets has the effect of tightening up the definition of corporate objective even further.)

Let us take a simple non-profit-making organization, Southtown School. The intended beneficiaries are children and the benefit is education (see Figure 4.2).

Figure 4.2   The Corporate Description for Southtown School

The Intended Beneficiaries	Children
The Intended Benefit	Education
Performance Targets	–

Plainly, however, this is not sufficiently precise: Are all the children from Southtown going to this school?, No, it is for the 5 to 11 year olds. Only from Southtown or is the village of Eastville included? What about handicapped children? And so on.

Identifying who the intended beneficiaries are is seldom difficult. If it is, that suggests the organization has well and truly lost its way and that this has become one of its elephants. I can see who might be the beneficiaries of the Ministry of Defence – the British. But who are the beneficiaries of the Minstry of Agriculture – farmers or consumers?

Now for the benefit – education. How are we to define education in such a way that we can set targets that can be independently empirically verified as being 'satisfactory'? Here the difficulty is acute. We are trying to solve a riddle that has defeated education authorities for centuries. It is doubtful if a satisfactory conclusion will ever be reached – that is, we may never be able to judge between schools as accurately and as universally as we can judge between companies. Perhaps we should set down, say, a dozen educational attainments that a child should be able to reach by a certain age. It turns out that this is not difficult and techniques of this sort are increasingly in practical usage. One such method used in UK is as follows: divide a school's total annual budget by the number of pupils who have achieved five 'O level' passes in the year. The result is the cost of turning out pupils of this standard of general education and each school can be compared with every other. One snag, among several, is differences in the raw material – schools in deprived areas cannot be expected to do as well as in wealthy areas – but at least we can compare like with like, we can compare deprived schools with deprived, village schools with village, nation with nation.

There remain several major elements in the definition of 'education' for children that cannot be easily assessed, perhaps not at all, such as behaviour, initiative, social skills, physical prowess and many others. Even if we could measure these intangibles we face the problem of weighting. How many marks do we give a school which produces ten children who can solve simultaneous equations at the age of 12 but where three of them are hooked on heroin? But is this really such a difficult problem? Surely a school riddled with heroin is not going to turn in such good examination results as one that is not? And surely the pupils in a school with high academic results will be reasonably well behaved?

This problem – the claim that one often cannot define the intended benefits sufficiently accurately to verify that they are being provided – is very common among NPOs. A hospital is for the benefit of the sick; the benefit is that they are cured. Easy, everyone knows that. But how does one judge whether this hospital is performing 'satisfactorily' or not. How does one judge this hospital against another serving a different population? In particular, how does one attempt to score a general hospital? A partial cure for cancer earns 30 points, a complete cure for a broken leg gets 6 points (7 if the patient is over 70)? Add them all up and divide by the annual budget? Something of the sort is actually used (see later), although it breaks one of my rules above, that corporate objectives must be simple.

It is interesting to note that the more specialized an organization is, the easier it is to verify its objectives. To judge between two hip-replacement clinics, say, is far less difficult than judging between two general hospitals.

The corporate performance indicator (CPI)

How are we to judge the long-term efficacy of the government of, say, a town? We could measure the rate of unemployment, how many swimming baths per thousand population, the crime rate, the rate of homelessness and so on, add them up – after weighting them for importance – and compare this index with other towns. It is essentially how we do it now.

However, even if we could score and weight all the items correctly we still have a measure that is a sum of the parts. This is like scoring a company, not on its return on capital – a single *overall* measure – but by calculating its market share, its output per man, its rejects per thousand, and so on, then weighting all these *operational* performance indicators in order of importance, adding them up and then trying to compare this total with that of other companies. What a complicated thing to do when we can use one single overall pointer – return on capital.

A sum of the parts indicator is not the same as an overall *corporate* performance indicator. Moreover, this type of objective breaks another of my rules: that they must be strategy-neutral. If the town's objective specifically includes all these criteria then the management have no option but to reduce unemployment, build more pools, recruit more police, reduce the homeless, etc.; the objectives tell them what their strategies are to be. It is another Trojan Horse.[5]

Would it be possible to devise more of an overall CPI, such as whether people want to come and live in that town; is it a nice place to live? That sounds a very 'soft' objective – how could we possibly measure this? Perhaps we could design numerical targets to reflect this by measuring, say, the growth in the total market value of the citizens' property per head compared with the nearest few similar towns. If the total market value of property per head has been rising faster in our town over the past few years than in our neighbours' then our town must be getting it right, surely?

The CPI should not be the tax receipts on citizens' property or income – these can be too easily distorted by the town government itself. It would have to be something that cannot be fabricated.

Also, it is 'value *per head*'; we do not want the mere increase of population to affect the indicator, we only want it to indicate the desirability of living there.

Would this measure the success of a local government unequivocally? If the market value of local property per head increases, does that unequivocally mean our town government is getting it right compared with neighbouring towns? And if they allowed the crime rate to rise, or the streets to become dirtier than the neighbours', or whatever; if it is 'not such a nice place to live' as Northtown; if people are moving out and not moving in, then, surely, the values would go down? I think it does (except for windfalls and tragedies – but companies get these too and have learnt how to adjust for them, and we are taking companies as our standard, remember, not something of infinite accuracy).

This type of overall *corporate* performance indicator, because it is strategy-neutral, invites the town management to search for strategies to enhance the average property value of its inhabitants. It does not tell them what the strategies are; it leaves that to the management. That's what managers are for.

Is every government's corporate objective something like, 'make this a better place to live'? From a village government right up to the European Community? The criterion being the market value of its citizens' property compared with neighbouring or similar villages or nations?

What about all the moral issues – freedom, the distribution of wealth, justice, health, and so on? I do not know. I suspect that most of these things come with wealth, perhaps all of them do. Look at the wealthy nations, then look at the poor ones. Which are more free, enjoy a more fair distribution, are more just, more healthy, more cultured, and so on? Or maybe it is the other way round, and wealth comes to the fairer, the more just, the more healthy. Anyhow, surely these are subsumed in the 'better place to live' criterion? We do not have to measure them at all, nor create a 'quality of life index', do we? It is all subsumed in the CPI.

I believe that, if we really tried, *someone, somewhere*, could devise an overall CPI for any town, any charity, any institution – any non-profit-making organization – which truly reflects what it is supposed to be doing for whom. I do not believe that people who found NPOs have such a hazy idea or such a complex concept that we cannot tell whether they are doing it except by vast statistical exercises. I think we have been looking in the wrong place for the wrong thing. We keep finding the wrong thing because we have not been looking for the right one.

Criteria for selecting the corporate objective

I would like to put forward certain principles (see Figure 4.3) for determining the corporate objective of NPOs. (For the sake of completeness I have had to stray into the criteria for Targets. I will explain these in detail in Chapter 5.)

Figure 4.3   Criteria for defining the corporate objective

Three elements must always be identified for any organization: the beneficiaries, the benefits and the CPI targets.

The intended beneficiaries

- It should be possible to state the identity of the intended beneficiaries in just a few words: 'The children of Southtown between the age of five and eleven', for example.
- The beneficiaries should be homogeneous. An organization formed to meet the wishes of two or more disparate groups will not be able to allocate its resources between them. Multi-purpose organizations are unmanageable. A single homogeneous group is essential. The more homogeneous they are the more readily will they agree on the performance of the organization and on trade-offs between one benefit against another if it is ever necessary for them to do this.

The intended benefits

- An organization should aim to provide the beneficiaries with just one homogeneous benefit. However, the more homogeneous the beneficiaries are, the more readily will they be able to trade off disparate benefits.
- It should be possible to state the benefits in just a few words. They must be sufficiently concrete to allow a target to be set and for this target to be verifiable by the beneficiaries or their representatives, by the management or any independent observer. If the benefits are numerous or disparate it will be impractical to allocate, or weight them, into a single overall corporate performance indicator.
- The benefits must be attractive to the beneficiaries and socially acceptable.

The corporate performance indicator (CPI)

- The CPI should reflect the corporate purpose – that is, it should be a restatement of the intended benefit *in figures* (or a close proxy). One CPI, or at the most two, should always be sufficient for this purpose. If more than two are required the benefit has not been correctly defined. A sum-of-the-parts target will not reflect the true purpose of the organization nor will any measure of efficiency.
- It must be dynamic. The target must call for a higher level of performance every year.
- It must be comparable – no performance can be said to be absolutely 'satisfactory', it is only satisfactory relative to a comparable organization.
- (See Chapter 5 where one further, highly critical, additional provision is required which has the effect of adding further precision to all these definitions.)

The following are intended as supplementary hints and tips which may sometimes help. They are in no particular order:

- Try the word 'unequivocal'. Which indicator is unequivocally good news for your organization when it goes up and unequivocally bad when it goes down (or vice versa). Thus, if fatal accidents per million miles goes down this can only be good news for a safety organization. It is not possible to think of any circumstances when it would be bad news. But an increase in sales is not *unequivocally* good news for a company so 'sales' is not a reliable CPI.
- Identify the closest competitive organizations to your own. Then ask how you would rate them compared with your own. Now, the criteria you have instinctively used in this comparison will be the ones, or very close to them, that reflect your corporate objective.
- Who would be entitled to the assets of your organization if it was wound up? They are probably the beneficiaries.
- Imagine that your organization was privatized. What would you then be selling to whom? What would your 'product' be? Who would be your 'customer'? These will probably be the benefit and beneficiaries respectively.
- What are the actual concrete changes that your organization is striving to bring about *in the real world*, on the ground, so to

speak, over the next five years. These will be the benefits. Who
will enjoy this change? They will be the beneficiaries.
● The most powerful lead into a definition of the true purpose of
any organization is possibly 'Tmin'[6] – see Chapter 5, where I
shall explain this as follows: if an organization knows what are
the signs that tell it that it is *failing*, then that organization can
claim to have at least some idea what it is supposed to be doing
for whom. So if you can identify (1) who would start complaining, and (2) about precisely what, then you will be very close to
knowing the corporate objective.

Re-formation

Now for the crunch statement:

> Any organization which cannot clearly define the beneficiaries,
> the benefit and the CPI, and which cannot demonstrate a
> satisfactory performance, should be closed down or reformed
> into a new corporate entity.

In other words, the burden of proof should rest with the organization. It should be up to them to tell us (1) what they are trying to

---

Figure 4.4   Three alternative organizational forms

---

(1)   Re-form to exclude all the beneficiaries except one homogeneous group. Simplify the benefits to just one homogeneous
type. Drop any secondary beneficiaries, or charge them for
services rendered. Or it may be necessary to fragment the
organization into two or more autonomous parts, each more
specialized and focused than the original, each serving one of
the original several beneficiaries.

(2)   Re-form into a profit-making organization. Charge the erstwhile
beneficiaries for the benefit. In other words, be privatized. It may
also be necessary to break up into more specialized segments.

(3)   Re-form into one or more project organizations where the
objective is stated, not as benefits to beneficiaries, but as a
particular task to be achieved by a set date. It thus becomes a
'throw-away organization' where it is disbanded (or re-formed)
each time it achieves its objective.

---

do for whom, and (2) provide us with the evidence that they are doing it satisfactorily. If they cannot do both, they should be reformed until they can.

Organizations that are aged, or large, or socially significant, or have been perverted, or have achieved their original objectives, or have very wide remits, or have simply lost their way, will find it particularly hard to meet these criteria and may need to be re-formed. How? Figure 4.4 contains possible alternatives.

I wish there was space here to continue this discussion which has very wide implications. I did comment earlier on mechanisms by which beneficiaries may control their organizations, and will comment later, extensively, on setting targets and on the structure of 'fragmented' organizations, but now I would like to make a few random comments on the above:

- The consideration that was uppermost in my mind in setting out these three forms was the impossibility, in my view, of running an organization with more than one intended beneficiary. That is why I recommended that organizations should be re-formed by dropping all beneficiaries except one homogeneous group.
- I am proposing, then, that all organizations with multiple objectives (including the very common double objective ones) should be broken up into autonomous parts, one for each homogeneous beneficiary. For example, to set and to verify corporate objectives for a teaching-cum-research organization is virtually impossible. To set and verify the corporate objective for a teaching organization and, separately, the corporate objective for a research organization is a practical proposition. (There is nothing to stop any person working for both.)
- An important result of this philosophy is that NPOs would become more specialist – in theory we would have two single-objective organizations where we had one double-objective organization before. Each would attend to the needs of a narrower sample of beneficiaries. This specializing trend would parallel the trend to niche marketing in the profit-making sector which began several decades ago.
- This would also allow us to identify when an organization has become too large or too general. An organization will have become so when it can no longer demonstrate whether or not it is achieving a satisfactory performance to the beneficiaries. If it

can still demonstrate this it is self-evidently not too big.

- Although I believe that 'privatization' – 'profitization' would be more accurate – is one solution for NPOs, it is not the only one. For some it is certainly not the best, for others it is out of the question, absurd – obscene, even. Highly successful though profitization may be, I consider it of intense importance that an alternative be found. To re-form as a single-objective organization, but still non-profit-making, rather than having to face profitization as the only alternative, seems a most valuable option.

- I shall refer to this again under target setting, but in all cases it is important to set 'dynamic' targets. This means that, every year, the beneficiaries should expect to receive an improved benefit – rather as shareholders expect continued growth every year.

- Also in the next chapter I shall suggest one single criterion for re-formation – if an organization can not identify, or does not exceed 'Tmin' then it should be re-formed.

- Comparability is vital. No organization is unique; every organization has its counterpart somewhere in the world. It makes no sense to select a corporate performance indicator that cannot be compared. The word 'satisfactory performance' can only mean 'more or less satisfactory than alternative organizations or than not doing it at all'.

- My proposal is that organizations be deemed guilty until they prove themselves innocent; it should be up to each organization to demonstrate to its beneficiaries that it is making satisfactory progress towards its corporate objective. Failure to do so should result in re-formation to providing a more specialist range of benefits to fewer beneficiaries. This is exactly what happens to companies which are showing a poor return on capital – they are slimmed down, rationalized and divested until the return improves. Why not NPOs?[7]

- A project organization is one which does not have a named group of people as its beneficiaries. It is formed to carry out a specific job – Save the Whale, Ban the Bomb – and when the whale has been saved, etc. (or when, on the contrary, it has not), the organization disbands. Motivation in such an organization is often electric. When the objective has been achieved, however, it must be disbanded or given a new, worthwhile task, if it is not to suffer the fate of NASA after the moon landing.

- Finally, I think I am saying something else, that these three are the only valid types of organization there are: a non-profit-making organization yielding a verifiable benefit to specific beneficiaries, a profit-making organization and a temporary project organization. No others are effective; all others are a waste of resources; all others should be re-formed into one of these three.

I see corporate planning as being a truly profound exercise which is supposed to go to the very roots of an organization. Alas, when they reach this stage, decide objectives, many organizations will skip over the fundamentals – and who can blame them? The task of giving an organization verifiable objectives is bound to be difficult and even disruptive, re-formation horribly so. Yet, in all honesty, most of our older and larger organizations ought to be doing exactly that.

Summary

I say in this chapter that I do not know whether to believe executives in NPOs who claim that it is not possible to determine their corporate objectives in a verifiable form. I would be tempted to retort that they have not tried hard enough, or that they had fallen into some of the traps I listed above, namely, that they have chosen a non-corporate objective, or they were pretending to be different, or were obsessed by efficiency, or, more likely, had confused objectives with strategy or were trying to be clever by adopting several objectives at once.

Anyhow, I am certain the founder of their organization knew very well indeed what he wanted it to do, what effect – what verifiable effect – it was to have in the real world. It would probably be something very simple, requiring little in the way of elaborate statistical surveys to establish. If the corporate objective is really not now known then it must have become overlain with bureaucracy, personal ambition or perversion.

I would go further. Unless they can prove to the beneficiaries that their corporate objective is verifiable, and that it is being verified, then their organization should be re-formed until it becomes possible to do this. One way to demonstrate that their organization does not need re-formation is to complete a 'corporate description' showing beneficiaries, benefit, CPI targets (and conduct) and to provide the beneficiaries, or their representatives, with an annual record of concrete progress towards the corporate objectives as specified. (In the next chapter one single criterion will be proposed for re-formation.)

This re-formation may take three forms, only one of which, and by no means the most appropriate, is to be privatized:

(1)   To break down into more specialized autonomous segments (or fragments within a federal organization) to ensure that the beneficiaries and the benefits were more homogeneous so that verifiable objectives could be set.
(2)   To be privatized. This usually means charging the erstwhile beneficiaries for the benefits they used to receive. Plainly this is appropriate for only some NPOs.
(3)   To become project organizations formed to achieve some specific task by a specific date and then to be disbanded or re-formed again.

For all socially important organizations a governing body is required for which certain structural rules should apply.

These propositions are put forward in the belief that the man in the street now expects non-profit-making organizations to shape up, just as the profit-making ones have had to do, and that many of our organizations do not, and cannot, meet satisfactory performance levels in their present form.

CHAPTER 5

Setting the Corporate Targets

Having identified the beneficiaries and the benefit they are entitled to expect from their organization, the next step in deciding the corporate objective is to set targets for these, together with some of the items in its code of conduct. To do this one must first select an appropriate corporate performance indicator (CPI) and then decide what level of performance the beneficiaries are entitled to expect.

As noted in the previous chapters, companies have the huge advantage that they have a ready-made CPI – profits – and target-setting has become second nature to many of them. It is therefore on companies that I shall concentrate in this chapter. Only when I have established an effective regime for target-setting in companies will I turn to the far more difficult subject of setting targets for non-profit-making organizations and for conduct. It will be observed, during this chapter, that although profit must be one of the most attractive and easily verifiable CPIs yet devised, it is certainly not without its defects and difficulties.

I believe that an organization can only be set a target correctly if the planning team go through a three-step process:

(1) Select a suitable CPI.
(2) Examine the organization's past performance.
(3) Decide targets for its future performance.

I shall now move through these steps for companies and then return to non-profit-making organizations at the end of the chapter.

Profits – the CPI for companies

I start with the assumption that companies have one simple corporate purpose – to make a profit for their shareholders. Assuming this is correct the next step, putting a figure on this aim, should be simple; you calculate the surplus income left over a year's operations and there you are!

Apart from a vast number of technical accounting problems (depreciation, revaluation for inflation, tax deferrals, 'exceptionals', 'extraordinaries' and many others which I do not intend to discuss in this book) there are a number of matters of principle. One of these is to remember that 'profit' can come from two types of transaction, income and capital. If a company spends £1,000 in a year and earns £1,100 it has made an income profit of £100. If it buys an asset for £1,000 and sells it for £1,100 it has also made a profit of £100 – this time it is a capital profit.

Some companies have no capital assets at all – a service company which rents its premises, for example. Others have no income at all – a property development company. Most companies have both. So we have to bear this in mind in selecting the CPI.

Another major issue is that beneficiaries are not just expecting a profit; they want a *satisfactory* profit. If I told you that a certain company had made a profit of £1m last year you would have no idea whether that was satisfactory or not. On its own it is a completely useless and meaningless figure. You could only judge if I also told you the previous year's profits, or compared it with another similar company, or compared it to the capital employed. I am going to suggest that for most companies we need to do all three of these tests before judging its performance. There is no such thing as an absolute target. All targets are set relative to something else, usually relative to the performance of comparable or competitive organizations. Nor is a single year's comparison adequate, one needs to see several years to even out the inevitable annual fluctuations.

The CPI statement that most companies chose is: 'The aim of this company is to achieve a satisfactory long-term growth in profits or a satisfactory return on capital or both.' If that is accepted we now have to select the precise method of calculation for growth and return.

Measuring 'profit'

As a general rule each company will do best to continue to use the definitions of growth of profit and of return on capital that they have traditionally used. If their traditional methods have served well, why change them – especially as we are discussing long-range targeting here where extreme accuracy is entirely out of place.

Figures 5.1 and 5.2 outline some of the many measures of profit, return and growth that companies use, together with some of the advantages and disadvantages of each of them.

Figure 5.1   Measures of profit

Measures of profit	*Advantages and disadvantages of each as a measure of overall corporate objectives.*
Trading profit	This will be readily understood by senior executives but does not include certain 'other income' (such as from investments) which, with skilful management, could become a major source of profit.
Operating profit	Also well understood but the definition does not include interest on loans. It must surely be a major function of management to manage interest on the company's loan capital and not to include this item is a serious drawback.
Profit before tax	By far the most popular and the best understood. Unfortunately it does not include tax – the management of a company's tax burden is also surely something the managers need to be judged on.
Profit after tax or 'earnings' or 'attri-butable'	This is the only measure that includes everything the managers should manage. Unfortunately, while it is widely used by quoted companies it is far less popular in small ones.
Dividends	No. Dividends reflect the immediate generosity of a company towards its shareholders. Dividend is the proportion of earnings that it decides to pay out rather than retain. It says little about the long-term performance of the company.
Reserves	Again this measures only a part of earnings – the part that is retained instead of being paid out.

Figure 5.2 Measures of return on capital

Measures of return on capital	Advantages and disadvantages of each as a measure of overall corporate objectives.
Return on capital employed or return on net assets	They both take operating profit (which *includes* interest on loans) and either express it as a percentage on equity plus loans (ROCE) or on total assets less liabilities (RONA). (Note that ROCE = RONA.) (It is usual to take average capital employed.)
Return on equity or on shareholders' funds or on net worth	Profit before tax as a percentage of shareholders' funds, i.e. this measures the profit, *after* interest on loans, as a percentage of the shareholders' equity.
Growth of earnings per share	The best. It not only measures performance after interest and after tax but introduces the concept of growth. Moreover, the market value of a company is directly related to growth of EpS. Unfortunately it is seldom used by smaller companies.
Growth of assets	This usually refers to book values. The problem here is that book values sometimes reflect replacement values, sometimes written-down values or even insurance values – seldom market values. So the *true* value of the company in a sale or bid or flotation is not measured.
Growth of market value	What most owners would really like to know is how much their company is worth in the market place in a bid, a float or a sale. Quoted companies can see what their 'market capitalization' is from their daily share price but, alas, private companies can only make rough guesses – too rough to be much use – because there is no way of estimating their price earnings ratio.

Non-financial readers, and those who come from non-profit-making organizations, will begin to glimpse that selecting a valid CPI is not so easy even for a company which, as I keep saying, is probably the least controversial of all organizations. For some companies it is almost impossible. Life assurance company profits, for example, like everyone else's, result from subtracting income from expenditure. The problem is that the company will not know for up to a hundred years how much it will have to pay out, so they have to fall back on confections like 'assessed values' and 'statutory profits'. Most unsatisfactory.

So what are the conclusions so far? Growth of earnings per share seems the least misleading of all the possible CPIs. Certainly most public companies now use this measure as their key criterion. Alas, most companies that are not quoted on a stock market seem to prefer return on capital and growth of profits before tax; I say 'alas' because (a) tax is surely something that managements should manage and to employ a CPI that does not include tax seems rather careless; and (b) the 'capital' often turns out to be a meaningless mixture of book values and replacement values – but I wish to avoid accounting technicalities and so I conclude that, if this is the measure that a small company management is most familiar with, then perhaps they should stick to it even though it does have certain avoidable dangers. But (c) there are problems with reconciling any two CPIs, such as growth and return, as we will see below.

Finally, I should warn against using growth of profit on its own, without ROCE; a company can easily double profits by, say, acquiring another company, but EpS could actually go *down* in some such circumstances, and so could ROCE. Profit on its own, therefore, can be positively dangerous.

Different CPIs for different companies

If not all companies see EpS as their best measure what are the alternatives? Figure 5.3 contains a list of possible measures for each different type of company starting with EpS for quoted companies.

Double trouble

One of the reasons I am so keen on EpS is that it may be used on its own, without ROCE, for, providing that a company's return on capital is satisfactory at the time the EpS target is set then, if its EpS is growing its return on capital cannot be declining. To be able to judge an organization by reference to one single criterion is immensely powerful. No trade-offs between two targets is called for and, as we shall see below, having to make trade-offs can create serious problems.

Figure 5.3   Different measures for different companies

Types of company	Suitable measures for profits and return on capital.
Quoted, or public, company	Growth of earnings per share. This is all that is normally necessary to provide a full and meaningful criterion of corporate success. Growth of market capitalization. The only problem is the huge swings in stock market values, otherwise it would be fine.
Groups	Growth of earnings per share for the parent company, but growth of profit and return on capital for its subsidiaries — and cash flows?
Private company	Growth of profits before tax and ROCE, or, for a company with insignificant capital, just growth of profits before tax.
Subsidiary company or profit centre	Operating profit (where the subsidiary is not held responsible for its loans) and ROCE. In addition, cash flow to or from the parent company.
A partnership	Growth of profit attributable to the partners including any salaries and fees they draw. Return on partnership capital, or on equity.
A co-operative	Growth of profit including any benefit in kind to the members (such as discounts on goods purchased from their co-operative). Return on members' cash investment into the co-operative.
Company with no or negligible capital	Growth of profit attributable to the shareholders including any salaries they draw.
Company with no or negligible income	Here the key target may be capital gains, as could be the case with a property development company.
A start-up	Profits and/or ROCE as above — except that sometimes these may only become important in later years. In the early years of a start-up the key target may be *cash*. How much cash are the backers prepared to invest each year? In which year do they hope to earn a return and by when will they abandon the project if no return is forthcoming?

Most companies prefer to set two targets – growth and ROCE. This creates the problem of reconciling the two figures. While I have no doubt that return on capital is theoretically the most fundamental of all, most managers see growth as equally important. They certainly like to see their company growing (so much so they sometimes make the inexcusable error of aiming for growth in sales rather than growth of profits). Suppose, then, a company wishes to set two targets, one for growth and one for return on capital. What are the dangers?

Take a company with the following financial results in Year 1:

£m	Year 1	Year 2
Capital employed	100	104
ROCE %	10	
Profit before tax	10	
Tax	3	
Profit after tax	7	
Dividends	3	
Retained	4	

What will be the capital employed in Year 2? Answer: £104m (the Year 1 capital employed will be increased by the retained profit of £4m). Assuming 10 per cent ROCE again, profits in Year 2 will rise to £10.4m – a growth of 4 per cent. In other words, in this company a ROCE of 10 per cent is compatible *only* with a growth rate in profits of 4 per cent on these assumptions. Of course it is possible to break this link – by borrowing, by altering the dividend yield and so on – but the fundamental fact is that a given ROCE is compatible only with a given rate of growth, other things being equal.

Many companies seem unaware of this link. One company I know had just begun to make a return of 20 per cent on capital after a period of decline but the family owners had no desire whatever to see it grow. 'Oh. In that case what are you going to do with all those dividends?' I asked. 'What dividends?' – and it took several calculations similar to the one above to convince them that 20 per cent return automatically gave 11 per cent growth (under their prevailing tax and other conditions) unless they paid out a massive dividend.[1]

And note this: once you select *two* targets you automatically create a third by default. Suppose a company wishes its return on capital employed to improve from 10 per cent to 18 per cent, and suppose it would like to see a growth in profits over each of the next five years of, say, 8.5 per cent. Those are the two targets, but a third – capital employed – is automatically created by the very nature of this equation. Furthermore, this third factor is going to do something very peculiar over the five years:

	Year 0	Year 5
Profits	£10,000	£15,000 (8.5% growth per annum for 5 years)
ROCE	10%	18%
Capital employed	£100,000	£83,333

Did the management know, when they selected these two target parameters, that this would inevitably result in a third one – their company's capital employed – shrinking by 17 per cent?

Multiple targets

The greater the number of targets one selects as CPIs the more confused and arbitrary does the target-setting exercise become and the more strategic decisions does one pre-empt – the less 'strategy-neutral' do the objectives become. Thus suppose, to the two already discussed, we add turnover, for example, then, including the derived ratios, we have the following targets: profit, ROCE, capital, turnover, profit on turnover ('margin'), turnover/capital (sometimes called 'asset turn'). Suppose such a company sets its five year targets as follows:

	Year 0	Year 5
Profit	£1,000	£1,800
Capital	£10,000	£12,000
ROCE	10%	15%
Turnover	£20,000	£30,000
Margin	5.0%	6.0%
T/C	2.0	2.5

Each time one adds another target figure one pre-empts a further raft of possible strategies. In this case the company, by selecting an *increase* in margins, has eliminated all strategies that might reduce the margins such as moving down-market, going for a major increase in market share, reducing value added, increasing discounts, improving customer loyalty by price cuts – a whole host of possibly major strategic decisions made in just the time it takes to say 'margins ought to be raised to 6.0 per cent'.

And they have done exactly the same by setting the ratio T/C. What is so special about a turnover to capital ratio of 2.5? Would it not be better if it was 3.5 – or 1.5? The answer is, we have not the faintest idea until we have gone through the planning process. And how do they know that the turnover target of £30,000 is better than say, £125,000 or £15,000?

One final word concerning 'growth'. Business managers are obsessed by it. 'If a business is not growing it is dying' is typical of the clichés one hears. It is not considered to be masculine to be running a company that is not growing. In fact, while I personally believe that growth should be the prime aim for businesses, and for nearly all other organizations as well, there really is no logical reason for its primacy. A company that declares no dividend but grows at 10 per cent per annum shows no better return to the shareholder than one yielding a dividend of 10 per cent with no growth or even one that is shrinking at 10 per cent per annum and paying a dividend of 20 per cent. Logical or not, growth does seem to be a very satisfying ambition to the professional manager. Technically, growth is far below ROCE as a target; psychologically it is streets ahead.

Examine past performance

Having decided which CPI they wish to use, the planning team should now study the past and present performance of their company's CPIs. To do this they need to decide how many years' history they wish to examine. I consider that anything less than five years is inadequate. Even if some momentous event has interrupted the normal sequence of figures – an acquisition, perhaps, or a financial crisis three or four years ago – I still think the full five years sequence should be shown, more if available. After all, if a discontinuity occurred a few years ago, it could occur again and this possibility may need to be taken into account when setting the targets – and let us not forget that we are still looking for elephants.

Figure 5.4 shows a typical example for a manufacturing company. Notice that they only need to show profits, capital and return – the CPIs they have chosen. Many members of planning teams like to see turnover and margins as well because these are the figures they are most familiar with. By all means show these, but they should be placed separately from the CPIs.

Figure 5.4   Five-year record for Sparrow & Co. Ltd
(Summarized from the annual accounts)

Year	−5	−4	−3	−2	−1	0
Profits £000	140	153	173	178	202	222
Annual growth %	–	9.3	13.1	2.9	13.5	9.9
Capital employed £000	1431	1491	1557	1631	1708	1795
Annual growth %	–	4.2	4.4	4.8	4.7	5.1
ROCE (year end) %	9.8	10.3	11.1	10.9	11.8	12.4

The planning team should ask themselves how they feel about this performance. Is it good or bad, does it provide a norm for the future performance of their company or must they do better? They cannot do this until they have carried out three checks:

● Should the record be adjusted for inflation?
● Are there any hidden anomalies?
● How did their competitors perform?

Adjusting for inflation

The first of these is simple: one adjusts the figures for inflation by using the Cost of Living Index or GDP Deflator. It is important not to use any of the specialist indexes such as the Building Materials Index (if the company is in the building industry) or the Capital Goods Index (if in capital goods). What is being discussed here is the past return to shareholders and they are entitled to measure this against a constant buying power, so it is the RPI that is relevant.

Figure 5.5 shows Sparrow's results, adjusted for inflation. The results for Sparrow's now looks rather poor. When we first saw the figures, as reported in their annual accounts, it appeared that profits had risen quite well – from £140,000 to £222,000 in five years, a rate of growth of nearly 10 per cent per annum. But now we know that inflation has been running at nearly 10 per cent annually

Figure 5.5   Five-year record for Sparrow adjusted for inflation

Year	−5	−4	−3	−2	−1	0
Annual inflation %	7.9	9.7	6.7	11.5	14.2	7.4
RPI	62.5	68.6	73.1	81.6	93.2	100.0
Real profits £000	224	223	237	218	217	222
Real growth %	−	−0.4	6.0	−7.7	−0.6	2.4
Capital employed £000	2290	2175	2128	2000	1833	1795
Real growth %	−	−5.0	−2.1	−6.0	−8.3	−2.1
ROCE %	9.8	10.3	11.1	10.9	11.8	12.4
Real ROCE %	1.9	0.6	4.4	−0.6	−2.4	5.0

Definitions: The RPI figures are adjusted to show Year 0 as 100.00. All figures are therefore in Year 0 values.

over this period and so, as we can see from the adjusted figures above, real profits have barely moved. And look at the return on capital – it has barely exceeded the rate of inflation and so the real ROCE (i.e. the return on capital employed as reported minus the rate of inflation in each year) has actually been negative in two of the years. Moreover, the purchasing power of the company's capital value has fallen.

The planning team should ask the accounts to check whether there has been any major change in accounting policy over the period and whether any anomalies have occurred. For example, if the dividend cover has deteriorated then, possibly, the profit trend will have been overstated in the above record. The company's performance may have been understated if, for example, the income gearing has significantly improved.

Comparing with competitors

We turn now to the third check to be made, how competitors have performed. This is often difficult because many of one's competitors are small and their accounts are either not published or are years late or are 'inaccurate'. Other competitors may be subsidiaries of very large companies whose accounts are not broken down into relevant divisions. Moreover, to be strictly correct, one should check that no anomalies exist in any of their accounts either – a considerable and time-consuming task. (I have to say that my suspicions are frequently aroused at this point. Many companies pretend they have no competitors with whom they can be compared – 'we are unique' they claim with a haughty smile. Yet, at the same time, they will excuse an awful profit record by referring to the 'vicious competition' they have been suffering!) So, it may be hard work, but it is usually possible to find enough reliable comparative figures to learn some useful lessons. These may be displayed in the form shown in Figure 5.6.

Figure 5.6   Sparrow's competitors: comparative performance figures

Year		−5	−4	−3	−2	−1	0
Sparrows							
Profits	£000	224	223	237	218	217	222
Capital	£000	2290	2175	2128	2000	1833	1795
ROCE	%	9.8	10.3	11.1	10.9	11.8	12.4
Competitor A							
Profits	£m	1.8	1.9	1.9	2.0	1.9	2.1
Capital	£m	15.1	15.7	16.0	15.2	15.1	16.1
ROCE	%	11.9	12.1	11.9	13.2	12.6	13.0
Competitor F							
Profits	£000	51	50	53	57	63	68
Capital	£000	281	267	280	333	328	349
ROCE	%	18.1	18.7	18.9	17.1	19.2	19.5

Note: Competitor F is foreign. His figures have been adjusted for changes in the exchange rate during the period. All figures in real terms.

There is one more problem. If we were concerned here with planning over a short time horizon – a year, say – we could very easily select suitable competitors with whom to compare our company. If we are a restaurant in Northtown, for example, we can compare ourselves with the one in Southtown. But this is strategic planning. One of our options over this horizon is to move into, say, industrial catering. So should we compare ourselves with a restaurant company or with a catering company? Or with the entire food industry? Or even 'industry'? And just your own nation or are you going to compare yourself with the world? It is a decision that has to be made. It is easy for IBM, it is easy for Fred's cafe in Eastville, but in between it has to be related to what is reasonable over the planning horizon. If a national company could become international within its five-year horizon, then, whether it intends to or not, the international criteria should be used.

Now at last it is possible to come to some conclusions as to the performance of the company over the past few years. In the case of Sparrow the planning team might make the comments contained in Figure 5.7.

Figure 5.7 Sparrow's past performance

Profit record	Poor. Profits have been static or falling while those of our competitors have risen.
ROCE	Poor. In real terms it has been close to nil.
Year 0	The same. Year 0 is still not as good as competitors.
Main explanation	We failed to control labour costs while prices fell because of low demand in our home market. Year 2 was hit by the bad weather.

Already some interesting facts are coming out, although whether they will prove to be elephants will not be clear until the end of the data-gathering stages. It looks as if Sparrow is rather dependent on the weather, for example, and the foreign competitor seems to have done better than those in the rather slack home market – could this point to a lucrative export market?

Parent companies

For subsidiary companies there is one competitor whose performance can certainly be obtained in detail, and which is possibly the most important competitor of all – their parent company! The subsidiaries of most groups are competing with all the parent's other profit centres, whether these are in the same business or in wholly different areas, for funds, for management and for attention. If a parent habitually hits a return on capital of 30 per cent for the whole group, any subsidiary who does not achieve the same may be in trouble regardless of the performance of its other market competitors. Not only is a parent company *doubly* important as a comparison (as the parent and provider of all things, and as a competitor) but its accounts and history will, unlike some of its market competitors, be available in minute detail. I question whether a target-setting exercise for a subsidiary can ever be valid if it does not start with its parent's comparative figures.

One question all planning teams should also ask themselves is whether the results for Year 0, the year they are taking as the base year (most companies take their latest financial year, or the one they are currently in, providing its outcome can be reliably predicted) are normal or not. If there has been some windfall profit or loss then this should be noted in the calculation of the starting figure for the CPIs. Similar advice holds for parents. They should check that the accounts for all their subsidiaries are on the same basis and that the 40 per cent return from the American Hotel Division, for example, is truly comparable with the 17 per cent from the Asian Engineering Division.[2]

Setting the targets

The planning team will so far have (1) decided the criteria by which they are going to judge their company's overall performance, and (2) examined how well it has performed over the past five years. Now they should set performance targets for the next five years.

This usually boils down to what figures they would like to see for growth of profit and return on capital over the next five years. Remember these are targets, not forecasts. A target is what one wants to see; a forecast is what one expects to see. Quite different. So the question is not, 'How well do you think the company will perform over the next five years?' It is, 'How well do you *want* it to perform?'

The problem with this question is that the sky is the limit! Managers want their companies to perform miracles. History is full of wildly ambitious targets being set, often to the point of hazarding the company. If it is so dangerous to set ambitious targets, ought we to set unambitious ones? Surely not. Then what are we to do?

I believe most textbooks have failed to understand that single targets are impractical. In real life no one gives himself a single target to aim at. No one says, 'I would like to be earning £100,000 a year before I am 40.' What they may say is, 'I would like to be earning £100,000 before I am 40 and I shall be bitterly disappointed if I am not earning £30,000. Of course, wouldn't it be marvellous if . . .' People feel a whole range of ambitions all the way from what they consider a major disaster right up to the nearly miraculous. For themselves, their families, and for their companies.

There are two points on this endless scale that seem to me by far the most significant. One is at the level that represents failure or perhaps just above it. The other is the level that represents 'satisfactory'. I call these two levels Tmin and Tsat: the Minimum Target and the Satisfactory Target. The first identifies a level of performance below which the beneficiaries of an organization would be entitled to dismiss the managers and to contemplate winding up the organization as a failure – they will contemplate it, please note, but will not yet be at the point of doing so; if they do so, that would suggest performance has been at Tmin for some time already. The latter, Tsat, represents a performance for which the management ought to be congratulated, where the organization may be seen as a success and where it feels it could move ahead into the future with considerable confidence, perhaps even expanding its activities into new areas.

Of course, there are other important points on the scale – Tfan for fantastic, Tmax for a level of profit so high that it might be deemed politically unwise, Trec for the record level of performance ever achieved by any competitor. None of these, in my view, have the significance of Tmin and Tsat. It may be felt that a 'satisfactory' performance is not sufficiently ambitious. Maybe, but, as will be seen later, having found strategies to achieve a satisfactory performance there is nothing to stop a company going on to find even more ambitious ones.

Surely this is the right way round. A management's first duty must be to underpin the organization's minimum performance; they must *not* allow performance to sink to the level considered to be a failure. Next they should underpin a satisfactory performance. Then they can find more strategies to take them to Tfan. Then to smash through Trec.

Strangely enough, I believe Tmin is the more important, not Tsat. I personally detest any organization which potters on for years or decades at a level of performance that brings nothing but disgrace to the management and despair to the beneficiaries – all those huge UK nationalized companies bleeding away our national wealth decade after decade, for example. Or our prison system. I believe it is vital for managers and beneficiaries of all organizations, especially non-profit-making ones, to have a minimum standard set for them below which violent and painful corrective action should be promised. So important do I consider Tmin that I would always set it before Tsat.

Let us try this concept out on companies. I am asking each planning team: 'What level of performance, over the next five years, would embarrass you, the managers, cast doubt on your competence and justify the shareholders taking action to change the management, and even threaten to dispose of the company?' Assuming a company selects return on capital and growth of profits (or EpS) as their key indicators, is it practical, in real life, to identify a figure that would represent Tmin?

ROCE targets

I have no hesitation in suggesting that Tmin for return on capital virtually sets itself. Tmin is the cost of borrowing. A company showing a return of 11 per cent on capital is not long for this world if the cost of capital is 12 per cent. In practice, companies using this approach prefer to state Tmin as 'prudently above the cost of capital (or borrowing)', where the word prudently means a percentage point or two to allow for the normal fluctuations of business life. I think that is all there is to it. For *all* companies Tmin for ROCE is: 'a prudent margin above our cost of capital'.

What about Tsat for return on capital? That is more controversial. For large, mature British companies in 1988 investors would like to see a premium for risk capital, or equity, of 7 per cent above long-term government bonds. So if bonds are yielding 10 per cent one would hope to see, say, 17 per cent from a large mature company. This premium varies with time, with the size and perceived riskiness of each company, within each nation and even with each adviser whose opinion you ask. Over the past sixty years the yield from equity (dividend yield plus the annual growth rate of the dividend) has averaged 6 per cent above government bonds but it has varied between 0 and 15 per cent over short periods.

Note that a German company yielding a return on capital of 8 per cent can be doing better than a Greek company yielding 21 per cent if German bonds are yielding 3 per cent (with zero inflation) while the Greek bonds are on 18 per cent with, say, 15 per cent inflation. Furthermore, if this German company has a subsidiary in Greece it might be very unhappy even with 21 per cent return because of possible exchange rate risks.

Beware, too, of changes in inflation rates and interest rates. When inflation is at 15 per cent a return of 30 per cent may be a sensible Tsat, but this 30 per cent becomes Tfan if inflation falls to 5 per cent.

Chairmen do not like cutting the targets they set to their companies but, when interest rates fall, that is just what they should do if they are not to saddle them with unattainable tasks. (I know one chairman, of a company employing 30,000 people, who refused to drop his 33 per cent ROCE target, set when inflation in UK was 18 per cent, even though his company had never exceeded 21 per cent, and inflation was now down to 6 per cent).

Beware, too, of returns that are too high. A return on capital of 40 per cent may well be too high. Why? Because (1) competitors will be attracted into a market that earns such a tempting reward, (2) the company that aims that high may find very few projects to yield such a tough 'hurdle-rate', (3) (maybe the most significant) it suggests that the company is so successful that it ought to expand very rapidly – with the inevitable, and not unwelcome, result that returns will fall (but not below Tsat, of course), and (4) it may mean that the company's assets are undervalued – perhaps because they are out-dated. In this case, then, the high return is bad news, not good; it is a harsh warning signal, not to be ignored.

In other words, and contrary to many people's understanding, a company's ROCE can be too high. As a crude generalization, a company with a high ROCE should inject a lot more capital into the business to expand it until the ROCE comes down towards Tsat. Conversely, a company with a low ROCE may have to contract the business, by not investing capital and even by writing some of it off until ROCE rises to Tsat. ROCE is a most ingenious ballcock.

A major, and sometimes painful, discussion will be required if the company has recently been making losses or has simply not been very profitable. This difficulty can be described as the 'peg in the ground' problem. Take a company which has shown a return on capital of, say, 20 per cent over the past few years and where the steadily rising profits have just reached £1m on the capital employed of £5m. Assuming the cost of capital is 10 per cent it is easy to set the ROCE targets on the £5m capital because the performance has been steady and unsurprising – here there is a peg in the ground, you know where you are on the conventional ROCE scale.

But imagine a company which has made no profits on its £5m capital for the past three years. Now the awful truth for this company is that it cannot take its £5m capital as a base because, for all we know, it should retrench down to £3m or £1m – or anything, or nothing. We know that it ought to aim at a Tmin of, say, 12 per cent on its capital, but we do not know on what capital! We have lost the peg in the ground.

Alas, the only way I know how to answer this conundrum is to move through a sequence of trial and error attempts as follows. First, make the assumption that the company can be turned round into profits without reducing its present size. A suitable Tmin might be, 'We must make a profit of at least £0.6m by Year 2 and at least £1m by Year 4', where the management give themselves two years to achieve a minimum ROCE of 12 per cent and a satisfactory one of 20 per cent within four years – all, hopefully, on the £5m capital. It may be that the planning team have only to voice these aims to see that, given the circumstances of the company, they are unattainable. Very well. Now try 12 per cent and 20 per cent on, say, £4m capital. Then £3m. As soon as they reach a level they think is practical they should then move through the rest of the corporate planning process to devise a strategy that will achieve these targets. If they cannot convince themselves that their strategies are practical, then back to the capital base again, for a further cut.

For companies who have not yet set themselves ROCE targets, and most have still not done so, I can say with confidence that they will find it an eye-opening experience – whether they are currently performing well or badly.

So much for setting Tmin and Tsat for return on capital. Now let us turn to Tmin and Tsat for growth of profits and earnings per share.

Growth targets

Consider a company making a profit in Year 0 of £1m. What level of performance over the next five years would be so poor that the shareholders ought to consider dismissing the managers? Suppose in Year 5 the profits were still £1m – would that warrant dismissal?

In my view it would, subject to a number of caveats. (Remember, by the way, all figures in this book are in real terms, in constant value £s. So in this case I am postulating a company whose profits have not improved at all *in real terms* in the five-year period.)

The chief caveat is that if other companies in the nation have stood still or fallen that might constitute an excuse. Should we also excuse the management if other companies in the same industry have declined while the rest of the nation's companies have grown? I do not think so. After all, we are talking here of strategic, long-range planning and it would certainly be within the management's brief to move out of a declining industry. It might well be in their brief to move out of a nation whose economy was in decline.

Does this mean that there is no excuse for a management whose profits stay static for five years? That in all cases they should be fired? Personally, I think so. I repeat, this is long-term planning, they should be searching for growth everywhere and anywhere in the world – but it is up to each company's shareholders to tell their managers what *they* think Tmin is.

In fact, many of the planning teams that I have seen consider that Tmin is 3 per cent per annum growth. Why 3 per cent? Because, they argue, the economies of most of the developed nations look like growing at approximately that rate for some years and not to grow as fast as one's national economy, containing as it does many organizations that are not even aiming to grow, would be a disgrace. One company I know, trading mainly with OECD nations, also chose 3 per cent because that was, approximately, the rate expected of those countries. Another chose '2–3 per cent' because this rate of growth is barely perceptible – 'we would be embarrassed if we could not achieve perceptible growth over five years', they said.

According to statistics in *Management Today* magazine, in 1987 half of Britain's top 250 companies achieved an annual rate of growth of 3.4 per cent over the previous decade. I hardly think, in the light of these figures, that 3 per cent growth for five years is anything less than reprehensible. (Note that these figures relate to *large* companies over a whole decade. Smaller companies often grow faster than large ones, and I am suggesting a *five*-year span, not ten.)

What growth rate is appropriate for Tsat? The statistics quoted above also show that one-third of these companies exceeded 7 per cent per annum – their (real) profits doubled in ten years. In my view, and this seems to be accepted by many planning teams in large mature companies, 7 per cent is at the bottom of the scale for Tsat; 12 per cent is at the top. Growth of 15 per cent for five years (doubling in five years) is, for large mature companies, well beyond Tsat and into Tfan.

Small, young companies could, if their owners wish to do so, aim at vastly greater figures. The highest target I have seen is 150 per cent per annum for five years set by a software company employing 200 people. I have seen 50 per cent for an insurance company employing 1,700 people – an aim I considered wholly irresponsible and far beyond Tsat, especially as it had 'only' grown at 35 per cent in the previous five years. It is an almost immutable law for growth to slow as size increases; not completely immutable, but so nearly so that I felt entitled to disbelieve this one.

The lowest Tsat target I have seen was zero growth (but, as noted above, the management insisted on coupling this with a 20 per cent ROCE target and modest dividends so it was not possible to achieve it!) The next lowest I have heard is 5 per cent. This was a large British company whose board persuaded its shareholders to grant a bonus of several million pounds to the executive directors if they achieved a 5 per cent real growth in earnings per share for the next five years. Normally I would say this is far too low a target to be termed satisfactory, or worthy of a major incentive payment. However, I have to acknowledge that this team had already raised their company's performance to a new high level, and, starting from that elevated position, a further 5 per cent every year for five years would be no small achievement.

Changing the targets

Does it really make sense to set targets like this? Surely it is not possible to foresee the course of the next few years with sufficient accuracy to endow these figures with any credibility. I believe that asking this question betrays a misunderstanding of what I am suggesting. I am not asking for a *forecast*; I am asking for a *target*. I am asking, 'Assuming nothing wholly unexpected happens in the world economy, what level of performance do you *want* from your company?'

But what if something does happen? Then we will have to change the target figures – that is what the Monitoring Stage is for. Please note, however, the target figures may *only* be changed because shareholder expectations in general change. The meaning of the word 'satisfactory' would no longer be a mere 7 per cent if every other company is growing at 12 per cent due to a lengthy boom. In a prolonged slump even 3 per cent becomes 'satisfactory'. It is *not* legitimate to change target figures just because your particular company, or your particular industry, is in trouble. If everyone else is growing at 12 per cent then 6 per cent is not satisfactory. It is if everyone else is growing at 2 per cent.

If you use the argument that you can change the target if you cannot achieve it, you are back to the idiot diagram in Figure 3.2. This implies that you change your target if you cannot find a strategy to hit it instead of changing the strategy to hit the target.

It is possible to duck out of setting actual figures. One can define Tmin as 'not below the average for our industry (our nation, or whatever)'. And Tsat becomes 'in the upper quartile for our nation/industry'. But using this method one cannot perform the very useful 'gap analysis' (see next chapter).

The best way to show any of these targets is on a graph. The simplest version is Figure 5.8, where the company made a profit of £1m in Year 0 and is aiming at a Tmin of 3 per cent and a Tsat of 10 per cent over the five years. So we have two exponential curves reaching approximately £1.16m and £1.6m respectively in Year 5.

Figure 5.8   A smooth set of targets

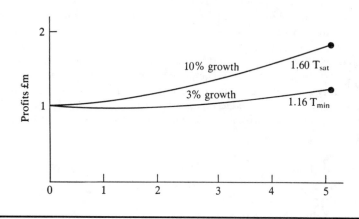

Sometimes there are complications. In Figure 5.9 the company considers that its Year 0 results were a freak and has adjusted them upwards by £100,000. But it also considers its recent performance to have been so poor that it must 'catch up' and so they have set a Tsat of 10 per cent growth for three years, then 7 per cent. Sometimes a 'slow down' sequence is indicated.

Figure 5.9   A more complex set of targets

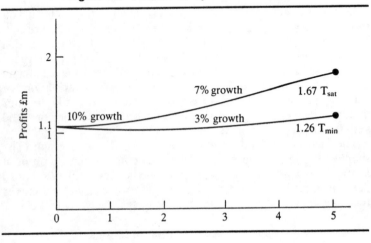

Care is required to check that the ROCE and the growth targets are compatible over the targeted five years and it is wise to ask the accounts department to run off a skeleton Profit and Loss and a Balance Sheet for each of the next five years on the assumptions (a) that these targets are achieved, and (b) that none of the company's other ratios change. Certain ratios in the resulting figures should be studied to ensure that no major anomaly is caused by adopting the targets. For example, imagine the following figures:

£000	Year 0 Actual	Year 5 Target
Profits	£100	£200
ROCE	10%	16.7%
Capital employed	£1000	£1200

You see that the planning team wants profits to double in five years, for the ROCE to rise to 16.7 per cent and therefore the capital employed will be £1,200,000 – it all looks very reasonable. But now calculate what this extra £200,000 capital has got to do – it has to generate an extra £100,000 profits! That looks like 50 per cent return on the new capital! But is that really so? Perhaps some of this improvement is due to the better use of the existing £1,000,000. In this case the accountants would need to check that the old *and* the new capital, profit and ROCE are all reasonable, bearing in mind all the circumstances.

They need to check for other anomalies, too. For example, if the ROCE target exceeds the concomitant growth targets then a cash mountain will develop, and vice versa. If the targets are excessively ambitious certain ratios will rise to an extent that cannot be believed. If the targets are too weak, other ratios will decline. These must all be checked.

Examples of target setting

The following examples from real life illustrate some of the points described above.

Teal Textiles Ltd   This was a family-owned textile company, which, as may be seen from its record in Figure 5.10, had suffered the switchback performance that characterized this industry in past decades. Six years ago the chairman, who was also chief executive, flew off to the United States one Thursday and purchased the company which supplied Teal with its man-made fibres for £8m. He returned the next Tuesday and held a board meeting at which he told his colleagues what he had done.

When they recovered from the news they gave their approval and, as can be seen, when the economic upturn came the following year, the effect on profits was quite remarkable. So remarkable, indeed, that in Year −4 the company persuaded its auditors to adjust the depreciation policy. The consequence was that the depreciation charge rose from approximately £2m per annum to almost £4m. Even so, profits exceeded £6m the next year, as may be seen.

Last year a recession again struck the industry and the new depreciation policy was abandoned. Profits were back to £2m this year, just where they had been (in real terms) five and ten years ago.

Figure 5.10   Ten-year record for Teal Textiles Ltd

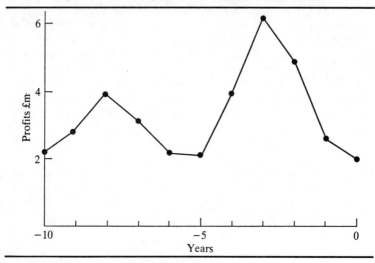

On being invited to set Tmin and Tsat for growth of profits the planning team first had to ask themselves where they were now – bearing in mind the alteration of the depreciation policy, were the profits in Year 0 actually £2m, as showed in the accounts, or £4m, or nil?

Having decided that the new depreciation figure of £2m was about correct (taking account of the likely life of the assets) and that therefore the profits really were about £2m, the team decided that Tmin for Year 5 ought to be £2.25m and Tsat should be £4m, as shown in Figure 5.11.

Their rationale was as follows. They thought it would be a serious reflection on their management ability if profits were not a little higher in five years time than they were today even if – and here is the point – *even if there was a recession in that year.* So they were warning themselves: 'We must organize our affairs in such a way that even if there is a recession in the next five years we will still improve our profits by at least 10 per cent over the whole period. Recessions are endemic in our industry, it is no good setting a target or selecting a strategy pretending that this is not so.'

They set Tsat at £4m, not at £8m, or some other ambitious figure that they might have chosen to compare well with the £6m they had

Figure 5.11. Profit targets for Teal Textiles Ltd

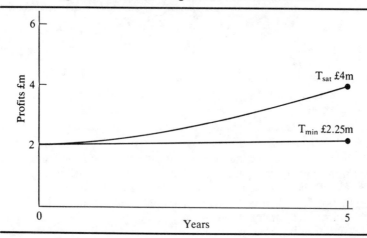

actually achieved many years ago. Why? Because this company employs 800 people in a town, 40 miles from any other town, with a population of 11,000. The working population is 5,000, so Teal employs 16 per cent of the town's working population and is easily the largest employer. 'We are heavily responsible for the economic welfare of our home town as well as our company,' said one member of the family. 'We simply must not play the fool with this company. We just have to accept our responsibilities and go for a modest target, not an ambitious one, which some of us might have preferred. By the way Charles,' he added, turning to the chairman, 'you are not thinking of another trip to the States are you?' The chairman assured him that he was not.

I am recounting this example because it was an unusual and difficult target-setting exercise bedevilled by three uncommon features – the extremely cyclical record, the entertaining accounting techniques, and the strong ethical considerations. I felt, after witnessing the long and sometimes heated discussions of this planning team, that if a Tmin and a Tsat could be agreed under these circumstances then they could be agreed under any. (Incidently, their profits reached £4m in Year 3.)

Pochin Paints Ltd   Here is another example. Figure 5.12 contains the first draft of Tsat for ROCE and growth for Pochin Paints Ltd.

Figure 5.12 Proposed Tsat for Pochin

£m	Year 0	Year 5
Profits	0.7	3.6
ROCE %	12	22
Capital employed	5.8	16.4
Sales	11.4	22.5
Margin %	6.1	16

Looking back at the past five years it was noticeable that sales margins had never risen above 12 per cent. Very well, they agreed, let us assume a 12 per cent margin instead of the 16 per cent shown in Figure 5.12. But now, to hit this target, sales turnover in Year 5 would have to reach £30m – no one believed this was remotely possible (quite apart from the effect on capital employed of a concomitant rise in working capital).

I thought this example illustrated very pointedly how an excessively ambitious target can be highlighted by a simple cross-check on a couple of ratios. I doubt if an elementary error like this would have been made if the company's past and present performance had been normal but, as can be seen for Year 0, it has been very poor. The team had lost their peg in the ground and a rather wild set of targets had resulted.

To complete this story, the parent company had told the chief executive that he must, absolutely must, achieve 22 per cent ROCE by Year 2, so the team tried Tmin as outlined in Figure 5.13. They were still very doubtful about achieving a 10 per cent margin in their increasingly competitive market (this is their Tmin, remem-

Figure 5.13 Proposed Tmin for Pochin, first draft

£m	Year 0	Year 2
Profits	0.7	1.32
ROCE %	12	22
Capital employed	5.8	6.0
Sales	11.4	13.2
Margin %	6.1	10

ber), yet every reduction assumed there meant a higher sales target – 9 per cent margin gave £14.7m turnover and 8 per cent gave £16.5m. This was quite unrealistic, they felt, so finally they bit the bullet with the Tmin contained in Figure 5.14.

Figure 5.14 Proposed Tmin for Pochin, second draft

£m	Year 0	Year 2
Profits	0.7	1.0
ROCE %	12	22
Capital employed	5.8	4.5
Sales	11.4	12.0
Margin %	6.1	8.3

It implied a substantial write-down and cut-back, but it looked realistic, it hit 22 per cent ROCE, and, importantly they felt, it took profits to £1m which ought to please head office.

Just as a subsidiary must ensure that the targets it sets itself are acceptable to its parent, so parents must set sensible targets to subsidiaries. The first part of the Case Study in Appendix E shows what happens if the parent fails to do this.

Let me end this section by reminding the reader of the distinction I am making between targets and forecasts: a target is what you *want*; a forecast is what you *expect*. The two are quite different. (Unfortunately, in a budget – which most managers see as the standard method of company planning – this distinction is not drawn at all.) So, a target reflects what the shareholders want the managers to achieve; a forecast is what the shareholders will get if the managers continue to run the business as they presently intend.

In the two examples above, the teams set targets at levels they thought they *ought* to achieve.

Targets for non-profit-making organizations

The aim of the planning teams of all non-profit-making organizations should, in my opinion, be to find a way of setting targets that approaches the power of the method described above for companies. This means that:

- Only one, or at the most two, overall measures of the organization's performance may be chosen. These CPIs must not be a mere weighted amalgam of departmental efficiency ratios but must reflect the magnitude of the 'intended benefit' generated by the organization for the 'intended beneficiaries'.
- The CPI must be as verifiable by the beneficiaries, the management and any interested observer, as 'profits' are, bearing in mind, however, that there are, in practice, many technical problems with the use of 'profit' and that few people would claim to be able to judge a company's performance over less than a few years.
- It must be possible to identify a Tmin performance level for this CPI – that is, it must be possible for the beneficiaries to identify when their organization has so far failed to yield an adequate benefit that they should begin to ask if the management should be changed or the organization closed down. This – identifying Tmin – is probably the most powerful of all methods of selecting a truly verifiable measure of corporate performance.
- Indeed, so vital is it for an organization to know its Tmin that one should lay it down that 'any organization which cannot identify its Tmin should be re-formed'. If an organization does not even know what performance is so bad that it should be closed down then it has no right to existence.
- It must be possible to identify a Tsat performance level for this CPI – that is, it must be possible for the beneficiaries to recognize when the performance of the organization is satisfactory. The word 'satisfactory' performance implies that no corrective actions are needed and, indeed, that consideration of an expansion of the activities of the organization might well be a sensible option.
- 'Satisfactory' can only be a relative term. The CPI must be comparable with CPIs of similar organizations.
- The objective must be desirable to the beneficiaries. The management and employees must be inspired by it or by something related to it – such as the satisfaction of knowing that they have relieved famine, helped the aged, saved a child from cruelty.
- One of the most powerful incentives is provided by a 'dynamic' objective such as an annual improvement, or a growth, target. It provides a challenge or 'stretch' for the management team.

I have no doubt that many organizations will have to be completely reformed before they can even get near these requirements. On the other hand, many will be able to sweep straight through to a satisfactory target as easily as any company.

I should draw special attention to the role of Tmin. As stated above, if an organization cannot say what is the lowest level of performance that would be considered tolerable by the beneficiaries then it is indeed in trouble. I think this may be true of the Church of England, the Arts Council, and many others, where no one has ruled a line under it, so to speak, and proclaimed 'thus far and no lower'. To ask, 'Who would complain and what would they be complaining about? (i.e. 'Who would know if we are approaching Tmin?') is another most useful route to the true corporate objective of any organization.

One advantage that the managers of non-profit-making organization enjoy over their counterparts in companies is job satisfaction. To strive all year to generate more dividends for the faceless shareholders is not very inspiring; indeed, it is so uninspiring that people go to great lengths to pretend that profit is not the objective of companies. Managers in many non-profit-making organizations, on the other hand, know they are working to save the panda from extinction, help the disabled, cut down crime or provide housing to someone who could not provide their own.

Conversely, what managers themselves feel they lack most in some non-profit-making organizations is the sense of achievement that company managers experience when they beat their competitors in the race for growth. Often this growth is achieved in a static or even declining market. For huge, mature companies like Unilever, say, to grow by over 10 per cent every year, in a market that is almost static, is a stupendous accomplishment that must be very gratifying to the managers. Presumably there are NPOs who achieve similar feats – a police force, perhaps, which, in spite of crime rising all around it, has found the means to keep it down in its own area.

The thrill of *doing it better and better every year* has to be experienced to be believed. This delight in one's own competence, and that of the organization for which one works, is not normally available to, say, the civil service, charities or learned societies. Most of these organizations do not set 'dynamic' targets for themselves which not only demand success this year but also build in a challenging annual improvement. Consequently, alas, they sometimes withdraw into 'administration' rather than management.

What a challenge all this is to the planning team of, say, a charity with the aim of 'bringing Christian values to the work-place'. If these aims really are genuine, really do have meaning and validity, as its executives plainly believed, then, they are going to have to find some way to measure it. If it is doing any good, we ought to be able to *see* it doing good. There should be certain concrete events actually taking place in this specific work-place to prove that Christian values are actually taking root. Is it really possible to quantify a thing like that?

Consider an organization looking after handicapped children. Imagine that it costs £10,000 per annum to provide for one child in the institution operated by the charity. One strategy is to leave the child there and simply look after him. Another is to adopt 'positive therapy' to reduce the child's disability. Suppose it costs £20,000 to employ the skilled therapists. Suppose it is then possible for this child to leave the institution and live in a sheltered home costing £5,000 a year per child – or maybe he even gets a job and starts earning. This seems to me an ideal example of how it might be possible to measure performance by using *real* figures, of what actually happened in real life, rather than using say, cost–benefit analysis to judge the child's happiness, or having to calculate such ratios as social workers per child.

I feel the principle is valid; if no material, physical, tangible evidence can be adduced *from the real world* that an organization is generating a satisfactory benefit then closure or re-formation seems right.

Some examples

Let me give a few examples of setting targets for non-profit-making organizations in accordance with the above principles. Imagine a charity set up in Northtown to try to stop young children smoking cigarettes. I presume the beneficiaries and benefit could be stated as in Figure 5.15. Without some form of quantification these statements are not verifiable so now, in Figure 5.16, we need to set the Tsat and Tmin targets.

Figure 5.16 declares that if this Society can show no *measurable*

Figure 5.15 Corporate Description for the Northtown Children's Anti-smoking Campaign

The Intended Beneficiaries	Children under 18 in Northtown.
The Intended Benefit	Reduce cigarette smoking.

progress towards its aims within five years it will consider closing down (that is what 'Tmin' means, remember). If, on the other hand, the number of smokers under 18 look like halving over the five years then the founders will deem the organization a success. They might think of starting up in Southtown, or whatever. Notice, the criterion is physical, in the real world – are fewer children smoking? It is not ratios or CBA or indices. As concrete a question as, 'Did the shareholders get more money through their letter-box this year than last year?' Just to show the next step required in order

Figure 5.16 Corporate Description for the Northtown Children's Anti-smoking Campaign

The Intended Beneficiaries		Children under 18 in Northtown.
The Intended Benefit		Reduce cigarete smoking.
Performance targets	Tmin	There must be some independent statistical evidence of a decline within five years.
	Tsat	To halve the incidence every five years.
Corporate conduct		We will only make statements in our campaigns that are scientifically correct. Etc.

to complete the full Corporate Description of this charity I have added an arbitrary conduct statement. A strategy statement will also be required when these are known.

Suppose a town government adopted the corporate objective I proposed in Chapter 4, it would look something like Figure 5.17. Remember these are *corporate* objectives, criteria by which the organization as a corporate whole should be judged, not just parts of it. The key criterion is the level of benefit to the intended

Figure 5.17   Corporate Description for the Northtown Town Management

The Intended Beneficiaries	The citizens of Northtown.
The Intended Benefit	Making Northtown a better place to live.
Performance targets Tmin	The total market value of property per citizen should increase no less rapidly than Southtown's or by at least 3 per cent per annum.
Tsat	As above, but more rapidly than the top quartile of (listed) neighbouring towns or by at least 5 per cent

beneficiaries, remember, and, if this cannot be measured directly then some proxy, such as property values to reflect the fact that people recognize it as 'a better place to live' compared to its neighbours, may have to be used. If it cannot be measured at all, then re-formation is indicated. If the town government either cannot identify its Tmin, or its performance falls below it, the government should be replaced or the town's boundaries be reduced, until performance rises above Tmin. I am suggesting that a similar format might be appropriate for village, metropolitan, national and international governments and their agencies.

Again, think of a professional association. I presume its Corporate Description would appear as in Figure 5.18.

Similarly, but much more controversially, I suppose the overall corporate objective for a school might relate to the number of students passing into the next level of schooling (compared with a similar school). The final school in the educational chain might adopt a CPI relating their ex-pupils' actual earnings in their first five years of employment (including any unemployed among them) to the cost of their last five years' education – certainly that might be the CPI for a vocational college or business school. But again, please note, this would be the actual figures these pupils are earning in real life, not the pupil–teacher ratio, not examination results, not the opinion of the inspectors.

Most targets for most organizations seem likely to be measured in money. Its no good being snooty about this: money is the only

Figure 5.18 Corporate Description for the Institute of Industrial Executives

The Intended Beneficiaries		Professional executives in industry.
The Intended Benefit		To enhance their professional life.
Performance targets	Tmin	The earnings of members should increase no less rapidly than other professional managers or by at least 3 per cent per annum.
	Tsat	As above, but more rapidly than the top quartile of other professions or by at least 5 per cent.

universal measure of value we have yet invented, so it is no use protesting that it is irrelevant because 'we are non-profit-making'.

Not all non-profit-making organizations' outputs would be judged by money. The corporate objective of a national health service might be 'improve the nation's health' and the unequivocal CPI might be quite simple, perhaps 'annual improvement in life expectancy compared with similar nations' or 'lost working time due to illness' is all that is needed. What is *actually* happening to the nation's health? And again, as a reminder of its importance, if no Tmin has been established, or if the health of the nation does not improve as fast as other similar nations, then the management should be replaced, or the health service re-formed into a smaller entity.

Suppose we could not find a verifiable objective for a particular organization, what should be done? My answer is that it should be closed down or re-formed until we can.

Finally, I should remind readers that the corporate objective and the targets must be strategy-neutral. Imagine someone who is disturbed by the extent of homelessness in his town. He might set up this organization:

Aims and objectives for The Northtown Homeless Society: to draw the attention of the public to the plight of the homeless in Northtown.

But this, I suggest, is only a strategy, not his true aim. His true corporate objective is to reduce homelessness, surely, and he is going to do this – a strategy – by drawing attention to it. So I believe his Corporate Description should be as in Figure 5.19.

Figure 5.19   Corporate Description of the Northtown Homeless Society

The Intended Beneficiaries	Homeless people in Northtown.
The Intended Benefit Performance	Find them somewhere to live.
Targets Tmin	To house 50 per cent of them by Year 3.
Tsat	To house 90 per cent of them by Year 5.
Strategy	By arousing public concern.

Now his corporate objectives are strategy-neutral. He has listed one strategy and it is plain now that there could be many more by which to achieve the objective.

Setting targets for conduct

Where appropriate the planning team ought to target some of their corporate conduct statements, too. The No Harm Principle may be helpful here. At the very least, organizations would not wish to cause any significant harm to any of its interest groups and this virtually sets Tmin. This means: 'If what we are doing causes significant harm to anyone we will stop doing it, even if this makes our corporate objective more difficult to achieve and even if it makes it unattainable.'

Tsat will probably be something like: 'To meet the reasonable wishes of the relevant interest groups.'

Summary

Companies are lucky. They know with great precision what they are trying to do for whom – make a satisfactory return on their shareholders' capital. In practice, however, it is not so simple. There are a dozen different ways to define profit and a thousand different snags in measuring it. Each type of company – private, public, partnership – requires a slightly different version. However, bearing in mind that this is corporate planning where we are concerned with quite lengthy horizons, it is possible to overcome all these technical difficulties and achieve highly reliable CPIs for measuring company performance. Almost without exception these will be return on capital and growth of profits or EpS. Seldom is any other measure required.

It is desirable to move through a sequence of steps to select a target for any given company. The planning team should examine the company's past performance, compare it with competitors – and with its parent company if it has one – before selecting a target figure. It is important to set two figures – Tmin and Tsat – to avoid the common difficulties associated with target-setting.

The planning team in non-profit-making organizations have a much harder task. Unless they have been highly rigourous in their definition of the corporate objective they will find it is difficult, or even impossible, to quantify it. They would have to return to this definition and sharpen it up so it could be translated into figures.

Tmin will be found to be a most instructive concept – it underlines for the planning team the level of performance that they *must* achieve for their organization. Tmin is also the key trigger to re-formation. If an organization cannot identify what its Tmin is – in figures, in terms that are verifiable in the real world – or if the performance of the organization falls below Tmin, then its management should be replaced or the organization should be re-formed into a more specialized unit.

In this chapter I have again suggested that many of the attempts to measure the performance of NPOs are on the wrong track – they are not *corporate* performance indicators, or not quantifiable or not even verifiable in the real world, or not dynamic.

If certain rules are followed, as described in this chapter, all planning teams will find this an extremely interesting and rewarding exercise to start them off on the corporate planning process.

The Fulmar Life Assurance Society

At the end of each chapter I attach part of the summary of a corporate plan prepared by a real company to show what it might look like at each major stage in the corporate planning process. This is to demonstrate the layout rather than the strategic conclusions this particular company reached.

Here are the first two sections of the corporate plan for Fulmar Life showing summaries of the corporate objectives, the targets and the conduct.

Corporate Plan for Fulmar Life Assurance Society
Summary Page 1. Objectives and targets

Corporate objective

Because this organization is a mutual society we consider that the Society's prime objective is: 'To increase the assets relating to participating policy holders over the long term.'

The planning team particularly wish it to be noted that this is a long-term aim. It would be all too easy to boost sales and net assets in such a manner as to appear to result in an immediate improvement of net assets for the policy-holders but which, in the long term, worked to their disadvantage. Accordingly, it is proposed to invite the actuary to comment annually on the long-term implications of our short-term record to ensure that it is sustainable.

The planning team selected this measure, net assets, since it is the sum of any growth in capital values and the accumulated income from premiums and investments, less claims, less the 'without-profits liabilities'.

Past performance

Standardized Net Asset Values

(Not adjusted for Inflation which declined from 12 per cent to 6 per cent over this period.)

Year	−5	−4	−3	−2	−1	0
£m	401	487	572	661	757	859
% growth	20	21	17	15	15	13

Our performance was about average compared with similar societies over this period.

Targets

We aim to grow as fast as our comparable competitors (Tmin) and to match the growth of the top quartile (Tsat). We estimate that this implies the following figures:

Tmin = growth of net assets of $7\frac{1}{2}$ per cent over inflation.
Tsat = growth of net assets of 10 per cent over inflation.

These targets require the following SNAV:

SNAV	Year	0	1	2	3	4	5
£m							
Tmin		859	923	992	1067	1147	1233
Tsat		859	945	1039	1143	1257	1383

. . . .

Corporate Plan for Fulmar Life Assurance Society
Summary Page 2. Corporate Conduct.

Stakeholders

We propose the following codes of conduct:

Policy-holders: To provide security of guaranteed benefits for all policy-holders, to treat all classes of and generations of policy-holder equitably, to provide an attractive range of products and services.

Agents: To pay agents a fair rate of commission, provide them with excellent and rapid service and to encourage them to grow.

Staff: To aim to unite the staff towards achieving the new common objective, provide an attractive work environment, help them to develop their careers and personal talents, provide security of employment.

Pensioners: To take an interest in our employees and their families after they have retired.

Suppliers: To discourage personal gifts or rewards from suppliers.

The community: To play a role in the local community and to encourage our staff to do so.

The industry: To play a role in the insurance industry and encourage our staff to do so.

Government   To co-operate with government agencies and abide by the spirit of their aims.

CHAPTER 6

Forecasts and Gap Analysis

Having determined their targets for the following five years the planning team should next make their five-year forecasts. So if, in their last meeting, they have selected growth of profits and return on capital as their two CPIs, they now need to meet again to determine how these two indicators might move over the next few years.

Remember, these are forecasts, not targets. They are entirely different. The reason managers find it so hard to make the distinction is that it is not normally made in textbooks or in budgetary control systems. I see this as a major defect and I want the distinction brought out here with great clarity. Any figure you see, anywhere, in any context, is either a target, a forecast or an actual. So far as I know, these are the only three types of figure known to man. But they are all different and, in long-range planning (and, in my view, elsewhere too) the differences are vital.

You *set* a target. You *make* a forecast. You *note* an actual. The target is up to you, it is in your control. The forecast is out of your control, it represents something that you think is going to happen in the world around you. There is nothing you can do about an actual either; it has happened. Whether you like it or not, it is too late. But if the forecast does not equal the target (i.e. if you suspect that things are not going to turn out as you would like), you *can* take action to bring the forecast closer to your target. This is what a *plan* is for, to change something that has not yet happened, to make the outcome suit you better.

Target, forecast, actual, plan. All are totally distinct. Blur them and you start to talk nonsense.

Long-range forecasts

Some people think that to attempt to forecast five years ahead in the uncertain world of today is absurd. Indeed, a number of corporate planning systems exist in which the forecasts are omitted for that reason. But, providing two simple rules are followed, such forecasts can indeed be made and this forecasting stage will reveal an astonishing wealth of knowledge about the strategic situation of the organization.

There are two reasons why these forecasts are so important in my scheme of things. One is to enable a 'gap analysis' to be performed; that is, to calculate the 'gap' between the target and the forecast. This will indicate how powerful any new strategies will have to be to close the gap and hence achieve the target. This is an incredibly useful thing to be able to estimate – indeed, not just important, it is essential. And yet there are planning systems which fail to include gap analysis at all.

The second reason is that, in order to make a forecast, one has to examine the past and that is where one may find some more elephants. I am constantly amazed how much planning teams learn about their company from this exercise. These people collectively enjoy an unrivalled knowledge of their company, yet still they learn new lessons of the greatest strategic importance as some of my examples will show.

In view of the massive arguments in favour of making these forecasts, I cannot understand how anyone dares to plan without them, and yet I have just been handed papers for a strategic conference for a company employing 3,500 people, to which I have been invited, in which no profit forecasts of any kind appears in any of the 230 pages.

And what weird views some people hold on the subject of forecasting! They range from those who simply state 'you cannot forecast the future' right up to the mystics who place their faith in the stars. The truth lies between these extremes: you *can* forecast the future, but the errors in doing so may be huge. Forecasts are often wrong, sometimes severely so, and you never know how wrong they will be. Of course, sometimes the future is known with almost complete accuracy – short of the Black Plague we know very accurately what the population of Britain will be in ten years' time, we even know the number of children aged 11 and how many widows will die in April 2021. But, in general, long-range forecast-

Figure 6.1 Key performance statistics for Sparrow's past five years

Year	−5	−4	−3	−2	−1	0	Explanation
			(Year 0 values)				
Turnover (£000)	2770	2901	3162	3304	3562	3968	Rising by over 7% pa
Profits (£000)	224	223	237	218	217	222	Static or falling
ROS %	8.1	7.7	7.5	6.6	6.1	5.6	Falling by 7%
Capital employed (£000)	2290	2175	2128	2000	1833	1795	Falling by 5%
ROCE (%)	9.8	10.3	11.1	10.9	11.8	12.4	Erratic, low but rising by 5% p.a.

(Assets were revalued in Year −2)

Conclusions: the main reason we have not done well is vicious competition which has caused us to slash margins (or ROS, Return on Sales).

ing is an immensely dangerous game. To make a forecast without acknowledging that it may be wrong is an absurd, and a most unprofessional, thing to do. Almost everyone does it.

I have developed a particular method of making long range forecasts which, as will be seen, presents us with yet a third reason for making forecasts – namely, specifically and deliberately to remind ourselves how uncertain the future may be. The sequence of steps the planning team should follow in order to make these forecasts is reflected in the layout of this chapter. First, examine the past, then make the forecasts, then calculate the gaps and note the strategic implications.

Examine the past

The first step in making any forecast is to learn the lessons of the past. We all know that the future will not be the same as the past but it is the only guide we can ever have.

The planning team should ask the planning assistant to prepare a report showing the salient features of the organization's history over the past five years – or, if necessary, ten. We want to know:

- How did the CPIs perform over this period?
- Why did the CPIs move as they did?
- What are the lessons for the future?

Consider the record for Sparrow's in Figure 6.1.

One needs to be extremely honest with oneself when making this sort of analysis. For example, Sparrows have blamed 'vicious competition' for their poor performance, but their turnover has risen very fast over the past years so have they been cutting their prices to buy market share? Might it not be their own fault that margins have dropped so dramatically – nothing to do with the market at all?

The five key figures used in Figure 6.1 above might be an adequate basis for making a forecast for a very small company, but in most cases considerably more detail would be required before the planning team could say that they really understand what were the main influences that had shaped their company's performance over the past few years. We certainly ought to see some more figures for Sparrow (Figure 6.2).

Figure 6.2   Additional data for Sparrow's

Year	−5	−4	−3	−2	−1	0
Units sold	1277	1400	1590	1669	1870	2061
Selling price (£ per unit)	2169	2071	1987	1977	1903	1926
Turnover (£m)	2.77	2.90	3.16	3.30	3.56	3.97
Cost (£ per unit)	1827	1740	1674	1668	1607	1636
Contribution (£000)	437	464	498	516	553	597
Overheads (£000)	213	241	261	298	336	375
Profits (£000)	224	223	237	218	217	222
Margin (%)	8.1	7.7	7.5	6.6	6.1	5.6
Capital Employed (£m)	2.29	2.18	2.13	2.00	1.83	1.79

What do you notice? In addition to the facts that we already knew (that Sparrow's turnover had been rising fast but that, because margins have fallen, profits have barely changed) we can now see several quite new features:

- Sparrows have cut their unit costs almost every year – down by an average of 2 per cent over the period. So now we know that rising costs were *not* the reason for the falling margins.

- One reason that margins have been falling is that selling prices per unit have fallen (by an average of approximately 2.5 per cent per annum).
- Overheads have increased by an amazing 12 per cent per annum. (If we needed to know why, which we probably would, we would need a further set of figures.)

And did you notice their asset utilization trend? Turnover has risen much faster than assets, or capital employed.

Capital utilization   1.2   1.3   1.5   1.6   1.9   2.2

How do you think Sparrows have managed to get so much more turnover out of so little more capital assets? Could they be 'overtrading' (expanding faster than their capital availability – a well-known danger sign of a possible collapse into bankruptcy)? Have the assets been written down and are, therefore, very old-fashioned? Either of these would be bad news. A more optimistic explanation of this trend might be that they have been using their assets more effectively. Sparrow's planning team would *have* to find out. They could not possibly make a forecast of the future without understanding such items in Sparrow's past.

Astonishing revelations

On the other hand, it should be remembered that this is corporate planning and we are only interested in trends and events that are of strategic significance. It is important, therefore, not to waste time with trivialities – especially as this examination of past trends should be performed not only on one's own company but on the figures for all one's significant competitors. Have their profits followed the same pattern? If not, why not? Did they recover more quickly from the recession? Have they all been improving their asset turnover ratios? If so, has there been a massive change in the whole cost structure of the industry? And so on.

My personal experience in using some of the published industry comparative figures is not encouraging. In several cases the figures have been wrong – and not just by a few per cent. In one case a company was surprised to find its very healthy ROCE shown as a negative in one widely distributed inter-firm comparison report! In another a company was listed as a competitor but was in fact a supplier. Authors of textbooks who call for detailed studies of competitors must have had better luck than I have – and better luck than many consultants have, judging by the errors in their reports to clients.

Figure 6.3 contains some typical figures (simplified and rounded) from this sort of analysis, this time from an engineering services company compared with its direct competitors.

Figure 6.3   Some key statistics for our two competitors

Year	−3	−2	−1	0
Sales £m				
Our company	27	29	31	33
Competitor A	123	131	132	141
Competitor B	11	13	12	14
Number of employees				
Our company	870	881	888	886
Competitor A	2095	2002	1788	1600
Competitor B	123	133	102	109
Capital employed £m				
Our company	21	22	24	26
Competitor A	78	81	86	91
Competitor B	5	6	7	8

A glance is sufficient to see that this company's turnover per employee and asset turnover is far below their competitors' – the difference is so dramatic one does not even need to calculate the ratios! A simple calculation further shows that this company has increased its turnover per employee half as rapidly over the years as the competitors. The figures for this company are so out of line as to be patently strategic because either the other companies quoted here are not true competitors (and everyone in this real life example accepted that they were) or this company's costs must be so much greater than theirs that an explanation is required as to why they are still in business!

This inter-company comparative analysis, which many companies do very thoroughly over short periods, often throws up new and surprising information when performed over these longer periods. A life assurance company discovered that its unit-linked business had not grown faster than its close competitors' over five years – it had been a widely held belief that it had. Company myths of this sort are something from which many companies suffer.

I have recently seen a company split into five geographical areas. The five-year record shows that in the area long considered to be the most profitable, capital employed has declined to £2m while turnover has risen to £40m. Meanwhile a new area, formed three years ago, now has a turnover of £20m but capital employed of £6m. It has suddenly dawned on everyone that the 'best' area's enviable 100 per cent ROCE is actually due to its equipment being grotesquely old-fashioned and undervalued. This revelation caused a further realization – that their finance function is incompetent.

And so on through an infinity of similar experiences. I do not think I have ever witnessed a long-term analysis of this sort without some discovery that astonished the top executives.

Another simple lesson: examination of past trends will show the planning team something the textbooks do not often show, that trends are seldom smooth. An industry in decline, for example goes downhill in jerks, not smoothly at x per cent per annum. A technique for showing this realistically in forecasts is described below.

Trend and ratio analysis

Figure 6.4 shows a list of the trends and ratios that may be used in this sort of strategic analysis. Naturally, in any given case only relatively few of these will need to be highlighted. The planning assistant will have to spend some time whittling away most of these criteria to get down to the important few for his particular company.

Many industries have their own critical ratios – banks have liquidity ratios, hotels have occupancy rates, retailers have sales per unit floor area – so the last item in the list below, special ratios, is sometimes of major significance.

A word of caution on inflation. Many textbooks suggest one should use such ratios as assets per employee or added value per employee. But to report any *true* movements in these over a number of years one would have to adjust for pay-inflation. That is

Figure 6.4 Trends and ratios useful in company analysis

Trends

Annual rise or fall in:

Units sold	Tax
Selling price	Dividends
Unit cost	Tangible assets
Sales turnover	Working capital
Contribution	Capital employed
Overheads	Capital expenditure
Operating profit	Borrowing
Interest paid	Numbers employed
Profit before tax	

Physical size (selling area, production capacity, number of branches, etc.)

Ratios

Movement over the period in:

ROCE (profit before interest and tax (pbit) as % of capital employed)
Net profit margin (Pbt or pbit as % of turnover)
Asset utilization (Turnover/Total assets)
Sales to fixed (Turnover/Fixed or tangible assets)
Selling costs as per cent of sales turnover
Capacity utilization of production facilities
Number of employees in each department related to activity
Quality criteria (Reject rates, etc.)
Stock turn (Turnover/Stocks or inventory)
Credit period (Debtors/Turnover × 365 days or × 52 weeks)
Credit taken (Creditors/Purchases × 365 or 52)
Working capital (Working capital/Turnover)
Current ratio (Current assets/Current liabilities)
Quick ratio (Debtors, cash, etc./Current liabilities)
Borrowing ratio (Total debt/Net worth)
Equity gearing (Shareholders' funds/Total debt)
Income gearing (Interest paid on borrowing/Pbit)
Tax (Tax as percent of Pbt or of earnings)
Dividend cover (Earnings/Dividend)
Profit per employee (Pbt/Total employee remuneration (TER))
Sales per employee (Turnover/TER)
Capital per employee (Capital employed/TER)
Fixed capital per employee (Fixed capital/TER)
Added value per employee (Turnover – purchases/TER)

Special ratios

why it is suggested in the list above that one uses 'Total Employee Remuneration' (TER) instead of *numbers* of employees to calculate these ratios. Inflation is thus included both sides of the equation.

It is important to retain simplicity at all times in the corporate planning exercise: publishing masses of detailed figures, attempts to achieve accounting accuracy and analytical complexity are three great enemies of truly strategic thinking. They all get in the way, partly because they hold up progress – it obviously takes ten times longer to analyze, present and discuss a hundred figures than it does a dozen – but worse, attention to detail is the first refuge of the executive who does not wish to consider strategy. He will deliberately spend an hour on one trivial day-to-day ratio, with which he is familiar, rather than dare to venture into something unusual but more fundamental.

The planning team must exert great discipline in selecting the trends and events that they decide to examine. The planning assistant, because he is often not a full member of the team, can exert considerable influence here by strictly rationing the flow of figures to his team.

Multiple analyses

A similar lesson has to be learnt in another dimension of this analysis into the past: the number of products, divisions and subsidiaries that one should examine. In the figures above the company was so simple that it was unnecessary to show its various different products separately, but plainly it makes little sense to analyze a group of companies without studying some of its key subsidiaries. I show below (Figure 6.5) the format that may be used to study parts of an organization. In this case the two products are so different that it would have made no sense to lump them together.

If there are three different products one may have to do a triple Figure 6.5. What about five, six? Please keep constantly in mind that the task is to search for *elephants*; the significance of the fifth (or even the third) product is likely to be very small in strategic terms. The same may be true of subsidiaries in a group, geographical areas of a charity, or whatever.

The more extensive Figure 6.5 becomes, the more likely it is that the planning team is not doing its job. To reduce the amount of

Figure 6.5　The past five years for Starlings Ltd

Year	−5	−4	−3	−2	−1	0
			Product Alpha			
Units sold	177	140	159	166	180	161
Selling price (£) per unit	3768	3888	3789	3661	3501	3499
Turnover (£000)	667	544	602	608	630	563
Cost (£) per unit	3127	3950	3124	3126	3146	3336
Contribution (£000)	113	−9	106	89	64	26
			Product Beta			
Units sold	3993	3911	4662	4986	4701	5602
Selling price (£) per unit	234	236	246	214	239	266
Turnover (£000)	934	923	1147	1067	1123	1490
Cost (£) per unit	151	168	162	183	111	118
Contribution	331	266	392	155	602	829
			Company			
Overheads (£000)	199	208	239	203	235	219
Profits (£000)	245	49	259	41	431	636

detail it is often possible to add together all the minor products, the ones that are not likely to be elephants, and bundle them in 'Miscellaneous' or even 'lose' them in related product figures.

I would be deeply suspicious of a forecast that showed more than half a dozen separate products or areas or profit centres. The team is not standing far enough back to see the company as a corporate whole. They will be blinded by detail.

Make the forecasts

Once the main factors affecting the past five years' performance have been identified it should be possible to judge how they might behave in the future. So, based on the past behaviour of these factors, together with what one knows about the future, the planning team is now going to make two forecasts for their company's performance over the next five years. *Two* forecasts? Yes: a pessimistic and an optimistic.

The reason for asking for two forecasts is that everyone knows perfectly well that one cannot forecast the future accurately. So, instead of pretending that one can, the Argenti System demands that one should deliberately and explicitly admit how inaccurate one's forecasts might be. This can be done by displaying the range between what the profits might be if things went rather badly for the company *and* if things went quite well – a pessimistic and an optimistic forecast.

The point here is that, when someone says, 'I can't forecast my profits five years ahead,' what he really means is that he does not know what is going to happen in the world. If he knew this he could fairly easily calculate how his company's profits might be affected.

Suppose, however, one makes a range of realistic guesses about the world – assume the economy is buoyant for the next five years *and* that there is a recession; assume that the company *does* get that big order from a major new customer *and* assume it does not; assume it *does* cut its overheads *and* that it does not – then the profits the company will achieve will lie somewhere between all these guesses. No one knows *where* in between but at least it shows where the extremes might be.

This procedure should be extremely useful for non-profit-making organizations where the art of forecasting is often more neglected than in companies. By making pessimistic assumptions about, say, famine in Ethiopia (or traffic flows in London, or government grant levels, or whatever), and then the optimistic assumptions, one can spell out the full range of eventualities with which the organization may have to cope. This is strategic planning, remember, where one of the things we are concerned with is how to set out our stall to deal with anything the future may throw at us.

See how Sparrow did the calculations in Figure 6.6 below. First, the planning team assumed that margins would continue to fall – actually they added a new element of pessimism because they also assumed that margins on a Defence Department contract would also be cut when it came up for renewal in Year 3, and that margins will fall even faster from then onwards. Then, in the optimistic forecast, they assumed that margins would *not* go on falling, and so on. As can be seen, they made a number of pessimistic and optimistic assumptions.

In making these forecasts the Sparrow planning team have assumed that they would not introduce any new strategies which had not been approved – no new products except those which they would normally have introduced under their present strategies, no

Figure 6.6   Two five-year profit forecasts for Sparrow's

A. Pessimistic						
Pessimistic assumptions for the pessimistic forecast (Fpes)	0	1	2	3	4	5
Turnover will rise at only 3 or 4% because the product is aging. (£m)	3.97	4.16	4.33	4.48	4.62	4.76
Margins will continue to fall due to competition. New contracts with the Department of Defence will be tougher from Year 3. (%)	5.6	5.3	5.0	4.5	4.0	3.5
As a result of these trends profits will be: (£000)	222	220	216	202	185	167
B. Optimistic						
Optimistic assumptions for the optimistic forecast (Fopt)	0	1	2	3	4	5
Turnover will continue to rise at 7% p.a. (£m)	3.97	4.24	4.53	4.85	5.19	5.55
Margins will stabilize in Year 2 due to an upturn in the economy and higher productivity. (%)	5.6	5.3	5.3	5.3	5.3	5.3
As a result profits will be: (£000)	222	225	240	257	275	294

change in markets served, except changes that would normally have been made under their existing strategies, no improvements in efficiencies except those expected from current policies, and so on.

Notice too, they did not assume a constant trend over the whole of the five years. Most trends will change over such a long time and one should take this into account wherever it is relevant. Of course, one never knows when these points of inflexion will occur so one assumes bad news will come early in the pessimistic and later in the optimistic.

A spread of forecasts

Notice that the two profit forecasts come out quite wide apart, but it is surely more realistic to show the great spread of expectations that one has from one's company's future than to pretend this uncertainty is not there. You may prefer to see this spread shown on a graph. Sparrow would show the figures in Figure 6.7 as a graph like this:

Figure 6.7 Sparrow's two profit forecasts

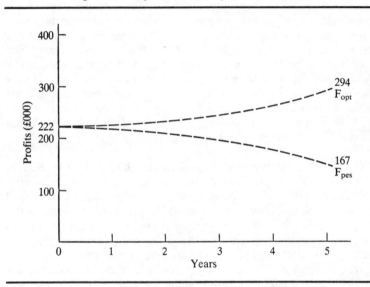

So Sparrow has a range of expectations for Year 5 that stretch all the way from £167,000 to £294,000. I would expect to see such a spread for a mature company in a mature market in the stable Western world. A small company in a developing market or in a developing nation might show a much wider scatter. This spread between these forecasts is a vital indicator of the riskiness of the company and, as will be seen a little later, the riskiness of a company is a major element in the type of strategy it should choose.

It is important to note the two rules which regulate this unusual method of forecasting – very few executives make *two* forecasts. Usually they make just one which they will defend to the death. To make just one forecast is tantamount to pretending that one has the power to foretell the future. Everyone knows it cannot be done, yet time after time senior executives, 'experts' and others in authority make these absurd forecasts, and such is the prestige of some experts that no one dares to challenge them. All single-figure forecasts are wrong. Senior executives who make single-figure long-range forecasts should be sacked.

Rule 1. It must be assumed that the company will continue to be managed as the management now intend. Assume no major changes of strategy, no new projects (unless they have already been launched or are just about to be). If, for example, turnover per employee has been static at £23,000 for the past three years, then that is where it will stay. But if the management normally opens two new branches every year then assume that this continues. If they normally improve productivity by 3 per cent per annum then assume this continues. If they habitually spend 3 per cent of sales on R & D, assume this continues, and so on. Rule 1 does not mean 'do nothing' it means 'do nothing new'.

Rule 2. Assume the world outside *does* change. If it is thought there will be a recession in the market then base the profit calculations on that – assume the recession comes earlier and deeper in the pessimistic and later and less severe in the optimistic. If a particular competitor may go bust assume that the company's share of his customers are acquired in Year 3 (pessimistic) or next year (optimistic), and so on. Do not just project the past into the future. Much will change – margins, costs, interest rates, legislation – and the management should show how they think these will change and how these will affect profits.

It is important to be reasonably pessimistic and optimistic. It would be absurd to be unreasonably so – unless something really awful or really magnificent is actually likely to happen. If the management believe that something of that magnitude might occur then they should *certainly* show it and take full account of it in the forecasts.

A most important principle which many professional managements adopt today is the 'No Surprises' rule. This says that, when discussing the future of one's company or department with one's boss, one tells him *all* the bad news so that, when it happens, he is not surprised. In much the same way, when a professional manager makes a forecast he ought to include all the bad news, even if it shows his company's profits declining. Now it takes some courage to do this in a budget or business plan because, in effect, one is saying to one's boss: 'I have studied the future, I have made all the decisions I can think of, but profits are going to fall and I don't know what to do about it!'. However, if one asks an executive to make a pessimistic *and* an optimistic forecast, and if it is on a no-change in strategy assumption, he is much more inclined to be honest – everyone knows that he was going to take action in good time. So this double method of forecasting is far superior to the traditional business plan in this respect.

An example

I recently saw this in a small group of companies (turnover £100m) in which the three divisions (each employing about 1,000 people) had recently completed their business plan which showed continuously rising profits. All the divisional managing directors had assumed that they would be introducing new products which would permit profits to go on rising, but when we used the double forecast method it revealed the fact that, quite by chance, and for different reasons, all three divisions faced a drop in profits in Year 3. Figure 6.8 shows their pessimistic forecasts, on a no-change in strategy basis, together with Year 0.

Figure 6.8   Group profit forecast (Fpes)

Year £m	0	1	2	3	4	5
Division A	7.1	8.3	8.6	6.3	6.6	7.2
Division B	0.1	1.3	3.7	1.4	2.5	2.1
Division C	−4.2	−2.1	−3.4	−4.6	−4.6	−4.8
Group	3.1	7.5	8.9	3.1	4.5	4.5

The group chief executive, on seeing these figures, protested that every company would show this pattern – if you look far enough ahead, all companies' profits decline if you assume 'no change in strategy'. Perfectly correct. But division A's profits may fall in Year 3 because an £8m contract may not be renewed – and this comes up in only eighteen months' time; Division B because one exceptionally large order for £12m will be completed by Year 3;

Division C because we must assume that the major new product planned for Year 2, and far outside their normal range, might fail in the market – as many others from this stable have done before.

This forecast was on the assumption, remember, of 'no change in strategy' – in other words, no strategies currently exist to bolster this downturn; lead times for new products are typically 18 months. The group chief executive faced the real possibility that the profits of his group, after an apparent recovery, might return to the current miserable levels (£3m profit on £100m turnover was considered appalling). His company would have to find an extra profit of £7m or so, by Year 3, to continue the recovery.

To return to the forecasting process, when the profit forecasts have been completed, two forecasts for return on capital should be made. Again, in the pessimistic forecast the pessimistic assumptions should be clearly stated and the same for the optimistic. For example, 'our return on capital should rise significantly as a result of our recently acquired machine tools and this is assumed to occur in the optimistic. The pessimistic assumption has to be that only 40 per cent of this advantage will, in fact, be realized.'

Sometimes it is easier to calculate the capital and then derive return on capital. One way to calculate capital is to relate it to turnover. Assuming there is no reason to expect a change in the asset/turnover ratio one can simply assume that if turnover is forecast to double then capital employed will double. Of course if, in the past, this ratio has been declining, then assume it goes on declining and show turnover rising that much faster than capital. But, be warned: a favourite trick of managers is to assume that capital employed will not rise as fast as turnover. They make the same assumption about overheads not rising with turnover. If one is as suspicious of such miracles as I am, go and see what happened in the past. Now how sure are you?

Finally, the profit forecasts, the ROCE forecasts and the capital employed forecasts should be displayed in a table.

The three types of forecast

Before we continue with the corporate planning process I should draw attention to the three different types of profit forecast that one meets with in planning.

'Foo'.   There is the projection, a very naive and primitive form of
the art which is used mainly as a 'ranging shot'. In this one examines
the past and projects the trends unchanged into the future. If profits
have been growing at 7.6 per cent per annum, say, then you assume
they will go on growing at 7.6 per cent as far into the future as you
like. It does have the merit that, because no assumptions are made
about the future, no errors are introduced, other than the obvious
one that the future is not going to be the same as the past. I call this
type of forecast the Foo (two zeros because neither the environment nor the company is assumed to change).

'Fo'.   The second type does assume the future will be different but
that the company will respond to these changes in the same way as it
always has responded. I call this Fo. ('Fo' because only one 'no
change' is assumed – a 'no change' in the company.) Obviously, the
ones I am describing in this Chapter are Fo forecasts.

'Fp'.   The third type assumes the company does make a new
response – the 'p' stands for plan – that is, this forecast both
assumes the world changes and that the company responds with a
new strategy. This is the forecast that will be made in Chapter 10
where we have to estimate what the company's Year 5 profits will
look like as a result of adopting the new strategies.

    It is worth taking note of these three types – I think all forecasts
are one of these and there is no fourth category – because terrible
confusion arises if the type is not clearly stated. For example, some
of the long-range national economic forecasts published in the
press are made on the assumption that the government does change
its economic policy and some are on a 'no change in policy' basis.

Psychological aspects of forecasting

So notoriously difficult is it to make long-term forecasts that a
number of checks should be made on them after they have been
prepared but before the planning team finally approves them. I
should warn that in no case I can remember has it been possible to
make these forecasts in one attempt. The executives on the
planning team find the conclusions that emerge from this exercise
so surprising and so full of new implication that, having used the
checks below, they will invariably want to recalculate their figures

several times to get them 'right'. This is true even where, as is the case with most companies today, they have already prepared long-term business plans. The difference between this exercise and standard business planning is that here the sums are (a) much simplified and (b) done twice (Fpes and Fopt), and this allows a far more truthful set of figures to be revealed. No executive would dare to admit, in his official business plan, that turnover might actually *decline*. In these exercises he would be heavily criticized by his peers on the planning team if he failed to show this possibility if it could, in reality, occur.

These psychological aspects of forecasting are as important as they are neglected. There is evidence that even expert forecasters build into their forecasts the answers that they believe their sponsors wish to see. The market research specialist who knows that his boss, the marketing manager, is keen to launch a new product will (subconsciously?) select the data for his report which tend to show that there will be a strong demand for just this product. (I know one boss who sacked his researcher because her figures showed that the project he had just approved would not be profitable.)

Again, who do you ask to do a forecast of, say, air traffic over the next ten years – a specialist in air transport, or someone who knows nothing about it? If you ask the expert, and it seems the sensible thing to do, he is sure to be personally interested in, perhaps even fascinated by, air transport and will (subconsciously?) select the data which shows it will increase the fastest. This time, then, he slants the data the way *he* wants it to go.[1]

Only by inviting someone to make a pessimistic and an optimistic forecast, with key assumptions clearly stated, can these little known, but extremely powerful, influences be countered.

Checking the forecasts

I do not think I have ever seen a forecast that has been error-free first time. Naturally, I do not mean one that has been perfectly accurate – that is too much to hope for – I mean human errors. The list opposite contains some of the checks that the planning assistant should make for his team.

I should comment on the accuracy required in these forecasts. The planning team will save a lot of time if they drop their standards of accuracy to well below that required in normal financial account-

Checks for long-term forecasts

- **Rule 1.** Check that Rule 1 has been observed – that is, in making these forecasts it must be assumed that there will be no change in strategy. One of the reasons for this rule is to prevent wild flights of fancy. Without this rule it would be possible to justify almost any optimistic forecast on the grounds that the new product (or whatever) was going to perform miracles. So no new products (unless the project has actually been approved). If productivity has not been improving, then you cannot assume that it will improve in the future. If margins have been falling, they will continue to fall.
- **Assumptions.** Check that the various pessimistic and optimistic assumptions are reasonable. For example, suppose a company wishes to take account of a possible recession in Year 3. Suppose the pessimistic forecast shows profits falling by 25 per cent from the previous year – is that reasonable in a recession? What happened last time the market turned down? Were conditions comparable? If profits fell by 40 per cent then, why assume only 25 per cent this time?
- **Consistent assumptions.** For example, in many firms the factory manager will estimate the expected rise in wages, while the personnel department will estimate rises in salaries. Have they both assumed the same rate of pay inflation?
- **Anomalies.** Very often one of the ratios will be seen to behave unexpectedly across the five-year sequence; perhaps gearing falls in spite of a major programme of capital expenditure, or perhaps the margins in the *pessimistic* forecast turn out to be higher than in the optimistic! As a matter of fact, because there will be two forecasts – Fpes and Fopt – the number of cross-checks one may perform is enormous and this makes it almost impossible to get away with any assumption that is not sensible. For example, capital employed may be checked three ways: it should rise each year by the retained profits (normally), it should rise in line with sales (normally) and ROCE should be reasonable – in *both* forecasts over all the five years.
- **Widening errors.** The further ahead one forecasts the more inaccurate one's forecasts generally become. This should be reflected by a widening of the spread between the pessimistic and the optimistic forecasts. Thus an Fpes and an Fopt for Year 2 of £1m and £1.5m (showing a 50 per cent spread between them) ought to become, say, £2m and £4m by Year 5 (a 100 per cent spread).

- **External checks.** Try to link company figures in these forecasts with something outside the company. For example, all forecasts of unit sales should be related to the market so that changes in market share are clearly shown. Check key ratios with those of competitors and ask if the comparison is reasonable.
- **The plus and minus method.** The method of forecasting suggested above is to make two forecasts, an optimistic and a pessimistic. But there is another way which, while not so reliable, may be used to cross-check this method. First, list the pessimistic and optimistic assumptions as above, then calculate the effect of each compared with the Year 0 profits. Add the pessimistic effects to Year 0 profits and the optimistic effects to Year 0. The result should be similar to Fpes and Fopt for Year 5 obtained from the above method.

  Thus suppose Sparrows calculated that all the pessimistic assumptions would reduce their profits by £60,000 compared to Year 0, and all the optimistic assumptions would enhance them by £70,000. This provides very good confirmation of their original forecasts of £167,000, and £294,000 because their current £222,000 minus £60,000 is £162,000 (quite close to £167,000) and plus £70,000 is £292,000 (very close to £294,000).

---

ing. I have just seen a company, operating in a declining market, now making a profit of £7.6m, where the optimistic forecast rises to £11.7m in Year 5 and the pessimistic drops to £5.5m. It really does not matter at this stage of the corporate planning process whether they round this off to '£12m and £5m' or '£12m and £6m'. This is not double entry book-keeping. The aim is simply to quantify their hopes and fears for the future, the better able to confront and address them.

The piston effect

Finally, there is a problem for companies who have to make forecasts for several parts of their organization, such as those with several different products or subsidiaries. Consider the case in Figure 6.9, where the group consists of three divisions, A, B and C (it could just as well be a company with three different products).

It appears that group profits in Year 5 could be between £16m and £39m depending on whether they experience bad or good

Figure 6.9   A group forecast

	Year 0		Year 5			
	£m		Fpes		Fopt	
	Sales	Profit	Sales	Profit	Sales	Profit
A	122	12	133	13	176	19
B	92	8	98	7	133	12
C	83	6	54	−4	97	8
Grp	297	26	285	16	406	39

fortune – a substantial spread. In fact, if each of these subsidiaries are all in the same business then this is indeed the sort of spread that this group might have to endure. Suppose, however, that none of these subsidiaries' businesses are related. It would indeed be bad luck if all of them were to be at their pessimistic at the same time. The pistons are not all going to be at bottom dead centre at the same time, surely?

How does one avoid adding together several pessimistic and optimistic forecasts to make something that is, frankly, outrageously pessimistic or optimistic? There are advanced mathematical techniques for doing this but I suggest these are not used. Unless the planning team are all mathematicians they will lose the 'feel' of the answers that these calculations provide. I suggest the following crude rules – to be modified at will according to circumstances.

If there is no link at all between the subsidiaries (or products) then take the figures for the largest (A in Figure 6.9) and assume these to be correct. Take the next largest and ask: 'What are the chances of B being at the bottom of its profit range at the same time as A?' Plainly, if there is no linkage at all between A and B then one takes the middle of the pessimistic and optimistic forecasts for B – sales of £115m and profit of £9.5m in this case. Assume there is no linkage with C either then the figures for C may also be averaged (at £75m and £2m). The total for the group is now as shown in Figure 6.10.

The group profit now shows a spread of £24.5m to £28.5m – a massive reduction in uncertainty from the previous £16m to £39m. Such are the joys of being a conglomerate. In a conglomerate there is no linkage (or synergy) between the various business activities. In

Figure 6.10   A conglomerate forecast

	Year 0		Year 5			
	£m		Fpes		Fopt	
	Sales	Profit	Sales	Profit	Sales	Profit
A	122	12	133	13	176	19
B	92	8	115	9.5	115	9.5
C	83	6	75	2	75	2
Grp	297	26	323	24.5	366	28.5

the real world there are no true conglomerates – most businesses have *something* in common with most others (the state of health of the world economy if nothing else) and so, in reality, we have probably understated the linkages above. In some cases, where two activities are truly contra-cyclical, for example, then one would *add* one's pessimistic forecast to the other's optimistic resulting in no spread at all between the two forecasts!

In real life the group above decided on the figures shown in Figure 6.11, which reflect the fact that there was a significant amount of linkage between the subsidiaries (the price of oil being highly important in two of them). The stabilizing effect of being a group is also evident from the reduced spread.

Figure 6.11   Related group forecast

	Year 0		Year 5			
	£m		Fpes		Fopt	
	Sales	Profit	Sales	Profit	Sales	Profit
A	122	12	133	13	176	19
B	92	8	101	9	115	11
C	83	6	66	0	84	4
Grp	297	26	300	22	375	34

It is interesting to note that a matrix of figures such as this gives ample opportunity for cross-checking. The management would look at the margin on sales, for example, and ask: Are they sensible, bearing in mind the nature of the businesses for each division and for the group as a whole? What about growth rates? Is it really possible that the above group's turnover might fail to grow at all over a five-year period? That profits might actually fall? (I can almost *hear* the other members of this planning team telling the managing director of Division B that the margin he has shown in his pessimistic is *far* too high compared to his optimistic: 'Oh come on, Tony; its more like 7 per cent.')

I hope it is by now quite clear why I attach such importance to making these double forecasts, Fpes and Fopt. While it takes twice as long to prepare as a single forecast I believe it reveals four times as much information about a company's future, especially its riskiness. Indeed, a single-figure forecast says nothing whatever about risk; it sweeps it under the carpet. This is quite mad, in my view, and I cannot think why the textbooks go on preaching single-figure forecasts. It is wholly unprofessional. I must repeat what I said above: executives who make these double forecasts – even if they have just completed a budget or business planning exercise – find them rich with new implications.

I said that one reason for making these forecasts is to reveal more elephants. In the real-life group above, two major elephants were revealed: the distinct possibility that Subsidiary C might run into losses within the next five years and, secondly, the remarkable effect of the price of oil on two of the subsidiaries of the group, where, quite by chance, if the price went up one subsidiary benefited while the other suffered. The extent was not identical but it was sufficient to afford some protection to the group from this large uncontrollable variable. I do not think anyone on this team – immensely and impressively professional though they were – had previously taken either of these phenomena on board. It made a major difference to the sort of strategies they then searched for.

Forecasts for non-profit-making organizations

Forecasting in non-profit-making organizations is sometimes no more difficult than in companies. Alas, because quantification is so much less practised in this sector, it will often be that much more difficult. In my view, this method of forecasting reveals such a profusion of information about the organization, the planning team should make real and genuine efforts to follow this part of the process.

Figure 6.12 shows an extract of the past few years' performance for a non-profit-making organization which, decades ago, was granted a government-backed monopoly on insuring the premises of small shopkeepers.

Figure 6.12   National Small Retailers Association Insurance Society

Year (£m)	−7	−6	−5	−4	−3	−2	−1	−0
Income from members	17	18	18	21	22	24	26	29
Investment income	6	7	9	10	12	13	17	19
Reserves	61	71	88	98	119	132	164	196

Because you are given only the three relevant figures you can hardly fail to notice what has been happening: every year the Society has been salting away part of the contributions they receive from their members in order to build up a prudent reserve. So while the members have paid premiums rising with inflation (8 per cent per annum over this period) the reserves of the Society have also increased – but *much* faster than inflation! In fact, income from these reserves has started to overtake members' contributions. Seven years ago investment income totalled only one-third of the premium income, now it is two-thirds. So while contributions have been rising at 8 per cent, investment income has grown by 18 per cent per annum.

What would a forecast tell us? First, that if there is no change in strategy, by Year 5 the annual income from the members will still be about £29m (in today's values) while investment income will have grown, at about 10 per cent per annum (real), to £30m; so it will actually exceed premium income by then. Now, if this was a profit-making organization the shareholders might be rather pleased with that, but it is not – it is a non-profit-making mutual.

Neither the management of this trade association, nor the shopkeepers themselves, have yet noticed this phenomenon (the three lines of figures I isolated for you normally lie buried in a mass of others in the annual report). In my view, this comes close to corporate perversion because the shopkeepers' premiums, intended to be used to protect their shops from certain hazards, have been used to build a huge investment fund. (Incidentally, who owns that £196m? The existing members? What about the past members, long since dead? When will they get their share?)

Two possible strategies are suggested by this forecast: either to cut the premiums very substantially or offer enormously better terms and conditions on the policies – and the Association should do one or the other fairly soon before their members realize what has been happening!

I suggested above that one reason for doing these forecasts was to search for elephants in the past and the future. The other reason is to carry out a gap analysis and to this we must now turn.

Gap analysis

Once both the targets and the forecasts are known the planning team will be able to calculate the 'gaps', that is, they will be able to see how powerful their new strategies will have to be to take their company from where it is going to be on present strategies to where they want it to be. It will also show them how urgently the strategies are needed.[2]

Normally the profit and the ROCE gaps are much more important than that for capital employed. So, first calculate the profit gap. It is much easier to visualise this if it is done in the form of a graph. All one needs to do is to place the graph for the profit targets on top of the graph for the profit forecasts as Sparrow did in Figure 6.13.

The gaps for ROCE are made in exactly the same way (see Figure 6.14).

Finally, the planning team should draw up a summary of the strategic implications of their gap analysis, perhaps under the headings shown in Figure 6.15. As can be seen, an extremely valuable picture of the sort of strategies the company will be looking for begins to emerge from this target–forecast–gap exercise.

Figure 6.13 Sparrow's profit gaps

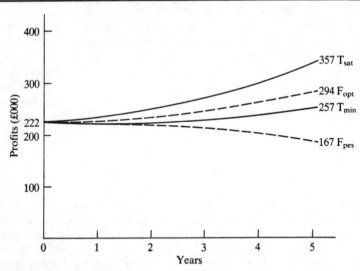

'Conclusions

If things go well for us (Fopt) then we will be safely above Tmin every year for the next five years, but we will miss our Tsat by £63,000 in Year 5.

If things go badly we will be well below Tmin each year and by Year 5 we could be £90,000 below Tmin – a terrible prospect.

The gaps in the early years are not too bad so we do have time to think. But if things go badly (Fpes) we will be an amazing £191,000 below Tsat by Year 5. Obviously, we need to make a major shift in direction compared with our present course.'

The message from the gaps

No two companies display the same two patterns. Some typical examples are described in Figure 6.16 – and I should draw particular attention to graph 4, which shows how this gap analysis sometimes reveals a high-risk situation that may require a risk-reducing strategy rather than the usual profit-improving one.

To simplify comparison all the graphs have the same Tmin and Tsat.

Figure 6.14   Sparrow's ROCE gaps

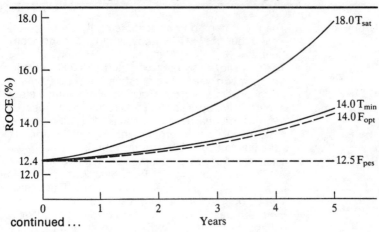

continued ...

'Conclusions

Even if things go well for us (Fopt) we will be just below Tmin every year for the next five years, and we will miss our Tsat by 4 per cent which is an enormous margin below the 18 per cent ROCE we want.

If things go badly we will be a little more below Tmin each year and by Year 5 we could be nearly 2 per cent below Tmin.

In the early years the gap between Fpes and Tsat is wide and it gets rapidly worse. It is quite clear that ROCE is the key problem for us.'

Examples

There is no limit to the variety of shapes in these gap graphs. Figure 6.17 illustrates a company which has been caught out by a change in technology.

A high technology company   Its old product, currently yielding a profit of £34m, is increasingly being rejected by customers in favour of a new design, already available from competitors, which this company will not have on the market for another three years. Mercifully, their research department started work on the new technology several years ago and, they believe, the new products will be available by Year 3, or more optimistically, Year 2.

Figure 6.15   The strategic implications for Sparrows

Urgency	The profit gaps do not become really serious until Year 3 but the ROCE gaps could be huge from Year 2.
Profits	The gap widens by approximately £30,000 a year in the next two years. We need an extra £100,000 to bring profits up from Fpes to something safely above Tmin by Year 5. To take us from Fpes to somewhere near Tsat we need £200,000. So we are looking for an improvement in the region of £100,000 to £200,000 extra by Year 5.
ROCE	This is the main problem. We need to improve ROCE very substantially from Year 2: it could still be as low as 12.5 by then and we want 18 per cent.
Risk	The company does not appear to be at great risk. Even the pessimistic forecast shows no sign of a collapse into losses. We seem to have an in-built stability.
Strategic implications	By far the most important conclusion is that we need to improve ROCE very substantially and very rapidly. *Any* strategy that calls for *any* capital expenditure in the near future is certain to be wrong. What we must do is *first* improve the use of our existing capital – or even divest some of it – and only then can we think of expanding the capital base.

Elephants may be found anywhere in the corporate planning process. As it happens, in this case all the elephants were found here, in the gap analysis. The first one for this company was the declining product. The second was the new product. The third was the absence of a product to fill the dip. The fourth was the realization that, because no more investment would be made in the old product, the company's cash flow would be strongly positive for the next three years. An obvious strategy, that this cash flow could be employed to accelerate the introduction of the new product, emerged with great force and clarity. There were other strengths and weaknesses, threats and opportunities, but the core of the company's problems are to be seen in the graph in Figure 6.17.

Figure 6.16 Various gaps

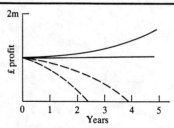

1. Even the F_{opt} sees a loss developing within a very short time. This is such a serious situation that corporate planning should be abandoned and an urgent rescue mounted.

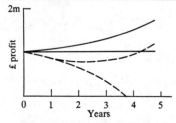

2. An unusually poor outlook. If things go badly for this company it could be making a loss very soon; even if all goes well for it, it will barely reach T_{min}. This pattern could imply that a massive retrenchment is needed to cut back to a profitable core.

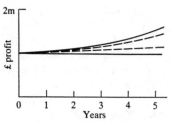

3. A pattern found frequently. With luck the company will come close to a satisfactory profit on present strategies but even without luck, performance will not be too bad. Suggests a steady, sensible strategy.

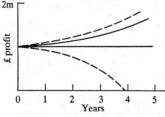

4. This shows a very wide spread between F_{pes} and F_{opt} indicating that the company is in a high risk situation. Their problem is not profits – with luck they will hit T_{sat} – it is the possibility of doing very badly indeed. This suggests a defensive, risk reducing strategy rather than going for growth.

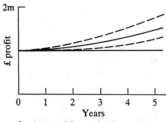

5. A very satisfactory situation; present strategies will take the company well clear of T_{min} even if things go rather badly and above T_{sat} if they go well. In theory the company does not need a new strategy at all – in practice the managers are likely to aim at something rather better than T_{sat} and are entitled to take some risks to achieve it.

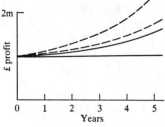

6. An extremely fortunate company. Even if things go against them their performance will be better than satisfactory. The managers can confidently go for a very expansive strategy to take them to $T_{fantastic}$ and they are entitled to consider a high risk strategy such as diversification.

Figure 6.17   A monstrous gap

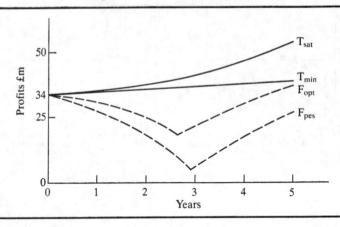

This phenomon is rare – elephants are usually well spread through the process, many of them appearing in the strengths and weaknesses analysis – but in the above example almost all the elephants that the company discovered could be seen in this gap graph.

A manufacturing company   One most impressive company displayed the profit gaps seen in Figure 6.18. In other words, 'even if things go badly for us we will still do very well'. It might be thought that this conclusion is too good to be true – surely the forecasts must be wrong. But, try though they did, they could not conceive of a situation where their profits would fall below £65m by Year 5. It is interesting to note that their Tmin (at 3 per cent per annum real growth) was not considered unduly low and that their Tsat (based on 9 per cent per annum growth) was considered entirely satisfactory for a company of this size.

I discuss a similar case in great detail in Chapter 12.

I recently saw a company with a gap of £1.8m in Year 5. It normally introduces two new products each year and, by tradition in this industry (retail personal hygiene) products have a turnover of around £1m and sell at margins of approximately 10 per cent. Will the company close the gap by Year 5? Plainly no – you can do the sum in your head. So its present strategy will have to be changed. The conclusion – that they needed a new product strategy – was so stark and simple that it hit the managers with great force.

Figure 6.18   Two negative gaps

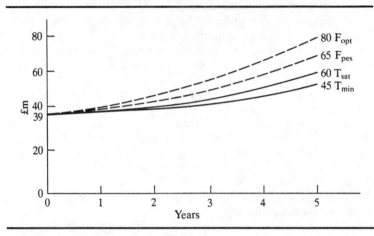

One very common strategic conclusion is provoked by the level of ROCE. If it is below Tsat – and certainly if it is below Tmin – then it suggests that strategies for growth should be postponed until the company has learnt to make better use of its existing capital. Conversely, the higher ROCE is above Tsat, the more likely it is that strong growth strategies will be indicated.

I can barely exaggerate the value of gap analysis for putting a planning team into the right mood for selecting their strategies. If the gaps are serious, if Tmin is at risk, this cannot fail to alert them to trouble ahead. If Tsat is not at risk, it tells them to find an aggressively expansionist strategy – to push the boat out. If there are no gaps for two years it tells them that, if they want it, they have two years before the strategies need to take effect, and so on.

Even more impressive is the effect the gap will have later when the planning team comes to select its set of strategies. Most corporate plans consist of a small, sequenced, set of strategies rather like a layer cake: at the base will be a defensive strategy to protect the organization against some threat perceived by the team, then comes a wedge of low-risk, profit-improving strategies, topped by a higher-risk, high-reward strategy to take the organization beyond Tsat. Each of these slices have to be sized and phased to close the gaps. The gaps tell you when you have done enough planning – when you have sufficient strategies to close the gaps, you have done enough.

I have just seen a company choosing between organic growth and acquisition – an extremely common dilemma – and their discussions were constantly peppered with remarks like, 'But, Tom, we will never get that off the ground by Year 3, which is where the gaps suddenly widen out.'

It amazes me that corporate planning systems exist with this gap analysis missing altogether.

Having completed the profit gap analysis, the same analysis should be carried out for ROCE and, perhaps, for capital employed. A further raft of strategic conclusions will spring from these gaps – but, unless otherwise indicated, the planning team should resist the temptation to jump to any final conclusions until the end of the internal and external analysis when the total strategic situation will become clear.

During the whole of the corporate planning exercise ideas for strategic action will occur to members of the planning team, prompted by the facts and figures that the process reveals to them. I am particularly concerned that no strategic decisions are taken until Stage 7. Once all the elephants have been collected together in one place, all labelled and agreed, then it is a relatively simple matter to see how to deal with them, taking account of all their interrelationships, as will be demonstrated in Chapter 10.

I would recommend that, rather than take any decisions here, the planning team keeps a running list of all the strategic ideas that occur to them and refers back to this list at the strategy-forming stages.

Summary

The planning team now needs to make a long-range forecast of profits and ROCE – or whatever CPIs they have selected.

The past may be a fragile guide to the future but it is all we have, so they (or more likely, the planning assistant) should carefully analyze the company's past performance to see what lessons there may be for the future. I hope I made it clear that they should still be looking for elephants; they should not waste time with trivia, otherwise this enquiry will take months.

Now comes a shock. Not only am I asking for a five-year-profit forecast '('I can't forecast five weeks!') but I require *two* of them!

The reason is that, although no one ever admits to it, all forecasts are wrong. Managers go to great lengths to hide the errors; it just is not honourable to admit you cannot see into the future. But I want the clearest possible admission of the true range of errors so that the team can see how vulnerable their organization is to the vicissitudes of the world we really live in. This forecasting procedure overcomes the profound psychological motives for over-optimism and over-pessimism.

The result of this double forecast, when compared with the double target from the previous chapter, is quite remarkable – a whole raft of strategic implications reveal themselves to the planning team and have a profound effect on the design of their strategies. For one thing, they will know that they must seek a two-dimensional strategy, one that takes them to Heaven if things go well but does not condemn them to the flames if things go wrong. This makes strategy formulation much more difficult but *very* much more realistic.

The Fulmar Life Assurance Society

Corporate Plan for Fulmer Life Assurance Society
Summary Page 3. Forecasts and gaps

Forecasts

The team found this forecast extremely difficult. It depends so heavily on interest rates, economic growth, claims experience and, above all, on tax changes. However, we believe the industry will grow at between 4 and 7 per cent, that our share will stay constant or increase slowly and that assets will therefore accumulate as shown:

Year	0	1	2	3	4	5
Pes	859	914	960	990	1010	1030
Opt	859	930	1000	1080	1170	1260
Growth % Pes		6	5	3	2	2
% Opt		8	8	8	8	8

Gaps and strategic implications

The calculations show that the gaps become significant towards the end of the period when, in Fpes, the tax changes begin to bite.

Instead of net assets rising to the Tsat of £1383m they might only reach £1030m. On the other hand, the gap may be as low as £123m. Indeed, we could actually exceed Tmin (£1233m) on present strategies.

CHAPTER 7

Strengths and Weaknesses Analysis

The previous stages in the corporate planning process – targets, forecasts and gaps – were designed to demonstrate to the planning team how urgent the need for new strategies is and how powerful they will have to be. The gaps will remind them that their strategies must not only achieve Tsat for the company but must also protect it against the awful stigma of falling below Tmin, so they will be looking for a two-dimensional strategy at the end of the exercise, not a one-dimensional one as called for by most planning systems. The chosen strategy must give them a satisfactory performance if things go well, but, if things go against them, it must not land them in trouble. Moreover, the gap analysis reveals the 'flavour' of the strategies they should be looking for, whether these should be risk-reducing and defensive on the one hand, or profit-seeking and aggressive on the other.

However, versatile though two-dimensional gap analysis is, it cannot show which direction the strategies should take. This is the function of the internal and external appraisals – the strengths and weaknesses analysis described in this chapter, and the threats and opportunities described in the next.

We have reached the point where the planning team attempts to identify what their company does outstandingly well or badly, what its special abilities and disabilities are, where its advantages and disadvantages lie compared with its competitors.

It is important to remember that this is corporate planning and that we are looking only for elephants – that is, factors that may condition the company's destiny for many years into the future. These will be unique features of the company which will distinguish it from its competitors and mark it out from the norm. It is highly unlikely that any company harbours more than half a dozen strengths or weaknesses of that magnitude.

I emphasize this point because many planning systems call for a *detailed* analysis of the company at this stage. I continue to believe that this is a mistake. What is needed is a very crude, coarse-grained picture of the company. We need to know only a minute number of facts about it to determine its strategies – indeed, as I have said before, the more information the planning team is faced with the more likely they are to miss the point of the exercise, which is to look beyond the normal small change of day-to-day executive concerns.

As I mentioned earlier, I have just been handed the 230-page briefing papers for a strategy conference for a company employing 3,500 people. It is in typical textbook style. Much of it consists of detailed analyses of competitors and their comparable competence profiles for all the significant critical success factors. Alas, two of the features that really matter to this company, its top management structure and its capital intensity, are not mentioned anywhere. This, I repeat, is typical of the way strategies are determined – the key points are missed because of the burden of detail. Detail *is* needed to develop a finance plan, a manpower plan or a marketing plan, but this is *corporate* planning. Keep the details out otherwise they will kill it.

Nor do we need very sophisticated methods of detection – elephants are fairly conspicuous! Most of the people in any given company will already be familiar with most of the elephants and, in some cases, will have been aware of them for years. Not always. Some will come as a complete surprise. Some, that have been recognized as elephants for years, will be found to be mere rabbits – of no strategic significance whatever! Some elephants will be very bad news; others will be excellent.

Assessing strengths and weaknesses

This stage is probably the most important of all the stages in the Argenti System. The reason for this rather bold statement is as follows. One of the fundamental principles underlying the design of my system is the open recognition that forecasts are often wrong and that long-range forecasts are often spectacularly wrong. If a company bases its strategies on a forecast that turns out to be wrong it could be in very serious trouble indeed, unless it had also based the strategy on its strengths, the things it does superbly well. If it had done that then it would have the relevant abilities to recognize when trouble was brewing and to take, and to execute, the right decisions to get the company out of trouble.

That is why this stage on strengths and weaknesses is so important, for it is here that the team identifies its lifelines into an uncertain world. The strategic strengths they find here are the pillars which will support the growth of the company as it reaches out into the future. In particular, if a company is going to diversify away from its traditional activities then it needs above all to step forward on its strongest leg – and that implies that the company knows which this is. A diversification must, I submit, have some link with a recognized strength, whether it is technological, market, management, products or skills – a link of some sort is essential. Knowing the strengths and weaknesses is a vital element in strategy formulation and I find it quite astounding how many companies devise their strategies without carrying out this internal analysis.

The emphasis I give to this part of the corporate planning process is another of those safeguards against uncertainty that I mentioned in Chapter 2 and which are summarized in Appendix D.

Some practical suggestions

Before describing the various methods by which this exercise can best be carried out a number of detailed practical hints may be useful:

- The reason this exercise is often called the Internal Appraisal is because strengths or weaknesses are defined as something *inside* the company, usually within its control. The External Appraisal, which concerns threats and opportunities, which will be considered in the next chapter, are usually outside the company in its environment and, usually, outside its control.
- Obviously a company that has yet to be formed has no history of strengths and weaknesses. The analysis for a start-up will therefore have to be performed on the people who are to manage it. Their collective skills, knowledge and experience will form the main strengths and weaknesses of the new company, plus their intentions as to finance, facilities, distri-

bution, marketing and so on. However, it might be prudent to place very little reliance on these until they have been tested in action.

- Some things are both a strength or a weakness at the same time; others are immensely important without being either. One should not be concerned with academic definitions. If something is important, list it. It does not matter, at this stage, where or how.

- As the planning team goes through the check-lists below they should seek to list no more than the top half-a-dozen strengths and weaknesses.

- If they find many more than that they are standing far too close to their company and are seeing every tiny operational detail. This is corporate planning; they must stand further back so they can only see the things that really matter. They should ask themselves: 'What are the five or six most important things I would tell someone to whom I was selling the company?' (And, presumably, the half-dozen things they would prefer he did not know!)

- Many textbooks on corporate planning invite one to examine the company's *market* strengths and weaknesses. I certainly recognize the importance of a company's market position – see the check-list below – but I believe that non-market issues are sometimes equally important. For example, a family business in which a hostile outsider has obtained 25 per cent of the shares may have as big an elephant on its hands as if the company had just introduced a faulty product, so the strengths and weaknesses check-list below covers every possible area of a company, not just marketing.

- The team should not concentrate purely on *physical* strengths and weaknesses such as the factory, the offices or the products. In many situations non-physical features are just as important, or more so: the company's reputation, its record of innovation, its culture, its intellectual property, and so on.

- The team should make the survey of strengths and weaknesses for *the company as a whole*; they should not try to make a list of strengths and weaknesses in each area. That is, they should produce one list of strengths and weaknesses for the company and *not* a dozen lists, one each for strengths and weaknesses in Finance, another for strengths and weaknesses for Facilities, another for strengths and weaknesses for the Western Region and so on. Only *one* list of half a dozen *corporate* strengths and half a dozen *corporate* weaknesses.

- A useful guide as to whether to include an item in the list is its potential effect on profits. Anything that is going to affect profits by less than 10 to 20 per cent over the next few years is unlikely to be an elephant, while something that might affect profits by 50 per cent is obviously a stronger candidate. One should not be surprised to find some of these features with the power to double or treble profits, or to reduce them by a half, or drive the company into losses – these would certainly be elephants and are very much the sort of item one should be looking for in this exercise.

- Another criterion is to compare one's organization with its competitors. If any strengths or weaknesses are significantly greater than one's competitors, then they should be listed as potential elephants. Some textbooks call this exercise 'analyzing competitive advantage', but this does not draw sufficient attention to a major class of possible elephants that may be only indirectly competitive, such as a poor Finance Department – one does not normally go round saying: 'Our Finance Department is a competitive disadvantage.' One would put it a little more directly than that.

  For non-profit-making organizations, the advice to compare themselves with competitors will remind them that they do indeed have competitors and that they should take full note of this – something few of them do. It would be hard to overstate the value of this competitor-comparative exercise to such organizations in which the culture is often non-competitive and even anti-competitive.[1]

- As a general rule a company with a satisfactory history of growth and profitability will display more strengths than weakness, and vice versa. When the planning team has completed this exercise the strengths and weaknesses they have selected ought to account for the performance that their company has actually achieved in recent years.

- Summarizing the three paragraphs above, there are thus these criteria for classifying a strength or weakness as 'strategic': that it has had a major impact on past performance, that it may have a major impact in the future, that it distinguishes this company from its competitors – and generally that the planning team feel they would be incompetent not to include it in their strategic thinking.

- The descriptions should be precise. to say 'communications are poor' is almost certainly quite useless. It is far too general. In what way are they poor? All over the organization? Only in the Eastern region? At general manager level? How does this weakness manifest itself? Give concrete examples which show how damaging this really is.

Check-lists for groups

As noted in Chapter 2, it is important to follow an essentially top-down movement in the corporate planning exercise and this means that in a group of companies the group corporate plan should be prepared first, followed by corporate plans for each subsidiary as required. (The same pattern should be followed for a federation and other umbrella organizations.)

Let us start with the check-list of strengths and weaknesses for groups (Figure 7.1). As may be seen it is rather brief, but it seems to cover most of the areas in which group elephants will be found.

Figure 7.1   Check-list for strengths and weaknesses for a group

---

Finance, legal
For example, profit record, gearing, strength of balance sheet, property, dividends, exchange rate exposure, cash, investments, articles of association, etc. (More details will also be found in the lists below for profit centres.)

BCG
The Boston Consulting Group (BCG) suggests that groups should categorize their operations in terms of four types of business – cash cows, dogs, stars and wild cats. The following is a simplified and modified description of this famous 'farmyard':

- A cash cow is a business, or a product, having a high market share in a low growth market, which will require very little investment of money or management, but will go on returning a positive stream of cash over the next several years. It will probably already be the foundation stone of the present business and the source of cash for the future.
- A dog is a business with a low market share in a low growth market which is not making a reasonable profit and probably never will. It may have to be cut or disposed of.

- A star is a business which, given (substantial) investment of resources, could gain, or already has, a significant market share in a market that is likely to grow rapidly. When the market eventually slows the star will become the next cash cow (unless it loses share and becomes a dog.)
- A wild cat is a business having a low share of a growing market. It is a moot question whether to invest heavily to try to gain share to make it a star, or, on the contrary, to dispose of it.

The distribution of these four categories in a business is a valuable strategic indicator; the use of this Portfolio Analysis approach in strategy formulation is described in Chapter Ten.

Not everyone agrees with the BCG classification. Might it not be more useful to classify businesses in the four categories which, it is said, is used by ICI: growth businesses, cash cows, problem businesses and new businesses? Views differ: my view is that *any* classification of this sort is a useful exercise for a group. The very act of classifying helps to crystalize opinions.

Geographical spread
The planning team should consider whether the group is represented in all the appropriate parts of its nation or of the world, and whether there are any advantages or disadvantages in the current geographical balance.

Business spread
The planning team should also consider the mix of business and activities. What is the mix? Why is it what it is? Have competitors done better because their mix is different?

Risk
One of the advantages of being a group is that the risks of the various constituent activities and businesses are spread. Is there any single trend or event – or two or three of them – which could seriously affect the group as a whole?

Structure
How is the group structured? Is it by product, by geographical area, by customer, by market? Why? What benefits does this confer?

The group executive team
Is the group executive team appropriately constituted? Are there enough members or too many? Are all major functions represented? Should there be any divisional or profit centre managing directors in the group team at all? If both functions and business areas are

represented on the executive team, does that present any organizational problems such as 'dotted line' responsibilities or 'matrix' management?

Management
Taking the top three or four levels in the group hierarchy (including divisions and profit centres) how does the planning team rate their management skills, organization and structure, training, age, planning ability, career opportunities, remuneration, etc.? To what extent was the executive team responsible for the performance of the group in recent years?

Size
How large is the group compared to similar competitors? Are there any profit centres which are so small as to be a disproportionate management burden, or so large as to overshadow the others? Any that are too small to compete or too large to be managed?

Skills
Are there any major skills spread around the group on which a substantial new leg of activity could be built – or are the skills all clustered within the individual profit centres? Is there a gradient of skill in the various subsidiaries – that is, are all the subsidiaries in low-tech engineering, for example, or are some of them hi-tech? Is this gradation desirable?

Strengths and weaknesses in the operating companies
The team should scan through all the profit centres, using the strengths and weaknesses check-list below, to determine if there are any strengths and weaknesses in any of the subsidiaries which are of such importance that they should be seen as *group* strengths and weaknesses.

There follow some typical, simplified, examples of complete group strengths and weaknesses statements. Most of them contain, as one would expect, two types of statement: those that refer to the group as a whole and those referring to major features of some of the larger profit centres.

Some examples

A conglomerate

- Weaknesses.
  Because the chairman and the group chief executive are both qualified accountants the group has been without a finance director for some years. For a group of our size (4,000 employees) this is now seen as a mistake.

  The chairman and the managing director are both active executives and have direct responsibilities for some of the smaller profit centres. The managing directors of the three major profit centres are also executive members of the group board. Because every member of the group board has executive responsibilities for subsidiaries they are all fully in touch with the real world. Unfortunately, none of them is responsible for the long-term future of the group as a corporate whole.

  We are very 'low profile' – for a group of our size we are not well known even in our own industry.

  The group consists of three major subsidiaries: one in processing, another in retail distribution, the third major profit centre is in construction. There are similarities between the processing and the distribution companies (and most of the smaller subsidiaries) but the construction company differs markedly in geographical area and capital structure. The only group director who understands it is its managing director. The stock market is not sure how to classify us and our Price Earnings Ratio is often said to be below what it would be if we were one thing or the other.

- Strengths.
  The group finances are very strong: £150m cash for investment is readily available, double that with prudent gearing.

  Our distribution business has grown very rapidly in recent years (20 per cent per annum). We are now Number 2 in the industry (we were Number 4 five years ago) and customers are constantly asking us to do more for them. This company now accounts for 40 per cent of group turnover and 50 per cent of profits. Margins are strong and rising, while competitors' are falling.

  Although the construction company operates mainly in the

North East, both the other main subsidiaries are truly national and distribution is spreading rapidly into Europe.

A manufacturing group

● Strengths.
   Our International Division has grown rapidly and now accounts for 50 per cent of sales, 40 per cent of profits.

   The selling functions in the three UK divisions – customer liaison, product design, product range, pricing, even down to the design of leaflets – are excellent. (The reason that sales have not been buoyant is due to the decline in the market, not through any fault in our sales departments. Our market share has risen in recent years from 11 per cent to 14 per cent.)

   Borrowings are not low but we could raise another £40m. The balance sheet is moderately strong. The financial situation of several competitors has deteriorated in recent years.

● Weaknesses.
   The share price is lower than a few years ago. We could be a bid target.

   No new products are in the pipeline. The present range is well liked and trusted by customers, but we have no replacements for Products D, F and M which are fast becoming obsolescent.

   We are overtrading. Margins in the industry have declined in recent years and our turnover has risen. As a result, the overdraft is rising towards the limit and the trend is worrying.

   Six of the top eighteen divisional directors will retire in the next four years.

A Latin American group.   We are the largest private company in the nation with a reputation for excellence in management, conditions of employment and, above all, technology.

We have huge cash reserves and a strong annual cash flow.

We have been criticized by the government for employing too many American-trained executives. We will have to set up a management training college staffed by our own nationals and open to officials in state enterprises.

Our steel division has been instructed by the government not to improve its productivity beyond that of the state owned steel companies.

The President has commented favourably on our interests in

hotels, tourism and construction. He has invited us to expand in similar labour-intensive businesses, in areas of high unemployment, which contribute to exports or which save imports.

Check-list for profit centres

The check-list in Figure 7.2, which catalogues a large number of areas where elephants may typically be found, and also displays a number of (simplified) examples, is intended for use in profit centres – that is, in companies and non-profit-making organizations which consist of an autonomous operation, managed by a general manager who is responsible for revenues as well as costs.

Most companies display the 'elephant' phenomenon – they have a few (always less than half a dozen) massive strengths and weaknesses which, because they tower over all the others, mark them out as unmistakable. Occasionally, however, a company will display a larger number of weaknesses, often over the entire range of its functions and activities. This may be due to one of two very different strategic situations. Either:

- The company has been growing so rapidly that the management have not had time to correct the problems of growth as they arise. This company will probably enjoy two major strengths to counterbalance all these weaknesses. It will display (a) one massive strength (a brilliant product, young vigorous managers, superb marketing, or whatever), and (b) its rapid growth will have given it considerable financial reserves. So this is generally good news – this company is in a very strong position although it may be in danger of over-expanding. Alternatively:
- The company has not been growing rapidly – indeed, it may have been in decline – and it does not have any massive strengths at all to counterbalance all those weaknesses. This is bad news. *This* company has been poorly managed for some years and is in danger of being caught out – that is, going bust – by some chance event before it can correct the weaknesses.

As stated above, these two very different cases may be seen occasionally. Apart from these, all companies conform to the 'elephant rule' – the list of strengths and weaknesses will be very

Figure 7.2   Check-list for profit centre strengths and weaknesses

Functional area	Possible items	Examples of strengths and weaknesses
Finance, Legal	Stability of profits, reliability of cash flows, level of gearing, major legal commitment, property, inventory or stock levels, creditors and debtors, dividend record, parent company's financial situation, leases, hire purchase, currency risks, inflation, contracts, overtrading, asset values, financial ratios, strength of balance sheet, taxation, foreign loans, government grants and subsidies, capital intensity, ownership and control, unusual articles of association, voting shares, loan agreements, floating charges on assets, etc.	'Our bank loans are far too high and interest payments absorb most of our profits.' 'We enjoy special tax status because of the way we write our pensions business.' 'Cash flow is high and very reliable.' 'We are a prime bid target.' 'When Uncle George dies, my side of the family will lose control of the company.' 'Our parent company has made it clear that we will get no more capital from them for several years. Meanwhile they want all the cash we can spare.'
Facilities	Modern or ancient shop, factory or office, costs compared to competitors, up-to-date or old-fashioned equipment and computers, recent levels of investment, cramped or surplus premises, capacity utilization, location, computer-aided design, technology, order book, production planning, costing systems, layout, scrap levels, working	'Our plant is among the most modern in Europe.' 'Our machine tools are decades old, the layout has not been improved for years and our costs are 20 per cent above most competitors.' 'We can beat most of our competitors because our computing systems are superb.' 'The factory is filthy.'

	conditions, site, standard of maintenance, security, fire risk, etc.	'Magnificent retail premises in prestige position.'
Purchasing	Buying materials and components, multiple and single source, extreme dependence on one supplier, vulnerability to supply breaks, credit terms, bargaining position, price variations, exchange-rate fluctuations, *force majeure* clauses, quality, depletion of natural resources, weather dependence, transport failures.	'We purchase one vital material from a politically unstable nation.' 'We purchase from a major competitor.' 'Huge variations occur in availability and price.' 'We are the only buyer in this country.' 'We do not purchase anything of strategic importance.'
Products	Where they come in the market, how many products in the range, gaps within the range and above or below it, extreme reliance on one product, the price range, the technology range, the quality range, 'relative quality', design, geographical availability, services offered with the goods, goods offered with the service, segments, niches, margins, unprofitable lines, volume, price elasticity.	'Our products lead in technology. They are by far the most expensive on the market.' 'There is nothing to distinguish our product from all our competitors.' 'We cannot offer a product at the top of the range as some of our larger competitors can.' 'We have far too many products. Some of them are real dogs.'
Research and development	Facilities, reputation, basic research, new product development (NPD), process development, product usage development, know-how, licenses, patents, intellectual property, copy-	'We are far too small to do any development work. We buy all our know-how, some of it from a competitor.' 'The patent expires in two years time.'

	right, computer technology, technologists, contracts.	'We simply do not have a proper NPD system.'
Marketing	Advertising, promotion, selling skills, sales force, customer services, packaging, display, market research, knowledge of the market, knowledge of competitors, attitude to customers in the company, market share, competitive advantage, customer base, exports, product development, market development, marketing strategies.	'We are market leaders in the North of the nation but weak in the South.' 'We do not know the size of the market, nor our share of it.' 'Our customers say our service is the best. But our prices are among the highest.' 'Our salesmen sell four times as much as anyone else's because they do not cold call.'
Distribution (how the products reach the final customer')	Physical distribution by means of road, rail, sea, fibre optics, satellite, warehousing facilities, ports and airports, etc. Delivery record, lead times, complaints. Distribution chain: wholesalers, retailers, agents, licensees, franchisees, branches, etc.	'We manufacture and we also distribute through our own retail outlets. Is this a strength or weakness? It is certainly unusual.' 'We are up with the leaders in electronic transmission of funds.' 'Our agents can no longer handle the volume.'
Employees	Trade unions, morale, age distribution, enthusiasm, discipline, motivation, skills, culture, education, absenteeism, communications, staff turnover, strikes, productivity, remuneration, pensions, recruitment, share-options, pay structures, career prospects, training, working conditions.	'Morale is high: no unions, low turnover, high productivity – profit per employee far above average.' 'Endless disputes, poor working conditions, strong unions have us over a barrel.' 'We are too small to attract specialists with the

		highest qualifications. They do not want to live in this area of the country.'
Management (supervisors, lower managers, middle managers, top managers, directors, non-executives, managing director, chairman)	At each level: managerial knowledge and skills, professionalism, age distribution, style of management, control data, management systems, budgetary control, business planning, centralization, delegation, innovation, career planning, training, organization structure, remuneration, share options.	'We cope well with existing problems but, without new blood at the top, we could not handle much more expansion.' 'No succession at the top.' 'Few of my staff have any bright ideas.' 'We are resistant to change.'
Position in the industry	The size of the company compared to competitors, its place in the market, in technology, price, quality, reputation, image, public relations, relations with press, with local authorities and industry regulatory bodies, political influence.	'We are the largest employer in this town.' 'We are just another small widget manufacturer.' 'In spite of our small size, we are known throughout the world as a leading fashion house.'
Others	Include here any statement which does not seem to fit elsewhere. List the critical success factors for your industry now and over the next five years and comment on those you do and do not possess.	'Our market share is 7 per cent. We do not know whether this is a strength or a weakness.' 'To succeed in this business we need to be good at "customer service electronic systems". It is quite obvious we lag behind most of the big competitors here.'

short and there will be a readily perceived cut-off between the items that are and are not of strategic significance.

Some examples

As a result of this analysis, then, each planning team will come to a small set of conclusions, such as the ones below, which encapsulate the internal strategic features of their organization and describe the current balance between its positive and negative attributes.

These cameo descriptions should reflect the company's recent performance. In the first example below, the company's forecasts show profits continuing their recent fall – we can see why from the balance between the strengths and weaknesses it displays. In the second the performance has been excellent – and again we can see why. This is an important test of the accuracy of these internal appraisals. If the performance of the company is not reflected in the balance then either the analysis is wrong or the past performance of the company has been due to outside influences – including luck.

An engineering company

- Strengths.
  We have been in business for many decades and enjoy a good reputation with our customers.

  The spread of our products – marine, industrial and educational – gives us considerable protection from downturns in any one area.

  Our mini-turbine design is known throughout the marine industries of the world. Margins remain high.

- Weaknesses.
  Following the decline in our fortunes two years ago our overdraft remains near its limit. We have no assets to back further loans except our premises which are mortgaged.

  Three of our ten senior managers are over 60. It is very difficult to recruit qualified people to live in this rather remote town. We have no career planning.

  The other three products, in the industrial and educational sectors, are less well known and have been in decline for some years. We have not updated them. Margins have fallen.

  Manufacturing costs are high compared to competitors. We sometimes lose tenders by a margin of over 50 per cent.

Marketing is weak. The department does not keep adequate statistics on customers or competitors.

A construction company

- Strengths.
  We have built up very substantial cash reserves. (So has our parent company.)

  We have a superb reputation in the industry for design, service, early delivery and trouble-free commissioning. Customers fight to obtain our services. Our margins are double or treble those of most competitors. We turn down twice the business we accept. Return on capital is hundreds of per cent.

  Employee relations are good. Unlike most competitors we have no unions or staff associations. Incentives are a substantial element of total remuneration.

- Weaknesses.
  We are too reliant on a small number of enormous customers. We find it hard to say 'no' to them although they know, as we do, that we are too much in each other's pockets.

  We have no idea how to market our wares: If we lost a major customer we would not know how to sell ourselves. Outside the present specialist customers we currently serve, we are unknown.

  We are too small to be able to purchase goods or services at below average prices.

  We have expanded faster than any of our key resources, especially management and technical skills. The new computer systems are already overloaded, offices overcrowded.

It may be asked whether this sort of analysis is appropriate to non-profit-making organizations. Certainly it is. Below is the strengths and weaknesses result for a building society and a 'Quango' (Quasi-autonomous non-government organization) – but all organizations of any sort should adopt this step in the corporate planning process. I believe corporate planning without this step is virtually useless. Certainly, the check-lists would require some modification for non-profit-making organizations, but, as emphasized above, they need that for the many types of company, too.

A building society

- Strengths.
  We are well known in our own area where we have 12 per cent of the market.

  Unlike many of our competitors, we have undertaken a number of mergers in the past six years and now have considerable experience of this.

  Our branch network is well managed.

- Weaknesses.
  We do not have any significant competitive advantage over the other large societies operating in our area.

  Our management expenses ratio – agreed to be a key ratio in our industry – is at the top end of the scale for large ('A2') societies.

  Results from the recent computerization have been disappointing.

  The market strategy we adopted three years ago has not increased our market share. We attempted to move up-market (from the C1C2 socio-economic groups to the BC1s) but most of our branches are in down-market areas, and all our products were geared to the C1C2 life style and they still are.

  We feel there is a lack of skill and ability among the middle managers.

  For historical reasons 10 per cent of our branches lie far outside our main area.

A non-profit-making organization

- Strengths.
  By Act of Parliament we enjoy a complete monopoly. We have substantial technical skills in house.

  The staff are enthusiastically committed to fulfilling a socially worthwhile function.

  We are supported by a wide range of nationally recognized organizations as well as by the sponsoring government department.

- Weaknesses.
  The organizational structure is plainly at fault. Fourteen people report to the Director-General. There have been a number of serious mix-ups with some of our recent major projects.

Communications are poor. We have no formal top-level gatherings. Only the D-G knows what is happening.

We are seen as being remote and bureaucratic by a significant fraction of our clients (last year's Image Survey).

Our budgetary control system consists of an edict from the Comptroller-General. There is no contribution from departmental heads and no discussion. No actions are required on the variance reports.

The computer is elderly, the systems antique.

The council, which supervises our activities six times a year, delays decisions, is politically motivated and indecisive. Most of its 46 members, because they are so part-time, lack any real knowledge of what we do.

Because of the extensive legislation affecting the financial services industry in recent years in Britain I have accumulated a miscellaneous collection of strengths and weaknesses from that area. The following remain in my mind:

- 'We are in the forefront of using Viewdata as a marketing tool.'
- 'We react slowly. We are not innovators. We missed out on several major changes in legislation in recent years. Our image in the market is reliable but old-fashioned.'
- 'Too much reliance on a narrow base of intermediaries and agents.'
- 'Severe doubts as to the abilities of our senior staff.'
- 'No career planning. Short of experienced staff at Head Office and at branches. We do not have the management capacity to expand nor to meet the new era in financial services.'
- 'The top management is excellent. They know exactly what is happening in the company and in the industry and act swiftly to reposition the company accordingly.'
- 'Slow decision-making, weak accountability, very high management expenses which are near the top of the league table.'
- 'Our experience in several mergers will be highly relevant to the way the industry is going.'
- 'Just another faceless medium-sized insurance company.'
- 'A major influence in our area where our market share is 9 per cent. Elsewhere we are nothing.'

- 'Most of our strengths are historical. Few are relevant to the new world of financial services. We are already living on borrowed time and past reputation.'

Who should make this analysis?

As will have been noticed above, some of the comments that come out of this analysis are somewhat sensitive – remarks relating to the competence of the management, for example, and the members of the governing body. The question obviously arises: how should this analysis be made – and by whom?

Over the past twenty years I have come to a very clear conclusion as to these questions but before describing how I now invariably carry out this enquiry, let me review some of the alternative methods.

Invite written comments from the employees. The results of such a survey are always patchy and often disappointing. Most employees do not appear to make any great effort to be objective nor to treat the questions seriously. Even when someone does make a comment worthy of attention it is necessary first to verify that it is valid and then to determine whether there are any counter-arguments which mitigate the opinion. It is no hardship to do this, although it does take time, but the method is stilted and lacks vitality and conviction.

Interview a number of employees. This may be done singly or in small groups. It carries far greater conviction than the above method, especially in small groups. It should be carried out by someone in a relatively neutral senior position such as the planning assistant.

Invite a consultant's opinion. It is said that this is the most effective because he will be truly neutral. As an outsider he will be well placed to gather opinions from the senior employees and will be able to place these alongside his own knowledge of other companies and industries. However, a consultant normally lacks detailed knowledge of the company and, unless he takes a great deal of (expensive) time, he may well misconstrue the significance of certain remarks made to him. My impression, from working with them and from reading their reports, is that consultants also have their own biases and these are often as eccentric as those of employees.

The procedure I recommend universally today, having now compared it with all the above methods, is to invite a number of senior managers to a half-day meeting for a structured discussion. It is scheduled as follows (and see Appendix A.):

- The planning assistant sends out invitations for a half-day meeting to the top executives of the organization. In small companies this may be limited to the planning team only, but in organizations employing more than, say, 200 people it would consist of the planning team plus all those who report to its members – from 15 to 30 people as a rule. The invitation stresses the importance of the meeting, explains that frank and forthright opinions are being sought and includes a check-list such as one of those above. The planning assistant also encloses a full description of the timetable as set out below.
- The meeting is held away from the office, perhaps in a hotel. It begins with the chief executive describing why he has launched the corporate planning process at this time, he introduces the members of the planning team to the others, explains their work so far and then invites the participants to break into discussion groups in separate rooms for a full and free-ranging discussion of the company's strengths and weaknesses. Each group will be composed of a wide mix by department, age, seniority, skill and personality. (The chief executive will not normally join a group lest his presence constrains the discussions.)
- After two to four hours the planning assistant calls them all back and asks each group to make a fifteen-minute report, backed by headlines on a flipchart, describing their conclusions to the full assembly. When all the groups have reported the planning assistant will invite the participants to re-form into informal groups round the table (that is, not in the same groups as before) and ask them to summarize the main points of agreement. After some further discussion the seminar ends.

It will be found that an astounding measure of consensus exists in the reports from the discussion groups. As a rule, a small number of key strengths and weaknesses will be mentioned, often in almost the same words, by all the groups and will appear as headlines on all or most of their flipchart summaries. Normally between three and six strengths and weaknesses will be identified with astonishing clarity.

In addition, there will be other items on which little or no consensus exists and these will be generally seen as reflecting personal views held by one or two individuals in one or other of the discussion groups. While these should never be ignored (they may indicate something amiss that a department head should take note of) they are probably not elephants for the attention of the planning team.

While I believe this method is by far the most effective a number of comments need to be made about it:

- It should not be attempted with fewer than three discussion groups because, if there is a disagreement between two of them, there will be no third group to facilitate a conclusion. Nor should there be more than five or six groups because by the time the fifth has reported – especially if there is already a marked consensus – the sixth report will be recived with some impatience.

- There should not be fewer than three members in each group, nor more than six – two people is not a discussion group, while more than six does not allow each member sufficient time for comment, especially if, as is often the case, one or two people in each group prove to be loquacious. In effect, these two rules limit the exercise to between nine and thirty people – three times three and five times six.

- In any case, there is presumably a limit to the contribution that the nth person in a management hierarchy can make. Below a certain level of seniority a manager would have experience of such a small segment of the business that his view of the corporate whole might be somewhat restricted. In fact, my experience casts doubt on this theory. For example, I conducted 'Introductory Seminars' (see Appendix A) for eighty-five of the top managers in a large company, the first for the top twenty-five, then two more for the next sixty. I was surprised to discover that the company strengths and weaknesses as perceived by the last thirty (which included managers who were six or seven levels down the hierarchy and ranked as low as 100th in seniority) were almost identical to the top twenty-five and the middle thirty. There was a gradient, but only in one respect. In spite of several similar experiences I think it would normally be wise to keep this strengths and weaknesses enquiry within the bounds of the top three levels. Nevertheless, my experience does suggest that people do have a remarkably sharp and intelligent view of the strategic situation of their organization even at considerable depth in the hierarchy.

- In a group of companies, especially if it is a conglomerate, one would expect fewer people to be in a position to perceive the group strengths and weaknesses and so one would tend to make these seminars even more rigorously exclusive.
- Great care is required in the preparation of such a seminar. It should possibly not be held if any person present is likely to be savaged by his peers. Instructions to the participants should make it clear that, although they must be truthful, they also need to be tactful. Indeed part of their brief is to find the form of words in which to make penetrating reports that do not give offence.

Finally, an obvious point: the great advantage of inviting so many people to participate is that their knowledge is cumulative while their personal biases cancel each other out.

This approach cannot be used in very small companies. This is serious because the top men in a small company probably know more about their company than the top men in a large one, but they will be even more biased, not to say obsessed. How does one reduce the bias in a small company? If the firm is very small then I strongly suggest inviting a close outsider – friend, relative, professional adviser – to join in the strengths and weaknesses exercise. However, some quite small companies employ a large proportion of bright people. A software company employing twenty people, for example, may well boast ten who could certainly play a useful part in this exercise. A textile company of twenty, of which fifteen are part-time shop-floor workers, almost certainly could not.

The planning team meeting

At the conclusion of this seminar the planning assistant should collect together all the flipcharts and use them as notes for a summary that he should make to the next planning team meeting which should be held within approximately two weeks. His summary should consist of a brief, but accurate, description of each of the half-dozen strengths and weaknesses that the discussion groups revealed to be of corporate strategic significance.

The planning team will approve some of the conclusions, reject others, and require further consideration of others. This is where they should ask either their own managers to form a small working party to establish the truth more accurately or invite a consultant to examine the specific area of doubt. (See Chapter 12 for a detailed example.) Management audits of this type are a common consulting service and certainly to be recommended. Some planning teams like to rank their strengths and weaknesses. If this is done (and it need not be, since there will only be half a dozen items, all of them elephants) then a comparatively simple system should be employed. Some specialists recommend a system in which weights from one to a hundred are given to each item. This might be appropriate if there were hundreds of item to rank, as there are in some corporate planning systems. I believe it is impossible to rank anything with such implied accuracy, and furthermore, I believe it is impossible to take the next step that some textbooks recommend, namely using these scores to select strategies. I prefer a three-level system where:

'A'   means that the item is of critical strategic importance and absolutely must be accounted for in the strategies of the company. Without this item in the strategies they would be useless.

'B'   means the item is of strategic importance and should be in the corporate strategies if possible. If not it must be attended to elsewhere by the planning team.

'C'   means the item is not of corporate significance but may be of departmental or sectional importance and should be dealt with by the relevant senior executive.

Care should be taken in the wording of the final versions of these strengths and weaknesses statements. The planning team itself may well come to use just a single word as shorthand for a well-defined item but the official final version of each agreed strength and weakness should probably be several sentences in length. It must *not* be much longer than this. A ten-page report on the failures of the marketing department is absolutely useless; a six-sentence summary could be extremely useful. Even more useful, assuming it leaves out nothing of *strategic* significance, would be a six-word summary.

This ends the description of this very important stage of the corporate planning process.

Additional techniques

There are a number of rather more technical and disciplined methods of identifying strengths and weaknesses, which are too time-consuming for the planning team to employ, but the planning assistant or a small working party might well find them useful in areas of particular concern.

Critical success factors

Some specialists recommend the use of 'Critical Success Factors' (CSFs). They suggest that it ought to be possible to make a list of, say, the top five things which a company needs to do well in order to succeed in its particular industry.

One approach is for the planning assistant to ask each of a number of senior executives the same two questions:

(1) 'What are the Critical Success Factors for our business and will they be different in five years time?'
(2) 'Rank our company's abilities in each CSF.'

He could also ask certain selected outsiders the same questions – academics, journalists specializing in the relevant industry, for example, or one's customers, suppliers, and so on. Typical conclusions may be:

- 'I have spoken to all our key executives about CSFs. The wide range of opinions is worrying – no particular CSF came top of the poll. We do not seem to know what these factors are for our industry.'
- 'Only two CSFs seem to be important: a friendly, confidential service to customers and real-time on-line financial data. Everyone seems agreed that these two are the key ones but that the customer's priorities are now changing. While the intimate, confidential style used to be important, what they are increas-

ingly looking for is sharp, up-to-the-minute advice on a wider range of financial matters. We are renowned for the former: Herons, on the other hand, are excellent at the latter and now have their remarkable real-time on-line 'expert' system which we do not have.'

- 'We have identified that our key strength is engineering excellence. According to an industry survey of CSFs carried out by Corncrake Consultants, however, this is seen by 75 per cent of customers as relatively unimportant. The really important CSF is delivering on schedule. Moreover, this factor has increased in importance since the previous survey four years ago because the concept of 'just in time' has gained in popularity. We certainly do not come very high in this area.'

- 'We have identified exports to the developing nations as being a major strength. The first CSF here, unfortunately, is the ability to make low-interest loans for the purchase of our products by these nations. We are too small to make significant offers ourselves and have to rely on the government who are plainly becoming less enthusiastic to provide this service. The second CSF is going to become "lobbying" government departments and here again we are very weak.'

As will be appreciated, this approach could well provide additional useful insight into the company's strategic situation.

Competitive position in critical success factors

One should also make this CSF analysis for one's competitors. Suppose a company in the defence industry identifies five key CSFs in this order of importance:

1   Engineering capability: the need to possess certain minimum plant and equipment, and associated skills, in order to achieve the very high technical standards required by the armed forces. (This factor scores 8 marks out of 10 for importance.)
2   Operating costs: the government has, in recent years, become obsessed by the cost of defence equipment. Almost without exception orders go to the lowest bidder (8 marks).
3   Quality: beyond the strict minimum quality criteria that the armed forces require they also respond to evidence of additional reliability (7 marks).

4   Lobbying: there is strong evidence that suppliers are not even considered for the 'tender list' unless their names are known among the higher ranks of the armed services and the sponsoring government department (5 marks).
5   Innovation: since the armed services lay down specifications for the product in such great detail there is limited scope for any supplier to attempt to improve on the product (3 marks).

The company should try to score the same factors for each major competitor (see the next chapter for Competitor Analysis) and then it is possible to draw up a 'bubble chart' (Figure 7.3) where the size of the bubble reflects the importance of each factor and the position of the bubble on the chart shows how the company compares with its competitors.

Figure 7.3   Bubble chart showing CSF against competitors

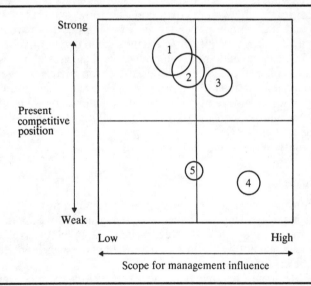

In the above case it is clear that they should throw their energies into improving their lobbying skills (4) and should not waste time on innovation (5).

I do not dismiss this technique out of hand – anything that forces a management to think systematically about their business must be a good thing, especially if it also makes them study their competitors more closely – but seeing it in action merely confirms my impressions of most of these highly systematized techniques, that it is too detailed, it obscures more than it reveals, it is inimical to strategic thought.

In the company where I witnessed its use it was virtually ignored by the senior executives, most of whom felt that little reliance could be placed on its accuracy. They did not agree the ranking that the planning department had ascribed the factors; some did not accept some of the factors at all, others proposed additional ones, others quarrelled with the place given to the company compared to its competitors, some wanted to add or subtract competitors from the list, others disagreed with the stated scope for management action.

Above all, this company had six strategic business units for each of which bubble charts had been drawn up and it is fair to say that the senior executives were completely confused and shell-shocked at the end of this analysis. No conclusions of any sort were reached. Not only did they feel unsure where they stood competitively in the SBUs but they failed to note three huge elephants standing just out of sight, hidden behind all the details: an obsolete management hierarchy, poor industrial relations and a parent company unwilling to invest in its subsidiaries – especially this one! Nothing of any strategic significance came out of these charts. On the contrary, strategic thoughts were suspended for the whole of the period that these charts were being discussed.

Measuring quality

For most managers, 'quality' means 'defects per thousand' or some similar measure. This has the merit of being simple to quantify and to control. Frequently, however, it is completely irrelevant. Quality means not what the production engineer says it means but what the customer says it means.

The Strategic Planning Institute has developed the concept of 'relative quality', by which they mean quality as perceived by the customer relative to how he perceives competitors' products. Suppose customers rank five features of a product in order of importance out of 100, and suppose two competitive suppliers, Pelican and Penguin, score as in Figure 7.4 for each feature.

Although Pelican's scores are slightly lower than Penguin's, they are highest where it matters most to the customer. Pelican will get the business. His *relative quality* score is a good 12 per cent higher than Penguin's.

Figure 7.4 Relative quality

Features	Rank	Pelican Ltd	Penguin & Co
		score out of 10	
A	45	9	6
B	25	8	7
C	15	7	8
D	10	6	9
E	5	5	10
Totals:	100	Rel. Qual: 795	Rel. Qual: 705

This PIMS analysis goes further. Their studies suggest that ROCE is strongly correlated with the perceived relative quality score. Why? Because selling prices are strongly related to perceived quality. But surely to achieve this higher quality the cost of the product would be higher? PIMS says not – certainly not always – because, for example, by improving quality you cut the costs of correcting complaints.

I ought to mention that 'relative quality' is not quite the same as 'differentiation'. In the example above the two products were remarkably dissimilar, especially in respect of features A and E. So although Penguin's product was very strongly differentiated from Pelican's its relative quality was below it. This also leads to an interesting strategic conclusion: it is not enough to be different, you have to be different in the important places!

Measuring management

It might be possible to measure how well a company is being managed by using another of the PIMS techniques.

PIMS assert that ROCE depends heavily on a small number of major strategic features. High market share has a strongly positive effect on ROCE; so has high relative market share (share of a market compared to the largest competitor); so has relative quality (described above), value added per employee, growth rate of the market and low marketing costs. On the other hand, investment intensity (the proportion of sales revenue that has to be invested in fixed assets) has a strongly negative effect. Suppose a company demonstrates all these positive features but still its ROCE is below average then that must reflect badly on the management. And vice versa.

By plotting 'Strategic Attractiveness' (using the above criteria) against 'Operating Effectiveness' (using ROCE, or maybe growth of EpS) one may observe how well a company is actually performing compared with how well it ought to be, bearing in mind its strategic situation. One reason for a company not appearing in the centre of the chart below, that is in its expected position, is the quality of the management – there are others, of course, including maybe, bad luck, for a time at least. Because of these other possible explanations care must be taken in apportioning blame and praise to a management. Please note that this would only measure current performance. It would not measure the competence of the management team who steered the company into its current strategic situation.

Figure 7.5   The PIMS assignment grid

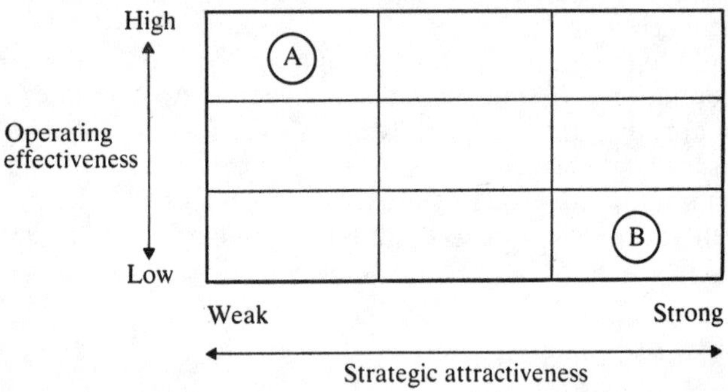

Company A somehow manages to have a high ROCE in spite of its frail strategic situation. B, on the other hand, has failed to capitalize on its good fortune. We all know companies that ought to be doing well but are not, and vice versa; perhaps this approach, taken with other evidence provided by the check-lists above, might help a planning team to reach a more objective assessment of the effectiveness of the management – themselves, in other words.

Clues from financial analysis

In Chapter 6 I suggested that the planning assistant should use trends and ratios analysis to search for further elephants. I give below a number of strengths and weaknesses that have been revealed in this way.

- 'Profits, dividends, dividend cover, and capital expenditure have moved as follows over the past five years:

Years £000	−5	−4	−3	−2	−1	0
Profits	123	127	121	133	167	141
Dividends	27	29	33	39	55	55
Cover	4.5	4.4	3.7	3.4	3.0	2.6
Capex	41	41	37	31	32	17

There may be another explanation but it looks as if the dividends have been taking an increasing proportion of the company's earnings leaving less and less available to be ploughed back in. Certainly, capital expenditure is now very low compared to earlier years.'
- 'Turnover is rising much faster than profits. The working capital to finance this expansion is growing rapidly and the interest payments on the bank loans are rising so fast that, in a couple of years, they will exceed the profits:

Years £000	−5	−4	−3	−2	−1	0
Turnover	1276	1399	1543	1776	1990	2274
Profits	109	112	121	143	134	135
Working Capital	398	444	481	541	598	782
Interest on loans	31	43	52	66	83	96

The company seems to be overtrading and this could threaten its existence within a couple of years.'

● 'The finance director says that the office has not been revalued correctly: its market value is not £4m, as shown in the accounts, but £12m. The balance sheet is really very strong indeed, therefore.'

● 'The company seems to be very capital intensive:

Years £000	−5	−4	−3	−2	−1	0
Turnover	128.8	139.0	143.2	154.3	167.2	177.8
Capital employed	141.2	158.8	165.4	171.1	184.3	201.3

There are great variations each year, but on average we need an extra £6m of capital to finance every extra £5m of turnover. We cannot find another company of our size with such a high capital intensity. With interest rates so high, this must be a weakness.'

● 'Our factory has a run-down appearance. The equipment seems to be old-fashioned compared with the industry (55 per cent of our machine tools are more than 10 years old compared with the average of 33 per cent). Capital expenditure has lagged behind depreciation for some years:

Years £000	−5	−4	−3	−2	−1	0
Depreciation	775	764	711	689	722	812
Capital spend	865	755	622	637	611	616

Several employees expressed concern at the lack of investment. The production manager said this was an exaggerated view. He has recently visited three competitors and says they are the same.'

● 'Sales per floor area is well above average. Industry figures show that we have been consistently in the top quartile for this and for turnover per sales assistant for the past five years.'

Strengths and weaknesses in marketing

One of the most controversial areas in which the search for strengths and weaknesses must be made is that of marketing. The problem here is one of definition, with two very distinctive meanings of the word being frequently used and misused:

Marketing techniques. These would include, for example, advertising expertise, packaging, product design, market research, competitor analysis, distribution, customer services, promotion, and so on – a long list of marketing techniques, many of which might be elephants in their own right. However, important though they are they are arguably less important strategically than marketing philosophy.

Marketing philosophy. This is more an attitude than a set of techniques. In a 'market orientated' company, the whole company is geared to the needs of the market – to the customer, in other words. The company will be aware of his needs from top to bottom. The chief executive will personally know all his opposite numbers in all the key customer hierarchies. The shop-floor worker and delivery man will know exactly how each customer likes his product delivered, when and where. Everyone in the company, from top to bottom, will struggle manfully to give the customer exactly what he wants, every time. Everyone is a salesman. Any mistake, any complaint from a customer about *anything* – an error in an invoice, a late delivery – all are treated as a major disaster, a dire reflection on the perpetrator.

It used to be said that a company could be considered to have embraced a market-orientated philosophy when it discovered, from market research, who the potential customer was, and exactly what he wanted, and then produced a product to meet that demand. A sales- or production- or technology-orientated company, on the other hand, was said to produce a product first and then try to sell it. But today the marketing concept has moved much further and commands the sort of universal dedication to the customer that I described above.

Typically, one obtains examples such as the ones below from an examination of marketing strengths and weaknesses:

- 'The planning team asked twelve managers to define "marketing". Most included "advertising" in their answers but only two knew that marketing should be the starting point for many of our decisions. Most believed that the Development Department ought to design the product and then the salesmen ought to go out and sell it.'

- 'We claim to have a range of high-technology products and we believe our expertise is superior to all the others. Why then do we have to cut our margins to make the sale? The Marketing Director says it is because we design the product according to good engineering principles and then try to sell it – alas, he says, it may be beautifully engineered, but it is not what the customer really wants, so we have to persuade him to buy it by cutting the price. If we made it to please *him*, not our engineers, he would pay the earth to get what he wants.'
- 'The planning team tried an old marketing trick; we asked six of our employees why they thought Drakes (our largest customer) bought our product and what were the features that he most valued about it. We then asked Drakes' chief buyer the same questions. As may be seen from the table attached [not shown], all our employees thought that "quality" (defects per thousand) was the top concern; Drakes obviously feel that delivering exactly on time is more important because of their cramped premises.'
- 'We are a small company. We try to compete on price. This must be self-defeating.'
- 'Our marketing is excellent. Our advertising, promotion, design, packaging – everything we do – convinces the customer that our product is different and better than the competition.'
- 'We do not seem to know very much about our market, its size, how fast it is growing, what our market share is, what our competitors are doing. Everyone is out selling, which is fine, but no one is studying market trends. We call it the Marketing Department, but is it?'

A very robust system

Before they experience this Internal Appraisal, executives sometimes express the fear that not all the elephants will be found, that some will be glossed over, that others will be exaggerated. But the procedure described here is very searching and very robust.

Executives who have employed the method of identifying strengths and weaknesses described in this chapter find it an exhilarating experience. Not only does it confirm for them the company's key features with remarkable proficiency but it leads to a major improvement in morale. This is true not only of companies which emerge with great strengths, it applies also to those with major weaknesses, for at the end of this procedure the executives have at last brought all these out into the open. Under the full glare of publicity the strengths sparkle invitingly, while the weaknesses seem less horrific than when they lurked under the more sinister lighting of prohibition.

I should, however, mention the case of an organization which was unable to find any strengths at all. I can hardly claim that in this case the morale of the planning team improved – it did not. However, it did result in a determination to do something about the strategic situation that had been revealed.

Having described this spectacular result – surely a maverick – I should balance it by noting the one opposite case I have seen – a company with no weaknesses. The explanation for this rare example of corporate perfection was that a new chief executive had been appointed 18 months earlier, had tackled the company's ills with great vigour (assisted by one of the 'Quality Management' techniques) and it was difficult to see what strategic weaknesses remained. The performance of this company in the past 18 months had been astonishing while the strengthless organization mentioned above had been in decline for some years and these two extremes provided dramatic confirmation for me that a correlation should be observed between the results of this analysis and the company's past performance.

Is there not a danger that the executives taking part in these analyses will attempt to fudge embarrassing problems, will embellish their strengths? Yes, there is that danger. But I believe the truth will out. I could give a dozen examples of how attempts to falsify the evidence have failed:

- One building society executive suggested this strength: 'Our branch network is excellent. The staff in our branches are very friendly.' It only required a colleague to murmur, 'More friendly than any of the competitors?' for this contribution to be dropped like a hot potato.
- When an insurance company went through the process one discussion group reported that the Underwriting Department constituted a major company strength. None of the other three groups had mentioned this feature and the reporter was invited to explain why his group had reached this conclusion. He referred the question to the Underwriting Director who had

been an influential member of his discussion group – amid much ribald laughter.

- The Research Director of a manufacturing company told his peers that his department had published eleven papers in learned journals last year – plainly a mark of excellence. 'You are not suggesting this as an R & D criterion are you, John? What about the new products that we didn't get again last year?'

I am impressed by the skill with which these groups of senior executives find forms of words to make their meanings clear wthout giving offence. I have lost count of the number of chief executives who have come under criticism for bias towards certain subsidiaries, slowness in closing down loss makers, pursuing too many projects at once, failure to reconstitute their executive teams, risking their companys' assets in prestige projects, etc. One managing director, listening intently to a critical report from a discussion group, noting the embarrassment of the reporter, said: 'Go on, George, I'm not about to go out and shoot myself.'[2]

Summary

I believe this strengths and weaknesses analysis to be the most significant of all the stages in the process. It is where the greatest number of elephants are found, of the greatest strategic importance and with the greatest clarity.

I have no hesitation in recommending the above highly participative procedure in all circumstances except three: where there is an autocrat, where there is a problem of such sensitivity that more harm than good might result, and where the company is too small to invite nine suitable employees and outsiders to form discussion groups.

I can almost guarantee that all the internal elephants will be found, described and agreed in one two- to four-hour participative session and that a four-hour meeting of the planning team will conclude the stage. The clarity of the consensus will be remarkable and will later allow the team to select a set of strategies that will use the strengths to take advantage of the opportunities and avoid the threats that will be discovered in the next stage of the process.

The Fulmar Life Assurance Society

Corporate Plan for Fulmar Life Assurance Society
Summary Page 4. Strengths and Weaknesses

Strengths

- Strong financial base.
- Investment record in top ten for past few years.
- Wide range of products, some gaps, especially pensions and unit-linked.
- Skilled staff, better trained than many competitors.
- High standard of service which has slipped lately.

Weaknesses

- Decision-taking; only executive directors take the decisions.
- Organization: too many committees.
- Market orientation lacking.
- Reliant on very few large agents.
- Not up to date on hardware and systems which are inflexible.
- Insufficient resources to diversify.
- Staid and fuddy-duddy.

CHAPTER 8

Threats and Opportunities

General

This stage is the mirror image of the previous one. There the planning team were trying to identify the elephants *inside* the company. Now they must turn their attention outside, to the External Appraisal, the threats and opportunities, the trends and events external to the company, which are usually beyond its control.

They will be listing those trends and events in the environment which they feel might have a major effect on the performance of their organization. Most of these will be in the future although some may already have occurred. Once again there will be very few of these items, half a dozen or so, and once again the team will not need to employ sophisticated detection equipment – they probably already know what most of them are.

There is one major difference between this stage and the last one, however. The search for strengths and weaknesses was conducted inside the company, a limited area, a finite zone, and one well known to the planning team. Here, however, they are being asked to scan the entire environment of the organization for several years ahead. While the former will take just a few hours, the latter can be much more extensive, much more complex.

As a result, this chapter is also more complex. In the previous chapter I recommended that the planning team, aided by the top three levels in the hierarchy, could identify and describe the elephants in just a couple of meetings. Here this will have to be broken into two distinct steps: first the elephants should be identified, then they should be described.

This chapter is therefore laid out in the following sequence: first I shall describe who should make this study and the sequence in which it should be made, then I will suggest a check-list of five areas in which to find the elephants, together with a number of simple examples, then I will examine the five areas again in more detail, giving more detailed examples and demonstrating some of the relevant techniques. I end by describing how the planning team pulls this part of the exercise together and I give examples of a completed threats and opportunities statement for a company and for a non-profit-making organization.

Who should make this study?

Although the threats and opportunities analysis has much in common with the strengths and weaknesses study – the planning team is again looking for elephants, the search must again be systematic and the more people who take part (up to a point) the better – it is plainly much less sensitive. This suggests that it is practical to pursue it by many different methods rather than concentrating on the single technique of a half-day seminar with perhaps two dozen of the most senior executives.

Having said that, it is my invariable practice to use this same seminar technique again. The reasons are, first, having consulted the top three levels in the hierarchy concerning the internal features, it makes sense to ask them about the external ones also. Secondly, having gathered them all together for half a day (a costly operation in terms of executive time) one might as well extend it by a few more hours to cover this additional area. Thirdly, experience suggests that the list of threats and opportunities these people will devise is as good as any. And finally, of course, even if it could be bettered by a search technique that did not involve them, their involvement is good for morale at the time of the seminar and will later enormously facilitate their acceptance of any strategies which the planning team eventually devises.

Because its scope is so much wider, however, this examination will also require supplementary methods. This is because, although those present at the Internal Appraisal will probably know more about the company than anyone else in the world, these same people will not necessarily know more about future trends and events in its environment than anyone else. This marks one key difference between the two appraisals.

Thus one would expect a very comprehensive and accurate list of the company's strengths and weaknesses to come out of a few hours' discussion among these top executives, a catalogue that will need little more than mere confirmation and polishing by the planning team. In the case of the threats and opportunities, however, substantial additional data may be required before the planning team can feel confident that the items have been correctly and fully described. The suggestion is this:

- Extend the half-day seminar with the top three levels of the hierarchy to include the threats and opportunities analysis. The seminar will thus take up a full day.
- Add to the participants any experts or specialists in any area which is expected to be of critical importance to the company's future. Thus a company in which technology plays a major role would invite several extra people from the technical departments in the company, or indeed from outside specialist bodies.
- Having gathered their views (using the same sequence of discussion groups, plenary discussion, then the second discussion session to list the consensus as described in the previous chapter) place them before the planning team who should then decide what further opinions to seek.
- Seek further opinions. Thus again, if the company is dependent on technology, it may be necessary to obtain a very detailed report from experts in that area to fill out the description of some particular technological element.
- Finally, the planning team should produce an 'authorized version' of all the major threats and opportunities complete with a description of each in whatever detail they feel is appropriate. See examples below.

Before presenting the check-lists I use I should like to enumerate a number of miscellaneous practical suggestions based on experience:

- Excessive reliance should not be placed on something being either a threat or an opportunity – some things are sometimes both at once, others are just immensely important without being either.
- The planning team should not identify more than half a dozen threats but perhaps a dozen opportunities.

- If they have listed more than this they are standing too close to their company and are seeing every tiny detail. This is corporate planning; they must stand further back so they can only see the things that really matter.
- A useful guide whether to include an item in the list is its potential effect on profits. Anything that is not going to affect profits by more than 20 per cent over the next few years is unlikely to be an elephant, but something that might affect profits by 50 per cent is obviously a stronger candidate. Some will double or treble profits – or halve them – and these will obviously be just what the team is looking for – elephants.
- Some of the threats or opportunities that will affect the company may already have made their appearance, some may not come to pass for years. The rule here is to include everything that might have a severe effect on the company. This is entirely a matter of judgement – the judgement of the planning team. Some events cast their shadow forwards for many years and even decades.
- Sometimes a negative statement is as useful as a positive one. It may make sense to say: 'There are no technological threats facing the company'; or, 'No significant competitors will enter our market in the next three years.' The fact that a team believes that something is not going to happen can be extremely important especially if they had previously thought it likely.
- One thing is certain, some of the employees, even those quite low in the hierarchy, know a great deal about certain specialist aspects of their company's business. Not to tap their knowledge, even though their viewpoint of the company is restricted to their specialism, is to waste an important resource.
- As will be seen from the examples below, this exercise is also very crude and unsophisticated. There are some techniques for use here – I describe many of them below – but I question whether they are sufficiently reliable to spend very much time on. Sceptics are invited to study the cases I show elsewhere (Chapter 12, for example) where I think it may be seen that some remarkably powerful strategies do come out of this rough and ready approach.
- Finally, the team should not rely too heavily on the check-list below. Companies vary enormously and some of the items below will be irrelevant while others that are vital are not even listed.

As may be seen from the above, collecting a list of threats and opportunities is very like collecting a list of strengths and weaknesses except that it may take very much longer – the strengths and weaknesses are inside the company and most of its senior executives know very well what their internal elephants are, but they will know far less about the elephants in the environment. Typically, at the half-day seminars, the initial discussion groups take four hours to identify and describe their company's strengths and weaknesses while the equivalent discussion on threats and opportunities takes less than two. So far as I can tell, this is *not* because the executives have made such a close study of their environment that they are able simply to regurgitate a predigested list of the elephants. On the contrary, it is because they have given it so little thought that they cannot do justice to the question at all.

I hasten to add that this does not vitiate the exercise – the seminars *do* identify all or most of the external elephants. What they do not do is to define and describe them to the same level of detail and confidence that is possible with the internal features. For this reason the planning team may have to meet several times before they have accurately described all the elephants and may need to consult a number of experts. All this takes time, typically several months.

A check-list for threats and opportunities

The check-list contained in Figure 8.1 is intended for use in groups of companies, in profit centres and in non-profit-making organizations. I have broken it down into five main areas of change: political, economic, social, technical and industrial. The first four are intended to catch general changes in the environment, the sort of trends and events that might affect any organization. The fifth is intended to identify upheavals in the planning team's specific industry.

Some examples

The following is an additional explanation of the four general categories above, together with some rather more detailed examples of threats and opportunities I have seen in recent years. At the end of this section I show a brief outline of some of the

Figure 8.1   Threats and opportunities check-list

Major area of change	*Possible items*	*Examples of threats and opportunities seen in a variety of companies*
Political changes (Consider the changes that may occur locally, nationally, and on a world scale.)	Next change of government, new legislation on safety, products, employment, liability, labelling, etc. Tax changes, controls, tariffs, quotas, embargoes. Nationalism, developing nations, developed nations, crises, terrorism, wars, revolutions.	'None of our competitors suffer from such tough local pollution laws; this handicap seems likely to get worse.' 'The very favourable tax treatment for small companies will continue at least until the general election in Year 3.'
Economic changes (Consider the changes that may occur locally, nationally, and on a world scale.)	Economic growth rate, inflation, unemployment, interest rates, exchange rates, costs of labour, materials, capital equipment, disposable incomes, consumer demand, prices, the stock market, availability of loan and venture capital, world trade, balance of trade, the European Community, the OECD, subsidies, grants, price of oil, gold, etc.	'Our local economy is booming in spite of the poor outlook nationally. But this cannot continue; the downturn could come next year, or not until Year 3.' 'Interest rates are bound to rise in the next year or two. We ought to meet our long-term capital requirements before this occurs.'

Social changes	Population trends, age distribution, births, pensioners, sex, ethnic, health, education, housing, mobility, equality, class, motivation, life-styles, leisure, part-time work, sport, religion, crime, security, holidays, working hours, conditions of employment, attitudes to work, to management, to wealth creation, etc.	'The local population is young, well-educated, skilled, ambitious – just the sort of people we need.'
(Consider the changes that may occur locally, nationally, and on a world scale.)		'The working week may shorten within the next few years so we may have to employ four teams of shiftworkers instead of three.'
Technological changes	Gradual technical improvements, breakthroughs, old technologies jumping into new areas. New products, new processes, new materials, new methods. Trends and events in biotechnology, in computing, in data transmission, in engineering, retailing, banking, space, etc. Costs and volume of R & D generally and by competitors, rising cost of technological sophistication.	'The cost/performance curve in our industry is rising exponentially at 25 per cent p.a. We cannot see this continuing much longer.'
		'The use of steel components is in decline. Demand for our products will continue to fall as this happens and we are far too small to follow the new composite technologies.'
		'No breakthroughs are even on the horizon. We expect a gradual technological up-rating at say 1–3 per cent p.a.'

Changes in your own industry (Consider the changes that may occur locally, nationally and on a world scale.)	More or fewer competitors, larger or smaller companies, more or less competition overall, mergers, demergers, failures, new entrants, the cost of entry, margins, discounts, market segmentation, specialization, niches, prices, market shares, maturity of the market, profitability, distribution patterns, marketing techniques, new customers, customer groupings, suppliers, supplier groupings, cartels, rings, etc.	'The entire market is in decline. By the end of the century we guess that only two or three companies will be left in the industry.' 'The industry seems to be splitting into giants and dwarfs.' 'Technology is driving prices down rapidly. We see the price as low as £5–£8 per unit by Year 5. The cartel of the big producers is likely to collapse within that time.' 'Delivery by road may eliminate rail entirely by Year 10.'
Other changes	You may feel that the five main categories listed above do not include some major areas of concern to your particular company. List them here.	

techniques that can be used in the External Analysis. Later I will return to the fifth category above – changes in the planning team's industry.

Political change

Political change includes changes inspired by politicians at the local level, nationally and on a world scale. These include something as concrete as legislation specifically aimed at a specific industry, or it might be something as intangible as a subtle change in the political atmosphere towards profit-making organizations. For most small businesses the most important ones are local and national; the larger the organization the more its focus of attention will swing to the national and world scenes. Any company which operates or trades in any other nation should consider possible political changes in that specific nation and, for example, European companies should know something of the political changes taking place in the Community. Examples of political threats and opportunities are:

- 'We are sole suppliers to the Army of Armoured Running Rings (ARRs) for the Mk V Battle Tank. The Government has decided to introduce the new Mk VI in Year 4 and this will cause the Army to look at their stock of spare ARRs for the Mk V. We know that they will discover that they have a stock equivalent to 54 years' requirements! There is a serious risk that they will cancel their annual contract with us as soon as they discover this. At any time in the next few years, therefore, we may lose 20 per cent of our turnover and 30 per cent of our profits.'

- 'The local government has finally decided to allow the development of the Northtown Retail Estate Complex. This means that the High Street will be further reduced in importance as a shopping area – a trend that has been going on ever since the C2 DEs started to own cars and held in check only by the local government's desire to preserve the status quo. In many nations the decline of the town centre has proceeded much further than here (in America it is called 'the hole in the doughnut'). Virtually all our business arises from people shopping in the town centre; all our branches are there and our staff live conveniently for this location and not for the new retail estate. We do not yet know what proportion of our customers, mainly C2 DEs, will shop in the High Street versus the new estate.'

- 'New legislation on product liability is scheduled in the next few years. The proposed penalties will be crippling and will make zero defects the only practical policy. Few companies of our size will be able to stand the insurance premiums which have already started to respond to the recent outcry over the Bewick case. Experts are talking of 300 per cent rises.'

- 'The Community proposes to harmonize trade throughout Europe by 1992. We have at present the most serious doubts that the legislation will be agreed by then – certainly the regulations relating to our industry will not. Either they will be rushed through, and botched, or they will be late. We must be ready for both eventualities. This has major implications for our decision, long overdue, as to the correct balance of our business between USA, Europe and the East.'

- 'By the mid 1990s some massive Pan-European companies will already be in place. Even Unilever will seem like a tiddler. If we do not do something soon we will be left behind.'

Economic change

Economic change includes changes at the local level, nationally and on a world scale. Once again, for most small businesses the most important ones are local and national, the larger companies more international, and any company that operates or trades in any nation should be aware of changes in the economic climate there too.

In most nations today there is a plethora of economic forecasts for the current year and many for the next three or five years – the newspapers and financial journals are full of them. Universities, banks, stockbrokers and consultants churn them out by the score on every subject under the sun. Most individual industries also boast official bodies who prepare statistics and forecasts. In other words, most companies do not need to make their own economic or market forecasts. Examples of economic threats and opportunities are:

- 'Our key competitor operates in a region that is in long-term economic decline where pay is low, skilled employees are freely available and rents are cheap. We operate in an area of continued prosperity where pay is high (40 per cent higher than his), rents are double and skills are almost unobtainable. We can see no reason why this dichotomy should not continue for at least five years even if the government launches an economic package for his area. Conditions are so different in the two areas he should be seen as a major competitor although he is, in all other respects, a very inferior operator.'
- 'Our business is heavily influenced by the price of oil. It is impossible to predict what will happen to this commodity over the next few years but the range may be as follows: the price

will not remain below $10 per barrel for more than a few months because below that level the North Sea, Alaska, much of Texas, etc., becomes uneconomic and, with this volume out of the equation the price would inevitably rise again. At the other end of the scale, if the Muslim Fundamentalists "win" in some way against the House of Saud the price could go to almost any level for a while, but it will not remain above $40 for more than a few months because this price would rapidly reopen most of the existing wells in the world and, within a year, new ones would be brought on stream. So we must expect this extreme range of prices and our *strategic* plans must be robust against both limits. For operating plans we will continue to use the range currently agreed: $15 to $25 until further notice.'

- 'Over the past few years the local town has crept nearer to our premises. So far our landlords have kept very quiet but it is clear that the site is worth far more for private housing than it is for light industry. Our property advisers have warned us that the rent may rise tenfold in Year 2 when the rent review is due. This would mean that rent would rise from 1 per cent of our total costs to 10 per cent. Worse, in a few years' time the owners might give us notice to quit which, under the terms of our lease, we would be obliged to do within 12 months. This was a perfectly adequate provision when we moved here, it would be a disaster for us today.'

- 'The entire world market seems set on an expansion which may last for several years – no one I spoke to could think of any reason why the boom in our industry should end. Disposable incomes are rising (for those in jobs), technology is bringing costs down very fast, demand seems set to rise at 7 to 12 per cent per annum according to most of the forecasts in the trade journals, but I am suspicious. We all know what happens to a company growing at 30 per cent per annum when the music stops.'

- 'The period of exchange rate turbulence that has plagued us for many years seems likely to decline now that inflation is down in most of the nations we trade with.'[1]

Social change

Social change includes changes at the local level, nationally and on a world scale. No universal definition of what is a social change has been generally accepted but the examples below illustrate some of the common areas. The number of social forecasts, often specifically designed for organizations going through the corporate planning process, produced by universities and other organizations, is increasing rapidly. Techniques are now developing in this area. For example, the socio-economic groupings – AB, C1, C2, DEs – that have stood demographers in such good stead are being supplemented by other groupings based on values, attitudes and life-styles rather than on 'social class', which, in many nations, is plainly undergoing some remarkable, possibly terminal, changes.

Marketing specialists have long been aware of how social change creates and destroys *product* opportunities. I suspect that not all senior managers have taken on board how these changes also affect the way they should be managing their 'human resources'. Examples of social threats and opportunities are:

- 'Our customers are down-market – mainly C2DE. Most of them are financially unsophisticated and this has meant that in the past we have had to limit ourselves to some very simple financial products which we have sold at very high margins. But increasingly, due to education and greater coverage in the popular media, they are asking more complex and relevant questions and this suggests they are becoming more sophisticated. One consequence is that we may now be able to upgrade some of our products. However, our customers may not tolerate the high margins that we have enjoyed for many years past. Even if they did there is a very great danger, now that we are quite well known in the community, that the media might accuse us of exploiting them.'
- 'Unemployment in this area has recently risen to new heights following the closure of the coal mine. We are now one of the most important employers – an extraordinary situation for such a small company. It will become very much easier to recruit, but far more difficult to dismiss, for the foreseeable future.'
- 'The local community has been invaded by immigrants in the past few years. Racial dissension has begun – and our site is exactly in the middle of this area.'
- 'One possible strategy – to move into defence-related software systems – would cause profound moral offence to several of our key systems analysts. One of them heard of our intention to enter this market under a new company name and stated flatly

that if we did she would leave. These views may come to be shared by an increasing number of young people.'

● 'As the population ages the number of elderly who will require nursing rises while the age group from which we recruit nurses falls. Over the next decade these slowly diverging trends will have a major impact. We expect the over-80s to grow by 50 per cent and the recruitment pool to decline by 20 per cent in the decade. That builds into a huge gap.'

● 'Employees are increasingly aware of how they should be treated by a modern organization. We can hardly claim to be up with the leaders in our employee policies and they are sure to find us wanting sooner or later.'

Technological change

Technological change knows no boundaries so the 'local, national and world scale' is not relevant. For most businesses the most important technological changes are new products, new materials, new methods of producing or distributing the product, new uses for the product and new technologies invading an old industry.

Plainly, the planning team should ask the opinions of any technologists within their company and any outside it who may be able to help. Again, trade journals and technical press will be helpful as will industry research bodies, government and international scientific agencies, and so on. Examples of technological threats and opportunities are:

● 'A major threat is "technological sophistication". As technologies advance, the products themselves, and the research and development facilities required, become increasingly complex and costly. So long as a company expands as fast as the cost of its technology there is no problem but in our case we have not been keeping pace.

'This is exemplified with the PW turbines, where we have gradually been producing fewer units each year. Each unit has a greater added value than the one before mainly due to the advances in electronic management systems. Development costs are nearly twice as high on the modern turbine as on those only three years ago and the commercial and technical risks on each unit are now very much higher than they were. The entire risk profile of the company has changed in the past few years and since there is no sign at all of the relevant technologies slowing down it will continue to do so.'

- 'So far as we can discover there are no major technical developments that may affect us.'
- 'We are plagued by "reverse engineering". A number of our competitors, especially in the East, are pirating our designs by working out from the product what the engineering specifications and production techniques must be and are then producing almost identical copies.'
- 'There is a widespread view in the company that our competitors are all catching us up – it is, after all, nearly seven years since our remarkable leap ahead of them. Drake & Co. may already be ahead of us now and there are rumours that their new range of products will have 20 per cent more power. If so, they will be far ahead of ours.'
- 'Most people in the company see the switch to optical systems as being completely in our favour. The research department estimate that this change will be practical for us in three years while the rest of the industry are thinking in terms of a decade. This appears to represent a major opportunity for our company.'
- 'On-line real-time systems are likely to develop much further: They will become more complex, networks will spread geographically and become more intricate, costs will fall with the rising volume. But all the necessary technologies are already in place for this revolution; no more major technical advances are likely in the next few years. Our detailed technical estimates are as follows . . .'
- 'The computer and its associated systems are becoming as important as management accounts and data processing were a few years ago. The time may come very soon when a 'Systems Manager' will join the top executive team as one of the four or five most important people in the company.'

Forecasting techniques

There are a number of systematic methods for making forecasts. Many of these, especially in the area of technological forecasting are very advanced, but a few of the simple ones are well worth considering. Many of these may be used for any area of change, not merely technological. I have to say that the number of companies actually using *any* of these is very small.

Trend analysis

In essence this is simply the study of the past behaviour of a trend to gauge how it will move in the future.

Suppose the number of fatal accidents per million passenger miles has declined by 12 per cent per annum since 1935 (which, remarkably, it has for American airlines – from one accident per 10 million miles then to one in 3,000 million miles in 1985) then one can reasonably forecast the same trend for the next few years. Moreover, judging by the spread in the actual rate of improvement from year to year in the past, one could even appraise how accurate this forecast might be for any given year or over any given period. (As I have noted before, to estimate the errors in a forecast is as important as making the forecast itself.)

I strongly believe in the value of doing something like this for any trend that is of strategic importance. As a crude guide I believe it is good enough to lay a ruler over the graph of the past trend and, using normal common sense, project it into the future, noting how wide the errors might be.

Very advanced computer programmes exist to separate out any number of trends with respect to any number of factors. My feeling is that none of these are relevant to the sort of forecasts one wishes to make for the broad, general viewpoint one needs in corporate planning and that, as I have said so often, masses of detail tend to cloud the issues and to gild them with spurious accuracy.

You can play with morphological analysis, envelope curves, time series, dynamic modelling and cross-impact analysis, too, if you wish, but be warned: nothing ever happens as you expect. The market for bottled milk has declined in many countries of the world at a steady rate for many years (in England at 4 per cent per annum). Someone should have told the Dutch – in Holland it disappeared almost overnight!

The 'S' curve

In the examples above it would be possible for the trend to continue indefinitely. Many phenomena have no ceilings: wheat yields could, in theory, continue to rise at 1–2 per cent every year for the next fifty years as they have for the past fifty; house prices could continue to rise indefinitely; car engine power output per litre might never cease to soar. Some trends, however, have a natural point of inflection. For phenomena in this category it is sometimes possible to observe a life cycle curve in the form of an 'S' which has a beginning, a period of growth, a mature phase and, perhaps, an ending. If one can discover where one is on this curve one can sometimes forecast what will happen next. Imagine the graph in Figure 8.2 represents the life history of a product.

Figure 8.2   An S curve

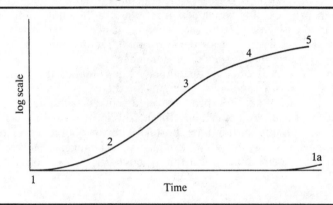

At (1) the product is launched and sells very slowly. Then gradually it becomes accepted in the market and sales rise rapidly for several years (2 to 3). Eventually, however, the market matures – perhaps demand falls to the replacement level, or for some other reason begins to tail off at (4). Finally the market is saturated, or a new product appears at (1a) and demand dies.

This pattern is extraordinarily common. Not only products but whole technologies follow the 'S' curve. It is occasionally possible to predict that a new product or an entire new technology will arise if one can predict that the existing one is approaching a point of inflexion on its 'S' curve life-cycle.

The problem is knowing where you are on the curve and how much further the growth phase has to go before giving way to decline. Where is the petrol engine on the curve, for example, a hundred years after its invention? Experts have been predicting that an entirely new technology will displace it for decades, ranging from diesel and electric motors and rotary engines to steam and nuclear. None of them have happened yet; the petrol engine goes chugging on to ever greater heights of efficiency. One suggestion is that the end of the curve is in sight when return on investment begins to decline (for example if your next product is less profitable than your last, the curve it is on may be about to level off; if the return on your current research project is lower than the last project the technology is near the top).

Sometimes there is a logical end point, a theoretical limit to a technology, perhaps, beyond which one may be sure that the graph cannot progress and which sets a natural point of inflection. But one may easily be caught out; technologies can jump! The transistor did not lie in wait for the valve-manufacturer further up the valve 'S' curve, it was on a different one!

The 'S' curves of some technologies are steeper than others, indicating more rapid development. In theory, if one's product competes with another product on a slower technology, that could be good news. Certainly the life-cycle of most products is today becoming shorter and shorter. The oft-quoted telephone exchange is a case in point: the manual exchange lasted for 50 years, the electro-mechanical for 20, how long will the electronic last?

Delphi

Both the above examples referred to trends – gradual, continuous changes over a long period – but what about forecasting sudden changes or discontinuities? It must be said that trends are difficult enough to forecast, events are nearly impossible.

One simple method, which may not be any more unreliable than other more complex ones, is to ask the views of a number of experts. Suppose one wishes to know if a certain breakthrough in technology might occur within a five-year planning horizon. First, one questions a number of people whose opinion on this subject is considered worth having. Care must be taken to phrase the question accurately. It would not be effective to ask for example: 'When do you think all-weather football will be practical?' Something more like: 'By what year will 20 per cent of professional football games be played irrespective of weather conditions' is required. One should add the supplementary question: 'And what are the reasons for your opinion?'

At this first round the expert's replies will reflect a wide spread of opinion, but at the second round each expert's rationale is circulated to all the others and the same question is asked again. This time each expert will have before him a number of facts he may have learnt from the others (a recent breakthrough in the economics of under-soil heating, for example) and so the spread of their opinions will now become narrower. It is possible to go to a third and more rounds, each time the consensus will sharpen until it reaches the desired level of accuracy. Statistical analysis may be employed throughout the Delphi process.

Scenarios

This is now a well-known forecasting technique. The principle is to recognize that one cannot forecast the future; the best one can do is to examine and list a whole range of trends and events that may occur and then do one's best to devise a strategy that is right for all likely possibilities – or, at least, that is not seriously *wrong* for any of them.

The scenario approach helps to define the 'envelope' of possibilities within which the strategies must maintain the company's performance. Rather than attempt to forecast which political party might win the next election, for example, one describes what might happen if each party won and then one devises a strategy which is right for any of these victories – or, rather, which is not seriously wrong. Thus, a privately run hospital would test its strategies against a left-wing, a right wing and a centre party winning the next election with the likely actions each party might take towards it.

The example describing possible movements in the price of oil, above, is a simple illustration of this technique. A simplified example is also given in the case study described in Chapter 12.

Industry analysis

The four areas for external analysis outlined above will reveal a number of specific elephants. This fifth area – trends and events in the industry itself – should be tackled after these four. I recount a number of typical threats and opportunities that I have seen in recent years.

Examples of changes in an industry:

- 'The industry is extremely mature and margins are under constant pressure; several competitors fail every year. The main threat seems to come from our suppliers. They provide us with nearly 80 per cent of our turnover and we add very little value – just final assembly and packaging. Two of our suppliers have recently acquired two of our competitors so the trend to vertical integration may have already begun. And, we have to admit, their cost of entry is trivial.'
- 'Mergers among our customers began seven years ago during the recession. We then had thirty customers, now we have twelve. If the theory is right we could end up with three. We used to be a major force with considerable bargaining power but now most of our customers are bigger than we are and they can play us against our sixteen competitors. Mergers amongst them are virtually certain – everyone expects Dove & Co. and Pigeon Ltd to merge soon. That will be just the start.'
- 'Since deregulation the industry has been in turmoil. New competitors appear every week but still everyone's business expands. Return on capital is over 25 per cent even for the very large companies (ours is 45 per cent) and so more competitors are bound to pour in over the next few years. At some point all this may crash. Sooner or later the weight of new competitors will become too great, or the boom will fizzle out, or both at once. We have to assume that this will come quite soon – within a very few years probably – and then there will be a shake-out. We anticipate that the winners will be the eight largest and the most highly specialized in the various niches.'
- 'The size of projects is increasing all the time. Even our largest competitors are having to enter collaborative ventures and this is the way we may have to go.'

Some of the answers one needs from this Industry Analysis are:

- What sort of industry are you in? Is it about to die, is it mature, dormant, or about to explode?
- Is it crowded with indifferent competitors or dominated by one superb one?

- Do others want to come in, or is everyone trying to get out?
- What do you need to be successful in it and have you got it?

There are a number of systematic ways of looking at any given industry. A few well known methods of Industry Analysis are briefly described below.

The experience curve

The well-known Experience Curve theory states that as a company gains experience in a product the cost of producing that product will decline. One school claims that there is a quite precise relationship here, namely, 'double the experience and costs will fall by 30 per cent.'

Suppose a company starts making widgets and finds that the first 10,000 cost £100 each to make. The next 10,000 will, according to this theory, cost only £70. The following 20,000 will cost only £50 each. The next 40,000 will cost £35, and so on. Note carefully, the theory does *not* say that costs fall at 30 per cent each *year*; it says 30 per cent each time experience *doubles*. Assuming the same output each year it would take one year, then two years, then four years, then eight, to achieve each 30 per cent drop. It has to be said that not many people believe this '30 per cent' figure – for some products it may be more but usually it is less. What most people do agree, however, is that costs will fall as experience rises. The graph contained in Figure 8.3 illustrates the principle.

Figure 8.3   The experience curve

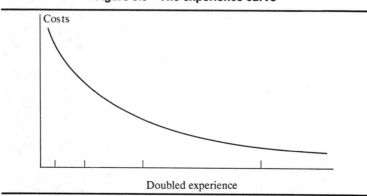

Costs

Doubled experience

How can this be applied to any given company? The main conclusion is that the first company to produce a particular product will be well down the Experience Curve before any competitors appear and by the time they do his costs will be lower than any of the newcomer's. So long as he continues to stay ahead of them in total volume they may *never* be able to produce as cheaply as him.

An interesting question for the planning team to consider when analyzing the future of their company within its industry, therefore, is where does it come on the Experience Curve? If it was one of the first on the scene or if it is one of the biggest producers it might have a chance of competing on costs (because in both cases it will be further along the Curve than most competitors), but if it is small *and* it was late into the industry there is scant chance of success with that strategy.

A second major implication is that one could buy a dominating, or even an unassailable, position in an industry simply by purchasing competitors. The more you buy the further down the Curve you move until no one can touch you for costs. At least one well-known firm of strategy consultants employ this concept as the core of their advice to clients: if you cannot dominate the market you are nowhere, they say. To dominate it you need to be Number One, to be Number One you need to be a long way down the Curve, you get there by acquisition.

A third implication is that if you cut your prices to gain market share this might not, as common sense suggests, result in lower margins. Why not? Because the increased volume you will gain takes you further down the Curve where costs will be lower, thus recouping the lower selling prices. This belief lies at the root of many 'increase share' strategies, so beloved of ambitious marketing men, but which, according to PIMS, can prove disastrous, mainly because competitors will respond, a price war breaks out, and everyone ends up back where the war started with everyone, except the customer, worse off.

Industry maturity

Another way to look at an industry is to ask what stage of development it has reached.

Each industry begins when the first product is launched. The company that launched it may well have made a loss in the earliest stages because of the cost of development, but then its profits soar because its costs would have fallen (the Experience Curve) and there would have been no competitors – an ideal situation!

Eventually, though, competitors would come in and start to erode selling prices. Finally the industry would reach full maturity when there were so many competitors that margins were only sufficient to support the most efficient companies (see Figure 8.4).

Figure 8.4   The four stages of industry

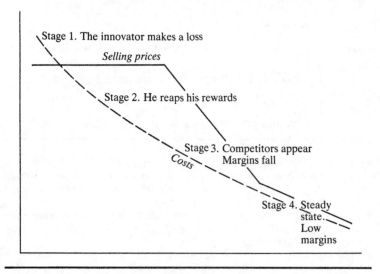

On this analysis the innovator may make a loss in Stage 1 but he will make substantial profits at Stage 2. At Stage 3 his margins will be cut by competition but, because he is further down the Curve than the others, his profits will still be reasonable.

An interesting position develops in Stage 4. The industry leaders, with a high market share, will beat their competitors on price (because they will be further down the Curve) and this implies that only the biggest will survive. (One theory says that at this Stage 4 there will eventually be only *three* companies left in the industry – the three largest). So what happens to all the other competitors in a mature industry? Some dip in and out of profits, many are driven out, but others start again at a new Stage 1 with a new product in a new segment of the main market. And so the whole story begins again in a more specialist segment of the industry.

One important question to any planning team, therefore, is: 'Where is your company *and* your industry on the Experience Curve?' In particular, if their industry is at Stage 4 and if the company is one of the leaders then it may be a sensible strategy to compete on price. If not, the company should search for some alternative strategy such as seeking a new specialist product to exploit in a new segment – that is, start again at Stage 1 of the Experience Curve.

Competition analysis

Another way to look at an industry is to examine the competitive forces at work.

According to M. E. Porter there are five main sources of competition (see Figure 8.5).

Figure 8.5   The sources of competition

- Existing competitors, at home and abroad.
- Suppliers – who are not only striving to cut your margins to their advantage, but may also decide to enter your market by forward integration.
- Customers – who are also trying to use their bargaining power to cut your margins. They may decide to enter your market by backward integration.
- New entrants – who may come from unexpected directions (banks offering auditing services to their corporate clients, for example).
- Substitute products which may appear from a quite different industry – fibre optics displacing copper cables, for example.

The team should think out which of these, in their particular industry, presents a serious threat (or opportunity). It may help to do this if they bear in mind the reasons why competition is stronger in some industries than others. These include the 'barriers to entry' listed in Figure 8.6 which deter competitors from entering any given industry.

Figure 8.6   Barriers to entry

- **Size.** In some industries one just has to be big (making jumbo jets, for example). This limits the number of possible contenders.
- **Customer loyalty.** A new entrant has to woo customers away from existing suppliers. Strong brand loyalty or a well-known, well-established product will be a useful defence against new competitors, but the will and the commitment of resources to defend one's position against new entrants will also deter them.
- **Access to customers.** The new competitor has to persuade retailers, agents and distributors, as well as the final customer, to take his new products.
- **The experience curve.** The fact that the new entrant starts well behind the entrenched competitors means he lacks certain skills and his costs may be very high.
- **Government policy.** Some governments protect some industries as a matter of policy (but others adopt deregulation as a deliberate policy to increase competition).

The team should ask itself which of these defences does their company have against competitors:

- Strong customer loyalty?
- Well-established distribution channels?
- Special expertise that competitors cannot acquire?
- Government protection for the industry?
- Size?
- Capital intensity on a major scale?
- Anything else?

It should also ask where the main thrust of competition will come from:

- Their suppliers?
- Their customers?
- Existing competitors?
- New competitors?
- Substitutes?

Competitor analysis

Among the most serious threats and opportunities that any company faces are its competitors. Most companies do not bother to buy their competitors' products in order to analyze them or even to obtain their published accounts: 'We know them intimately – we compete with them every day of the week.'

'Competitor Analysis' is the name given to a systematic study of what they are doing and what the strategic implications might be. What follows is a summary of some of the ideas of M. E. Porter.

Porter suggests that there are four main areas in which information on competitors might be usefully collected in a systematic manner: their goals, their current strategy, assumptions about them and their capabilities.

First is is necessary to list the competitors who it is intended to study. This certainly includes the more obvious direct competitors, but also firms which may come into the industry through merger or diversification (see Figure 8.5 for sources of competition).

Next consider each competitor's goals. What is he trying to become? The industry leader? Is he attempting to capture a particular niche? How would he behave in a price war? What sort of people run the company – ambitious, lazy, elderly? Are they going to diversify? What financial aims do they have? Do they have a parent company and will it support them in a downturn? Does the parent see them as a cash cow, a star, what?

What strategies do you think each competitor is pursuing? Is he gradually spreading his influence into the North? That new product he launched recently – why that particular product, why was it so different (so similar) to his normal range? Why is he renting such an enormous new office? What did the chairman say in the annual report about that new loan?

Then look at the assumptions that the competitor himself and the rest of the industry makes about him. For example, as a low-cost producer? As having the best technology? Does he see himself as a champion of his local community, as a wheeler-dealer?

Finally look at his strengths and weaknesses, an exercise identical to the strengths and weaknesses analysis described in Chapter 7, except that it is that much more difficult to obtain the data.

Now, once all this data has been assembled it should be woven into the strategies as described in the next two chapters. Thus, if

your company is the leader but the next two competitors, com-
bined, could overtake you, this would have to be stated as one of
the elephants, especially if the above analysis indicated that this
merger was probably in the minds of the two companies. Or,
perhaps an opportunity presents itself because the current leader
has made a strategic error and a new niche market has become
available to you.

None of this will be possible, however, without a systematic
process for gathering competitor intelligence. How is this
achieved? There is nothing magic about it, just systematic: the sales
force, engineering staff, suppliers, distribution agencies, advertising agencies, staff hired from competitors, conferences, trade
journals, journalists, trade associations and stock market analysts
may all provide unpublished data. As for what is published, there
are articles, advertisements for staff, government documents,
public announcements and speeches by managers, regulatory
agency reports, patent records and court records.

Obviously one's marketing director and the marketing department should be in a position to assist with many of these questions –
they normally collect a mass of *tactical* marketing data. Ask them to
extend their examination to this *strategic* data. Every industry
today has its own specialist outside observers. As stated above, the
number of published reports relating to every industry is remarkable. There are surveys by stockbrokers, universities, marketing
consultants, banks, international governmental agencies, trade
journals, the EC, OECD, the World Bank – the list is endless and
endlessly growing.

A Competitor Profile Chart may be useful to summarize the
salient points from the dossier of each competitor along the lines of
Figure 8.7.

Customer analysis

I often hear companies say that their customers are loyal. When I
ask why, no one seems to know. I find this odd. Surely one should
know exactly why your customers come to you and what stops them
going to your competitors?

I wonder if an analysis such as the one above, but for key
customers, would prove rewarding. Their goals, their current
strategy, their strengths and weaknesses would seem to be sensible
areas for a methodical enquiry.

Figure 8.7   Competitor profile: Drakes Ltd

Head Office   Nebraska
Ownership   Duck International Inc
Sales last year   Product A = $44m
                                   Product B = $21m

Profits $4.3m last year after losses
                                   for two years.

Market focus   N. America only, no exports

Strengths	*Weaknesses*
Good production engineers.	Set up for high volume.
Products are made-to-print.	Shallow technical know-how.
Government subsidies from	Limited customer support.
defence contracts.	

Recent events
Their failure on the Penn Contract is rumoured to have cost them
$7m. Their balance sheet is now weak and they are unlikely to try
anything on this scale again.

Strategies
Their position could be bad enough for them to look round for merger
(Goslings?). If not, they will surely avoid hi-tech adventures and stick
to current contracts in USA.

Product opportunity analysis

The idea of forming a matrix or table is most helpful in all these
systematic surveys. For example, suppose there are a number of
possible product opportunities in a number of related markets. It
may help to sort out and to rank some of these by drawing up a table
such as the one contained in Figure 8.8, although one should
always design one's own version to suit one's situation.

The planning team meetings

Because the threats and opportunities analysis is so much more
extensive than the strengths and weaknesses analysis it will require
several meetings of the team.

Figure 8.8   Product opportunities for a financial services company

Product opportunity	Market opportunity	Ease of Entry
Traditional mortgage lending.	Market booming. Profitability declining. Building societies losing grip on customers.	Difficult.
Secured personal lending.	Buoyant market.	Customer base development offers good opportunity.
Commercial lending.	Unknown.	Unknown.
Credit card.	Market maturing.	Very strong, large, entrenched competitors.

The first one will probably be with the other senior executives in the seminar at which the key external issues will be identified but, inevitably, not adequately described. The second will be a few days after this where the team will probably decide to call for special reports on a number of these issues either from specialist working parties inside the organization or from outside experts.

If they have called for a number of major reports the planning team may need to meet several more times before they are satisfied that they have both a complete list of strategic items and that each one has been adequately described, complete with the likely range of error and uncertainty. At their final meeting they may also like to rank each item by probability and by impact. That is, rank them according to the chances of the threat or the opportunity actually taking place *and* by the impact it would have on the company if it did.

They should not try to be too scientific about it, however. It really is very difficult to put probability figures on to such events as which political party is going to win the general election in Year 3. So classifying a trend or event as 'High', 'Medium' or 'Low' (H,M,L) is the best that mortals can do both for the probabilities and the impacts. If they follow this idea then the various threats and opportunities will be classified like this:

HH   This is obviously an enormously important threat or opportunity because it is both very likely to occur *and* will have a great impact on the company. Plainly it is something of such outstanding importance that the strategy which they devise in Stage Seven *must* take it into account. Without it the strategy would be useless.

HM or MH Also very important because it is either highly probable *and* will have a considerable impact on the company, or it is quite likely to occur *and* would have a major impact if it did. The strategy *must* take account of *any* threats and opportunities to which they have given either one or two Hs.

LH   This is a trend or event which they think is unlikely to occur but they believe it would have a most severe impact if it did. So while they may not have to include it in the main strategies they *must* do something about it – perhaps they will have to devise a 'disaster plan' or a 'contingency plan' (see Chapter 10).

HL, LM,   If they can include these in their main strategies then
ML, MM,   they should do so, but these are probably not sufficiently important to need further very serious consideration in the corporate planning exercise and might be better dealt with ad hoc by the company's other senior executives.

LL   Not worthy of further consideration in the corporate planning exercise. Ask an executive to deal with these operationally.

Some examples

When they feel ready to do so they should summarize their final views on all their threats and opportunities somewhat as below;

A manufacturing company

	Items	*Ranking*	
		Probability	Impact
•	Threats		
	The home market is mature and is now declining. Forecasts by the government indicate that demand will fall by 2–6 per cent each year for the next five years. Tax changes will, if anything, accelerate this.	H	H

Foreign competitors are now operating here at extremely low prices and this trend seems likely to continue. They could take a substantial share at the lower end of the market – perhaps 30 per cent by Year 5. M H

Software costs seem likely to rise again in the near future. They are already 7 per cent of our total costs and could go as high as 12 per cent. H M

- Opportunities.
Over the past few years the top end of the market has fragmented. We expect this trend to continue and that a large market for many new high-priced, high-margin variants of the basic product will appear throughout the developed world. H H

The economy is likely to grow steadily for several more years. Experts see disposable incomes rising very fast (perhaps 3–6 per cent p.a.) and this will fuel demand for high-priced products in this country. Most developed nations seem likely to share in this trend. H H

Remarkable advances have been made recently in technology which lowers the price of our product. But the computer design and manufacturing systems that are now being developed will give the same boost to the top end of the market. H M

The trend to part-time home-working seems likely to continue. Its effect will be to cut our direct and indirect costs substantially. M H

A non-profit-making organization

- Opportunities.
There will be a rapid growth in the number of clients due to government legislation. We expect requests for services to increase by 25 per cent over the next two or three years.

There will also be a shift towards the larger organizations in the south of the country.

The recent decision to delegate much more to the regional offices is working well. We see this as an opportunity to solve many of our head office problems and deficiencies.

- Threats.

A private sector organization has obtained permission from the government to offer services to the same clients – to do exactly what we do – and has already started to recruit staff. We have been told that their fees will be substantially lower than ours.

The decline in government funding, together with the above competition pushing down service fees, presents a major funding problem. We could lose 50 per cent of our income in the next five years.

We have been warned by the government that a marked downturn in the incidence of service may occur beyond Year 3 if their present legislative intentions are maintained.

Over the past decade a number of the bodies represented on our Council have declined in national importance, while others which have gained in significance have no place on it. There is a growing problem here: when offering service we have to appear to be even-handed but the organizations that are represented on the Council resent us offering service to non-members.

With the completion of this stage the data-collecting part of the corporate planning process is complete. All the elephants, both internal and external, should now be known, listed and fully described. The planning team should now move on to discussing the alternative strategies that are available to deal with the overall strategic situation that they have now revealed.

Summary

The suggestion made in this chapter is that having invited the top three management levels to describe the strengths and weaknesses of the organization – something I believe they will achieve more effectively than anyone else – one should then ask them to attempt the External Appraisal as well.

They will not do this as effectively as the Internal Appraisal; the areas to be covered are too vast to make this a practical proposition. They should be invited to *identify* the threats and opportunities, but the planning team will have to call on other methods to *describe* them.

A considerable number of techniques for forecasting and for the analysis of one's industry have been devised. The suggestion here is that these should be used although not in quite the detail proposed by their authors. The reason for this is that they, the authors, each believe their approach represents the complete corporate planning exercise and that the full weight of their methodology should therefore be employed. I am suggesting that in fact these are just segments – albeit very important ones – of a corporate plan and that many other pieces go to make the complete jigsaw.

In general it will be the planning assistant and the members of specialist working parties who use these techniques, not the planning team.

I believe the threats and opportunities analysis should include a survey of five main areas in any of which any organization may find issues of strategic importance. Once located, listed and described they should be ranked by probability and by impact.

The Fulmar Life Assurance Society

Corporate Plan for Fulmar Life Assurance Society
Summary Page 5. Threats and opportunities

Threats

- The removal of the tax advantages that life assurance currently enjoys.
- Changes in the way life companies are taxed.
- Competition from financial institutions not at present in the market. Some very large with economies of scale.
- Agents, now our main source of business, may be by-passed by new routes.
- Change in commission structure: rise in rates.
- Technology: we lag now, we could fall far behind.
- Declining margins.

Opportunities

- Personal 'portable' pensions.
- Become a financial supermarket.
- New methods of selling, especially to the mass market.
- Products to fill the gaps in our range.
- Europe: harmonization by 1992?
- Technology: an essential route to efficiency.

CHAPTER 9

Alternative Strategies

With the end of the External Appraisal the data collection stage of the corporate planning process is complete.

The team will now know how urgent the strategies are, they will know how large the gaps are, they will know their outstanding abilities and disabilities, they will know something of the trends in the world around them. They are still not ready to make the final strategic selections, however, before they do that there are two more steps to take.

The first is to stand back and review what they have now learned about their organization. What does it all mean? How does it all fit together? Does it tell a lucid and consistent story? Does it lead to any obvious conclusions? The second is to list all the various alternative strategies – the more innovative and imaginative the better – that might possibly help them in their situation.

In this chapter I shall first describe how the team can ensure that their strategies will be relevant to the needs of their organization, then how to enhance the diversity and variety of their strategies. I shall end by discussing a number of strategies which I have come to distrust.

The overall strategic totality

What the team has been doing, in the data collection stages, is to build up an overall picture of the company within its long-term environment. The final set of strategies which they must soon devise must meet the specification contained in Figure 9.1.

This is a very demanding specification. While it is important for any set of strategies to be fresh and inventive, it is even more critical

Figure 9.1 Specification for a set of strategies

- It must be imaginative, strictly practical and relevant to their precise strategic situation.
- It must give their company a very good chance of hitting Tsat and even exceeding it.
- At the same time, it must not expose their company to such risks that its performance might fall below Tmin – a two-dimensional strategy, bringing success *and* avoiding failure when things go wrong.
- It must make full use of all the company's most impressive strengths, certainly all those they ranked with an 'A'.
- It must correct or neutralize all major weaknesses, certainly those ranked 'A'. It must not build on these weaknesses, nor even those ranked 'C'.
- It must either eliminate or reduce the impact of all the threats they ranked as 'HH' and those with any 'H' in their ranking.
- It must exploit any opportunity ranked 'HH' and perhaps any with an 'H' in their ranking.

---

that they be truly relevant. Nothing will be gained if the team devotes its creative talents to devising wonderful new strategies that have no contact with the company's real situation. There is bound to be one permutation of strategies that will come closer than any other to meeting this specification and *this* is the one they will have to find. Let them use their ingenuity to find this set.

Relevance comes first, then creativity. To channel their thinking into the relevant direction the team may find it useful to set out everything they have concluded so far in a table called 'The Total Strategic Situation' (see Figure 9.2)

For the sake of brevity only about ten 'strategic factors' (strengths, threats, and so on) are shown in Figure 9.2. In a real-life company one would probably see twenty or more of these. As soon as they have drawn up this table it will begin to dawn on the planning team that in fact there are going to be remarkably few strategies that are relevant. Most of the strategic ideas that members of the team might have been harbouring, perhaps for years, often with passionate conviction, will at once be seen not to be relevant.

Figure 9.2 Total strategic situation for Crake and Bunting

Year 5 targets	Tmin profits = £1.2m Tsat profits = £1.8m
	Tmin RoC = 5% real Tsat RoC = 10% real
Year 5 Forecasts	Fpes profits = £0.9m Fopt profits = £1.3m
	Fpes RoC = 4% Fopt RoC = 7%
Gaps	Recent performance has been poor and although our RoC gaps are not bad we certainly require some improvement. We are not in a high-risk situation but we must have an extra £0.3m profits to be sure of Tmin by Year 5. We need an extra £1m to make sure of Tsat.
Strengths	All aspects of our marketing are ranked (A). The distribution of some of our products through merchants (B).
Weaknesses	The factory overhead costs (A). No facilities for product development (A). Several obsolescent products (B). No experience of operations abroad (B).
Threats	Continuing decline of our industry (HH). Emerging overcapacity of production facilities (HH). Foreign competitors (HM).
Opportunities	Huge markets abroad, some very unstable politically (HM). Home market ready for some new products (HM).

If their strategic situation is not already clear to them the team may be able to sharpen the focus as follows:

(1) For the time being, in order to simplify the task, leave the targets, forecasts and gaps out of the discussion. Targets, forecasts and gaps usually determine the *size* and *urgency* of the strategies that are going to have to be chosen, and so they are very important and must be taken fully into account when the final strategic decisions are made but, for the time being, ignore them.

(2) Consider only the other strategic factors – the strengths and weaknesses, threats and opportunities. These will determine the *nature and direction* of the strategies.

(3) Summarize these strategic factors, using just a word or two for each, in a Cruciform Chart to demonstrate their balance.

Figure 9.3 shows the Cruciform Chart which Crake and Bunting prepared from the data in Figure 9.2.

Figure 9.3   The cruciform chart for Crake and Bunting

S		W	
Marketing	A	Overheads	A
Merchants	B	Development	A
		Dying products	B
		Abroad	B

T		O	
Declining industry	HH	Abroad	HM
Over-capacity	HH	New products home	HM
Foreign competitors	HM		

The remarkable simplicity of the chart often reveals features and nuances that have previously been buried by the volume of data.

Notice first the unfortunate balance: not only are there more weaknesses than strengths but there are also more threats than opportunities. So in terms of the *number* of items the balance looks rather depressing. But look also at the weight and importance of the items as shown by the rankings – it is clear that in this case both the number *and* the weight of the weaknesses and threats out-balance the strengths and opportunities. There are a total of two A and two B weaknesses against one A and one B strength, and five Hs against two Hs for the threats and opportunities.

With an adverse balance like this one would not expect Crake and Bunting to have done too well in recent years and the gaps statement in Figure 9.2 did make this point. The flavour of the strategies that this company would adopt, therefore, is likely to be rather defensive: both the gaps and the chart are against it.

It will be appreciated that this approach is merely a method of getting the team to think about all the strategic factors together in a single overall picture of their company's strategic situation. There is nothing magic about it, the Cruciform Chart will not answer their strategic questions like some miraculous computer, but it might help to establish the *tone* or flavour or accent of their strategies. If their Cruciform Chart shows a disappointing balance then they should be prepared to have to select a set of rather defensive strategies; the more favourable the balance the more adventurous they may be able to be. The gaps usually reinforce these messages.

The Cruciform Chart might reveal much more than this, however. No doubt the team noticed in the chart above that the word 'abroad' appeared in two sections, in the weaknesses and in the opportunities. (It occurs again in threats in the words 'foreign competitors'.) Whenever the same factor appears more than once in a Cruciform Chart one may be sure that this feature will lie at the central core of their strategy.

There are also usually some interesting relationships between some of the items. In this case Crake and Bunting is good at marketing, the home market is receptive to some new products *but*, alas, the company has no means of developing new products. That trio of market area statements cries out for a solution. There is another trio: factory overheads are high, there is over-capacity in the industry and the industry is still in decline – obviously Crake and Bunting's production costs can only get worse as the industry degenerates. Costs will rise as volume declines; as the product becomes more expensive, volume will decline again.

It is clear that Crake and Bunting's strategies are going to have to be rather defensive *and* they are going to have to address the main areas of concern: production and new product development (NPD).

The key strategic issues

The team should now try to reach a clear and concise conclusion as to exactly what the final list of elephants is going to be. They have so far been allowed to play with a couple of dozen elephants or 'strategic factors', now they must get down to the very few that form the core of the strategic situation. As I said in the first chapter, where I explained what corporate planning is, at the core there is sometimes only one of these key strategic issues, often two, occasionally a few, never more than six.

What is required here is a crisp, clear statement of the conclusions of the planning team concerning their overall strategic situation. Note that no strategic conclusions are required yet. What is required is a statement of the strategic problems. If there is only one key issue then a statement as stark as this is sometimes required:

- 'We are in a real mess. Unless a miracle occurs the whole industry will disappear in a few years.'

- 'The recent licensing agreement with Eagle – the industry leader – is a breakthrough for us. It will result in a prolonged, massive growth for our company.'

Or perhaps the salient feature to have emerged in their minds is that the company should protect itself against some future shock, in which case they might say:

- 'We have for years been heavily dependent on exporting to Germany. So far we have been lucky with the exchange rate, but at any time in the next few years this might turn against us and this could decimate our profits. We must do something to protect ourselves against this.'

However, most companies seem to face more than just one key issue and I can think of many cases where there were two:

(1) We have failed to bring sufficient talent on to the main board. This is becoming acutely urgent in view of the age of the members – all over 60.
(2) One division has plainly not performed as well as the others and seems unlikely to do so. As it forms over half group turnover the matter is serious in the extreme. A recession in this industry may occur in less than two years time.

(1) Our parent company is not only our banker but is also our major customer. They constantly complain about our service to them.
(2) Our facilities are poor, the computer is aged and must be replaced soon. The offices are threadbare – all because the parent has starved us of capital. There is nothing wrong with the product, but we cannot improve service without consider-able investment. So we have a vicious circle: our service is poor so the parent will not trust us with further capital: we cannot improve the service without more capital.

(1) The company has far too many types of product. It is absurd for a company of our size to try to do five different things to the same standard as our major competitors.

(2) Apart from the planning team no other managers have any qualifications, no one has ever been on a management course, no one knows what marketing is: they have all come up from the shop floor. This company is becoming too large to be managed by amateurs.

Once this most important step has been made – stating the key strategic issues that have been distilled from all the previous stages – the team should begin its search for imaginative solutions.

Extending the list of strategic ideas

By this stage in the process most of the strategic ideas that the team will have been considering will now be seen to be incapable of meeting the company's strategic specification. What is needed now is an opportunity to enhance the residue of ideas, a chance to widen the list of alternative strategies.

The team will not be well served, however, if they merely allow their imaginations to run amok: really effective strategies demand brilliance *and* relevance. A strategy sparkling with novelty is useless unless it also fits the specification. One of my criticisms of strategy formulation by certain consultants is that although their ideas are extremely intelligent, and even brilliant, they are not geared to the needs of the client.

It should be possible to guarantee relevance if the various strategic ideas that the team have so far considered are listed under each Key Issues Statement, perhaps on the lines of Figure 9.4.

Figure 9.4   Possible strategies for Godwit & Co

A   Major strategies
It is clear that our strategies should be related to these two key issues and should take account of the current relatively difficult financial situation;

(1)   correcting our poor production facilities at Northtown, and
(2)   reducing the company's dependence on Product P.

Taking these two key areas in turn the alternatives we have so far considered include:

(1) The production facilities:
    (a) Spend £1.5m on a new factory.
    (b) Spend £0.5m on new equipment.
    (c) Lease a new factory near Southtown and install £1m new equipment.
    (d) Close down the facilities in Northtown, sell them and lease new ones in Northtown.

(2) Our over-dependence on Product P:
    (a) Increase the selling price of Product P and cut the price of Product Q.
    (b) Launch several new products similar to Q.
    (c) Licence a Product R which is unlike P or Q
    (d) Withdraw Product P from the southern area where competition is increasing.

B   Other strategies
A number of other miscellaneous strategies have also been mentioned:

(3) Improve financial controls especially in Product Development.
(4) Abandon sales in the South entirely, concentrate more resources in the North-East of the country.
(5) Appoint someone to supervise training, recruitment, pay, etc.

It is important for the team to remember why they are being asked to expand their list of strategic ideas: in a very short time they are going to have to make a number of decisions which may determine the course of their company for many years into the future. The direction they choose ought to be selected from as wide and as imaginative a range of strategies as it is possible to conceive. It would indeed by a sad outcome if, in a couple of years time, someone suggested a brilliant new strategy that they could have thought of now!

Also, of course, the company that is first with a new idea sometimes gains a remarkable advantage. This is true not only of new product ideas but *any* new idea. The company which first offered shares to its employees, first used computers to schedule the factory, first used the 'poison pill defence' against being taken over – all these ideas gave them an edge.

There are a number of techniques for widening and enlivening an otherwise rather dull and narrow list of strategies. Some of these are excellent and yield several bright new ideas while others might yield nothing at all – one can only try them to see if they suit one's particular circumstances. They are:

(1) 'What business are we in?'
(2) Opinion surveys.
(3) Imitation.
(4) Variations on a theme.

It will be interesting to see how the above company (Godwit & Co.) was able to enhance its list of strategies by moving through some of these alternative-generating techniques.

As with all the stages in the corporate planning process, the team would be well advised to draw a number of other people into these discussions.

Method (1) 'What business are we in?'

The aim here is to try to widen the definition of one's business activity. For example, imagine a company which describes itself as 'a pencil manufacturer'. The alternative products this company might produce would be longer pencils, fatter ones, harder, softer, round, square, personalized pencils, red ones, blue ones – frankly, a rather obvious and uninspiring list. But suppose the definition of this business was widened to 'graphic materials'. Now it could consider not just pencils but pens, inks, artists' brushes, paper, paints, maybe even word-processors.

Other examples might be:

Present product or service	*Wider definition of business*
Electric lamp bulbs	Illumination
Wallpaper	Interior decorating
Rat poison	Pest control
Pumps	Fluid engineering
Banking	Financial services

It is important to note the status accorded to this 'What business are we in?' question. In some textbooks it has been promoted to a method for deciding diversification. Thus the wallpaper company above, having recognized that wallpaper is a subset of interior decorating, might be tempted to become a paint manufacturer. My impression is that a number of companies, presumably managed by idiots, have swallowed this kind of advice.

A company making wooden pallets for fork-life truck operations tried to decide which business it was in: making pallets or making things out of wood. If it was the former it ought to diversify into making pallets out of materials other than wood; if the latter maybe it should make cheap furniture. In my view, both answers were wrong. They did not have the abilities to tackle either.

Another company, making doors, was solemnly advised by a well-known business school that it 'was in the business of filling holes in walls'. Mercifully this was not sufficiently meaningful to lead anywhere, but such was the stature of this school that the company would have followed its advice wherever it had led.

Another company, who assembled venetian blinds, could not decide whether it was in the business of keeping the sun out, in light assembly or in interior decorating. This merely illustrates that most companies are in several businesses at once.

In my view, the question, 'What business are we in?' is entirely valid as an aid to thought. As an automatic strategy generator it is potentially disastrous because it entices one to go rushing off into fresh green pastures, regardless of one's ability to do so, and it does not always work. I have just seen it used by a company supplying a small range of 'personal freshness' goods to supermarkets. The obvious cliché is 'We are in the hygiene business' and so they decided to increase their range of hygiene goods. Later they realized that, in fact, they were also highly adept at satisfying their customers' warehousing needs. But they did not recognize this when they asked themselves the 'What business?' question – that just led to hygiene products; they only realized it when they asked 'What are our key strengths?'

As a generator of strategic ideas it is sometimes prolific. If any organization has not asked itself this question recently it should do so now.

Method (2) Opinion surveys

The suggestion here is that the team carefully and deliberately makes a list of people whose opinion they respect and goes and ask them what they think the company should do. They will have to take some trouble to explain the key strategic issues to them.

Suitable people might include their own colleagues in the hierarchy, industrial journalists, suppliers, customers, academics, and, for small businesses, friends and family. So this is a very elementary suggestion – but one can be too close to a problem to see the best way out for oneself. It is a method made more powerful if one goes about it systematically; list the people who might have useful ideas and question them each methodically.

Method (3) Imitation

Being the first in the field is a splendid strategy for many companies: 'innovation', 'market leader', 'trend-setter' are words that spring enthusiastically from the pages of management textbooks. However, unless a company happens to have that particular spark of genius that allows it to take the lead, an attempt to gain leadership could prove an expensive failure. If one cannot lead, why not simply follow? In other words, the team should look around to see what their most successful competitors are doing and copy them.

If their most successful competitor has recently acquired some real estate they should ask why. If he has just opened an office in Japan, launched a share option scheme for his senior staff, closed down his foundry, offered credit cards, or whatever, the team should ask if these might be useful new directions in which to take their company. They should survey successful companies in similar fields as well, not just direct competitors.

Once again, the key is to be methodical. Make a list of companies that are deemed to be leaders, study what they are doing, note the relevance to one's own company's strategic situation. Be systematic.

It goes without saying that if a company does have the spark of originality, then it should employ it with vigour. Even if it does not have it, creativity can be deliberately developed. One very sensible strategy would be to alter the culture of any organization that is not innovative so that it becomes so (see Attitude Strategies later). If this spark is not there and cannot be fostered, then a non-innovative strategy is indicated. The world is full of companies who have not taken a glamorously inventive route but have stayed steadfastly and boringly good at what they already do – and enormously profitable.

Method (4) Variations on a theme

The idea here is to take all one's strategic ideas and to develop themes and variations on the originals.

For example, suppose a company in Eastville has listed one possible strategy as: 'open a branch office in Westville'. Variations on this might include:

- 'Open another branch in Eastville instead.'
- 'Double the size of the existing branch in Eastville.'
- 'Share a branch in Westville with Competitor A.'
- 'Employ an agent in Westville.'

Or try 'doubling and halving'. Suppose a strategy has been proposed to miniaturize a product. One might consider such variations as 'make a micro version' or 'double it' or 'make a jumbo version'.

Or suppose one possible strategy is 'increase the selling price'. Consider such variations as 'double the price over the next two years', or perhaps even 'quadruple it'. Or instead of 'we must close two branch offices in each of the next three years' try 'close all branches and sell through agents'.

The team could try a 'brainstorming session'. It is claimed that these sessions can yield dozens, perhaps hundreds, of new ideas. Experience suggests that very few of them will, on inspection, be found to be practical and relevant, but it may be worth doing even if just one idea proved useful.

Notice how much more imaginative the list of Godwit's strategies have become after using some of the above simple techniques (see Figure 9.5). Notice too, that all the new ideas relate to the key areas of concern. The last thing Godwit's planning team needs at this stage is a mass of ideas, however scintillating and innovative, if they are not relevant to their overall strategic situation.

It is interesting to notice how much wider and more imaginative some of the new added ideas are compared with the rather dull and narrow-minded list which Godwit & Co. made before they went through this stage. Even more interesting is the new strategic conclusion that seems to be emerging: instead of fiddling about with minor modifications to the factory and to the two products, the planning team is now thinking of not correcting the factory problems at all but getting out of production altogether and becoming essentially a sales organization with a much wider range of related

Figure 9.5

Final list of strategic ideas for Godwit & Co.

A   Major strategies
It seems clear that our strategies should be related to two main areas of concern: (1) correcting our poor facilities, and (2) reducing the company's dependence on Product P.

(1)   The production facilities
Alternatives considered so far include:

    (a)   Spend £1.5m on new factory.
    (b)   Spend £0.6 on new equipment.
    (c)   Lease a new factory near Southtown and install £1m new equipment.
    (d)   Close down the existing factory, sell it and lease a factory in Northtown.
Add: (e)   Close down the existing factory and licence a company in Hong Kong to manufacture for us (this is what Competitor C has done). (We might even go to the same Hong Kong supplier as Competitor C because they will now have the necessary know-how and may have ironed out some of the problems.)
    (f)   Halve the size of our Northtown factory. Sell half the site. Buy half our requirements in the world open market.
    (g)   Spend £4m to fully automate the Northtown factory to the highest world standards.

(2)   Our overdependence on Product P:
Alternatives so far considered include:

    (a)   Increase the selling price of Product P and cut the price of Product Q.
    (b)   Launch several new products similar to Q.
    (c)   Licence a Product R which is unlike P or Q.
    (d)   Withdraw Product P from the southern area where competition is likely to increase.
Add: (e)   Redefine our business to include products such as R and S as well as P and Q. Do not manufacture these ourselves, of course – buy them in.
    (f)   Cease to be manufacturers. Become merchants for products P, Q, R, and S. Expand geographically.
    (g)   Become leaders in Product P – stop worrying about our overdependence on Product P!

B   Other strategies
A number of other miscellaneous strategies have also been mentioned:

(3) Improve financial controls, especially in product development.
(4) Abandon sales in the South entirely; concentrate more resources in the North-East of the country.
(5) Appoint someone to supervise training, recruitment, pay, etc.

Add: (6) Offer share options to Tom, Dick, Harry and George. Split the company into three geographical profit centres under Tom, Dick and Harry; George to be Group Finance Director.
(7) Competitor D has installed a new IBM information system especially developed for this industry. It would suit us.

---

products selling into a wider geographical area. The managing director also thinks that the company could be run on a day-to-day basis by his three senior colleagues with himself and his finance manager, George, retaining overall control of the company at the centre.

Finally, having listed all the alternatives that have come out of the use of these techniques, the planning team should then eliminate all the strategies which they feel will not be practical in their strategic situation. They should try to reduce this residue to just half a dozen or so. A very few of these will relate to the core of the strategic situation while the others will relate to the more peripheral concerns. I shall describe this selection process in the next chapter.

I have to add that, in practice, very few of the ideas that come out of this stage – enhancing the alternatives – will turn out to be relevant to the company's strategic situation. Indeed, there will be very few strategic ideas, from whatever source, that are seen to be relevant. This is because the specification is now so tight, so precise, that only very few possible strategies can pass the relevance test. (Mathematicians will recognize the term 'Degrees of Freedom' here.)

The planning team is now ready to move into the final stage of strategy selection described in the next chapter.

Some classic strategies

In my view, all planning teams should be on the alert for a number of strategies that have attracted considerable popular attention. Some of these are excellent and powerful – I shall discuss these in the next chapter – but there are several to which I have developed some feelings of apprehension. I recommend that teams who find any of these in their lists at this stage should carefully consider whether to exclude them. I hasten to remind the reader that my specialism is not devising strategies for clients but devising a system for clients to determine their own strategies. I am not a strategy consultant, only a process consultant, so the remarks below should be treated with some reserve.

Diversification

Diversification is the *wrong* strategy for most companies. One problem with this strategy is that when a company moves into a new field it begins competing with companies who have been in it for a long time and who will beat any newcomer (because they will be much further down the Experience Curve) *unless* it has some remarkable ability that they do not have. This reason for being wary of diversifying is well known.

Another problem is that the resources (especially top management time) spent on moving into the new field of business will not be available to the existing business. This may result in the company falling behind in its core business and meanwhile its current competitors, who are not diversifying, will still be putting *all* their resources into their core business. It will not be long before they beat the diversifying company in his own back yard. If he runs into trouble in the new area *and* is overtaken in his traditional business as well, that could be very unpleasant. This argument – the effect on the existing business of deflecting resources into a new area – is seldom noted in the literature, but must be counted a major anxiety.

A third reason is that diversification may sometimes be used as an excuse for not tackling the problems in the current business.

The general rule is, do not diversify. However, there are two, perhaps three, good reasons for diversifying:

(1)   When a company has built up such a surplus of resources

(money in the bank, management skills, technical expertise, or whatever) that it would be impractical to employ them all in their existing business area for the foreseeable future. If the team thinks they can stay ahead of their present competitors in their present area of business *and at the same time* can channel some resources into the new area, then diversification may be a sensible strategy.

(2) When the prospects for the existing business is so poor that it makes no sense to continue investing resources into it, not even into a related niche. In this case there may be no alternative to diversifying and, provided the move is taken early enough it may be successful. If it is late, however, and the company has already entered a decline, then the diversification will be made from a position of weakness – hardly a good base for a venture into the unknown – and this will result in a period of very great danger to the company.

In both these cases the diversification should be as close to the existing business as possible and should be capable of employing at least one key strength so that, when things go wrong, as they certainly will in a field that is new to them, the company will have some relevant skill to help them get out of trouble.

Some experts state that it may help to acquire an existing company in the new business area rather than expand into it from scratch. In that way, they suggest, it is possible to acquire the necessary skills in the new area. But this may miss the point, the point being that when things go wrong *the diversifying company* does not have the skills. One of the things that may go wrong is that the management of the acquired company will fail – or leave – and then it will be *their* management that is called upon to put it right – but they know nothing about it.

A third acceptable reason for diversifying is:

(3) When the team wishes to build a conglomerate. The definition of a conglomerate is that none of its businesses have any intended links (i.e. there is no synergy) with any others. The advantage of this form of structure is that it is robust – no single event can cause it great damage. It is a perfectly legitimate form of business although it does require special management skills.

I am aware that diversification is widely recommended by other consultants. My concern is that it has acquired a superficial gloss and glamour which some planning teams may find attractive. There most certainly are occasions when a company should diversify, I am asking only that the alternatives – moving into a niche market within the existing core business, for example – are not lost sight of.

My experience firmly shows this: the list of strengths and opportunities that most planning teams find in Stages 4 and 5 are usually so exciting that any thoughts they may have had on diversification disappear without trace.

Acquisitions

Textbooks on corporate planning usually contain a major section on acquisition as a means of growth and diversification, but these are generally written with larger companies in mind. As a rule, acquisition is far less appropriate for small companies. This is partly because most large companies are quoted and so may use 'paper' to finance their purchases. It is partly because large companies are owned by shareholders willing to sell out at an economic price – which the owners of small businesses often are not because they value their independence too highly. It is also because of the way income and capital is taxed for institutions and individuals. So, while there are no concrete rules, acquisitions are generally a less appropriate method of expansion for the smaller company.

I sometimes wonder if it is an appropriate strategy for any company. A number of studies suggest that most companies which have acquired others and have been acquired show no improvment in the various significant ratios – market share of the post-merger company, profit on sales, return on capital, growth of earnings per share or return on the outlay for the bid. It continues apace, however, and it seems unlikely that any activity that is so widespread can be solely due to corporate perversion. Even so, over half of all the acquisitions made by the largest companies in America during 1950 to 1980, and 75 per cent of the acquisitions made in a field unrelated to the acquirer, were later divested. That is a devastating failure rate yet still they do it – not just the ignorant, but huge, professionally run companies too.

While I remain suspicious of it in general, I certainly concede that a most cogent reason for making an acquisition is to augment some *specific* strength or opportunity or to elude some *specific* weakness or threat. The more precisely one has defined the specific reason for acquiring a specific company, and the more accurately the acquired company meets this specified feature, the more likely is the acquisition to be successful. Once again, this brings into focus the importance of the Internal and the External Analysis. To acquire a company in order to correct a specific weakness or exploit a specific opportunity depends on having carried out this exercise correctly in the first place.

In one case a company seriously considered acquiring another in order to obtain their very attractive range of products. The chief executive finally decided against it: 'I do not see why I should buy a whole company just to get these products,' he concluded. 'Why should I buy the chief executive (we've got one of those), the chief executive's secretary, the secretary's wordprocessor . . . Moreover, we know he has trouble with his employees. Why should we buy a discordant labour force?' What he did instead was to license this competitor's products.

I suspect that this chief executive's remark is an important comment on the concept of 'synergy' or '2 + 2 = 5'. This suggests that if two complementary businesses are put together the result will surpass the two separately.

One can imagine two companies in the same business, one dominant in the North and the other in the South, merging to make use of the fact that they both have certain skills but neither can penetrate each other's area; put them together and make use of the synergy. Or a company running hotels merging with one running hospitals. In some cases synergy certainly occurs, in others two and two make three because of the costs of the merger, the unwieldy size of the merged organization or because the two are less compatible in other matters, such as their corporate cultures. Because the theory of 'synergy' does not specifically allow for these very common difficulties, the concept is open to misuse.

Synergy is not further discussed here, partly because it is thus flawed, but also because it is subsumed in the much wider concept of seeking a strategy that accords with a company's 'total strategic situation'. This prescription not only reveals synergistic opportunities but much else besides, as will be seen in Chapter 10, including strategies that are perfectly valid even though no synergy is involved. A merger can, for example, be valid with no synergy at all; merely to reduce competition or alter a perceived risk is sometimes a good enough reason to put two companies together. I imagine the creation of a true economic community in Europe will necessitate the building of some immense organizations by acquisition but the motivation will not be synergy so much as the need to match the size of the market.

This leads me to comment on Strategic Business Units or SBUs. An SBU is a grouping of operations in the same area of business, which have been brought together for some good reason, including that of synergy. Thus all groups of companies have a portfolio of businesses; as new businesses are acquired these will be placed into the various 'divisions' under divisional managing directors. Sometimes the grouping is purely a matter of convenience, often it is geographical, sometimes it is designed to take advantage of the experience of a particular group executive. Another reason is synergy and this would be the ideal foundation for an SBU.

However, in my view, the concept of the profit centre is more useful than that of the SBU. It seems to me more in accord with the way the world is moving to break organizations down into autonomous units rather than build them up into larger ones. Group plans that call for a restructuring should use profit centres as the building blocks rather than SBUs.

To return to acquisition as a strategy, my impression is that most companies, when they have completed their list of opportunities, will find such a wealth of them that they will obtain all the growth they want without making any acquisitions at all – the case in Chapter 12 is typical. I would almost dare to suggest that if a company is thinking of growth by acquisition it has not looked very thoroughly in its own back yard.

It would be silly to generalize. Some of the worlds most successful companies have grown almost entirely by acquisition. Equally, some of the world's most successful companies have grown without making any bids whatever (other than for a few tiny specialist firms). Some acquisitions are wildly successful, others are disasters. All this suggests that the planning team with 'acquisition' on its list should beware.

One word of warning: I cannot prove it but I suspect I have seen a number of cases where company brokers have sold companies to acquirers because they happened to have them on their books. They persuaded the acquirer that 'synergy' would result from the match. The best safeguard against this practice is to make a strengths and weaknesses and threats and opportunities analysis and see if the proposal fits the overall strategic situation.

Gearing

High gearing is *always* dangerous.

The word gearing is usually defined as the ratio of borrowings to equity capital. If a company with shareholder funds of £5m has borrowed £1m from an institution or bank then the gearing is said to be 1 to 5, or 20 per cent. (Or, confusingly, 1 to 6, or 17 per cent). The most compelling definition of debt capacity, however, is 'Interest Cover'. This measures the factor that really matters – the company's ability to pay the interest on the loan. If a company makes a profit of £6m and has to pay interest of £2m on its loans then the Interest Cover is 3 to 1.

A company whose gearing is high or whose interest cover is low is in danger. It only takes a trivial mistake, or a shallow downturn in the business, or upturn in interest rates, or for a customer to delay payment, or any stroke of bad luck, and the company would have to go to the bank for more loans, but if its gearing is already high the bank may refuse to increase the loan and that could be the end of the company.

So the definition of 'high' gearing is quite simple: if the company could still significantly increase its borrowing then gearing is not yet a constraint; if not, then gearing is already too high.

If gearing is too high then this is a strategic factor of such significance that *no* set of strategies can be right unless it includes some measure to reduce the loan, or cut the company down in size, or retrench, or sell an asset, or increase the equity, or reduce the exposure of the company to risk or *something* to address this problem. It could be *fatal* to try to expand, to introduce a new product, to modernize, to do *anything* that might go wrong, without first reducing the gearing.

If gearing is so dangerous, why does anyone use it? The answer is very obvious: it is one of the most powerful tools for expanding a company ever invented. All the best run companies make prudent use of it when conditions are appropriate. Unfortunately, Murphy's Law states that bad luck always strikes when one's gearing is at a 'temporary' peak.

Overtrading

Overtrading and overexpanding are dangerous.

These two are not quite the same. *Overexpanding* is when an expanding company runs into a resource problem – management ability, lack of space, inadequate staff recruitment, and so on. Companies always have to be wary of this, especially if their planning team is very ambitious, because it is so difficult to judge when it might happen. How does one estimate the management capacity required to cope with any given expansion?

Difficult though it is, if a planning team has set an ambitious growth target for a company which has a number of serious weaknesses then some anxiety should be felt on this score. The planning team should take a second look at the strengths and weaknesses analysis and ask themselves if the company is really in a fit condition to expand at the rate they have set.

Overtrading is a special form of over-expanding which relates to the company's *financial* capacity. As a company expands it needs more capital for stocks, new computers, extra staff, and so on. Normally the expansion itself provides the extra cash needed because profits usually rise at the same rate as volume. But suppose they do not? Eventually the company would run out of cash. It would go bust.

Overtrading can result if profit margins decline relative to volume (and one easy way to get expansion is to cut these margins) and as a result the cash to finance the expansion might not be there when it is needed.

Another way to overtrade is to use the cash elsewhere. Suppose a company is expanding at 30 per cent. If its profits are also expanding by 30 per cent that looks entirely satisfactory. But it would not be if some of the cash was used for something not strictly related to the current business such as moving to a prestige office block, taking it out in dividends, using it to diversify, and so on. The cash required to finance the expansion would not be there when it was needed.

'Overtrading', then, may occur when the cash or the capital required for expansion does not arise from the expansion. 'Over-expanding' relates to a deficiency in the resources required to achieve rapid expansion. Both need watching by ambitious planning teams.

Grand projects

I define a 'grand project' as 'any project which, if it went wrong, in the manner of such projects, could cripple the company'.

The most obvious way to increase the rate of growth of a company is to undertake a very large project. For a company aiming at, say, 30 per cent growth, a single project to boost volume by that amount would be most tempting, but the planning team should seriously consider whether any such project could go so badly wrong that it would severely damage the company.

Notice the words '... if it went wrong *in the manner of such projects* ...' Some projects can go more wrong than others. A company that has built hundreds of houses is unlikely to fail from building a few more, but it could be broken if it decided to build a whole new town and *that* went wrong. Technological projects are notorious: they can be overspent ten times their estimates, enough to break most companies.

Most people have heard of the Sydney Opera House (estimate, $8m; actual, $106m) and Concorde (estimate £150m; actual, £1,200m), not to mention similar horrors at San Francisco Bay Rapid Transport System and elsewhere. These were unique, and often leading-edge, projects, never before attempted. Particularly unnerving, however, are the routine projects that fail – projects similar to ones the company may have successfully concluded many times before but which, with no warning, suddenly go wrong. One example happened to a very large Scandinavian oil company. In 1986 they decided to extend their refinery at a cost of $550m. It actually cost $860m. They assumed a selling price for the oil-based product of $100; they actually had to sell it for $50. Note that this was not a high technology, greenfield project, it was merely an extension to an existing plant using existing technology.

It reminds one of the Edsel debacle in the mid 1950s, one of the most notorious failures in recent economic history. Ford introduced a new car – something they had done dozens of times before and since with enviable success – but, for some reason to this day no one understands, this one, the 'Edsel', flopped. It was a routine project, supervised by a capable, experienced project manager, involving a routine mid-range car with admittedly some unusual features – but nothing anyone thought at the time would be decisive. A completely unpredictable disaster, even with hindsight.

Again, during the 1980s, a number of British companies bought a number of American ones. Fine, a good idea, even though there was obviously an exchange risk which did indeed materialize in the shape of a decline in the value of the dollar of 50 per cent or so in just a couple of years. Two of these acquisitions went seriously wrong, however. One was a bank, purchased by a major British bank, the other a hotel chain acquired by a major British conglomerate with leisure interests. I do not think either of these were foolish. Everyone else, with hindsight, now derides them, of course, but if a bank cannot buy a bank and a leisure conglomerate cannot buy a hotel, what is left for anyone? What they did wrong, in my view, was simply the scale. Both companies broke my rule: 'Never enter an obligation which, if it goes wrong – and you never know when it will – will materially damage the company.' These projects were just too big.

The message is, be careful. One never knows when the next project will prove a disaster even if it is just routine. A crucial step in the selection of any list of strategies is this consideration, therefore, and the planning team should be ready to ask this question: 'How badly wrong could this strategy go and what would happen to the company then?'

I go so far as to suggest that all the textbook words of wisdom relating to acquisitions, mergers, diversification, launching new products, high technology projects – almost any of the risky operations any company can undertake – could be ignored, provided the size of the act is not such that 'if it goes wrong, in the manner of such projects, it could materially damage the company'.

It is, one assumes, in the last resort, up to the owners of the company to decide if they wish to take the risks involved, but it is surely up to the management to draw attention to the risks. One obvious reason why they might not do this is, of course, the prestige that goes with size.

Low margin, high volume

In most industries the various competitors can be seen as occupying different sectors of the market. Some will be serving the upper end, where selling prices are high in recognition of a product that has achieved a high perceived quality or differentiation, others are more down-market where volume is often higher and prices lower.

In some cases the positioning of each competitor is very evident – Rolls-Royce cars, for example, or Harrods obviously serve the top end. Others are plainly down-market. In other cases the market is not segmented in that way at all – there are no 'down-market' manufacturers of airliners, for example, whose products are sold at bargain prices because they keep falling out of the sky.

While it may make sense for a large company to adopt a high volume and low margin strategy, as a general rule all other companies ought not to try to compete on price. Certainly, if a small company is having to cut its margins, if it is constantly having to increase volume to make a profit, if its products are not seen by the customer as having some special quality, some unique selling proposition or 'USP' that justifies a higher price, then it may well be wrongly positioned in its market place.

Some studies show that a company can adopt a low-cost strategy *and* at the same time differentiate its products. The PIMs study (mentioned in Chapter 7) suggests that achieving a high degree of product differentiation does not always cost more and that going for 'quality' can actually reduce costs by eliminating the need to rework rejects or to remedy customer complaints. If high quality allows one to charge a higher selling price, and if it does not always increase costs, that makes it a very attractive strategy!

As a general rule, however, in most industries, the only competitors who are wise to compete on price are the big ones. They can produce in high enough volume to be able to sell at low margins.

Consequently, I am worried when I see a less than huge company competing on price and when I see a corporate plan based on cutting costs as a key strategy. Of course, all companies should do their best to keep costs down – obviously. What worries me is when a company bases its entire strategy on a low selling price.

The trap is one which Woolworths fell into in the 1960s and 1970s, when, in their efforts to maintain the lowest prices – they were, after all supposed to be a dime store – they lost many of their customers who, during those decades, began to be able to afford superior products. The same thing happened to the British National Health Service – it started as a low cost service and stayed low cost when we began to want something better.

I suspect this 'Woolworths Effect' is a major peril for many organizations, especially non-profit-making ones. Low cost is thought to mean high efficiency and sometimes it does; at other times it means poor quality or service. Most of us do not want that any more.

This is not the place to enumerate all possible market strategies – that would need another book – but strategists might bear in mind the alternatives suggested by the old adage, 'do it cheaper, do it better, or do it different'. To the extent that this cliché is correct –

and it is probably too simple to be more than a guide – then each company has to decide which of the three lines it is going to take. Very crudely:

● To decide to be big is tantamount to deciding to go for the high-volume, low-price end of the market and to go for this end is to decide to be big.
● Deciding to be small is deciding to go for the 'be different' market; 'being different' is not so easy if you are big.
● Deciding to do it better is available to all companies, large or small.

So, bearing in mind that this is a rather crude generalization, I feel the planning team of any company, except the largest, ought to be worried if any of their strategies proposed are based on high-volume, low-margin products.

Of course, 'products' includes services here as it does throughout this book. A small bank which offers standard financial services at a low margin has probably got it wrong; a big bank which did this may have got it right. Just like a small widget manufacturer who is making standard widgets at a low margin has probably got it wrong; a big one may do this successfully.

This ends the list of strategies towards which I have developed a nervous scepticism. I go as far as this: if the set of strategies that a planning team have proposed for their company contains any of the above types of strategy – diversification, an acquisition, high gearing, overtrading, a grand project, a low-price-high-volume strategy – then they should look at it again.

The grounds for this caution are simply that all these strategies, while highly effective in skilled hands and in certain specialized conditions, are, in other circumstances, either ineffective or positively dangerous.

Summary

Having completed the data-collection stage in the corporate planning process, the planning team should gather all its conclusions together in some methodical manner such as a Cruciform Chart or a table showing the 'strategic totality'. This will assist them to reach a very succinct description of their organization's key strategic issues.

There is sometimes only one of these, often two, sometimes as many as five or six, but never more.

Planning teams will discover that surprisingly few of the strategies they have listed would meet the very accurate specification they have now drawn up. They may find it helpful, therefore, to enhance this catalogue by employing creative techniques which sometimes draw attention to additional possibilities.

There are a number of strategies which, while perfectly valid in certain circumstances and in suitably skilled hands, should be viewed with some distrust by most planning teams. These include diversification, acquisition, high gearing, overtrading, the grand project, and low-price-high-volume strategies.

The Fulmar Life Assurance Society

Corporate Plan for Fulmar Life Assurance Society
Summary Page 6. Alternative Strategies

- Recruit additional marketing expertise.
- Move strongly into personal pensions.
- Enter the unit-linked market with own or other fund.
- Modernize the computer and the systems.
- Expand non-agent routes.
- Recruit more staff until systems are ready to halt decline in standards.
- Set up direct sales force.
- Use direct mailing.
- Advertising in press, sell off the page.
- Reorganize to give personal, named, accountability.
- Impose tighter control of costs.
- Improve training at branches.
- Reduce the number of branches.
- Increase the number of branches.
- Appoint a project director for the computer and systems.
- Acquire several small societies.
- Merge with a large society en route to 1992.
- Recruit a large number of smaller agents.

CHAPTER 10

Selecting the Strategies

This is where the planning team formally make their final strategic decisions. I said 'formally' because in many cases they will already know what the strategies are going to be. By now the logic of the facts and figures that they have carefully collected and agreed over the past weeks and months will already have broken through the emotional barriers to decision-making that exist in every organization.

Or not! There is a phenomenon, which I call The Fog, which is too common not to mention here. As teams approach these late stages in the corporate planning process a state of confusion sometimes arises: 'What does it all mean? How does it all fit together? Does it mean that we do diversify – or that we do not?'

I assume what happens is that the list of strategic factors, numbering two dozen or more, together with a dozen or more alternative strategies, is just too much for our brains to absorb in one sitting – and many of these items are closely interrelated, too. You have to let it soak in. All I know is that, quite suddenly, someone finds the end of the ball of string and the first, then the second, then all the strategies become perfectly obvious to all concerned and they wonder what the hold-up was.[1]

The strategies emerge

By now the planning team will have before them the gaps, the cruciform chart, the key issues and the list of alternative strategies. It is now a question of matching these up to determine which set of strategies will best attend to the key issues and close the gaps. As noted above, this procedure is sometimes difficult and long drawn out; on other occasions the strategies come out with complete lucidity long before this formal strategy-forming stage is reached.

Figure 10.1   Crake and Bunting's strategic summary

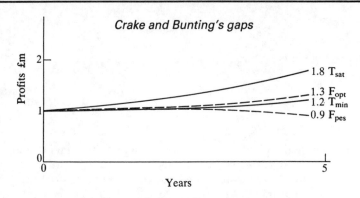

Crake and Bunting's gaps

Crake and Bunting's cruciform chart

S		W	
Marketing	A	Overheads	A
Merchants	B	Development	A
		Dying products	B
		Abroad	B

T		O	
Declining industry	HH	Abroad	HM
Overcapacity	HH	New products home	HM
Foreign competitors	HM		

Crake and Bunting's key issues

'In view of our poor past performance, and the balance in the chart our strategies will have to be rather defensive. They must address the two main issues we face: the costs of production and our lack of new product capability.'

Crake and Bunting's list of alternative strategies

(1) Reduce our selling prices to expand our volume sharply and to keep out foreign competitors.
(2) Purchase one of the merchants through whom we sell some of our products in our home market.
(3) Merge with a foreign competitor, sell his products in our home market, ours in his.
(4) Recruit agencies to sell abroad including the high risk areas.
(5) License products from a foreign competitor for us to manufacture and sell in our home market.

As an example of the birth of a strategy, let us return to Crake and Bunting. Their gaps, chart, key strategies and alternatives are shown in Figure 10.1.

Now the team have to select the best set of strategies for this company. One method for doing this very effectively is to go through all the alternative strategies and check each of these against all the high-ranking strategic factors.

As an example look at the first strategy which Crake and Bunting listed in Table 10.1. This was: '(1) Reduce our selling prices to expand our volume sharply and to keep out foreign competitors.' The team should test this strategy against their list of strategic factors; so, in this case, they should ask: 'Would this strategy make use of Crake and Bunting's main strength, the marketing skill?' Yes, obviously it would. 'Would this strategy help to solve the problem of the factory overheads?' Yes, it would (by increasing volume through the factory). So already this looks quite a promising idea: it has scored two 'yes's'. But does it deal with the other main issue – new products? Obviously not.

Now try the second strategy: '(2) Purchase one of the merchants through whom we sell some of our products in our home market.' Would this 'integration forwards' strategy employ the main strength? No, it would not – Crake and Bunting's main strength is marketing and it would be silly to waste this talent by selling through merchants. What about the factory overheads? No, this strategy does nothing about this either. Does it help with new product development? Obviously not. So Strategy (2) looks much less promising than (1).

The strategic scorecard

This technique of checking each strategy against each of the strategic factors can be done very conveniently in a table like the one in Figure 10.2 which I call the Strategic Scorecard. Each strategy for Crake and Bunting appears on the left, each strategic factor that this strategy employs is shown in the centre column and the factors it fails to use are shown in the right-hand column. (I strongly advise planning teams not to use the more sophisticated techniques involving complex scoring systems. To be frank, even my approach is too methodical to use for all the factors all the time – you just cannot squeeze all the factors you meet in real life into these restricting logical boxes.)

Figure 10.2 Strategic scorecard for Crake and Bunting

Alternative strategies	Strengths used, weaknesses corrected, threats averted, opportunities exploited.	Strengths not used, etc.
(1) Cut selling prices	Uses marketing (A), merchants (B), corrects overheads (A), reduces threat from foreign competitors (HM), helps counteract decline in home market (HH), uses up some overcapacity (HH).	But does nothing about product development(A), old products (B), foreign markets (LH), new products in home market (A). (Note: it may spark a price war.)
(2) Acquire a merchant	Partly counteracts declining home market (HH) by increasing revenue.	Fails to use any strength or exploit any H opportunity. Reduces no threats (except decline in home market).
(3) Merge with a foreign competitor.	Uses marketing (A), the merchants' network (B), corrects product development (A), obsolescent products (B), counteracts decline in home market (HH), foreign competitors (HM), uses capacity (HH), exploits some markets abroad (LH) and new products (HM).	May do nothing about overheads (A).
(4), (5), etc.		

The team can see very clearly from this table how useless Strategy (2) really is. On the other hand, Strategy (3) seems to be the easy winner – it kills nine birds with one stone, and misses only one. It looks like an excellent example of a 'multiple warhead' strategy. And it deals with both key issues.

Some practical considerations

The following observations may be of practical use:

- Many companies find that they need to devise a 'sequenced set of strategies' rather than just one single strategy as in the over-simple Crake and Bunting case described above (where 'merge with a foreign competitor' dealt with almost all the strategic factors on its own). A 'sequenced set of strategies' consists of a small number of major strategic decisions, nearly always fewer than half a dozen, but carefully phased and scheduled over a period of years.
- The reason for trying to limit the number of strategies is to cut down the demands on management resources. It would be so easy to list a couple of dozen brilliant strategies the team was going to carry through in the next two years, but the reality is that managers just do not have the capacity to do everything at once. One must be realistic. One should plan to do what one can do, which is not very much on the strategic scale.

  It is, for example, sensible to avoid devising a strategy for every individual strategic factor. Suppose a team has listed twenty strategic factors – they would have twenty strategies! They would never be able to carry them out – the management would be exhausted by the time they had done half of them and so would their capital! The best course is to try to find a set of one, two or three strategies which are carefully and skilfully tailored to deal with all their strategic factors. Strategies to 'kill several birds with one stone'; or think of them as 'multiple warheads', each strategy designed to hit several targets.
- Often a contingency statement has to be included in a set of strategies ('... so our strategy is to do ABCD; but if xyz happens we will do ABCE instead') because, as I have stated many times before, the world is an uncertain place and the team has to admit they do not know what is going to happen. So they may have to put most of their resources into the main strategies, but leave a little over for a 'side bet' just in case.
- They may also need a 'disaster plan'. One of the elephants that often emerges from this process is the realization that the company is not fully protected from a disaster that could cripple it overnight – a fire at their main premises, a media attack on their company, their product injures someone, the computer

wipes out their data, a scandal. These are often ranked 'LH' and demand not a full strategy, nor even a contingency plan, but the team may wish to form an emergency committee of trusted people to meet within minutes of such an event to decide how to limit the damage. (Such committees often include a lawyer, but beware of relying on the top executives because they may be part of the disaster!)

- Some textbooks recommend that strategies be selected by allocating marks for importance to each of the strategic factors and deciding which strategy is the 'winner' by adding up the marks it scores for using each of the factors. My experience suggests that one should not attempt to do this; the three-level ranking (A,B,C and H,M,L) described in Chapters 7 and 8 goes quite far enough in this direction and sometimes even this is too mechanical.

- Normally the team will find their strategies form into two layers: one or two of them will represent a major new shift in the strategic structure of their company, the others are often subservient to these major core strategies and will form themselves into a logical sequence with the main ones.

- As a crude generalization I expect to see between three and six strategies for each company. This, in other words, is the number of strategies that are needed to deal with the average number of elephants in an average company. Of these, two or three will be related to products, markets or customers, one will refer to the employees, one to the management, while the remaining one or two might relate to almost anything – the objectives, production facilities, IT, the finances, purchasing, interest groups, or whatever – a galaxy of possible concerns.

- Equally crudely, out of half a dozen strategies, one of them will almost always have to be defensive: planning teams nearly always find something they have to protect the company against. Several strategies will be aggressive. These are the means by which the team hopes to drive the organization into higher levels of performance. Look at the corporate plan as if it was a layer-cake. At the base is a strategy to defend the organization from decline; then there is a strategy to keep it above Tmin and moving towards Tsat; then a more exciting one to take it above Tsat; then a layer of icing with some candles to blast it to the moon.

At this stage in the process the strategies are still very bare. There is little detail. This is entirely desirable, the detail will not be required until the next stage. There will be few figures. A strategic statement without any figures at all is probably not valid because some indication of the intended size of the proposals is essential. However, a mass of figures may merely serve to blunt the sharpness of the strategic decisions.

Some examples

I give below a number of examples. In each case the set is complete, although somewhat simplified.

A manufacturer supplying retailers direct

- **Strategy 1** The entire new product development (NPD) system, which has let us down badly in design and timing several times in recent years, has to be recast. The whole NPD process from market research, through design, launch, to customer service, as outlined in the NPD report (not shown here), will come under Mr Heron. New product specifications have been outlined, with launch dates and volume and margin targets, for the next three years as follows (not shown).
- **Strategy 2** None of these new products will become available within 18 months. Accordingly, we shall buy Competitors A and B to furnish us with their recently introduced products which accurately complement our proposed new range.
- **Strategy 3** The factory is severely outmoded. Costs are among the highest in the industry. A major modernization must take place at a cost of £7m to increase output and cut direct costs by 20 per cent. The main areas of expenditure have been agreed as follows (not shown).
- **Strategy 4** The managing director, who built the company up from nothing, is to retire in three years time. A successor is now to be sought.

A regional building society

- **Strategy 1** There is a most difficult relationship between the executives and the directors. The chairman still effectively runs the society but is becoming increasingly out of touch. The executives have now resolved to address this problem by a personal approach to certain selected opinion formers in the Society and those in the wider community known to be receptive.

- **Strategy 2**   A substantial reorganization among the top executives is required; in particular, the department which still reports direct to the chairman should report to the general manager. The six other departments will be merged into five as follows (chart not shown here) with savings of £150,000 over the next 15 months.

- **Strategy 3**   The geographical spread is too wide. We are losing market share at the fringes and approximately seventeen of the outlying branches are uneconomic. The branch modernization programme will be heavily overspent if these branches are modernized as at present intended. The long-term strategy is not to expand geographically; on the contrary, we aim to take advantage of our strong regional position where we aim to increase our market share to 12 per cent through the existing traditional selling networks.

- **Strategy 4**   The new products directed at executive estates have done well and will be supplemented with equity dealing services, pensions, house, contents and personal insurance, secured and unsecured lending. The direct sales force will be strengthened to take advantage of this major new niche market.

- **Strategy 5**   A merger with a major neighbouring Society is almost certain to be required in the next few years. We will open discussions with the three obvious candidates this year to examine what the advantages might be. It will be necessary to explain to them that this strategy will not be viable until Strategy 1 has been achieved.

A Third World conglomerate

- **Strategy 1**   As the largest and best known company in the nation we have to behave with the strictest decorum and with a strong sense of national interest. Although we would prefer to diversify geographically, no developments will be allowed outside our national boundaries. Imports must be kept to the minimum while exports and import-savings are maximized. Expansion in labour intensive industries and in areas of high unemployment will be favoured.

- **Strategy 2** We would have preferred to expand our steel interests. Unfortunately we are so successful there that it has embarrassed the government-owned steel corporations and we have been asked not to expand in this area. Moreover, we have been asked not to improve productivity any further in view of the problem of unemployment in the region of the nation. A major fuel efficiency programme is to be launched.
- **Strategy 3** We intend to expand at a moderate rate in leisure, hotels, tourism, chemicals and construction. These are all areas in which we already have substantial interests and skills and they have been approved by the government as being in the national interest and not yet in competition with state owned enterprises. However, our role in these areas is already significant and it may be politically provocative to expand in this area too prominently.
- **Strategy 4** The most significant new development is the creation of an entirely new division formed to develop a complete, integrated mining and processing industry for the nation using the indigenous reserves in the country. The processing sectors will be sited in areas of high unemployment. A number of soft loans are being prepared by the development banks. By Year 15 its contribution to group profit should equal the steel operation.

A software house (doubling in size every year)

- **Strategy 1** Growth is so rapid, and reorganizations so frequent, that the staff are beginning to resent the numerous changes. We will form a 'group board' of four people to whom the existing project managers can report. This should allow not just the present project managers to report to them, but any number of project managers may do so in the foreseeable future.
- **Strategy 2** The remarkable success of three previous products has our dealers crying for more. We will go ahead with two new products each written for DOS, Unix and certain mainframes. Total turnover: £25m by Year 3; margins 25 per cent.
- **Strategy 3** The hardware manufacturers are developing an appetite for bundled software to differentiate their products. Jerry Plover will head a small sales force to visit all these from IBM down. He will report to the new 'group board'. Target: £5m at 20 per cent by Year 3.

- **Strategy 4**   Banks, accountants and financial services companies are all expanding rapidly. Jane Lapwing will form a sales team to reach these outlets, starting locally and spreading out geographically as success dictates. She will report to the group board.
- **Strategy 5**   We handle customer enquiries badly; there are daily complaints. In future these will be handled by the software writers themselves and Tony Kite will form a training group for improving their customer contact and support.
- **Strategy 6**   The office is far too small. The splitting of the group into project teams conveniently allows piecemeal expansion.

A national mutual insurance company

- **Strategy 1**   The key to achieving our corporate objective – a competitive return to participating policy holders – is investment management. We shall reform the investment management department into a separate profit centre and introduce performance related profit sharing for the staff.
- **Strategy 2**   We have increased all our growth targets. We will expand the sales force by 80 to capitalize on our excellent product range. We will continue to update and improve this range, but for the time being will not expand it.
- **Strategy 3**   We have decided not to employ direct sales techniques, but instead to concentrate on the intermediary market. However, this is not to be restricted to the traditional brokers, accountants, and so on. There is great uncertainty as to how this aspect of the market will develop and we must keep this under careful review.
- **Strategy 4**   The computer is currently by far the most serious hindrance to new product development. We have to recruit a new computer manager at a very high level in the hierarchy and several more staff; they then have to redesign the systems and relational data-bases so we may participate effectively in the new intermediary networks as they develop, they have to remove the inhibition on new products, and they have to switch to a new manufacturer. It is because of this massive catch-up computer schedule that we have had to design the above strategies to build on our

strengths while recognizing that we cannot introduce any major products without the new computer systems – a possible two-year delay.

Notice that these strategies should be precise enough to have practical meaning but not so detailed as to usurp the role of the action planners. A strategy is a task specification for the action planners – sufficiently defined to ensure there is no misunderstanding as to what is required but not so exact that their initiative is constrained.

A strategy with no figures in it at all, no names, no completion dates, is probably too bland to be much use.

Some important strategies

Over the past few years a number of companies in widely different circumstances seem to me to have adopted remarkably similar strategies. I have repeatedly warned that each company is in a unique strategic situation and that each must select its own set of strategies on its merits. Yet, because we all live in the same world, it is possible that, at any given moment in its history, it may be right for many companies to adopt similar strategies. Something like this occurred in the 1960s when a great many companies launched merger programmes and some of the great conglomerates were built – and again in the 1970s and 1980s when many of them divested.

The strategies listed below seem to me to follow the arrows of time into the direction they are currently pointing. I am not recommending these strategies, but I am advising planning teams – including those of non-profit-making organizations – that they should look at their strategic decisions again if none of these are present in their set.

Specialize

Consider these three statements:

(1) One notable trend, which appears to be true for all industries and all nations at all times, is the tendency for markets to segment.

(2)	In most industries competition is severe and increasing all the time. Only those companies which can achieve very high standards of satisfaction to their customers are likely to make good profits.

(3)	It is also reasonable to assume that no company, however large, can be proficient at everything; certainly small companies cannot.

Now if these three statements are true, it follows that every company will have to become increasingly expert in everything it does if it is to compete successfully for the customer's increasingly exacting favours. Few companies have the ability to excel at everything they do, however, and to remain competitive, most companies will have to specialize – in other words, the race for the customer will be won by those companies which concentrate on becoming excellent at *fewer* things.

If this argument is correct then most companies should continuously be developing strategies which rely on a *narrower* product range, a *narrower* range of activities, *fewer* suppliers, and so on.

Imagine a company which produces four different products. Product A is well known and respected in the industry while B, C and D are less profitable and less successful. The conclusion is, drop B, C and D in the most advantageous manner and concentrate all resources on making A the best there is in its area, its nation, and finally the world.

Is that not a dangerous strategy, though – what about 'putting all your eggs in one basket'? Yes, it is dangerous, but it may be less dangerous to have one magnificent product than to try to beat one's competitors with a number of products that are merely average. Of course, this does not necessarily mean that the company sells only one *version* of its product, although it did not seem to damage Coca-Cola to do so over many decades. It can market any number of variants for niche markets – left-handed ones, round ones, ones suitable for high-temperatures, the quietest, pink, jumbo-sized, nobbly, watery, for dogs. . . .

One way to balance the risk of having fewer products, of course, is to sell in wider markets. I imagine we are going to see many mergers in Europe in the next decade. Some will be huge general conglomerates, but I expect to see more pan-European *specialist* companies selling a small range of highly specialized products, probably strongly branded, throughout the Community. 'Fewer products in wider markets' seems a useful strategic slogan.

The same argument may hold for activities. If an engineering company is superb at machining special steels but not so good in the design department, then close that down and use the best design consultants available. If a manufacturing company's production costs are high, get out of manufacturing and become a distributor – purchase the product from the best manufacturer in the world. If a finance company's computer operations are less than excellent, use the most efficient contractor in information technology facilities management available.

The same argument may hold for suppliers. If a company purchases the same item from several suppliers, one of which is much better managed than the others, then single-source from him.

And so on. Whatever is excellent in the company, expand it. Whatever is not excellent, get someone else to do it – and get the best there is. This is one reason why I accord so much prominence to the strengths and weaknesses analysis; it must always be right to build on one's strengths – the greater the strength the more heavily should the strategies be based upon it. If a company does something supremely well then this should be the main plank of its strategy, perhaps even the only one. So study the strengths and weaknesses analysis, select the product which reflects one's greatest strength, and concentrate on this one, or, if the company already has only one product then move into a niche market. How? By studying strengths again and linking them with relevant opportunities. If 'costs' is a strength go for the markets that thrive on low cost; if 'technological leadership' is a strength, go for the relevant hi-tech niche.

Plainly, a 'specialize' strategy is the reverse of a 'diversify' strategy. So 'specialize' will *not* be appropriate for a company if the three reasons for diversifying given in Chapter 9 are valid: (1) if it has resources that are surplus to its present business, (2) if its leading product is threatened, and (3) if it wishes to form a conglomerate.

In his excellent study, *Competitive Advantage*, Porter describes how a company may select one of three generic strategies (low cost, differentiation and focus) and how it may develop these in detail, using its competitive position, the position of other competitors, technology, the state of the industry, the concept of the value chain and other factors. As an exposition on marketing strategies, as opposed to corporate strategies, his book can hardly be bettered.

The problems of the increased risks associated with narrower specialization have to be addressed – a specialization strategy could be defective and dangerous to the highest degree without consideration of this vital aspect.

Risk control strategies

Risk is inherent in all organizations. Small companies, however, have fewer customers, are more specialized, serve a smaller geographical area, have access to less advice and enjoy lower financial staying-power than large companies. A set of strategies for any business which does not include a risk control strategy is probably defective, but for a small business it could be disastrous.

In order to design a risk strategy one needs to identify the source of the risks. The gap analysis should have done this very effectively at Stage 3. As noted above, however, the strategies themselves may introduce additional risks – a company which decides to specialize runs the 'eggs in basket' risk; a company which decides to diversify runs the risk of the unknown. So alongside all the profit-improving strategies that the team will be considering they should certainly be thinking about the need for a specific risk control strategy.

A typical strategy of this sort would be as follows: suppose Curlew & Co. sells both its products, A and B, into Northtown and Southtown. Suppose it decides to drop Product B and concentrate entirely on A – plainly the overall riskiness of the company could thereby increase. How could Curlew restore its corporate riskiness to nearer the previous levels? The following alternatives might occur to them:

- Concentrate all their resources into Product A to reinforce its place in the market. If this product becomes superb then perhaps the overall risk will be lower than with two mediocre products.
- Market Product A in Eastville and Westville as well as in Northtown and Southtown. Thus Curlew, having decided to increase the product risk, would be spreading their market risks.

- Reduce the overdraft so that if something does go wrong they would have enough financial fat to give them time to take corrective action.
- Reduce the price of Product A to assure its place in the market.
- Offer generous customer service guarantees for Product A.

No doubt a brainstorming session would yield a number of new ideas if the question was framed as: 'In how many ways could the company reduce the risks inherent in dropping Product B?'

I would go as far as to say that a set of strategies for a business which lacks an explicit measure of risk reduction is just plain wrong. Textbooks tell you to 'exploit opportunities'. Of course, that must be right, that is where the main thrust of a set of strategies must lie. Yet every organization has at least one threat against which it must protect itself. It should be possible for the planning team to point to at least one strategy, or one part of one, and say, 'that is where we deal with our threats'.

Added value strategies

Consider these three broad generalizations:

(1) One of the most notable trends in developed economies is the way products become increasingly sophisticated. This is related to market segmentation, advances in technology, rising living standards and other factors.
(2) World trade is increasing. A major problem for companies today is the way *foreign* companies are entering their home markets, but the threat from importers is heavily dependent on the rate of exchange of their currencies.
(3) Third World countries, where wages are low and industrial discipline is high, can often undercut producers in the developed nations.

To the extent that these statements are correct it follows that the producer of any simple, low cost, product is not only likely to be left behind by his increasingly sophisticated customers but he will be exposed to the risk of competition from the Third World and, when exchange rates do move, often with unexpected rapidity, the effects on him may be sudden and severe.

It is quite obvious what a producer in the developed nations should do – he should add value. This will help to protect his product from Third World competitors and, because of its higher margins, from exchange rate fluctuations, as well as offering the increasingly sophisticated customer what he wants. I am amazed at the number of UK companies which turn over only £30,000 per employee; I believe that figures exceeding £100,000 are more the level required today (see Productivity below).

There are many ways to add value. The problem is to decide the most effective way for each particular product and each particular company. In this respect the strengths and weaknesses analysis should be immensely useful. Thus if 'technology' has been listed as a strength, then the product should be given a technological lift to place it further up the market to take it out of reach of more competitors. If 'skilled and well-trained sales assistants' is listed as a strength, then the services they offer to customers could be further enhanced – give them some special additional advantage over the competitor's assistants such as a 'smart' computer terminal. If 'innovation' and 'excellent design facilities' are strengths, then the added value could come in this case in new products with special design features.

It is difficult to imagine a set of strategies for any company, certainly not for a small one, that does not include a statement along these lines: 'We will set up a team of managers who will be responsible for continuously up-rating our products . . .' Everyone is aware that all companies, large and small, need to introduce new products – but that is not the message here. This message is that for companies in the developed world, especially small ones, any attempt to compete on price by lowering sales margins is likely to prove fatal: one's large competitors in the home market *and* both large and small competitors in the Third World will be able to cut their prices further and for longer. What they may not be able to do is to add value in terms of design, technology, packaging, marketing, service or rapid delivery – whatever it is that one's company happens to do better than most competitors. So the message is not just 'introduce new products' it is 'add value' – either to existing products or in new ones.

The trend to added value strategy is very strong today. One consequence of this broad trend is that although world trade continues to expand, the trade in primary products remains relatively depressed. This is because so much of the extra business being done in the world consists of adding value (including services) to these primary products. The primary producers – mainly Third World countries – are well aware of this and are struggling to enhance their own added value.

Productivity

Some companies achieve such eminence in the market place that their costs are almost irrelevant. A world-famous hotel, for example, or a fashion house with a royal warrant, can charge almost any price for its services. An attempt to cut costs would be almost indecent.

Apart from these enviable few, however, costs are such a major concern that they will often be the subject of a corporate strategy. This often takes the form of a long-term productivity target for any item of cost that is significant. The most significant is often the costs of employment and so, among the small set of strategies that most companies develop, a strategy for improving employee productivity is commonly seen.

Some companies are as much concerned with productivity per square foot of sales area, or productivity of raw materials, or of electricity – whatever is an important element in the make-up of their costs. In many companies today 'productivity' is almost synonymous with 'computers'. In factories a programme of electronic automation is often the key element, while in offices it is the development of IT systems.

As a rule, these strategies call for a long-term gradual improvement in productivity, typically 3 or 5 per cent per annum. Sometimes, where productivity is perceived to be very low compared with competitors, a major two- or three-year blitz is called for and, occasionally, some really amazing increases are possible – one financial services company doubled its turnover *and* halved its employees in a four-year period by the use of advanced computer systems.

The number of techniques available in this area is now enormous: Just In Time, Quality Circles, MRP (Manufacturing and Resource Programming – a highly computerized system), Right First Time, Logistics, CIM (Computer Integrated Manufacturing), Zero Base Analysis, FMS (Flexible Manufacturing System), Customer Contact Training, CAD, Total Quality Management. There is not much excuse for not having a thoroughly effective long-term productivity strategy these days.

The targets for these strategic exercises are fairly obvious, too. I often hear companies say that it is difficult to increase selling prices at the same rate as employee costs are rising. The Tmin target for productivity is obviously the difference between these two.

However, the mere improvement of labour productivity is not the sole aim of these long-term programmes. Because of the time horizon it is possible to tackle problems that cannot be addressed in a short-term programme, namely plan for changes in methodology. Thus if a meter-reader can currently read 160 water meters a day the company should not only be asking him to read 180 in two years' time but should be developing a form of meter, or a form of invoicing, that allows him to read 300 in three years' time – or eliminate this entirely.

As with many of the others in a company's sequenced set of strategies, this one will require the appointment of a named person to take charge of its implementation, a budget may have to be allocated to it and criteria will have to be determined by which progress can be judged – see Action Plans and Monitoring in Stages 9 and 10.

A productivity strategy, then, is likely to be one of the set of strategies that the planning team will be proposing.

Attitude strategies

I continually meet companies with attitude problems. Several of the examples given in this book refer to the problems subsidiaries experienced with their parent companies and vice versa; other examples refer to difficulties and deficiencies with employee attitudes; others with poor customer relations and misunderstandings in that area; others have problems with protest groups, governments, suppliers or the local community. In all these cases the company finds itself in a situation where a key threat or opportunity is a psychological one, not a physical one.

Typical is the engineering company manufacturing a product that is so far advanced technically that no competitor can touch it. Yet the company is not prospering. Why not? Because the employees are under the impression that the company is about to announce redundancies. Of course, it is not – order books are immense – but the employees *believe* that it is, so they are careful not to improve their productivity.

Then there is the engineering company whose employees are

devoted to engineering excellence when the new customers really only care that the product is cheap, is delivered on time and does not fall to bits inside a month. It is going to hurt the pride of those skilled men to be told the truth.

One company has a magnificent growth record – 35 per cent per annum over the past six years. The parent company has set it a target of 50 per cent growth for the next five years. It is a wholly absurd request but so great is the gulf of understanding between the parent and subsidiary management that the managing director has no alternative but to touch his cap and agree to it – the last time he tried to explain the workings of his subsidiary the misunderstandings multiplied into utter confusion.

The building society chairman who does not trust the general manager to manage, the trade union official who does not understand what 'profits' are and is disrupting the company's plans for expansion, the quality inspection department which overreacts to the skilled workers whose output they supervise, and so on, endlessly. Some are elephants on their own, others add up to elephants when taken with similar attitudinal difficulties in the company. Such problems are so common that it is surprising there is no collective noun for it; nor are there any general remedies, although there are a number of specific actions that one can take.

Many of the forms of systematic communication techniques are useful here: Quality Circles and Briefing Groups are two of the best known, Quality Management is another. These are designed to change attitudes by systematically informing the target audience (employees and managements in these particular examples) what the realities of the situation are and inviting their assistance to solve the problems thus exposed. The response and effectiveness of some of these schemes is quite remarkable.

An outline of one specific strategic remedy to one particular company's employee attitude problems is given in Chapter 12. Another company felt that productivity was low because morale was low because the top management (i.e. the members of the planning team themselves) did not know how best to treat their employees. They decided to embark on a long-term, systematic programme which would include:

Business-related awards for all employees wherever possible; openness and frankness from the managers on all matters; involving the employees far more on all shop-floor changes, even

if these are technical and financial; improving working conditions; breaking the organization down to small working units;
encouraging innovation, perhaps by brainstorming sessions,
perhaps by a suggestion scheme with very large rewards where
appropriate; quality circles and briefing groups; identification of
'opinion formers' who may be able to help; 'customers needs'
education for all front-line employees; accurate accountability
statements; improved selection, training, career planning and
rewards.

In this case, then, as in so many, the corporate planning exercise
revealed a major area of weakness in employee relations requiring
a complete overhaul of this relationship starting from the *top* – that
is, placing the blame firmly where it must be placed, with the top
executives. The key feature is that the solution is required on a
strategic scale. This company was not talking here about a need to
improve certain aspects of personnel policy – this was to be a major,
very long-term change in thinking about their employees and their
attitude towards them. It was more a change in attitude in the top
management than at the shop floor – indeed, there was full
recognition that if, in five years' time, their employees still wanted
to join a union, then the strategy had failed; it should be to the
managers that the employees want to turn for improvements in
their working lives, not to the union.

Another area in which the attitude of employees may be
changed is innovation. Such actions as introducing a high-profile,
full-reward suggestion scheme in which an employee can earn
very large capital sums for a really bright idea; top managers
displaying an evident interest in employee ideas; frequent use of
formal and informal techniques in this area – brainstorming, for
example.

Exactly the same attitudinal remedies are frequently needed for
other groups of people. Subsidiaries who need to improve relations
with their parents face exactly the same problem. There must be a
recognition among the team that something strategic needs to be
done. There must be the setting of objectives for the project
('exactly what do we want our parent to think of us, and by
when?'). Who are the opinion formers in the parent, what are we
going to say to them, can we think of a sparkling new way to say it,
who is going to say it, when, how? What benefits will the parent
gain from this new relation with us? And so on.

Here is yet another example of parent–subsidiary communications:

> Out of ten subsidiaries in a group, only one does not have a group executive on its management team. This is because its profits have recently amounted to only 2 per cent of the group's total, but this year profits will be 5 per cent, and next year perhaps 10 per cent. No one at group executive level knows anything about this subsidiary and the board have refused its requests for capital because they did not believe the figures.

The same with customers. Why do they not use our product? What do they want? To whom should we target our message? What do we want them to think about us? How can we improve the way we handle customer contact?

I saw one company whose appalling service had infuriated its sole customer over a period of years. To restore confidence the company not only had to improve service but to mount a carefully targeted propaganda exercise to make sure the customer realized that the service had now improved.

The same with protest groups. What are they objecting to, exactly? What do they want us to do or not do? Who are the opinion formers? What do we want them to think? How should we behave towards them? The same with one's public image – and so on. Many of these questions are the same over and over again; the difference is the target audience. In each case the problem faced is a major one demanding a long-term, systematic, strategic attack on a negative attitude towards the company over a broad front, very professionally carried out.

There is a danger that 'changing attitudes' will merely become an exercise in propaganda. The intention here is that genuine changes should take place – some of them hard and long-fought – so that, when people's attitudes change for the better it is because they have recognized that the realities have changed for the better.

Size strategies

One of the consequences of growth is, of course, size. Since growth is invariably among the very highest ambitions of almost every executive I have ever met (not many executives go home and boast to their wives that they have been put in charge of a *smaller* project than last time), size is a critical strategic consideration. Many small companies aim to grow very fast – growth rates of 100 per cent per annum are not uncommon. A company employing 20 people today could quite easily employ over 500 in a few years time. Although obviously more acute in small, rapidly growing firms than in mature, medium-sized ones, this problem must also be considered by companies that are already large. There are at least three problems associated with size:

- **Flexibility.** Small companies can run rings around large ones. In a world that is changing with ever-increasing rapidity, this is an advantage that growing companies ought not lightly to throw away.
- **Management.** At some stage in the process of growth it is necessary to introduce formal methods of management: pension schemes, performance incentives, staff assessment, capital expenditure budgets, lines of authority, and so on. Many experts say that this stage comes at around 100 to 200 employees but it is probably different for every type of company. The skills required to manage these formal organizations are quite different to the entrepreneurial dexterity needed to develop a typical smaller business.
- **Social responsibilities.** Any company that becomes large enough to be socially significant in its community has to take on certain responsibilities. There is no escaping these; many of them are no longer voluntary in the modern world because society will demand these as of right and a dozen protest groups will be at their door if a company fails to meet their expectations. Even small companies can become socially significant in a small community.

These three consequences of growth can be so serious that the decision to grow may require careful thought.

There are a number of size strategies that may help to address this problem:

- Decide to grow but recognize that action is needed to meet these major problems. This means (a) having strategic plans to alter the way the company reacts to change in order to preserve its flexibility (see 'Strategic Management' in Chapter 11), (b) having plans to formalize and systematize the management processes, and (c) preparing a statement of the social responsibilities that the company is likely to have to meet. This strategy, then, accepts growth and its consequences and systematically prepares for them.

- Aim not to grow *physically*. An alternative to growth is not to grow! One's *profits* could be made to grow very rapidly without incurring any *physical* growth at all if employee efficiencies, sales per floor space, and so on, improved rapidly. This growth decision obviously has to be married to a widespread and effective productivity strategy.

- Alter the profit target. Some owners are content to take the company's earnings out mainly in dividends instead of ploughing the cash back for growth. Thus although the rewards from the business could still be substantial, the business itself would not grow, or would grow slowly. Obviously, this would only suit those owners who were content with high dividends and low growth. Incidentally, a 5 per cent dividend which grows at 20 per cent each year gives exactly the same return as a dividend of 20 per cent growing at 5 per cent each year.

- Spawn small offshoots. For some types of business there is a minimum viable size – to succeed in some industries you just have to be big. For many modern businesses, however, this is not the case (especially in service industries and where capital intensity is low) and it may be possible to launch a completely new offshoot, or subsidiary company, whenever the original company reaches the 'size threshold'. Just before the problems of size become serious then, it may be possible to start a completely new profit centre in exactly the same business area, owned by the same people, overseen by the same people, but run day-to-day by a different management, possibly in different premises.

- Something like the structure shown in Figure 10.3 might prove appropriate to the company which wishes to grow while retaining flexibility – it has been adopted by a considerable number of companies, large and small. It will be seen that the company has a small head office where the group executives, aided by a few assistants, have four main tasks described below. No profit centre would be allowed to become so large that it required formal management methods (often assumed to be 100, or possibly 200, employees), that is small enough not to have to install such formal management techniques as staff appraisal, career planning systems or salary review bodies. The managers know their staff well enough to act on these issues without the formal techniques so beloved of professional managers.

Figure 10.3   The 'federal' or 'fragmented' company

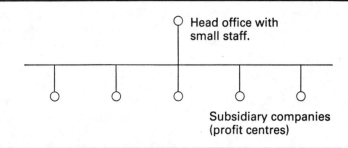

Head office with small staff.

Subsidiary companies (profit centres)

In accordance with the way the world is moving today both the group and each profit centre would be managed by a small team of managers whose lack of formal management training would be more than counterbalanced by their intimate knowledge of the business, reinforced by their ownership of some of the shares. Each team would be assisted by a minute staff of accountants and other specialists. I call this the 'Lean Team' philosophy; it is lean both at head office and the profit centres.

I should add that the above structure seems to me not only appropriate for small companies which are expanding and spinning off little offshoots, but is even more appropriate for large, sleepy companies and, above all, for large, sleepy non-profit-making organizations. To splinter down into specialist, informally managed profit centres, seems to me one of the most sensible things a large organization could possibly do in the modern world. Moreover, to strip the top executives of responsibility for individual businesses would allow them to run the group as a corporate whole, something not always possible when each group director is fighting for his own corner.

This treatment seems valid not only for operating departments of large companies but also the functions. Many large companies maintain training departments, for example, whose effectiveness is either not measured at all or is judged by means of such dubious formal techniques as quality assessment or routine staff appraisals. Why not make the training department a profit centre? The other managers would be very quick to make use of its expertise, at a full economic price, if they found this improved their own department's profits. More significantly, they would not if it did not.

Not just training departments, of course: typing, catering, despatch, internal post – indeed every department including, say, the general engineering shop. The accounts department should become a profit centre too, just like an outside firm of accountants. I am suggesting that large companies should 'privatize' their internal operations so as to become a 'federal' or 'fragmented' company.[2]

As for non-profit-making organizations, I remain convinced that these should be broken up into smaller units or geographical areas, each with one single homogeneous group of beneficiaries, one single benefit and one single CPI. How will they be controlled and regulated? Either by boards of governors, as described in Chapter 3, for those who enjoy total autonomy, or by the 'group HQ', as described above, for those who chose to shelter in a federal organization.

The duties of a group chief executive and his small staff at 'head office' in one of these 'disintegrated', of 'fragmented', or 'federal' companies, would be limited to four main ones:

- To monitor progress in the various profit centres of the group.
- To act at once in a 'firefighting' capacity, when necessary.
- To select, appoint, motivate and supervise the managers of the profit centres.
- Most important, to determine the overall group strategies.

The problems that growth may bring are severe. A set of strategies for a small rapidly growing business could be defective if it did not include a clear strategic statement showing how the management was going to tackle these. A set of strategies for a large organization that did not propose a strategy of disintegration would be strongly suspect. In all cases, however, there is one caveat: if 'financial controls' is listed as a weakness that should be put right first. The smaller the profit centre, the more specialized it is, the more unstable it will be, the more susceptible to random business hazards. The more essential it is, then, to ensure that effective budgetary controls are installed.

I have made clear that no two companies are the same, no two companies will ever require quite the same set of strategies. However, experience suggests that there are some patterns. While certainly not to be taken as an infallible guide therefore, I make this statement:

If the set of strategies proposed for their company does not contain any of the above types of strategy – that is, a strategy to specialize, a strategy to add value, a strategy to attend to risk, a strategy to improve productivity, a strategy to alter attitudes or a strategy to deal with the problems of size – then that set may be defective.

I think I would go further: most businesses should not merely adopt one or two of these strategies but all of them. A company which specializes (concentrates all its resources into the few things it does exceptionally well), adds value (steadily and systematically upgrades its products), raises productivity to progressively greater heights (by employing fewer resources per unit of output), strengthens positive attitudes (by systematically improving communications) and which attends to the problems of growth (perhaps by splitting itself into smaller profit centres) will be highly successful in the modern world.

This will not be true of *every* company, however. How will one know if these strategies are wrong for any given company? By studying the message from the gap analysis, strengths and weaknesses and threats and opportunities; by studying its total overall strategic situation.

Governance

Finally, I must refer back to Chapter 3 where I discussed the composition of the governing body and a system of governance. I noted there that textbooks on management discuss *management*. None of them seem to consider the beneficiaries, how they are to make their views known to the management, how they are to exercise control over their organization. They seldom even mention, for example, the difference between a chairman and a chief executive (see Figures 3.8 and 3.9).

I expressed the view then, and I repeat it now, that this aspect of organizational theory and practice, *governance*, seems to have been buried under the more glamourous topic of *management*. I believe it is more important than management, certainly for non-profit-making organizations. Attention to the problems of governance is, for many organizations, a legitimate and highly significant strategy.

Other methods of strategy formulation

I have explained my antipathy towards highly technical methods of strategy formulation. They may work very well for market strategies and in other second level decision areas but I think they are too mechanical, too detailed and too sophisticated to gain the confidence of senior executives. I do not think they come out with strategies of sufficient clarity to break through the emotional barriers.

Having thus warned, I recount below some of the best known methods of strategy formulation. I suspect that they they all deliver much the same message: try to match up you company's internal capabilities with the market.

While BCG and Shell have developed highly formalized techniques to help one to do this, other specialists in the field have come to the same conclusion: A. D. Little (consultants), for example, categorize a company's position as being 'weak, tenable, favourable, strong or dominant' and they categorize a market as 'embryonic, growing, mature or ageing'. Their advice: develop strategies to match them up.

In my view, however, all these have fallen into the same trap: they think 'strategy' means 'marketing strategy'. What about all those other vital issues in my check-lists? I believe that companies need strategies for them, too, but they do not come out of any of the techniques reviewed below. I recommend matching the company's capabilities not just with the market but with the environment. In other words, I believe these grids are useful for analyzing only about half the strategic problems that most companies have and for devising about half the strategies that any company needs.

Portfolio analysis

The Boston Consulting Group recommend the use of a grid to determine strategic changes to a company's portfolio of activities. I have already briefly described the BCG 'Farmyard' as a means of analyzing group strengths and weaknesses in Chapter 7 but here I wish to describe how the grid is used to formulate strategies for a group with a portfolio of businesses.

To draw up a portfolio matrix (Figure 10.4) one plots the market growth rate (in per cent) up the vertical axis, the logarithm of the relative competitive position along the horizontal, and shows each business by a circle proportional to its size. (The logarithm reflects the effect of the experience curve over time and the 'relative competitive position' measures the size of the company relative to its largest competitor.) Figure 10.4 shows a nicely balanced group of companies: a number of large cash cows, some stars and not many dogs or wildcats.

Figure 10.4　Portfolio grid

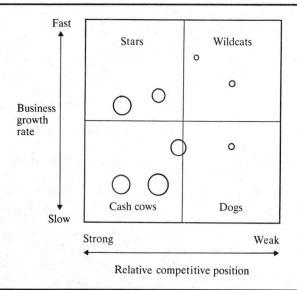

Now just because this portfolio is nicely balanced, this does not mean the group should treat each business alike. To set all its subsidiaries the same ROCE or turnover or growth target would be absurd. Alas, as I have noted above, this is exactly what many groups do and it demonstrates an extraordinary lack of understanding of strategy formulation.

In the case above, a more sensible strategy would be more discriminatory. For example, the group executives might well insist on the stars maintaining their market share even at the expense of some current profits (because they are only just in the 'star' category and, if they lose share, they could become dogs when the market declines). The cows should go for profit today; the dogs must yield cash; each wildcat requires a special target depending on its detailed situation.

This matrix is very useful. One may tell at a glance how profusely one's company is blessed with cows and stars. I have recently seen one company with no stars at all and one dying cash cow. I have seen a company with more stars than cows – and no dogs. The matrix instantly confirmed for each group planning team that their groups were, respectively, in serious trouble and most fortunate.

For each a completely different group strategy was required. We did not need, in either case, to draw the matrix in the detail described above – the strategic situation was spelt out with great clarity with a crude diagram on the back of an envelope. The balance of the businesses in these groups was well known to the top managers but – and here is the point – they had not seen the overall disposition clearly, as they did as soon as they drew the matrix.

I should add my usual warning: this matrix is essentially intended to design a portfolio of activities; it does not attend to strategies for people, for the computer, for tax, for all the other elements in a group of businesses that may need attention on a strategic scale.

The directional policy matrix

This is another portfolio technique, devised in the mid 1970s by Shell. The examples below are therefore taken from the oil industry. Like the BCG technique above it uses a matrix – with nine squares rather than four – but here the classification of businesses is by a rather wider set of criteria than in the BCG grid which concentrates on market criteria. This one includes production facilities and so it takes one welcome step towards the breadth of my own system.

The technique requires one to identify what are the main criteria by which one's business sector may be judged and those by which the company may be judged (see Critical Success Factors in Chapter 7). These are then quantified and the company's position plotted in the matrix. (Naturally this technique, like BCG, is intended for use where the company operates several businesses; it is a *portfolio* technique).

Shell suggests that there are four criteria by which their company's markets, or business sectors, may be judged:

(1) Market growth rate over the planning horizon (say five years). Shell awards no points to a market growing at 0–2 per cent, 2 points for 4–5 per cent growth, and the maximum of 4 points to over 7 per cent growth. (Each industry will be different, of course, but the 2 points score should be awarded for a sector with average growth for the industry.)

(2) Market quality; that is, the reliability of profits in this sector over the past years and into the future. Here stability of margins, the number of competitors, absence of powerful customers, the ability of customers to add value to the product in their hands, low risk of substitution, – and so on. Each industry is different; score up to 4 for a very high quality sector.

(3) Feedstock; plainly this relates to the oil industry but each industry will have its equivalent situation relating to suppliers or to some other key aspect. Award up to 4 points.

(4) Regulations; government controls, actions by protest groups, public opinion. Here score 2 where the industry is neutral, 4 where these effects are mainly beneficial.

Now turn to scoring the company. There are again four categories, each scoring up to 4 points, although differing sectors may demand different weightings. The scores should be related to competitors:

(1) Market position. The key here is market share. One scores 4 for the market leader, nil for a negligible share, 2 for being just below the top league.

(2) Marketing capability. Relations with customers, credit control – everything except production, and all compared to competitors.

(3) Production capability. Costs of production, capacity, locations, feedstock – compared to competitors.

(4) R & D. Product range, quality, successful launches, and so on compared to competitors.

Now plot the position of each profit centre on the DPM matrix as in

Figure 10.5 (actually the DPM is vastly more complex than I have shown it). I have shown a company which has scored very poorly in the market and for itself – see 'A'. Plainly a company appearing in the top left hand corner like this would be of very doubtful value and the word 'disinvest' appears there. Just to the right is a zone called 'phased withdrawal', another called 'try harder' is further to the right, and so on. I have also shown two competitors in a sector of the market. One is the leader, having scored 80 per cent of the maximum points, and the other is number two.

Figure 10.5   Shell's directional policy matrix

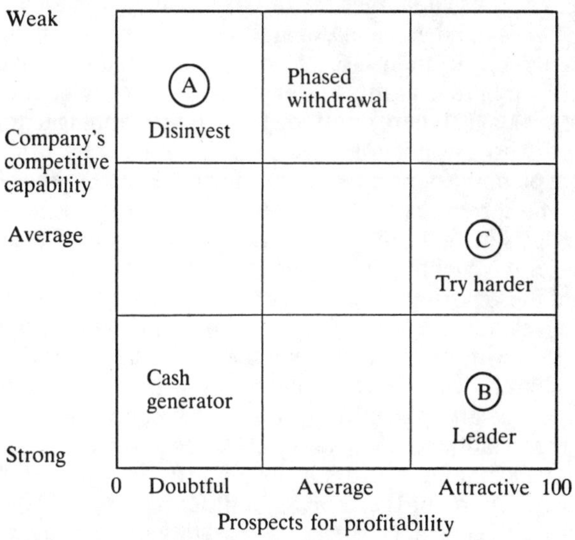

I have to add that I feel this matrix is actually a step backwards! In one respect it approaches my system in which the planning team takes the trouble to identify all the most important strategic factors relating to their company and to its environment (not just market- ing). However, whereas in mine the team devises their strategy directly from this list (in the cruciform chart), in the Shell method they then attach scores (a very arbitrary thing to do), then they add the scores together – dangerous again, because the weighting is arbitrary – so that now the words have become numbers. Thus the meaningful sentence 'major mergers will occur in the American market' in my system here becomes the coded '2' or whatever. Moreover, the matrix tells the management what to do – 'disinvest', 'try harder': In my system *they* decide what to do! Thus I suspect that the DPM twice risks taking the 'feel' out of their hands, first by quantification and then by mechanizing the decision. Also, where are the comments relating to the group itself? The portfolio shows details of all its businesses but it says nothing about the group itself, its structure, the quality of management, its financial state, the size of head office or the shareholders.

In the portfolio method, the portfolio *is* the system, this is all there is to it. It has no target-setting stage – an incredible omission, in my view – and no gap analysis stage to tell the planning team the size and urgency of their task. Also, crucially, the explicit analysis of the risks inherent in the strategies, so clearly highlighted in my gap analysis stage, is here omitted. There is no planning team either. The firms who use portfolio techniques are usually so large that they have planning departments to draw them up; thus the decision-makers, the top executives as opposed to planners, lose the 'feel' for their decisions – for the third time. I find it very hard to share the enthusiasm this technique once generated.

Should these portfolios not be used? I think they should be used, but, I suggest, as a much simplified, limited, technique within my system. I show its use in this role in the case in Chapter 12. Notice, incidentally, crude though the analysis was in that exercise, the basic problem of the group's portfolio was thrown up with great clarity.

As I understand them, the authors believe these techniques to be a corporate planning process in its entirety. I view each of them very much as parts of the process, quite small ones. They lack so many of what I consider to be key steps – targets, gaps, non-market phenomena – that I cannot take this claim seriously.

Summary

Now the planning team have at last reached the point where they have to make up their minds. They have to decide in which direction they wish to take their organization over the next several years. I believe this decision is best made by simply studying the essence of the strategic situation. This will be spelt out to the team by the gaps and the other strategic factors, together with the list of possible strategies they will by now have prepared. In spite of the efforts they will have made to retain the extreme simplicity that I have recommended throughout this book, some teams find the strategic decision exceedingly difficult, but then, quite suddenly, the fog lifts and the strategies become clear to them. Many teams will have reached their strategic decisions long before this stage in the process is reached.

An essential feature of this process is the attainment of complete lucidity and simplicity in the description of all the strategic factors and in the final statements of the overall strategic situation of the company. Only in this way, I suggest, will it be possible for a team of executives to see a clear way forward for their organization, hampered as they often are by their own personal emotional prejudices, opinions and feelings. These are difficult decisions on which the long-term prosperity of the organization depends; they have to emerge with such force as to overcome the natural impediments to strategic decision-making.

There are a number of strategies which appear to me to be particularly appropriate to the modern world. These include specialization, risk control, added value, productivity, attitude and size strategies. I would add that the design of the mechanism by which the organization itself is governed and appraised is also crucial, as is the composition of the beneficiaries' governing body.

In view of my definition of corporate planning – that it is a very much wider subject area than marketing and that it includes even such issues as governance – I would expect it to be more difficult to reach 'strategic' conclusions than other corporate planning specialists would expect. This is a further reason that I recommend eliminating all but the very few most important strategic issues.

While I am sure that some strategic planning techniques are valuable pointers to strategic decisions I suspect that most executives feel they are too sophisticated to be trusted and, in my view, they attend to only specialist areas – mostly marketing – within the wider corporate strategic arena. That said, they are helpful tools for use within a wider corporate planning process.

The Fulmar Life Assurance Society

Corporate Plan for Fulmar Life Assurance Society
Summary Page 7. The selected strategies

The overall strategic situation

Our performance has been average. If we do nothing we may remain average or, more probably, fall behind due to our two main weaknesses compared with our close competitors: reliance on a few large agents and our old computer systems. The whole industry is threatened by tax changes, much greater competition, and, very significant for us, a diversification from agents to many other selling routes. On the other side, our financial strength and our investment skills are above average and there are many opportunities in the market place, personal pensions and our own unit fund being the obvious ones.

Strategies

- **Strategy 1**   Immediately recruit more staff. Promote some of the very competent existing staff (John Teal, Ian Widgeon, etc.) to senior positions. In recent years the volume of business has expanded much faster than staff numbers and we will be unable to do any of the things we need to do with the present staff.
- **Strategy 2**   Substantially increase the expenditure and advance the phasing on the computer and systems. One of the reasons we have to rely on only a few large agents is the lack of computer capacity and the inflexibility of the systems. If we are to make use of the new routes – especially mail shots – we must have a large, fully relational data base, etc. A major shift in priority is indicated here.
- **Strategy 3**   As soon as we have the staff, move at once into pensions and unit-linked products (we should have been there a long time ago). We have decided, subject to Strategy 4 below, who should be responsible for NPD and for selecting and designing the new selling routes, including a direct sales force: An enlarged marketing department is indicated; the details are attached [not shown].

- **Strategy 4** Reorganize the top three levels of management. This is partly to encourage greater devolution of operational decision-making, partly to allow the top executives to spend more time planning, but also to accommodate into the hierarchy the new, more senior as well as more numerous, computer executives and marketing specialists. The organization chart is as follows: [not shown].

Special note

If there is one major single conclusion from this book it can be summarized in one word – devolution.

I believe that except for organizations run by autocrats and those in severe trouble (and therefore requiring a strong, centralizing turn-round man to rescue them) all organizations should be breaking down into smaller and smaller units. This is partly because managers and people capable of managing are now so abundant – we have a huge educated middle class in which managers are vastly more numerous than a few decades ago. We should give them the authority which they can so patently put to good use. It is also because we have effective control systems based on firmly established accountancy principles and the recently developed information technology. In addition, every aspect of life has become very specialized, requiring organizations themselves to specialize.

Finally, formal human resource management systems have fallen into disrepute and small informal 'lean teams' appear to be the best way to manage people today.

Many companies know all this and have already begun the process of re-forming into smaller independent autonomous companies or semi-autonomous profit centres within a 'federal' group. This is why buy-outs, demergers, franchising and licensing are such popular activities. Of course, not all companies have joined this tide and very few non-profit-making organizations have yet followed companies into specialization. They remain generalists, struggling to achieve seven impossible aims before breakfast. Unless they are re-formed into their component parts we cannot tell if they are being properly managed. Increasingly we need to know this. I believe that many should become autonomous and, where they are of social significance, should have their own simple form of governance, or become semi-autonomous inside an umbrella organization.

I hopefully predict a third revolution in management. The first was marketing – now understood and absorbed by a large number of organizations. Then came information technology, still in progress and about to erupt into the boardroom where it is not yet understood. Now, I hope, there is devolution – a great surge of smaller, single-minded organizations, either semi-autonomous within a grouping or autonomous with their own governance.

I see this organization strategy, this move from a command-like structure to a franchise-like one, as far more significant than the learning curve, for example, or diversification, or competitive advantage or going for market share. All these may or may not be valid, but get the structure of an organization wrong and none of them will rescue it; get it right and the best strategic route will become self-evident.

CHAPTER 11

Evaluation, Action Plans and Monitoring

The design of this corporate planning process will have ensured that the broad strategic ideas that will have now emerged are all highly relevant to the company's overall strategic situation. The team can be reasonably sure that, providing they courageously accepted the truth about their company in the earlier stages, the general strategic direction they have now chosen will be pertinent to their needs.

However, they have not so far made any detailed calculations to demonstrate that these strategies will be powerful enough to lift the company's performance up to, and even beyond, the Tsat level they chose in Stage 2; they do not know what might happen to their company if, having adopted the proposed strategies, one of the threats or opportunities they expected to occur either occurred in a different form or not at all. They do not know whether they have had their feet on the ground all this time; they do not know if the strategies are really practical; they do not know if they have the resources of money, management and skills to carry them out; they do not know how long it will all take.

Evaluation of strategies

In other words, they are now going to have to make quite sure that the strategies they have chosen are really going to work. It is therefore time to add some practical details to the ideas, to put some figures on them and to evaluate them. Evaluation is not only a vital and important stage in the Argenti System, it is also quite a complex one because so much detail is involved. I have so far deliberately avoided asking the team to grapple with masses of figures and detailed calculations so that they could see the wood for the trees – a concern of overwhelming importance, in my opinion – but now that they have the strategies, they must take a very close look at them before they commit their company to them.

Is it not rather dangerous to allow the team to have reached this advanced stage without any thought as to the practical difficulties? Remember who they are: the top executives. No one in the world knows more about their business than they, no one else is better placed to ask if they do not know. All through this exercise they will be discussing the practicalities of their strategic proposals – 'Not in France, George, we could do that in Italy, though.' Not always. I give an example later where they completely misjudged the scale of their strategies, an error that was picked up by the evaluation stage (see 'An example' on page 330) as it is intended to do.

If the team has not recently drawn their subordinates into the decision-making process this presents a magnificent opportunity to do so. The detailed knowledge of the organization that resides at the next few levels in the hierarchy could now be invaluable – not to mention the effect on morale of those whose opinions are invited.

Decide the evaluation criteria

The question the team is now being asked is: 'What facts and figures do they need in order to satisfy themselves that the strategies they have selected will really work?' They need to know such things as: will the company hit T_{sat} if things go reasonably well – without falling below T_{min} if things go wrong? What might go wrong? Have they used all their main strengths? Have they done enough to correct their weaknesses? What assumptions have they made and are any of them unrealistic?

As an example of the kind of data required, see Figure 11.1. This shows parts of the evaluation report for a company providing warehousing services to a small segment of the food industry in the north of its nation. The company has decided to move into the south of the country as well. This move is its main strategy; certain other strategies that this company has also adopted are not mentioned in the figure for the sake of simplicity.

Figure 11.1   Evaluation report for Pelican and Co.

A. *Strategies to be evaluated*	The strategic decision was: 'to launch a new operation in the South similar to our traditional operation in the North with the aim of doubling profits within five years.'
B. *The salient facts*	*The market.* The market in the South is four times the size of ours by volume and, because transport prices are 20 per cent higher, the sales value is five times that of the North. The market is expanding at 6–10 per cent p.a. while the North may now be declining. Competition is not by price, as ours tends to be, but more by service to the customer.
	Sites. Premises are difficult to find. Rents are 40 per cent higher than in the North.
	Employees. Salaries are 30 per cent higher — more in areas of low unemployment. There are strong cultural differences; employees in the South are much more independent, less union-ized, more demanding on the managers, expect to be rewarded for effort.
	Etc. (Other information would be shown . . .)
C. *Resources required*	*Capital.* Each warehouse will cost £2m to equip and we are scheduling for four by Year 5. Stocks (higher than in the North to ensure a better level of service) would cost a further £3m at each site. Total capital required: £20m over the five years and well within our financial capacity.
	Management. This is the big problem. In addition to a site manager at each site we will need a South Region manager. We do not have anyone in the company of this status and will have to recruit him.
	Skills. We have all the skills needed: We are certainly more cost-efficient than any of our southern competitors but all our skilled men are in the North.
D. *Major assumptions*	No change in taxes or regulations. No new competitors. Economic growth in the nation will continue at 2–4 per cent p.a. Fuel costs will rise faster than inflation. Salaries in the South are 30% greater than in the North (etc.).

The *pessimistic* assumptions are that turnover in the North will decline but productivity will improve. In the South competitors will cut their prices by 10 per cent in response to our arrival in their market, the first warehouse will be three months late, etc.

The *optimistic* assumptions are that ... (not shown).

E. *The calculations*

The figures below show the pessimistic and optimistic forecasts for the company's existing operations in the North together with the salient figures for the new project in the South. As will be seen, the pessimistic forecast shows profits that exceed Tmin; the optimistic shows profits that exceed Tsat.

Pessimistic forecast

Year	0	1	2	3	4	5
£m	*North*					
Turnover	18.5	18.0	17.5	17.0	16.5	16.0
Profits	2.36	2.4	2.4	2.4	2.4	2.4
	South					
Sales:						
Customer P		1.0	2.5	3.0	3.5	4.0
Customer Q		1.0	2.0	2.2	2.4	2.4
Customer R		0	3.0	4.0	5.0	6.0
Others		0	2.3	4.7	6.9	7.5
Total turnover		2.0	9.8	13.9	17.8	20.0
Contribution		−0.2	0.2	1.2	1.8	2.0
	Total					
Turnover	18.5	20.0	27.3	30.9	34.3	36.0
Profits	2.36	2.2	2.6	3.6	4.2	4.4
RoC %	15.5	14.6	15.4	15.7	18.6	20.6
	Gaps					
Tmin profit	2.36	2.43	2.50	2.58	2.65	2.73
Gap	−	−0.2	+1.0	+1.0	+1.5	+1.7

(The optimistic version is not shown here. Notice that although there are some detailed figures here – sales for each major customer, for example – many others would be needed such as cash flow calculations, estimates of capital costs in each year, a detailed split of turnover between products, the costs in both regions, ROCE gaps, etc.)

F. *What might go wrong*	*The weather.* The whole project is heavily dependent on the weather. If there is a poor summer in Year 2 the cash flow could be delayed by three months resulting in an overdraft of over £2m.
	Competitor reactions. The most likely reaction to our incursion is for them to cut prices. Although we are better able to compete on price than they are it could cause a drop in Year 3 of over £1m. If this continued for several years it could be very serious. However, there are two factors: (1) we are probably too small to cause any reaction at all, certainly not a price war, and (2) the strategy is for a *sequence* of warehouses – the total penalty would be £2m if we had to withdraw after the first warehouse and £3.2m after the second, very serious but not crippling.
G. *What might be disastrous*	There could be a major recession just as we are at our most vulnerable. Calculations suggest that turnover would have to shrink by nearly 20 per cent for this to cause us real concern, but we *must* recalculate this before committing each warehouse.
H. *What happened before*	Several competitors have made this move and all are now well established in the South.
I. *Dangerous strategies*	We are not proposing to do anything imprudently dangerous: We have included several items under risk control and gearing is not a problem. We have based the strategy firmly in our operating strengths; the risks are geographical and cultural.
J. *Conclusions*	The strategies look promising. Unless we have completely misled ourselves the strategies will take us well above Tsat and are most unlikely to drop below Tmin (except in Year 1 which we are prepared to accept as a cost of moving to the South). If we are being too optimistic we should find out as soon as the first warehouse opens, so we will ensure there is a 'firebreak' – in other words, we will not commit ourselves to the second warehouse until we have proved the first one.

Further practical considerations

The evaluation exercise is quite a substantial one, as will be appreciated. Furthermore, there are a number of other questions the planning team may need to ask about the strategies, including:

- Which of their close competitors are the most successful and the most unsuccessful? Have any of them adopted a strategy like the one proposed – and what happened?
- Do the proposed strategies, taken together as a set, make use of all the A strengths and H opportunities and do they reduce or obviate all the A weaknesses and H threats? Is the planning team *sure* they have been used? It is very easy to fudge some of these answers. For example, the statement 'We are certainly more cost efficient than our Southern competitors' may be valid for Pelican's operations in the north but will it still be true when they move to the south? Consider this: if their costs are low because their facilities in the north are written down and old-fashioned, their proposed green-field facilities in the south may be very high-cost, surely? On the other hand, if these low costs are due to some special know-how that they have but southern competitors do not then it might be true. It looks a bit thin – and their strategy is quite heavily dependent on this being correct.
- Do they need to check the strategies against any 'social responsibilities' statements?
- In Chapter 9 I listed a number of strategies that worry me. Does the company's set of strategies include any of these? (They were: diversification, gearing, overtrading, grand project, low margin-high volume.) Should it worry a team if they have selected any of these?
- Should the team worry if their set of strategies does not include several of the strategies I said were more in line with the modern world? (They were: specialize, risk control, added value, productivity, attitudes, size.)
- There is also a check they must make if their company is aiming for rapid growth – say more than 15 per cent per annum. Rapid growth can turn to disaster in just a few months if several adverse factors conspire together. Most companies can stand one major setback, but two together, especially when the company is growing rapidly, could kill it off. The problem

arises because, to grow rapidly, one has to commit the additional resources well in advance – the new offices, the extra staff, stocks of new products ready for launch. If a recession, a new competitor, a computer failure – any random event – occurs by chance at this critical time, just when they are most exposed, disaster may strike with amazing swiftness. If two such events occur...! Should they draw the shareholders' attention to any potentially fatal combination of this sort?

- Where do they think special attention should be paid to obtaining more detail? For example, Pelican's forecast for sales in the south includes estimates for the first few customers, P, Q and R. Is that enough detail? Should Pelican have made more effort to estimate demand from other customers in the south? Has someone from Pelican actually been to see P, Q and R and obtained firm orders, or is it all just a guess? Just how realistic are some of their estimates? Do they think any of them should be filled out with more detail to check their validity?
- How long are the strategies going to take to put into action? Look at each of them and check whether the forecasts properly reflect realistic lead times. The lead times in the pessimistic forecast ought to be longer than in the optimistic. Are they?
- What else do they think *must* be checked before the strategies are put into action? What are the really critical things that the company *must* get right if these strategies are to be successful.

The calculations in Section E of Figure 11.1 are very similar to the ones that were made in the forecasting stage (see Chapter 6). Then the team would have been making the forecasts for the company on the assumption that there would be *no change of strategy*; now they know what the new strategies are to be and so they need to make new forecasts with the effects of these included.

They should start by reminding themselves of the figures for the past five years so they can use them as a base for the new forecasts just as they did before. They should remember to be *reasonably* pessimistic and optimistic, they should not assume that *everything* goes badly wrong (or right) all at once (unless this *is* a serious possibility).

A number of other checks may be made on these forecasts:

- Consistent assumptions. They should check that all the forecasts are made on the same bases, that inflation is included or excluded everywhere, that if the price of a raw material is expected to fall, the price of the product falls also to leave the margin unchanged (unless they believe it would not). If lending rates fall, so will borrowing rates, unless they believe otherwise.

- Consistent results. The margins and ROCE in Fpes ought to be lower than in Fopt (except sometimes where demand for a product is falling, the company may stop investing in that product resulting in a *higher* ROCE and margin for the Fpes than the Fopt at least to begin with). Are interest charges rising faster than profits? Why? Watch out for anomalies of this sort in the calculations.

- Ratios. They should check that all the major ratios remain unchanged unless they are explicitly expected to change due to the new strategy. For example, check that the asset utilization has not changed (unless the past five years' experience shows that it should). In other words, make sure that if turnover rises by, say, 39 per cent over the five years, that capital employed does too – unless one of the strategies is specifically directed to altering this ratio.

- External checks. They should try to find some way to check the forecasts by referring to something outside the company. If they know the size of the market (many firms do not) they should calculate what happens to their market share to see if they believe it. Check the key ratios of competitors: do theirs look reasonable compared to these?

They should then calculate the gaps as they did in Chapter 6. It is devoutly to be hoped, now that they have a set of strategies, that the gaps will all be virtually closed as they were for Pelican above. If they are not, there is not much point in continuing to evaluate this particular set of strategies.

An example

I shall end this section by describing the evaluation carried out by one company on two rival strategies.

The planning team was split between two different sets of strategies relating to the proposed rate of growth of the company. One strategy called for an expansion in sales of 4 per cent per annum which was also the rate of growth expected in the market. So this strategy aimed at a constant market share, at maintaining a reasonably high price for the product and, crucially, it included a major modernization of the company's two very old fashioned factories. The alternative proposal, advocated by half the team including the chief executive and the marketing director, called for a 10 per cent growth in sales – obviously aiming at a powerful penetration of the market – a much lower selling price and a completely new factory on a green field site.

Both strategies seemed to match the company's strategic situation very well and it was just a matter of how ambitious they felt they ought to be. The team turned to outside consultants to evaluate the two strategies. They first costed out the two alternative factory strategies in more detail than had previously been attempted by the team. Then they asked the top managers in the firm for a consensus on various costs and for an opinion on the

Figure 11.2 Evaluating rival strategies

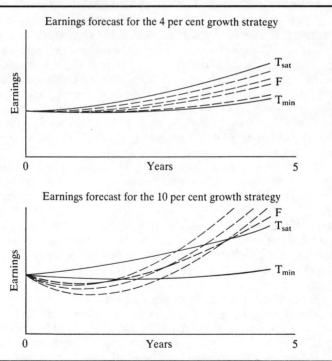

difference in the product price required, firstly, to maintain market share, and secondly, to gain share rapidly as implied in the second strategy.

They made a number of different forecasts, on different assumptions, for the earnings (not profits, please note, earnings – i.e. profits after tax and after interest on loans) that could be expected from each of the two strategies. Four of these forecasts are shown in Figure 11.2 for the two strategies.

As may be seen, the first strategy fails to hit Tsat at all although it certainly keeps them well clear of Tmin. The second strategy takes earnings *down* substantially for the first two years, because of the interest due on the very large loans they would have to obtain while building the new factory. This came as a complete surprise to the team. They had not fully realized what the cost of building a complete new factory was going to be and they had also assumed, wrongly as it turned out, that the sale of the two present factory sites would yield cash in time to pay off some of the loan.[1]

It is clear from these calculations that neither strategy will do. The first is too weak to get them to Tsat; the second is so ambitious that it would cause a drop in their earnings per share – not something the stock market would appreciate – although it does, of course, have a spectacular result in the end. The consultants suggested a revision: instead of building the new factory as one project, split it; take the warehousing to the new site first, then build the furnaces (the main expense). Many variations were considered but no *practical* scheme was found to improve the loan interest phasing significantly.

The consultants then made a final calculation to test how robust the two strategies might be to a number of uncertainties in the future. They could find no event that would take the first strategy below Tmin for more than a few months. It was robust. But they found three events, all distinctly possible, that would take the results of the second strategy well below the threshold of pain – in one case the cash flow calculations showed the company would be in breach of its current loan agreement with the bank (see Figure 11.3).

One of these was the possibility of a price war, another was the possibility of a strike by the contractors building the factory just before it was due to start. Another danger, though less probable, was a delay in the commissioning of the plant, and the third was the possibility of a tax imposed on the product – something that had

Figure 11.3   A strategy shown not to be robust

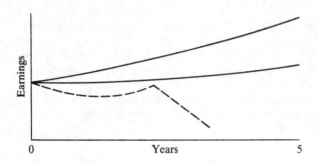

been threatened for years and which the company had displayed prominently in their threats and opportunities analysis.

The end of the story is that the two warring factions both admitted their strategy was inappropriate and they all decided to go for a modest market penetration implying growth of 6 per cent and to modernize both factories and build and extension to one of them – a fine British compromise.

The value of this evaluation stage as a method of scaling and phasing the strategies is well illustrated here – see the Fulmar case at the end of the chapter where it is demonstrated again.

Once the strategies have been evaluated many organizations will require the planning team to put their proposals forward for formal approval by a board of directors. Having cleared that hurdle the next stage is to put the strategies into action.

Action plans and business plans

In the evaluation stage sufficient detail was required to judge the practicality and suitability of the strategies that had been chosen. But now, in order to put these decisions into action, the senior executives are going to have to give instructions to a large number

of people and to do that they may have to add still more detail to
ensure that they fully understand what they are to do.

The company will need to draw up a large number of individual
plans: finance plans, product plans, manpower plans, and so forth.
They will probably appoint a number of project managers to carry
out specific parts of the overall plan and these managers will each
need their own detailed project plans. The planning team will want
to see what might be the effect of all these strategies upon the
company as a whole and so they will need a business plan – they will
certainly need one of these if the company is of any size or if they
need to raise additional capital, since almost all finance houses like
to see a business plan before they agree to lend.

Drawing up an action plan

Suppose one strategic decision is: 'Export Product A'. A plan will
be required showing, for example, how many units of Product A
they hope to sell in each new nation over the next few years, at what
prices and discounts, to which customers or markets, through
which agents or licensees or other outlets, and so on. The team may
need to specify who is going to be in charge of this project, how
many extra employees he will need each year as the volume builds
up, the cash flows, where the products will be made, at what cost,
how they will be transported to the customers in these new nations,
customs and duties, currencies and credit arrangements, and so on
– a mass of detailed decisions is usually required. Most important,
the project manager needs to know by what criteria he will be
judged, what profits this new venture is to earn each year, the
minimum result that will be tolerated before the project is abandoned as a failure (the so-called 'abort buttons' often seen in
modern project specifications), the rewards and penalties he is
being offered.

Suppose the strategy requires the company to build a new office
in Year 2. Where will it be built, by whom, who will be the project
manager, by what criteria will his performance be judged, and so
on?

A typical, rather simplified, action plan to reduce selling prices in
a family business is shown in Figure 11.4.

It will be appreciated that although I have insisted throughout the
planning process that the number of strategies be kept as low as half
a dozen, the number of action plans or project plans now required

Figure 11.4   Action plan for Ruff & Sons

Name of Project	Cuts in selling expenses
Targets	Tsat = save £200,000 each year to Year 3
	Tmin = save £100,000 each year to Year 3
Project Manager	John Ruff
Description of project	The company's corporate plan requires that selling expenses be substantially reduced over the next three years. This is to be achieved by closing down three of our smaller outlets and by transferring customers to the remaining seven outlets. But this must be achieved without losing business.
Resources allocated to this project	John is not to incur costs exceeding £60,000 in achieving this aim. This includes all severance and relocation pay for the staff and the legal expenses for breaking the leases.
Completion dates	Each outlet to be closed in August each year when business is slack.
Review dates	Progress will be reviewed every six months.
Failure criteria	The project will be deemed a failure if sales turnover falls by more than £50,000 or if net savings of £100,000 are not made.

may be substantial. This is because the corporate plan 'unlocks' a large number of decisions which could not have been taken until the strategic elephants had been decided. A hierarchy of decisions may be made once the main strategic decisions have been determined so that a whole cascade of plans may then be formulated.

Some of the action plans may relate to the major strategic decisions themselves, such as looking for a company to acquire or launching an entire new range of products, while others may be very much less significant in size and importance but will nevertheless now be required as part of the cascade.

The planning team may wish to draw up some of these plans themselves, as a team. Styles differ; some managing directors would ask the proposed project managers to draw them up on the grounds that one way to judge the ability of a person to act as a project manager is to see what sort of job he makes devising the plans for the project, and, equally important, the person who is going to carry out the plan ought to have a major say in its formulation. On the whole, then, managing directors tend to prefer that the team itself merely supervises and co-ordinates the preparation of these detailed plans rather than draw them up themselves.

Preparing a business plan

The main purpose of a business plan is to show how all the proposed projects dovetail together into a single coherent plan for the company as a whole. It will show the company's existing activities, the new projects, the new products, the effects of any cost-cutting exercise, the resources required to carry out the plan, any new loans, any extra employees – all the features that the team feels they need to include in order to convince themselves, and their directors, that the company as they now see it – the company of the future – is a viable proposition and that it will achieve the sort of performance they want to see for it. For anyone who is going to lend to the company this business plan is also a most important piece of evidence that the managers know what they want for their company *and* how to get it.

In Figure 11.5 a somewhat simplified example is given of the summary pages of a business plan for Puffin & Son. Notice that it is divided into sections: a section showing a few key figures for the existing business, most of which, in this case, will continue much as in the past; a section for each of the major new projects (three, in this case) and a section totalling some of the salient figures for the company as a whole including overall profits, ROCE, margins and – very important if the business plan is to be used to raise capital – a cash flow calculation. Finally, there should be a 'What might go wrong?' section.

It may sometimes be desirable to prepare both an optimistic and a pessimistic version of a business plan. However, the details required in such a document are often so extensive that to prepare two versions is too much of a clerical burden and so it is recommended that only one is normally prepared – the 'most likely' version. In this the team selects the figures they feel to be the most realistic.

In many cases the team will feel that the business plan, because it is in considerable detail, need not cover such a long period of time as the corporate plan. In Figure 11.5 the managing director decided that a horizon of four years was necessary to study the implications of the proposed acquisition.

Figure 11.5   Business plan summary pages for Puffin Ltd

(All figures 'most likely'. Inflation ignored throughout.)

Year		0	1	2	3	4
Existing company activities						
Turnover	£000	983	1000	1020	1100	1150
Profits	£000	111	119	122	126	131
Capital employed	£000	606	647	633	681	708
ROC	%	18.3	18.4	19.3	18.5	18.5
Overdraft	£000	85	120	100	110	110
Capital expenditure	£000	30	70	30	40	40
Margin on sales	%	11.3	11.9	12.0	11.5	11.4

The new strategies

Strategy 1   The new product

		0	1	2	3	4
Turnover	£000	–	–	250	300	350
Profit	£000	–	–	25	36	49
Capital expenditure	£000	–	120	80	–	–
Margin on sales	%	–	–	10	12	14

Strategy 2   The factory improvements

		0	1	2	3	4
Capital expenditure	£000	–	–	120	60	20
Savings	£000	–	–	10	20	30

Strategy 3   Acquire competitor

		0	1	2	3	4
Capital expenditure	£000	–	–	–	–	500
Turnover	£000	–	–	–	–	600
Profit	£000	–	–	–	–	40

Total for company under the new strategies

		0	1	2	3	4
Turnover	£000	983	1000	1270	1400	2100
Profit	£000	111	119	157	182	250
Margin on sales	%	11.3	11.9	12.4	13.0	11.8
Capital employed	£000	606	672	720	980	1283
ROC	%	18.3	17.7	21.8	18.5	19.5
Overdraft	£000	85	150	50	20	0
Long-term loans	£000	0	100	300	0	0

Capital expenditure	£000	30	190	230	100	560
Equity issue	£000	–	–	–	500	–
Number of employees		23	24	22	20	32
Turnover per employee	£000	43	42	58	70	66

Targets and gaps

Profits Tsat	£000	111	127	146	169	194
Gap	£000	–	–8	+11	+13	+56
ROC Tsat	%	18.3	18.0	18.0	18.0	18.0
Gap	%	–	–0.3	+3.8	+0.5	+1.5

What might go wrong

(a) The new product only achieves £200,000 turnover by Year 4.

Turnover	£000	–	–	100	150	200
Profits	£000	–	–	0	10	20

Effect on company:

Profits	£000	–	–	–25	–26	–29
ROC	%	18.3	17.7	18.3	15.9	17.2
ROC Tmin	%	18.3	15.0	15.0	15.0	15.0
ROC Gap		–	+2.7	+3.3	+0.9	+2.2

(b) Savings from factory modernization come through a year late.

Savings	£000	–	–	–	10	20

Effect on company compared with most likely

Profits	£000	–	–	–10	–10	–10

(c) Etc.

In a real-life company the business plan would probably continue for several more pages showing additional details, especially for those operations where the planning team may have had some special anxieties and wished to see the key factors in greater detail to convince themselves that the calculations were realistic.

Only one thing remains to be done, to put the strategies into action. In fact, most managing directors would already have started to do this. There is little point in waiting for weeks for someone to prepare a business plan if the team has sufficient confidence in their selected strategies to go ahead with some of them without it. Seeking authority for the strategic plan from the board and putting the plans into action are usually considered to be executive actions and not part of a planning team's brief; some believe that drawing up the action plans is not a task for the team, either.

The planning team having completed its task, its members revert to their more usual role as executives. In very large companies they will decide to retain the planning assistant on a permanent basis to act as their strategic eyes and ears, to make strategic studies, to search for acquisition targets, new business areas, and so on – all the duties of the traditional Planning Department. In smaller businesses they will almost certainly take exactly the same view, except, because of their size, they will invite him to act in these capacities part-time. It is almost inconceivable that a team, having learnt to appreciate the value of the corporate planning exercise, will choose not to post a strategic look-out in this way.

Monitoring

The act of 'monitoring' does not just mean checking results or watching the progress of the strategies, although these are very important aspects of monitoring. What it really means is 'testing the team's continued confidence in the strategies they have chosen'. The purpose of monitoring is to give them the opportunity at regular intervals both to control the strategic progress of their company *and* to review the whole strategic direction they have taken. I recommend that monitoring meetings of the team should take place at three-monthly intervals. It makes sense for the planning assistant to make the preparations for these meetings.

Regular testing of confidence

Suppose two years ago Whimbrel Ltd had decided to open one new branch of their business in a new town every year for the next five years – that was their strategy. The monitoring stage would raise two questions:

1   To review how well the new branches are doing.

Has Whimbrel actually opened two new ones, as called for by the strategic plan? Are they as profitable as they expected? How advanced are the plans for the third one? And so on – a number of relatively detailed operational questions which the chief executive and his senior colleagues would already be watching in their executive roles. Depending on this review they may decide to make some alterations to this strategy – perhaps they would decide to open two branches next year and none in Year 4, or whatever, but no change to the strategy of opening branches.

2   To review whether the strategy of opening branches is still considered the best way to hit Tsat.

Plainly this is the more fundamental question, one that is intended to raise Whimbrel's entire strategic direction. This is not a matter of making minor, nor even major, modifications to the strategy, it raises the whole question of the 'open more branches' strategy itself. This would be seriously reconsidered if it was felt that the present strategies will not take the organization to Tsat. (If they will not even take it to Tmin, someone has plainly blundered for this fact should have been picked up months ago.)

This stage is important for another reason also. I suggested in Chapter 4 that one of the reasons non-profit-making organizations find it difficult to use the concept of well-defined corporate objectives is not only the problem of selecting a suitable CPI but also, for some of them, that it takes so long to observe progress towards the target.
   The monitoring procedure acts as an early warning system. It relies not just on verifying progress towards the targets themselves but also, as will be seen below, a large number of other factors as well. It is this multiplicity and variety of features that makes the monitoring stage such a sensitive indicator of progress towards long-term targets.
   As with all other stages in the corporate planning process this one also needs to be thoroughly systematic.

Deciding which factors to monitor

First the team should decide which items they wish to monitor. The simplest way to make this list is to look through the corporate plan. Many of the decisions recorded there should be reconsidered at each monitoring session. For example, imagine a company that is two years into its strategic plan. The team may wish to consider the following:

- **Targets**   The team should ask themselves whether the targets they originally chose in Year 0 continue to look sensible. Do they feel that the Tmin they then selected still represents the lowest level of performance? Do the Tsats still represent a satisfactory performance? There is a legitimate and an illegitimate reason for revising targets. It is legitimate to revise Tmin or Tsat if something has happened to make the original targets inappropriate – if their whole industry has performed better or worse than expected, then what was thought would be 'satisfactory' might not now be considered to be so and it might be right to revise the figures. But suppose their company, alone in their industry or nation, had performed worse than expected, then their management must *not* cut the target but rather find a new strategy to hit the original one. Of course, if they are above target they do not need to weaken their strategies!

- **Forecasts**   They will want to ask themselves if they still believe the forecasts they originally made of the likely performance of their company under the strategies they have adopted – they will have specified this performance in considerable detail in their action plans and business plan two years ago.

- **Gaps**   They will need to know whether the gaps have widened or narrowed since they last reviewed progress. If they have widened then their confidence in their strategies will decline and vice versa.

- **Strengths and weaknesses**   They ought to review the strengths and weaknesses they said they had in order to determine whether anything has happened since Year 0 to alter their confidence in any of them. What has happened to confirm that their strengths are as they said? Are their weaknesses being corrected?

- **Threats and opportunities**   Again, they should study the threats and opportunities they relied upon when they determined their strategies two years ago to check that the expectations then expressed are still credible.

- **Alternative strategies**   What were the alternatives they considered in Year 0? Should they reconsider any of them in the light of what has happened since? Has anyone made a viable new strategic suggestion since then that they ought to consider?

- **Strategies selected**   They should study the list. They will have to ask how they feel about each of them in the light of everything that has happened.

- **Action plans** They should examine the list and any critical criteria (completion dates, etc.). It will be crucial for the success of their company that the actions which they asked everyone to take are on schedule.
- **Horizon** The team should remind themselves of the horizon they chose for the corporate planning exercise. They may need to change it.
- **Inflation** The planning assistant will have to make a number of calculations to adjust all the Year 0 figures to the current year.

With the planning assistant – or an entire planning department – watching all these factors for the team it would be very difficult for any organization not to know if it was heading off course, and, as I said above, this makes the monitoring process an ideal early warning system. Use this and no organization has to wait very long to know if they are drifting off target. One does not need to wait to see the CPI; if the threats are turning out to be more severe than the team thought when they drew up the strategy, if the weaknesses have not been put right, if the executives have not yet carried out an action that they should have completed by now then they already know. This is a most valuable feature of this corporate planning process and mitigates one of the main concerns of the managers of non-profit-making organizations, namely, that they cannot check their progress towards their target as easily as a company can.

Having decided what they want to monitor they have to decide how best to do this. Two questions usually predominate; Who will monitor the items? How frequently?

Who monitors what?

I suggest that the team asks the planning assistant (or the planning department) to carry most of the burden here. Because he may not be qualified to watch each individual item himself he should discuss with the team who might be the best person to do this. If it is a matter relating to competitors, for example, the marketing director or the sales staff are the obvious choices; if it is a technical factor then the technical department or the local university, or whatever. He should discuss each item with these people to determine exactly what it is they are supposed to be watching. It is no good asking the finance director to 'let him know if everything is OK'. The planning assistant needs to spell out very precisely which financial items are of strategic significance. If cash flow is one of the key factors in the planning team's strategy then, 'warn me if the overdraft is likely to exceed £2m' would be closer to the standard required. But remember, it is not the planning team's job (and certainly not the planning assistant's) to second guess the executives. All the planning assistant is entitled to ask for are the items listed as strategic.

Something like this would be needed for all the items of strategic significance – probably as many as several dozen items. Correctly defining the criteria does call for some care and attention. Examples include:

- 'Until Year 2, when our new product is launched, please ask the sales force to report any new competitive software package based on the new G4 languages.'
- 'Please watch the yield on bonds. We need to know as soon as the financial markets feel the dollar is likely to stop its long-term fall and to start rising again.'
- 'As Project Manager please tell me as soon as there is likely to be a cost over-run of more than £10,000 in any month.'

The team will appreciate that they will not be able to make specific requests of this sort unless they and the specialists concerned have put some thought into deciding exactly what their confidence depends on. 'If we are to have confidence in this strategy we must make sure that . . .' is the question they need to discuss.

Environmental scanning

It is rare, even in quite large companies, to find systematic monitoring systems in operation. Many companies do not even methodically examine their competitors' products, for example. They do not examine their competitors' accounts. They do not systematically scan the technical press. Now is the chance to set up a proper 'environmental scanning system'.

It may even be possible to devise some 'early warning' criteria by which the company may be alerted in advance to changes that may affect its strategies. To give a few rather obvious examples:

- Many governments expand their national economies before an election and rein them in again afterwards – not always but, if such an expansion has taken place before an election, then look for the first signs of a squeeze afterwards. This could materially affect the timing and sizing of any major capital expenditures in one's strategies.

● A salesman or a serviceman visiting a customer can sometimes pick up strange rumours. Over a period he may be able to form quite an accurate impression of any key customer's financial state, especially if he is carefully and methodically instructed what signs to look for. (A list of such items was discussed in Chapter 8 under '4. Competitor Analysis'.)

● The recruitment of certain categories of specialist by a competitor may point quite clearly in a specific direction (for example if a software house starts advertising for a hardware salesman).

When they have decided who should be watching and for what, they should record their conclusions as in Figure 11.6.

Figure 11.6   List of items being monitored by senior executives

Name	Who is watching what	Early warning signs	Date of report
Marketing Manager	Competitors' response to our price-cutting strategy.	Our sales force are to ask customers for their reactions.	Before May.
Professor Starling of North-town University	Development of laser-graphics in our sector.	Mention in learned journals. Its use by major competitors.	As soon as it appears.
Technical Director	Rise in price of oil above $25.	Any rise in price from current levels. Tension in Middle East. Stock levels.	Not worried after Year 3.

Strategic management

If a company adopts this very systematic monitoring system they will be well on the way to what is called 'strategic management' where, instead of waiting until something dramatic happens before preparing a new corporate plan for their company, they plan continuously.

In essence 'Strategic Management' consists of the following features (most of which are already built into the Argenti System):

- The organization sets up a system for monitoring the company and the outside world. This does not consist of an occasional glance, it requires a *system* of scanning the items that have been singled out as strategic in nature.
- It therefore requires the posting of skilled 'look-outs' who have been properly briefed what to look for. Their brief would include any early warning signs or signals that might herald a new strategic trend or event.
- A most important feature is that this *scanning* system must be firmly plugged in to a *planning* system such as the one described in this book. It is not much use knowing that some momentous event may happen next year if the company is not geared up to develop a strategic response to it.
- Therefore, the company must be organized in such a way as to allow it to act strategically once the strategy has been devised. This suggests that there must be a small management team at the top (including the chief executive) whose job explicitly involves making strategic decisons – see 'Size Strategies' in Chapter 9 where a possible organization structure is considered. The essence is that these top executives, whether they have day-to-day responsibilities for parts of the organization or not, consider themselves the strategic planning team for the *corporate* whole.

Strategic management, then, consists of an integrated system composed of many of the features described in the Argenti System. The company systematically and deliberately watches what is happening to itself and to the world outside and systematically and deliberately reacts to trends and events quickly – even, perhaps, while they are still emerging.

Frequency of monitoring

This second question, how frequently should the team monitor their strategies, is not usually very difficult. I suggest that, as a rule, they should gear their monitoring process to a three-monthly cycle. If they monitor more frequently than this there may be a tendency to respond to every little wobble in the plan. It could damage their strategic plans to keep changing them every few weeks. On the other hand, if they monitor less frequently they may miss major trends or events or they may not recognize them before their competitors do.

The planning assistant should submit a report to the planning team a few days before each monitoring meeting perhaps on the lines suggested in Figure 11.7 for a company in the second year of its plan.

Figure 11.7   Year 2   Monitoring report for Sandpiper & Co.

Original or latest version of the corporate plan	*Recent trends, events and results including planning assistant's comments*
Targets	
The Tsat profit target for this year was £0.98m. For Year 5 it was £1.2m. (Tmins were £0.70m and £0.90m.)	Inflation has again been 5 per cent this year so the target for this year should be raised by 10 per cent – i.e. to £1.078m. Year 5 will be £1.32m in this year's values.
The Tsat RoC target was 18 per cent throughout. (Tmins were 15 per cent)	The original RoC target assumed inflation at 8 per cent so we could reduce Tsat for RoC to 15 per cent and Tmin to 12 per cent.
Forecasts	
On the strategies we adopted in Year 0 we thought that profits (in *this* year's values) would be between £0.88m and £1.08m this year and between £1.2m and £1.4m by Year 5.	Profits so far in Year 2 look like reaching £1.1m by the year end – better than forecast and just above Tsat for this year.
	RoC may achieve 17 per cent this year – much better than Tsat adjusted for the drop in inflation.
	It is too early to say much about Year 5.

Gaps

We expected that our strategies would close all the gaps up to Year 4 at least.

The results confirm this view very strongly so far.

Strengths and weaknesses

These were recorded as: excellent products, poor marketing, inadequate computer facilities...

Our traditional products continue to sell well. Those recently launched are well above target. This suggests that the products are still excellent and that the marketing department reorganization has worked well, but the new computer is far behind schedule.

Threats and opportunities

Recorded as: competitors, economic recession in Year 2, new safety regulations...

Our largest competitor has published a terrible set of figures for last year. The economy is still buoyant; economists now forecast that it will slow down in Year 3. Our new products successfully exploited the new safety regulations exactly as intended. A new threat now looms, a change of government next year.

Strategies selected

We decided on: the new safety products, modernize our computers, reorganize marketing; acquire a small competitor in Year 3.

We should be feeling very anxious about the computer which is now extremely out of date. We should start planning the acquisition – we have still not decided whether to acquire Starlings or Plovers Ltd next year.

Roll forward

I propose to roll all the targets and forecasts forward to reveal the gaps in Year 6 ready for the next meeting.

Inflation

Inflation seems likely to decline.

We have to watch this – we may need to reduce the ROC targets as inflation falls.

The monitoring meeting

The team is now ready to have the monitoring meeting with the planning assistant and any executives they have co-opted. The purpose of this meeting is to work through this monitoring report and to take certain decisions. Essentially these are of two types: executive actions and strategic decisions.

Executive actions   These relate to the various actions that are needed to give effect to the strategies and to keep the plans on course. They do not really come under the heading of corporate planning but this monitoring meeting seems the obvious place for these matters to be reviewed.

Strategic decisions   There are probably only three possible strategic outcomes from a monitoring meeting:

- The team could decide to do nothing. This would imply that everything was on track, that they have considerable confidence that there are no new factors to throw the original strategies badly out of gear, that it would be safe to leave the strategies unchanged at least until the next meeting in three months' time.
- They could decide that something significant has happened or that it is expected to happen. In this case they need to decide how to handle it. Will they call the next monitoring meeting in two months instead of three? Or ask the planning assistant to prepare some further data on the problem? Or take some vigorous executive action to hurry something along? Or make some major change to a strategy?
- They could decide that they have lost confidence in the original strategies. If so, this will not merely demand changing a few figures or adding some ingenious twist to an old strategy, it will require a completely new corporate planning exercise beginning again at Stage 1. This represents the ultimate monitoring decision and marks the end of an era for the company; an entirely new sequenced set of strategies will have to be determined from scratch.

Four conditions may lead to such a final loss of confidence in a set of strategies:

- If the original set has been completed successfully as when, for example a company achieves its target of obtaining 50 per cent of profits from exports and does not wish to see this proportion exceeded. A new strategy may be needed to determine what, having attained this strategic goal, the company should aim to do next.

- When the original strategy is seen to be a failure. Not only would the strategy itself be a failure but the 'strengths' on which it was presumably based would obviously also be suspect. Plainly, in this case, a new strategy is required; just tinkering with the present one, or attempting to boost it back into life with some vigorous executive action, is not going to be sufficient – the team have presumably tried all this already, hence their loss of confidence now.

- When a gradual accumulation of minor changes over the years renders the original corporate plan inappropriate. This may be observed if, at each successive monitoring meeting, a gradual widening of the gaps is observed. Confidence in the original strategies would be gradually eroded. It is a matter of judgement when to declare the strategies defunct.

- When a sudden, major, unpredicted event occurs. Confidence falls suddenly and catastrophically. The oil shocks of 1973 and 1979, when a great many corporate plans had to be abandoned all around the world, are obvious examples. It is usually all too clear when such an event has occurred. A complete new sequenced set of strategies will be required.

It was, you may remember, an important aim of the Argenti System to devise a set of strategies that would be valid and viable for a number of years. It is most unusual for a set to have to be recast in less than two or three years and some may remain valid for a decade or more. Of course, as carefully explained before, all strategies require modification almost continuously to meet minor changes in the company's circumstances. What should not change, however, are the strategies themselves.

This ends the monitoring stage. However, please note that every year the team should ask the planning assistant to roll the strategic plan forward for one more year to see if the gaps in the added year are likely to alert them to a problem looming on the horizon. As soon as such a gap appears, of course, they will need to reconsider their strategic position.

Every year they should ask themselves if the Tsats and Tmins for profits and ROC are likely to change in principle for the new additional year. Depending on this answer, the planning assistant may simply extrapolate from the last year of the existing plan (Year 5 for a five-year plan) to the next one (Year 6). Thus, if they are in Year 1 of a plan, and if profits in Year 0 were £1,000,000 and the Tsat was 10 per cent growth then the Tsat target for Year 5 would have been £1,610,000 and so for Year 6 will be £1,770,000. The planning assistant would then extend the forecasts on the basis of no change in strategies (that is, he assumes the current set of strategies continues unchanged for another year) and he may then calculate the gap for the sixth year. Depending upon how this appears to the team their confidence in their strategies continuing to serve them for another year will depend.

Summary

The planning team will have completed the most significant part of their work when the strategies appear as described in the previous chapter. However, they still have three more tasks to perform: they must evaluate the strategies, they must put them into action and they must monitor them.

To evaluate them the team needs to quantify them – to define them in considerable detail and to ascribe realistic figures to all these features. If the strategy is 'To attack the market in France', figures will be required for the costs of launching the product in France, the timing of each major step, likely revenues in the first years, the threat from exchange rate changes, and so on. This calculation will show the team whether the strategies are proof against falling below Tmin if things go wrong. It will also show clearly if the phasing and scaling of the strategies is realistic.

Drawing up action plans is a further extension of the evaluation exercise and even more detail is required. Here most chief executives prefer to hand the detailed work over to their executive team leaving the planning team merely to supervise and co-ordinate all this activity. The business plan is an unsurpassable device for summarizing all the strategic consequences for the organization as a whole.

Finally comes the monitoring process, the importance of which should not be underestimated. Not only does it permit the team to

follow the progress of their strategies; and provide a mechanism for
alerting them when the strategies require revision, it also tells them
when to restart the entire corporate planning process again –
hopefully not for several years.

The monitoring stage is something else as well. It is not just the
final stepping-stone in the corporate planning process, it is also the
first in the next stage to 'strategic management' where a team of
executives continually act as corporate planners for their organization, constantly scanning the environment for new trends and
events, continually thinking about the long-term future direction
for their organization.

The Fulmar Life Assurance Society

Corporate Plan for Fulmar Life Assurance Society
Summary Page 8. Evaluation

The planning team evaluated the probable effect on the Society of
the four strategies listed above. We report two evaluations in order
to demonstrate the problems we encountered with the first of these.

The effect of the first two strategies – the rapidly increased staff
and the much greater expenditure on the computer – has a most
adverse effect on cash flow for the first two years.

Thereafter the introduction of the pensions and unit-linked
business (and the new routes) would increase income by a substantial volume quickly and would form over 25 per cent of our
business by Year 5. This surge takes our standardized net asset
value well above Tsat if there are no tax changes and just above
Tmin if there are:

SNAV £m	Year	0	1	2	3	4	5
	Pes	859	900	920	960	1100	1260
	Opt	859	910	1020	1220	1480	1720
Growth	% Pes		5	2	4	14	14
	% Opt		6	12	34	21	16

This evaluation gave us cause for concern. While we are convinced
that something has to be done about the computer and the staff

shortages, the virtual halt to the expansion of SNAV in the early years is not acceptable. No other society is likely to slow so dramatically and it would cause eyebrows to be raised throughout the industry and might even provoke an enquiry from the regulatory authorities. Nor is the team comfortable with such a huge rise in business from pensions which are in danger of overbalancing the traditional life business.

We conclude that the strategies are right; the volume and timing shown above are wrong. The following phasing is acceptable: the staff and the computer strategies are phased over three years rather than two and the new products, although introduced in Year 2, achieve only 15 per cent of income by Year 5. This produces the following SNAV:

SNAV £m	Year	0	1	2	3	4	5
	Pes	859	905	960	1025	1130	1260
	Opt	859	920	1020	1180	1360	1560
Growth	% Pes		5	6	7	10	11
	% Opt		7	11	16	15	15

The team considers this much more realistic. These calculations suggest that the timing of the strategies is going to be almost as important as the strategies themselves. We shall need to watch this aspect carefully both in the action plans and when we start monitoring.

CHAPTER 12

The Woodcock Group

This case study is related in much greater detail than the mini-cases quoted in the text. There my aim was to illustrate one particular point at a time. Here I wish to convey something of the flavour, complete with breakthroughs and setbacks, which one experiences while going through the complete corporate planning process in an averaged sized group of companies.[1]

Background

The company was founded by Mr Woodcock in 1926 when he invented a method of controlling the flow of hot metal in steel mills. His equipment very soon became standard in many of the world's steel companies and by 1939 his company employed 300 people. With the outbreak of war the demand for steel soared.

His contact with the government during the war led him into supplying components and electrical equipment for a range of military vehicles and a variety of mechanical handling products. After the war he began to make civilian versions of many of these products as well as continually updating his products for the steel industry.

The company went public in 1977. By 1980 all senior executives were professionals, many brought in from the outside, and the company no longer employed any member of the Woodcock family.

In the 1980s the company, then employing 22,000, was split into a Steel Division, an Electronics Division, a Defence Division and a Mechanical Handling Division. Since then, as may be seen from Figure 12.1, it's performance has been mediocre.

Two years ago a new group chief executive was appointed, a young, extremely able, finance specialist. He pushed through a number of short-term measures, including some severe pruning at the Steel Division which, as may be seen from the figures, considerably improved profits and ROCE. However, as he reminded his colleagues, this was just a 'quick fix'; the long-term strategic decisions had yet to be made.

That none of them knew where the long-term growth of the group was coming from was clearly shown six months ago when he had asked the divisional managing directors to submit their long-term plans to him. None of them, except Steel, had made any really concrete proposals at all, partly because none of them knew what their role should be within the group, how ambitious they should attempt to be, nor what resources group would be willing to make available to them.

He decided to introduce corporate planning at the end of Year O. The group organization chart showed the following senior positions:

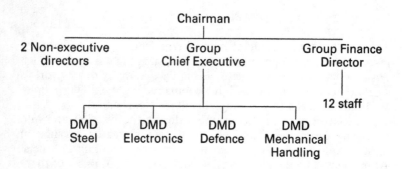

Apart from six secretaries and their supporting office staff the group headquarters consisted of these twenty-one people, three of whom – the chairman and two directors – were part-time and non-executive. The group board consisted of the five people shown at the top of the above chart and did not include any of the divisional managing directors.

The finance director's staff consisted of some highly qualified financal specialists and their assistants who prepared the group budget from the budgets put up by the forty-three profit centres in the four divisions, monitored performance against these budgets, made financial analysis for the group executives, commented on major capital expenditure proposals, etc.

Forming the planning team

In January of Year 1 the group chief executive invited the finance director and the four divisional managing directors and an outside consultant to join him in a planning team. The finance director was asked to take the role of planning assistant, chiefly because he and his staff enjoyed a wide knowledge and experience across the whole group.

A major difficulty encountered at the first meeting in February was the planning horizon: should the group plan be designed to look ahead five years, or was ten more appropriate? One of the divisions, Defence, habitually dealt with projects a decade or more ahead (some defence equipment takes a number of years to design, several years to build and prove, then as much as three decades in service plus another two decades in which spares continue to be required). On the other hand, the Mechanical Handling division seldom looked ahead for more than three years while, in electronics, technology was advancing so fast that some products had a profitable life of months.

The divisional managing director of Steel felt that five years sounded more sensible than ten. He felt that ten would introduce so much uncertainty into the exercise that it would render it impractical, especially as this was to be the first time the group had looked formally beyond a year or two. This view prevailed. It was noted that the horizon could be altered at any time during the exercise if necessary, at least in the early stages.

Following this discussion the whole question of the design of the exercise was raised. Surely, it was asked, it would not be possible to devise a group plan without knowing what the divisions were going to do? The group chief executive pointed out that they *did* know what the divisions were going to do – the divisional managing directors had told him this six months ago and their answer was: more of the same.

'We have to start somewhere,' he exclaimed, 'and we are starting this exercise where we are now and with the plans we all have now. One of the things we need to know is: where will our present plans lead us? When we know that we can see what else we need to do, maybe at group, maybe at the divisions, maybe both at once. We just don't know. We damn well ought to know. That's why we're here.'

The next question on the agenda was whether the team saw any urgent deadline for the end of the exercise. It was quickly agreed that there was none – the group was in good health and no massive decision was pending other than routine decisions that these executives normally determined. It was made clear that if any major decision had to be made before the plan could be completed then it would be taken in the normal way, having regard to any conclusions the planning process had thrown up by then.

Finally, it was agreed to hold an introductory seminar to explain to the next levels in the group hierarchy what the planning team was intending to do and how they might all help. The participants were selected with some care and their allocation into discussion groups made with much consideration for the spread of skills, knowledge and seniority as well as place of employment. The Finance Director commented on the final list that it contained fourteen engineers, three finance men and two marketing men plus a number of miscellaneous skills. The divisional managing directors, who were all engineers, explained that this was because this was an engineering company, thus reminding the chief executive that they had only recently overcome their hostility to him for not being an engineer.

The seminar

The seminar was held in April (along the lines described in Appendix A). It was attended by the planning team and sixteen others, a total of twenty-three. Five each were drawn from the two largest divisions and three each from the smaller ones. Most were profit centre managing directors but a few deputies or finance executives were also invited. They were provided with Figure 12.1 as background along with other papers ten days before the seminar.

The participants were divided into four discussion groups, moved through the corporate planning process and came to the following conclusions.

Figure 12.1 The Woodcock Group's five-year record.
Competitors' five-year record.

Year (Year 0 values)	−5	−4	−3	−2	−1	0	Average annual growth %
£m			The Woodcock Group plc				
Turnover	511.6	499.3	524.3	536.5	564.2	565.7	2.1
Profit	59.3	59.1	63.0	66.4	68.3	71.1	3.7
Capital employed	369.1	394.4	421.5	449.9	479.3	422.2	3.0
ROS %	11.6	11.8	12.0	12.4	12.1	12.6	1.6
ROCE %	16.1	15.0	14.9	14.8	14.3	16.8	1.3
			Steel Division				
Turnover	141.1	128.8	128.7	107.3	102.7	87.2	−9.0
Profit	12.6	10.6	9.3	9.5	9.2	6.7	−11.3
Capital employed	121.6	126.1	130.1	134.2	138.1	63.5	−8.2
ROS %	8.9	8.2	7.2	8.9	9.0	7.6	−2.1
ROCE %	10.3	8.4	7.1	7.1	6.7	10.5	3.4
			Electronics Division				
Turnover	78.1	81.8	87.3	98.9	109.2	124.3	9.8
Profit	9.6	9.8	11.3	13.3	15.5	17.1	12.5
Capital employed	44.8	49.0	53.9	59.6	66.2	63.5	7.4
ROS %	12.2	12.0	13.0	13.4	14.2	13.8	2.5
ROCE %	21.3	20.0	21.0	22.3	23.4	26.9	5.0
			Defence Division				
Turnover	176.2	178.3	199.1	208.9	221.0	225.3	5.1
Profit	31.5	32.9	37.0	37.4	38.2	41.0	5.5
Capital employed	168.9	182.9	198.8	214.8	231.2	248.8	8.1
ROS %	17.9	18.4	18.6	17.9	17.3	18.2	0.4
ROCE %	18.7	18.0	18.6	17.4	16.5	16.5	−2.4
			Mechanical Handling Division				
Turnover	116.2	110.4	109.2	121.4	131.3	128.9	2.3
Profit	5.7	5.8	5.3	6.2	5.4	6.3	2.7
Capital employed	33.9	36.4	38.7	41.4	43.7	46.4	6.5
ROS %	4.9	5.3	4.9	5.1	4.1	4.9	0.8
ROCE %	16.8	16.0	13.8	15.0	12.4	13.6	−3.5

(Note: ROCE is calculated here on year end capital employed for simplicity of presentation. Woodcocks used the average figure.)

Competitors

Year	−5	−4	−3	−2	−1	0	Average annual growth %
The Peregine Steel Supply Company							
Turnover	186.6	182.3	166.4	135.6	143.8	116.4	−8.5
Profit	13.1	13.1	10.5	9.4	8.8	8.3	−8.5
Capital employed	108.0	113.6	118.1	122.1	125.9	129.5	3.7
ROS %	7.0	7.2	6.3	6.9	6.1	7.1	0.9
ROCE %	12.1	11.6	8.9	7.7	7.0	6.4	−11.8
The Penguin Engineering Company plc							
Turnover	879.5	801.1	868.2	888.2	908.2	997.3	2.8
Profit	98.5	85.7	75.5	89.7	101.7	117.7	4.6
Capital employed	424.6	461.4	493.8	532.3	575.9	626.4	8.1
ROS %	11.2	10.7	8.7	10.1	11.2	11.8	1.8
ROCE %	23.2	18.6	15.3	16.9	17.7	18.8	−3.2
Partridge Electrical Engineering plc							
Turnover	303.3	309.4	311.1	341.7	355.6	377.8	4.5
Profit	26.7	23.2	24.0	29.4	32.7	38.9	8.6
Capital employed	107.2	117.2	127.4	140.0	154.1	170.8	9.8
ROS %	8.8	7.5	7.7	8.6	9.2	10.3	3.7
ROCE %	24.9	19.8	18.8	21.0	21.2	22.8	−1.1

Targets

It was widely accepted that the group should be judged on growth in earnings per share. It was agreed that the company had not performed well compared with its two closest competitors whose profits had grown faster and whose ROCE had remained higher than Woodcocks over the past five years. It was noted that the competitor supplying the steel industry had suffered nearly as badly as the Steel Division.

The consensus was that Tmin should be 3 per cent per annum growth of EpS for five years and Tsat 7½ per cent (one group suggested 10 per cent). Tmin for ROCE would be 18 per cent and Tsat 25 per cent. Profits in Year 0 were £71.1m and, therefore, assuming for simplicity the same growth as for EpS, this implied that:

Tmin for profits in Year 5 is £82m.
Tsat for profits in Year 5 is £102m.

Forecasts

Figure 12.2 shows the consensus forecast – that is, the planning assistant's attempt to amalgamate the four rather varied forecasts of the discussion groups (these ranged from Fpes in Year 5 of £65m to Fopt of £130m). It was, incidently, quite clear from some of the presentations that there was some confusion as to the definitions of ROS and ROCE, and EpS. The finance director privately invited his colleagues to note the lack of financial knowledge among the engineers.[2]

A number of important points were brought out by the discussion groups, including something not generally known to the planning team, namely that the Defence Division already knew what their turnover was likely to be for the next six or seven years having recently obtained two very large contracts. No further similar orders were on the horizon so the range of forecasts in the case of this division was known with unusual accuracy.

As may be seen, the group forecasts range from £93m to £109m (Fpes to Fopt). Three of the discussion groups drew attention to two particular matters: the fact that group ROCE would be looking quite healthy without Steel, and that on the pessimistic forecast Defence profits would account for 61 per cent of group profits by Year 5 – even more than the current 58 per cent.

Gaps

The profit gaps showed that, on current strategies, even if the group experienced some misfortune, its profits would be well above Tmin (Tmin is £82m, Fpes is £93m). With luck, profits would be slightly higher than Tsat (Tsat is £103m, Fopt is £109m). In other words, either the growth targets were too low (no one thought so – Woodcocks, they argued, was quite a large, rather conventional engineering group, not a bunch of whizz-kids, and a growth of $7\frac{1}{2}$ per cent per annum was certainly satisfactory), or the company did not need any new strategies (no one thought this either), or the

Figure 12.2 The Woodcock Group's consensus forecasts

£m	Pessimistic							Optimistic						
	Year 0	1	2	3	4	5	% change	Year 0	1	2	3	4	5	% change
The Woodcock Group plc														
Turnover	565.7	575.5	607.0	622.0	662.6	693.8	4.2	565.7	595.7	638.0	664.6	717.7	762.6	6.2
Profit	71.1	72.8	78.4	80.9	88.1	93.4	5.6	71.1	76.6	84.4	89.6	99.7	108.6	8.9
Capital employed	422.2	453.4	487.1	521.8	559.5	599.6	7.3	422.2	455.1	491.3	529.7	572.5	619.1	8.0
ROS %	12.6	12.6	12.9	13.0	13.3	13.5	1.4	12.6	12.9	13.2	13.5	13.9	14.2	2.5
ROCE %	16.8	16.1	16.1	15.5	15.7	15.6	-1.5	16.8	16.8	17.2	16.9	17.4	17.5	0.8
Steel Division														
Turnover	87.2	81.1	75.4	70.1	65.2	60.7	-7.0	87.2	83.7	80.4	77.1	74.1	71.1	-4.0
Profit	6.7	5.9	5.3	4.7	4.2	3.8	-10.7	6.7	6.4	6.1	5.9	5.7	5.4	-4.0
Capital employed	63.5	66.1	68.3	70.4	72.2	73.8	3.1	63.5	66.2	68.9	71.4	73.8	76.2	3.7
ROS %	7.6	7.3	7.0	6.8	6.5	6.2	-4.0	7.6	7.6	7.6	7.6	7.6	7.6	0.0
ROCE %	10.5	9.0	7.8	6.7	5.9	5.1	-13.4	10.5	9.7	8.9	8.3	7.7	7.1	-7.4
Electronics Division														
Turnover	124.3	135.5	147.7	161.0	175.5	191.3	9.0	124.3	139.2	155.9	174.6	195.6	219.1	12.0
Profit	17.1	18.6	20.3	22.1	24.1	26.3	9.0	17.1	19.9	23.2	27.0	31.5	36.7	16.5
Capital employed	63.5	71.5	80.2	89.7	100.1	111.4	11.9	63.5	72.0	82.0	93.6	107.1	122.8	14.1
ROS %	13.8	13.8	13.8	13.8	13.8	13.8	0.0	13.8	14.3	14.9	15.5	16.1	16.7	4.0
ROCE %	26.9	26.1	25.3	24.7	24.1	23.6	-2.6	26.9	27.7	28.3	28.9	29.4	29.9	2.1

Defence Division

Turnover	225.3	230.0	255.0	262.0	293.0	313.0	6.9	225.3	240.0	265.0	272.0	303.0	323.0	7.5
Profit	41.0	41.9	46.5	47.7	53.4	57.0	6.9	41.0	43.7	48.3	49.6	55.2	58.9	7.5
Capital employed	248.8	266.8	286.7	307.2	330.1	354.6	7.3	248.8	267.6	288.3	309.6	333.2	358.5	7.6
ROS %	18.2	18.2	18.2	18.2	18.2	18.2	0.0	18.2	18.2	18.2	18.2	18.2	18.2	0.0
ROCE %	16.5	15.7	16.2	15.5	16.2	16.1	-0.4	16.5	16.3	16.7	16.0	16.6	16.4	-0.1

Mechanical Handling Division

Turnover	128.9	128.9	128.9	128.9	128.9	128.9	0.0	128.9	132.8	136.8	140.9	145.1	149.4	3.0
Profit	6.3	6.3	6.3	6.3	6.3	6.3	0.0	6.3	6.5	6.8	7.1	7.4	7.7	4.0
Capital employed	46.4	49.1	51.8	54.5	57.2	59.9	5.2	46.4	49.2	52.1	55.1	58.3	61.6	5.8
ROS %	4.9	4.9	4.9	4.9	4.9	4.9	0.0	4.9	4.9	5.0	5.0	5.1	5.1	1.0
ROCE %	13.6	12.8	12.2	11.5	11.0	10.5	-5.0	13.6	13.3	13.1	12.8	12.6	12.4	-1.7

horizon of five years was too short to demonstrate the true situation of the company. On the other hand, the ROCE targets would apparently be missed by a substantial margin. (Tmin was 18 per cent against Fpes 15.6 per cent. Tsat was 25 per cent against Fopt 17.5 per cent). It was felt by some that, judging by current performance of the group and its competitors (16.8 per cent, 18.8 per cent and 22.8 per cent respectively) these ROCE targets might be too ambitious.

The conclusion from the discussion was that the planning team would need to consider these matters carefully. Plainly, some most important implications were going to flow from this analysis.

The internal appraisal

The following consensus emerged from the lengthy discussions in the groups and in the plenary session after the presentations.

Strengths

- Finance: the group balance sheet is strong and plenty of borrowings would be available if needed.
- Products: several of the company's major products (four in particular) were recognized as leaders in the market place. Two divisions were seen as 'cash cows' or perhaps 'stars', but Mechanical Handling and Steel may be 'dogs'.
- Reputation: the group name stood for quality and great reliability. Relatively few companies can reach the level of dependable technology that is required in the rugged conditions found in hot steel, in battle conditions, etc.
- Employees: very stable labour force.

Weaknesses

- Too dependent on Defence (well over 60 per cent of group profit if the defence work in Electronics is included), or, more widely, too dependent on a few large customers.
- Productivity: low. Strong trade unions disrupt and slow down change.
- Slow to develop new products. Followers, not innovators.
- No presence in USA.

- Divisional structure limits moves into new areas and prevents the development of a focused marketing strategy for the group. There is no group marketing strategy.

The external appraisal

The following threats and opportunities were identified as the key external elephants:

Threats

- The continued decline in the world steel industry.
- Cuts in defence budgets in UK and Europe.
- The barriers to the huge market in USA including a decline in the dollar and protectionism.
- Economic threats, especially a general recession and exchange rates.
- Japanese electronics companies rumoured to be entering defence markets.

Opportunities

- Rise in defence expenditure in Europe.
- Break into USA by any or all our divisions.
- Growth in electronics world wide, including the move to the use of electronics in other Woodcock divisions.
- Acquisitions to fill specific gaps in knowledge and business areas – several identified.
- One very large defence contract (codename 'Swallowtail') which the Defence Division must win for Year 5.
- Huge markets in Third World, not at present supplied.

Strategies

There was not sufficient time for a full discussion on strategies but the following were briefly mentioned:

- Appoint a senior executive to supervise the group's ventures into America.
- Defence Division to recognize 'Swallowtail' as a 'must win' contract.

- Use financial resources much more aggressively to expand the 'stars'.
- 'Put our house in order' by improved industrial relations.

The participants were plainly most satisfied with the seminar. It was the first time that these top management levels had met together to discuss the future of the business. They felt a much sharper appreciation of the relative importance of the various parts of the company and enjoyed the shared pride in their obvious engineering skills. They were particularly excited by the prospects for the group as a whole as revealed by the opportunities – they had, they felt, not found a very large number of them but the ones they had found were very significant and highly relevant to their skills.

The planning team meetings

The planning team met two weeks after the seminar. Before turning to the main item on the agenda they considered if any of the internal or external items raised at the seminar should be investigated in further depth before they themselves considered them. They decided to set up three working parties from the next level in the hierarchy to examine:

- Productivity: how do the group's divisions compare in productivity with their competitors here and abroad? What should be done?
- Industrial relations: are the group's industrial relations poor? If so, why?
- Stars and dogs: classify the group's forty-three profit centres into the four BCG boxes.

Targets

The team then turned to the targets. There was immediate agreement that growth of EpS was the prime target for a quoted company. The rest of the team were inclined to leave EpS as the sole target but the finance director insisted on ROCE being included because the group's ROCE would obviously have to be increased – EpS alone is probably sufficient, he explained, only when ROCE is already satisfactory, which ours is obviously not.

It was agreed that these two indicators were a marked advance on the one they had previously used – turnover. It would, they commented, result in a major shift in focus if they could get 'profits' into everyone's minds down the hierarchy instead of volume.

The team had to agree with the seminar conclusion that, judged by any criteria, the group performance over the past five years had not been good. On the other hand, the company had not shown anything like the same collapse in the recession three and four years ago as some engineering companies at home and abroad. All three close competitors had actually suffered a drop in profits, Woodcocks had not (Figure 12.1). 'Resilience' might well be added to the 'strengths'.

The team also agreed the two growth targets chosen at the seminar: a 3 per cent Tmin, taking EpS from its current 82.1 pence per share to 95 pence and profits to £82m in Year 5 (assuming no change in gearing); and a Tsat of $7\frac{1}{2}$ per cent taking EpS to 118 pence and profits to £102m.

In reaching this decisions the team discussed certain alternatives. Several members stated that as the forecasts showed that the group would *exceed* these targets without any change of strategy the targets, surely, should be raised. It was eventually agreed, however, that, in fact, $7\frac{1}{2}$ per cent growth would be very creditable for a company of this size and that, to raise Tsat to, say, 12 per cent would be to set a target considerably more ambitious than 'satisfactory'. 'But shouldn't we do just that?', suggested some members. The group chief executive reminded them of their past performance; growth had been 3.7 per cent per annum, the Electronics division – which everyone acknowledged to have performed magnificently (far above 'satisfactory') – had only registered $12\frac{1}{2}$ per cent. Again, Partridge's performance was recognized as entirely satisfactory and they had achieved 8.6 per cent. He also reminded them that ROCE had to rise substantially as well over the next five years – it is quite an ambitious task to grow *and* to raise ROCE.

It was agreed to accept $7\frac{1}{2}$ per cent but it was also noted that the new strategies ought to achieve something well above that. They then turned to the ROCE target. It was agreed that, with returns on Government Stock at 12 per cent and the average for manufacturing industry at 17 per cent, Tmin for ROCE could not be set below 18 per cent. On the other hand, they thought that 25 per cent was more than satisfactory, especially as the upper quartile of manufacturing industry showed only 21 per cent.

Tmin at 18 per cent and Tsat at $22\frac{1}{2}$ per cent were agreed. The finance director commented that, subject to detailed calculations, he guessed that 12 per cent growth (i.e. $7\frac{1}{2}$ per cent real growth plus the then $4\frac{1}{2}$ per cent inflation) was probably compatible with $22\frac{1}{2}$ per cent ROCE. (Subsequent calculations on the company spreadsheet confirmed this, assuming continued low inflation.)

The team agreed the following description of the past few years:

- Although the group had proved remarkably resilient to the recession three and four years ago this may have been a fluke. The profits of both the Steel and the Mechanical Handling Divisions had fallen and the group had been saved by the growth of Electronics and a fortuitous jump in sales in Defence. However, fluke or not, the group had benefited from its diversity.
- ROCE in Year 0 was enhanced by the cut-back at Steel. If this had not occured ROCE for the group might have fallen again – for the fifth year in succession – to a new, intolerably low level. No further cut-backs were planned.
- This poor ROCE may be linked to the low productivity that was identified at the seminar. But the whole group was becoming more capital intensive while continuing to show a low ROCE, a combination of trends that seems likely to lead to disaster in the long run. These trends had been hitherto unnoticed because of the performance of Electronics in the opposite directions. (In other words, it is only in Electronics that capital employed has been rising less rapidly than turnover.)
- The competitors showed the same trends of lower ROCE and greater capital intensity, but Partridge and Penguin had grown faster.

Forecasts and gaps

At the second meeting, in May of Year 1, the finance director presented the forecast figures prepared by the discussion groups at the seminar which, he explained, his department had 'clarified'. The discussion groups had neither the time nor the expertise to tidy up their forecasts during the seminar but it was, nevertheless, quite plain what they had intended to say (see Figure 12.2).

The team studied these carefully and concluded as follows:

- They did not believe that Steel might only decline to £3.8m profit in Year 5. By then a large loss would be entirely possible if margins continued to be slashed as in the past 18 months. They accepted the Fopt of £5.4m, however.
- They could not accept that, having lifted ROCE for the past five years, Electronics should suddenly allow it to fall as shown in Fpes. They thought zero improvement for Fpes and 5 per cent per annum for Fopt would be more reasonable assumptions.
- The Defence Division was seen as reasonable. It was noted that the new orders virtually set the figures in concrete – not only for turnover but for ROS and ROCE as well because the Ministry of Defence would be carefully monitoring these as part of the price variation clauses in the contract. Severe penalties could be imposed for exceeding 18 per cent margins and 16 per cent ROCE on defence contracts. Once granted, these contracts were, after all, very low risk.
- On present strategies Mechanical Handling would, they agreed, deliver a performance similar to that shown.

The team asked the Finance Department to recalculate the forecasts as above and submit them to the next meeting. Meanwhile they concluded that the consensus at the seminar was probably correct, that, even on present strategies (described by one member as 'carry on as best we can') the group was going to perform very well indeed in the next five years, thanks largely to the Defence and the Electronics Divisions. If confirmed it gave them a secure base from which to launch a somewhat more adventurous policy.

The revised forecasts

The revised forecasts confirmed this conclusion (Figure 12.3). The resilience of the group was well illustrated because, even though no account had been taken of the Piston Effect – that it was most unlikely that all four divisions would be at their Fpes or Fopt together – the group's profits in Year 5 would lie between £91m and £116m – a range of 1 to 1.27. They decided to try to estimate what this Piston Effect would be.

If they assumed that the largest division, Defence, was at its Fpes (£57m), what are the chances of each of the other divisions also being at that level? The answer, thought the team, was very low –

Figure 12.3 The Woodcock Group's revised forecast

£m	Pessimistic							Optimistic						
	Year 0	1	2	3	4	5	% change	Year 0	1	2	3	4	5	% change
	The Woodcock Group plc													
Turnover	565.7	571.1	599.1	611.3	649.7	679.2	3.7	565.7	595.7	638.0	664.6	717.7	762.6	6.2
Profit	71.1	72.9	77.1	78.8	85.6	91.1	5.1	71.1	77.1	85.8	92.2	104.3	116.1	10.3
Capital employed	422.2	447.4	473.7	501.4	532.4	565.8	6.0	422.2	455.3	492.0	531.3	575.6	624.6	8.1
ROS %	12.6	12.8	12.9	12.9	13.2	13.4	1.3	12.6	12.9	13.4	13.9	14.5	15.2	3.9
ROCE %	16.8	16.3	16.3	15.7	16.1	16.1	-0.9	16.8	16.9	17.4	17.4	18.1	18.6	2.0
	Steel Division													
Turnover	87.2	76.7	67.5	59.4	52.3	46.0	-12.0	87.2	83.7	80.4	77.1	74.1	71.1	-4.0
Profit	6.7	5.4	2.7	0.6	-1.0	-2.3	-60.6	6.7	6.4	6.1	5.9	5.7	5.4	-4.0
Capital employed	63.5	60.0	55.0	50.0	45.0	40.0	-8.8	63.5	66.2	68.9	71.4	73.8	76.2	3.7
ROS %	7.6	7.0	4.0	1.0	-2.0	-5.0	-55.2	7.6	7.6	7.6	7.6	7.6	7.6	0.0
ROCE %	10.5	9.0	4.9	1.2	-2.3	-5.8	-56.7	10.5	9.7	8.9	8.3	7.7	7.1	-7.4
	Electronics Division													
Turnover	124.3	135.5	147.7	161.0	175.5	191.3	9.0	124.3	139.2	155.9	174.6	195.6	219.1	12.0
Profit	17.1	19.3	21.7	24.2	27.0	30.1	11.9	17.1	20.4	24.6	29.7	36.1	44.1	20.9
Capital employed	63.5	71.5	80.2	89.7	100.1	111.4	11.9	63.5	72.2	82.7	95.2	110.3	128.4	15.1
ROS %	13.8	14.2	14.7	15.0	15.4	15.7	2.7	13.8	14.7	15.7	17.0	18.5	20.1	7.9
ROCE %	26.9	27.0	27.0	27.0	27.0	27.0	0.0	26.9	28.3	29.7	31.2	32.7	34.4	5.0

Defence Division

Turnover	225.3	230.0	255.0	262.0	293.0	313.0	6.9	225.3	240.0	265.0	272.0	303.0	323.0	7.5
Profit	41.0	41.9	46.5	47.7	53.4	57.0	6.9	41.0	43.7	48.3	49.6	55.2	58.9	7.5
Capital employed	248.8	266.8	286.7	307.2	330.1	354.6	7.3	248.8	267.6	288.3	309.6	333.2	358.5	7.6
ROS %	18.2	18.2	18.2	18.2	18.2	18.2	0.0	18.2	18.2	18.2	18.2	18.2	18.2	0.0
ROCE %	16.5	15.7	16.2	15.5	16.2	16.1	-0.4	16.5	16.3	16.7	16.0	16.6	16.4	-0.1

Mechanical Handling Division

Turnover	128.9	128.9	128.9	128.9	128.9	128.9	0.0	128.9	132.8	136.8	140.9	145.1	149.4	3.0
Profit	6.3	6.3	6.3	6.3	6.3	6.3	0.0	6.3	6.5	6.8	7.1	7.4	7.7	4.0
Capital employed	46.4	49.1	51.8	54.5	57.2	59.9	5.2	46.4	49.2	52.1	55.1	58.3	61.6	5.8
ROS %	4.9	4.9	4.9	4.9	4.9	4.9	0.0	4.9	4.9	5.0	5.0	5.1	5.1	1.0
ROCE %	13.6	12.8	12.2	11.5	11.0	10.5	-5.0	13.6	13.3	13.1	12.8	12.6	12.4	-1.7

the linkage between the divisions was slight, they each served quite different industries with different cycles. Therefore, instead of adding the other three Fpes together, it would not be unreasonable to take the average between their Fpes and Fopt (or perhaps a little to the pessimistic side to allow for a general recession), and add this to Defence. Now the average of the three divisions' Fpes plus Fopt is £45.6m – less, say, £5m to be a little pessimistic – which is £40m to add to the £57m from Defence, making the group Fpes £97m.

Similarly, the group Fopt would come to approximately £109m, making the likely range £97m to £109m, a range of 1 to 1.12.

The strategic conclusions from this gap analysis are as follows:

- On present strategies the group will perform well even if a number of unfavourable events occur as assumed in Fpes.
- Profits in Year 5 will rise to between £97m and £109m which represent an annual growth of between 6.5 and 9 per cent in real terms – well above Tmin and Tsat respectively; indeed even Fpes (£97m) comes quite close to Tsat (£102m).
- The implication is that the group is well placed for further expansion based on its low-risk situation. It would be possible to contemplate either a much faster rate of growth than currently planned or one involving greater risks, such as diversification.
- On the other hand, ROCE is unlikely to exceed 18 per cent in Year 5. This compares with Tmin of 18 per cent and Tsat of 22½ per cent. The implication is that, until ROCE in any division has been lifted towards 22 per cent the group should invest capital sparingly. In practice, this meant that Electronics could invest freely while the others could not. Indeed, further retrenchment at Steel and perhaps Mechanical Handling seemed probable. The team made a note, however, that 34 per cent ROCE was difficult to believe even for the Electronics Division (Figure 12.3).

The internal appraisal

The team next met in June to begin the strengths and weaknesses analysis. They had before them the three reports they had commissioned earlier which led to the following conclusions.

Productivity The report showed the group's position compared with other engineering companies. While there were some very large discrepancies in the four surveys that had been conducted in the industry in recent years, the message from these, said the report, was:

- In terms of turnover per employee the group was 15 per cent below average and far below some similar companies who turned over as much as £60,000 per employee compared with the group's figure of £26,000. Following the cut-back at Steel their turnover had risen to over £40,000, Electronics were at £35,000, and this implied that Defence and Mechanical Handling were considerably overmanned with figures of £21,000 and £24,000 approximately. Added value per employee appeared to be above average for the industry – a somewhat anomalous statistic.
- ROCE, as has been noted above, is average for the industry. However, capital employed per employee was one-third of the national average – a figure the team had great difficulty in reconciling with their capital intensity. (Some of the published figures swung wildly from year to year. One survey showed Woodcocks far below average for one year and far above it the next. Another showed one of their profit centres having one-tenth the capital per employee compared to the industry average – absurd. Another showed the group to be making a negative ROCE – plainly incorrect.)
- Sales per asset was fully 20 per cent below average, making the group that much more capital intensive than the average. The team rejected the implication that the report drew from this that the group used its capital inefficiently; it seemed more likely that the group was more capital intensive because it aimed for high quality. In other words, the team thought that labour productivity alone, not capital productivity, accounted for most of their problem. A correction of perhaps 20 per cent was needed in labour productivity.

Industrial relations   The report on industrial relations was disturbing. It firstly noted that industrial relations in the Electronics Division appeared to be excellent, partly because most of the companies were very small, averaging about 200 employees (the division consists of eighteen autonomous profit centres) and partly because there were so few unions. Most of the companies were young and employed a very large proportion of professional and skilled people.

In the three other divisions the report saw a consistent pattern of strong trade unions, weak lower management who had been given virtually no training in industrial relations, and low levels of skill on the shop floor (contrasting with high levels in the design departments where the latest computer design technologies could be found in profusion).

There was, the report said, a feeling that working for the company was easy, undemanding, unexciting, even unrewarding – although, because of its paternalistic attitude, by no means unpleasant. Labour turnover is exceptionally low (one half the industry average), absenteeism well below average, in spite of the fact that, in some companies, working conditions were downright poor, uncomfortable and dirty. (The report working party had carried out an opinion survey in order to establish some of these data.) Statistics were sketchy but seemed to confirm that working days lost per employee due to disputes were a little higher than average.

The report explained the current industrial relations position as follows: during the 1960s and 1970s the group expanded rapidly under the genius of one man, Mr Woodcock, but at that time the trade unions gained enormous power throughout the nation and as the company grew so it incorporated this union power within its structures (the Electronics Division was not even formed until 1977). In the three divisions there was approximately one trade union representative for every 25 employees which compared with 30 for other firms the working party surveyed and one to 160 for the Electronics Division. As a result, whenever a dispute occurs on the shop floor, the managers stand back and allow – indeed encourage – a team of personnel managers to arbitrate between the union and the management. Even today, whenever senior management wish to communicate with the employees, the union is informed first, and it is they who inform the employees and then, if anyone remembers to do so, the supervisors are told.

The report ended with the thought that smaller companies have fewer industrial relations problems: and many of the group profit centres, it noted, were rather large.

The team members were much impressed by this report and accepted it as a skilful analysis of a phenomenon they had all recognized without really giving it much thought. It had always been like that in this company. They now recognized this too: it was no longer like that in most of industry in Britain and had not been for many years; it was certainly not like that, and never had been, with some of their international competitors, and it was not like that in the best performing division in the group – the division which, some of the members noted privately, the other divisions were competing with for the group's resources. One divisional managing director remarked that if, in the modern world, the employees needed a union to protect them from their employer, then the employer must have got something very wrong indeed.

Stars and dogs   This report, compiled by the Finance Department, attempted to classify the group's forty-three profit centres into the BCG categories. In summary, this showed that 20 per cent of group turnover was from 'dogs', 25 per cent each from 'wild cats' and 'stars' and 30 per cent from cash cows.

The planning team decided not to pursue this very detailed analysis at the profit centre level, but to concentrate on the divisional. This analysis showed the following percentages by turnover:

Steel   (Four profit centres. Turnover £87m.)

Dogs	50
Wild cats	0
Stars	0
Cash cows	50

Electronics   (Eighteen profit centres. Turnover £124m.)

Dogs	0
Wild cats	60
Stars	40
Cash cows	0

Defence   (Eleven profit centres. Turnover £225m.)

Dogs	0
Wild cats	20
Stars	40
Cash cows	40

Mechanical Handling   (Ten profit centres. Turnover £129m.)

Dogs	60
Wild cats	10
Stars	0
Cash cows	30

Very considerable interest was aroused by this report. The finance department had carefully consulted everyone concerned so there was little disagreement in the team as to the classifications. What did arouse debate was the remarkably different distribution within the divisions suggesting that each needed to be guided by a different set of strategies.

The vast size of the dogs was worrying – £120m turnover would either have to be slimmed down into niche product companies or be disposed of, if the BCG theory was correct. On the other hand, the total of the stars and wild cats came to half the group turnover; for a company looking for expansion, with the financial resources available, this should give plenty of scope.

The team now turned to consider the other strengths and weaknesses thrown up in the seminar.

Finance   The group balance sheet is very strong. In particular, there are no loans at all and the overdraft has exceeded £20m only on rare occasions in the past three years. Cash flow calculations suggest that at the end of the current year (Year 1) there will be a cash surplus of £25m. By Year 5 the cash balance would approach £70m according to Fpes, £40m in Fopt, the interest from this invested cash making a significant contribution to profits in the later years.

The Finance Director estimated for the team that the current loan capacity of the group might be as high as £150m. This would take the gearing to 30 per cent at the end of this year. If the forecasts are correct the group could have borrowed £200m by Year 5 on present strategies, equivalent to a steady, prudent build-up of loan capital of, say, £40m each year. This contrasts with current group capital expenditure, over and above depreciation, of approximately £20m per annum – i.e. capital expenditure could be more than doubled and this ignored possible equity issues.

Products   The team agreed that the group could boast a number of market leaders but felt that the BCG description subsumed these under stars and cash cows. Nevertheless, the team agreed that it must not lose sight of the importance of these remarkable assets.

Reputation   The team agreed that this was an important strength. They noted, however, that its value was limited to its particular specialist markets and did not extend to areas beyond these. For example, the company's name was completely unknown in the aircraft industry, undersea warfare or aerospace, to mention a tiny number of the markets in which its particular engineering expertise (reliability under extreme conditions) would be particularly advantageous.

Employees   The team worried about this item. The seminar had suggested that the workforce was 'stable'. Certainly the figures quoted in the industrial relations report confirmed that turnover and absenteeism was low for the industry, but could this really be an elephant? The team thought not. They were not even sure that, compared with their competitors, which is how many strengths or weaknesses should be defined, it was really so low. Two members of the team had worked with competitors and they felt it was much the same as theirs.

The team turned to another aspect. The industrial relations report suggested that the company did not treat their employees with very great regard and yet the employees seemed willing and loyal. 'Maybe, if we treated them better – trained them properly, gave them proper supervisors – they would respond with enthusiasm,' said one member.

Dependence on defence   The team could not disagree with this, it was obvious – 58 per cent of the group's profits came from the Defence Division plus 6 per cent from the Electronics Division's defence work. (Compare the contribution from Mechanical Handling and Steel, two huge divisions turning over 40 per cent of the group total, employing 7,500 people and yielding a mere 18 per cent of profits.) The danger was that if the Defence Division rose to Fopt while the other divisions fell to Fpes it could rise to 65 per cent of group profits (Figure 12.3).

It was quite clear that a major strategic dilemma was emerging here: did the Group want to exploit this very obvious star or was it too dangerous to do so? The team noted the size of this elephant.

Slow to develop products   This required no discussion. The longest serving divisional managing director recounted how the group had, for three decades, startled its competitors with its innovations. How else does one achieve market leadership, he asked rhetorically, before pointing out that the group had brought not one single new product to the market for a decade. What do we get for the £20m of private venture development we spend each year? What did we get for the £5m we gave that German company for 'know-how'?

The others could only agree. Not even in Electronics had any major new products been launched. The success of this division was founded on buying small innovative companies and giving them the resources they needed to market their ideas. Even there, few new products had appeared after the companies had been acquired.

The team noted 'NPD' (New Product Development) as a major weakness, this term to include the fact that none of the divisions had the necessary mechanisms to take products through a systematic classic NPD process: market research, design, development, launch, sell, service and update.

No presence in USA   The team agreed that for a company with such substantial market presence in Europe, the USA was a notable vacuum. The group chief executive pointed out that although 35 per cent of the company's turnover was exported, mostly to Europe, this did not make the company very large in Europe. The group market share of the UK defence budget, for example, was less than 1 per cent! In no area, except the world steel industry, was our market share more than peanuts, so it could be said that the UK and Europe were also major opportunities. He agreed, however, that the USA was a glaring opportunity. It was also correct that we have no one whose knowledge of the markets there is substantial.

This item was rejected as a lone elephant but was treated as a part of the next one.

No group marketing strategy   Because the group was broken into divisions, each of which was expected to employ its own marketing department, the group as a whole had no group marketing policy. Not only did the group have no idea whether it should develop in the USA – or, on the contrary, not do so but continue to concentrate in Europe – it also had no idea whether its growth was to come from the existing four areas of business or from a completely new area in which, as had often been discussed in the past, high engineering reliability was at a premium, such as aerospace.

Again, although 77 per cent of turnover came from original equipment (OE), 32 per cent of the group's profits come from spares and repairs (SR). As all engineers know, SR traditionally returns higher margins than OE but it is now threatened by new long-life products, especially electronic compononents, by modular design (allowing parts to be thrown away rather than repaired) and by closer stock controls (JIT, MRP, etc.) which reduced the clients' need to hold stocks of spares. It seemed inevitable that margins would drop. No marketing response from the group had been devised for all this although it had been discussed for years.

The team agreed that this lack of marketing at group might well be an elephant. It was then noticed that not only did group not have a marketing presence, but there was no group personnel function either, nor an R & D function. Were all these elephants too? It was agreed that all these were exactly the sort of questions that the corporate planning exercise was supposed to sort out – though at this stage the team was not sure how this would be achieved.

The external appraisal   No further strengths and weaknesses were proposed by the team who felt that the seminar had successfully flushed out all the important items. The strengths and weaknesses discussions took the team a total of fourteen hours and it was now August. They then turned to threats and opportunities.

Steel   The long-term decline of the world steel industry was discussed and a number of reports were tabled by the divisional managing director of Steel.

Virtually all the reports agreed that demand for tonnage steel world-wide was likely to decline over the decades for a number of reasons, the decline in shipbuilding being one significant factor, while demand for special steels and alloys would increase. The reports differed strongly on the likely rates for all these trends. They did all agree that the centre of gravity of production had shifted to the Third World producers and would not shift back.

These trends spelt out clearly that the products of the Steel Division would decline or, at best, remain static in volume. Competition from the Eastern Bloc would continue to gain ground in the less developed world. Meanwhile, the three other competitors in the West would continue to cut each other's throats with price reductions.

These three competitors each had approximately the same production capacity as Woodcock's Steel Division and together could supply world demand twice over. So far as is known, all four companies were making profits and all were investing heavily in new electronic controls while at the same time taking spare capacity out of use.

The German competitor was owned by the Vogel family, known to be anxious to get rid of it. The Belgian firm, now absorbed into the Swiss conglomerate, Oiseau S.A., had closed down a number of manufacturing units in recent years. The American producer, part of the huge Bird Inc., was known to be considering renewed rationalization.

The team formed the impression of a declining industry in which there were four very evenly matched contestants.

Defence   Here the level of uncertainty was acute. Half the Defence Division's turnover was exported, half of this to Europe and the rest to Australia, India, etc.

In the past, demand had risen strongly while America and Europe had been 'catching up' with the Russians, but this was now over and a new possibility of détente and mutual disarming had emerged with the appointment of Mr Gorbachev as the Russian leader, and his realization of the need to cut their expenditure on arms for urgent economic reasons.

There were many scenarios of which two extreme possibilities were: (1) the East and West Blocs would come to trust each other increasingly, in which case, spurred on by economic necessity, over the next decade orders for conventional arms could actually decline; or (2) another hitch would occur, as it had on so many previous occasions (Gorbachev could lose power to the Russian 'hawks', another Afghanistan, a 'U2' and so on), and the world would be off on another round of re-arming. There were, within these scenarios, many others relating to swings between nuclear and conventional arms, technological shifts, the balance between US and European burdens of defence expenditure, and so on.

In attempting to quantify possible demand over the next ten years (the team decided that for this industry, five years was not a sufficient horizon) they noted that, according to one method of estimating, the USA spent as much as 6 per cent of GNP on defence, the UK 3 per cent and Europe approximately 2 per cent. It was easy to believe that popular demand might force a future, or even the current, British government down towards 2 per cent, resulting in a huge cut in UK expenditure. The team thought it was wholly unlikely that UK expenditure would rise, but it was possible to imagine the Americans weakening their resolve to pay for the defence of Europe such that Europe might collectively have to spend up to, say, 3 per cent of GNP.

Bearing in mind also the possible swings in air, land and sea warfare, and the place of the Defence Division's products in these theatres, the team concluded that turnover could rise or fall by at least £100m over and beyond the figures in the Fpes and Fopt forecasts. Thus the team's more detailed and longer-range deliberations had significantly widened the range of forecasts implied for the Defence Division at the seminar – the range was now down to only £340m in Year 10 and up to £550m.

Barriers to the USA and the dollar   For years, probably decades, Woodcocks had eyed the huge American markets for defence, steel, mechanical handling and electronic products. Each division had, at one time or another, tried to enter this market, only to be rebuffed. Turnover in the USA for the entire group was currently only £20m.

Recently the belief had grown in the company that if the group was to enter this market it would have to do so on a group scale, complete with a proper office, top quality native management and administration, and above all, market research facilities.

The problems were obvious. The Steel Division was unlikely to do very well there – Bird Inc. supplied the whole of the USA, Canada and much of South America's steel industries. The Defence Division would have a hard task to sell defence equipment to the Pentagon – the most nationalistic purchasing organization known to man. That left Electronics and Mechanical Handling. The Electronics Division was already expanding there at a very substantial rate while Mechanical Handling's range of products were barely up to UK standards, let alone US. It was beginning to look as though the USA was not, except for Electronics, quite the bonanza they had thought.

Above all, there is the dollar. It had fallen 30 per cent in the past year, having risen 50 per cent in the previous few years. Where would it be in one year's time, not to mention five? Might the group buy a US company for, say, £100m, only to find it worth £50m in the balance sheet in a couple of years? Did they have the skills to get into the USA where so many had failed? They thought not. Could they acquire the skills? Certainly, but . . .

Recession and the £ sterling   The team noted that neither Steel nor Defence were likely to be affected by a national, or even a world, economic recession; capital expenditure by the steel industry lagged many years behind normal recessions and defence was, if anything counter-cyclical even in these non-Keynesian days.

It was conceded that both Mechanical Handling and Electronics were sensitive to economic conditions. However, the recession three and four years ago, one of the most severe for several decades, apparently caused a drop in turnover and profits of only a few per cent. 'Recession' was therefore deleted as a group elephant although any individual business might consider it to be one.

Figures showed that the group's exports went to a considerable number of different nations of which West Germany, £17m, was the greatest. It was concluded that the group was not exposed to exchange rate risks for any one currency. It was felt that exposure to a general shift in the value of sterling was, however, an elephant, since a 10 per cent rise could wipe out the margins on all of Mechanical Handling's and some of the other divisions' exports; a fall in profit of fully £10m was possible, at least in the short term. The team felt some anxiety about making foreign acquisitions since they had no experience of this, and the swings in exchange rates, so much a feature of business today, worried them.

Japanese competition   It was agreed that this title was shorthand for Japan and other low-cost producers including, for example, South Korea. Taking the divisions in order, Steel felt it was unlikely that any new competitors would be emerging in their field, not in any nation. Electronics believed that competition would grow vigorously, but the divisional managing director made it clear that his companies' special skills lay not in the mass production of components – where volume was rising and costs were falling at 20 to 30 per cent per annum – but in applications where, if one was clever enough, one could use standard hardware and specialist software to provide customers with highly specific 'smart' equipment and systems. Defence recognized that the threat was very real. The

Japanese spent a tiny fraction of GNP on defence but, as the memory of war faded, the divisional managing director was sure they would be asked to make a far greater contribution to 'Western' defence. However, it would take a full ten years for them, or anyone, to make an impact on Defence Division products starting from a green field. (Oddly enough, he added, countries like Brazil and India have more embryonic competitive products than Japan, but neither are expected to compete significantly in world defence markets for many years.)

Mechanical Handling noted that the Japanese had already set up a plant in Holland and their products were becoming a nuisance. The divisional managing director feared there would be more such attacks on his market.

Electronics The market for special applications, such as the companies of the division specialize in, seemed likely to grow very fast; various reports estimated the rate at between 5 and 50 per cent. The market is so diverse and fragmented that no overall figure makes sense. Growth seemed likely to be rapid, prolonged and to widen into every imaginable field of human activity.

It is moving in every direction at once, explained the divisional managing director. For a time there is a massive surge in 'space invader' machines for the leisure industry, then a wave of enthusiasm sweeps over the car industry for engine management or active suspension, then it is off to hotels for security systems and to defence for 'smart' weapons guidance or stealth. The director explained that this is why he had adopted such a fragmented organization – it was essential to be small and alert. 'You all laugh at me because I have eighteen MDs, eighteen marketing directors, eighteen factory directors, and so on; but you should see the motivation!' He had no doubt at all that the 12 per cent growth in the 'optimistic' forecast was highly pessimistic (Figure 12.3).

Acquisitions The team began to list suitable companies for acquisition. The rules of this game, suggested the group chief executive, were to state clearly what the precise reason for making an acquisition was. He would not allow acquisitions to be made just for the sake of growth.

One obvious candidate was an American electronics company whose product range mirrored one of the Electronics Division's companies. Another was a French company which manufactured a similar range of products to the Mechanical Handling Division. Both these had been in the group mind for several years but no decision had ever been made. A large number of other suggestions were made and it was noted that several of them were private companies which might require a cash bid. Woodcock's price earnings ratio is 14:1 compared with the sector average of 11:1.

The Swallowtail project   The Ministry of Defence had advised the group, under the usual terms of the Official Secrets Act, that a major new defence project had been approved in outline and that the Woodcock Group would be one of four companies permitted to tender for certain elements of this. The specification showed that if the Defence Division won this contract it would be worth £700m over the period Year 3 to Year 11. (A small fraction would go to Electronics Division, but most of the contract was for mechanical and structural engineering.)

Unfortunately, the Government had decided not to subsidise the development work in the early years and this would cost Woodcock approximately £12m in each of the next three years. Although this project was plainly within the technical competence of the Defence Division the Ministry had never before included them on the tender list for such a major project. Thus Woodcocks could, if they wished to put up £36m private venture money, join the very select club of major defence contractors in this field.

The cruciform chart

The planning team had taken 17 hours to discuss the various reports on these threats and opportunities submitted to them by the various divisional specialists (the group chief executive and the finance director had devoted many more hours between the meetings). It was now late September and they felt that a clear picture of the strategic situation of the group was beginning to emerge. They summarized this in Figure 12.4 as an aide memoire.

The strategic situation

The team decided that the elephants were as follows:

1   The fact that there were no gaps, coupled with the very considerable strengths, especially the financial one, together

Figure 12.4 Woodcock's strategic situation

The gaps

Profit targets	Tmin	£82m
	Tsat	£102m
Profit forecasts	Tmin	£97m
	Tsat	£109m
ROCE targets	Tmin	18%
	Tsat	22.5%
ROCE forecasts	Tmin	16%
	Tsat	18.6%

Gap analysis   There are no profit growth gaps. Even if a number of trends and events move against us, our performance will still be better than poor and it could be excellent. But our ROCE is too low now and, on present strategies, stays too low throughout.

The cruciform chart

Strengths	*Weaknesses*
Finance	Productivity
Reputation	Industrial relations
25% stars	20% dogs
6 world leaders	Dependence on defence
25% wildcats	Slow NPD
30% cash cows	Group marketing
Stable profits	USA know-how

Threats	*Opportunities*
Steel industry	Defence
Defence	Electronics market
Dollar	Acquisitions
Competition	USA
	Swallowtail

---

with the almost limitless opportunities – all close to existing business areas – suggested that the group could be substantially more adventurous than it currently intended.

2 The stars and wildcats might well provide enough growth in the three areas of opportunities – defence, electronics and Swallow-

tail – to drive the company forward well beyond its present targets without going outside its core strengths. Diversification – even acquisition – looked unnecessary.

3 Simply dealing with the dogs would considerably improve the profits (by perhaps £6m per annum, if their ROCE was enhanced to Tmin levels), and if it was necessary to dispose of all of these this would add perhaps £30m to the already substantial cash available.

4 The group would have to attend to its four weaknesses: industrial relations, productivity, NPD and group marketing policy.

5 There was a major interlinked decision to be made on Steel and Defence. If Steel continued to decline and Defence to expand – especially if they won Swallowtail – the group would become massively dependent on defence, *and defence was listed as a threat.*

At this point the divisional managing director of Mechanical Handling made a profound and, for him, lengthy contribution: 'It seems to me that we have only three elephants. A very welcome one is that we could, if we wished, grow very much faster than we thought – and with virtually no need to diversify beyond our present skills or geographical area. The second is whether we want to become a defence group, an electronics group, or stay as an engineering conglomerate. Personally, I vote for electronics; it is the market of the future and Electronics Division has the shape of the future – a lot of small virile companies. And the third elephant is industrial relations, productivity and a couple of other internal inefficiencies that we must put right – but the point I am making is, I see this third bunch as just one elephant. They all stem from the failure of the group board to generate the relevant group strategies over the past few years.'

These comments were greeted with acclamation. He had summed it up for everyone.

Strategies

The team felt that a number of strategies did not require any further discussion and that immediate action could be taken on the following.

Industrial relations and productivity There was strong agreement that these two were intimately connected. It seemed that three of the divisions had failed lamentably to move with the times and that a complete overhaul of the way they treated their employees was needed.

It was equally clear that any attempt to tackle this would require great care – the slightest hint that they were mounting a 'Smash the Unions' campaign would be disastrous; this was most certainly not the intention. It had to be an 'Improve Employees' Career Prospects' campaign or 'Towards Personal and Product Excellence'; or whatever. The aim was to win the confidence of employees, to convince them that we, the management, would lead them to a more satisfying working life. Everyone recognized that a 'culture change' of this magnitude could take many years.

Three main limbs of the strategy could be discerned: the systematic introduction of human resource techniques such as Quality Circles and Team Briefings; the introduction of productivity techniques such as Quality Management, JIT and MRP; and, where practical, to cut the size of some of the larger profit centres – the group chief executive particularly mentioned one of the companies in Defence which employed over 3,000 people in one site on which several entirely different products were made. Surely that could be fragmented, he asked.

The group chief executive decided that he and the three divisional managing directors most concerned would form a team to interview consultants to help draw up a detailed schedule and to select a project manager. Mr Finch, for whom the team had great respect, was the obvious choice. Setting targets for him would also be an essential part of their task.

These considerations led to the next strategic decision.

The group structure   If three divisional managing directors and the group chief executive, already fully occupied, were going to give adequate attention to the industrial relations project, and all the others that would come out of the corporate planning exercise, they would need to alter their job descriptions. Moreover, they had all noticed that not one single idea for group expansion had lain outside the four present business areas represented by the four divisions. No one had mentioned medical electronics, space engineering, high pressure hydraulics or a dozen other areas of business which they were not currently in. It was as though there was a no-go area between the four business areas.

Again, they all remarked on the cohesion that had developed

Figure 12.5 Woodcock Group's third forecast

£m	Pessimistic							Optimistic						
	Year 0	1	2	3	4	5	% change	Year 0	1	2	3	4	5	% change

The Woodcock Group plc

£m	Year 0	1	2	3	4	5	% change	Year 0	1	2	3	4	5	% change
Turnover	565.7	572.2	614.1	595.4	672.5	737.2	5.6	565.7	606.9	732.5	805.3	936.9	1067.6	13.6
Profit	71.1	73.1	79.3	84.7	98.1	109.5	9.1	71.1	79.9	103.2	118.1	147.0	178.4	20.4
Capital employed	422.2	464.6	507.3	455.0	509.2	551.7	5.8	422.2	467.8	568.5	613.6	734.5	835.3	14.7
ROS %	12.6	12.8	12.9	14.2	14.6	14.9	3.4	12.6	13.2	14.1	14.7	15.7	16.7	5.9
ROCE %	16.8	15.7	15.6	18.6	19.3	19.8	3.7	16.8	17.1	18.2	19.2	20.0	21.4	4.9

Steel Division

£m	Year 0	1	2	3	4	5	% change	Year 0	1	2	3	4	5	% change
Turnover	87.2	76.7	67.5	0.0	0.0	0.0	—	87.2	88.0	90.0	92.0	94.0	96.0	1.9
Profit	6.7	5.4	2.7	0.0	0.0	0.0	—	6.7	8.1	9.1	10.1	11.3	12.5	13.5
Capital employed	63.5	73.5	76.0	0.0	0.0	0.0	—	63.5	73.5	76.0	78.0	81.0	83.5	5.7
ROS %	7.6	7.0	4.0	0.0	0.0	0.0	—	7.6	9.2	10.1	11.0	12.1	13.0	11.4
ROCE %	10.5	7.3	3.6	0.0	0.0	0.0	—	10.5	11.0	12.0	13.0	14.0	15.0	7.4

Electronics Division

£m	Year 0	1	2	3	4	5	% change	Year 0	1	2	3	4	5	% change
Turnover	124.3	135.5	159.6	199.4	243.5	286.2	18.3	124.3	138.7	181.3	223.5	265.5	329.0	21.7
Profit	17.1	19.3	23.4	30.0	37.5	45.0	21.5	17.1	20.8	29.0	38.0	49.0	65.8	31.1
Capital employed	63.5	75.5	90.0	108.6	131.8	159.7	20.3	63.5	76.4	94.4	117.9	148.3	189.1	24.4
ROS %	13.8	14.2	14.7	15.0	15.4	15.7	2.7	13.8	15.0	16.0	17.0	18.5	20.0	7.8
ROCE %	26.9	25.6	26.0	27.6	28.4	28.2	1.0	26.9	27.2	30.7	32.2	33.0	34.8	5.3

Defence Division

Turnover	225.3	230.0	255.0	262.0	293.0	313.0	6.9	225.3	242.3	313.7	331.9	408.5	461.9	15.8
Profit	41.0	41.9	46.5	47.7	53.4	57.0	6.9	41.0	44.1	57.4	61.4	77.2	89.6	17.3
Capital employed	248.8	265.2	286.7	287.6	314.0	324.0	6.0	248.8	267.3	342.7	357.0	438.6	489.6	6.0
ROS %	18.2	18.2	18.2	18.2	18.2	18.2	0.0	18.2	18.2	18.3	18.5	18.9	19.4	1.3
ROCE %	16.5	15.8	16.2	16.6	17.0	17.6	1.3	16.5	16.5	16.7	17.2	17.6	18.3	2.1

Mechanical Handling Division

Turnover	128.9	130.0	132.0	134.0	136.0	138.0	3.7	128.9	137.9	147.6	157.9	169.0	180.8	7.0
Profit	6.3	6.5	6.7	7.0	7.2	7.5	3.4	6.3	6.9	7.7	8.5	9.5	10.5	10.8
Capital employed	46.4	50.4	54.6	58.9	63.4	68.0	3.7	46.4	50.6	55.4	60.7	66.6	73.1	9.5
ROS %	4.9	5.0	5.1	5.2	5.3	5.4	1.3	4.9	5.0	5.2	5.4	5.6	5.8	3.5
ROCE %	13.6	12.9	12.2	11.5	11.0	10.5	−0.9	13.6	13.6	13.9	14.0	14.2	14.4	1.1

between them. They no longer came to board meetings just to fight for their corners, but to work for the interests of the group as a whole. These thoughts led to the implications that (a) they should act more as a group board, (b) they needed a group staff, in addition to the purely financial staff under the group finance director, including someone capable of market research, especially geographical opportunities and acquisition studies and technology evaluation for the group as a whole – a 'planning department' in other words, (c) none of the divisions had the expertise to set up and supervise an NPD system – someone at group level, perhaps a consultant on assignment, should give them a hand to do this, and (d) the divisional managing directors needed to delegate more to the their profit centre managers.

Very tactfully the group chief executive added another point. It had become clear that the balance of business in the group was going to alter significantly and it would help to spread the load on some divisional managing directors if they took up additional group responsibilities as their divisional duties declined. For example, it was clear that someone was needed to supervise several of their strategic projects – industrial relations and productivity, for example – and the divisional managing director of Mechanical Handling was ideally qualified to do that.

The team then turned to the more complex strategies.

Growth   It was agreed that the group should make full use of all the good news: the copious finances available and obtainable, the stars and world leading products, the rapid growth in some of their markets. The finance director produced a new forecast (Figure 12.5) based on the following assumptions:

- That the group invested all its cash flow in the stars and leaders in Electronics, Mechanical Handling and, to some extent, in Defence. This meant annual capital expenditures of almost double the currently proposed rate.
- That the expansion in Defence was restrained so that its profits did not exceed 50 per cent of the group total by Year 5, but this would have the effect of raising its ROCE. The Swallowtail project was excluded from these calculations.
- That the dogs be trimmed as described below.
- That loans to bring the gearing to 20 per cent by Year 5 be obtained, subject to rigorous year-by-year review.

Figure 12.6   Summary of the third five-year forecast

| *Woodcock Group* | *Year 0* | | *Year 5* |
	£m	Fpes	Fopt
Turnover	565	737	1067
Profits	71	110	178
Capital employed	422	551	835
ROS %	12.6	14.9	16.7
ROCE %	16.8	19.8	21.4

The team were startled by the figures. They showed a pessimistic rate of growth of 9 per cent and an optimistic one of 20 per cent per annum. They also showed Electronics, currently yielding 24 per cent of group profits, rising to 40 per cent with Defence dropping from nearly 60 per cent to 50 per cent. While rejecting the actual figures as being unbelievably optimistic, the team did feel that they represented the general direction in which the company could and should be moving.

Swallowtail   The group had deliberately never previously allowed itself to undertake any major project of such a size. Everyone agreed that £700m turnover from one project, out of the group total of less than £10bn over the next ten years, was out of proportion; to adopt this project would jeopardize the group's enviable reputation for profit stability. Furthermore, to move still deeper into the clutches of the Ministry of Defence – with their rigid control of pricing and ROCE, and their growing sophistication in purchasing decisions, not to mention the £36m that would have to be invested, and the possibility of not being awarded the contract as well as the group's already heavy dependence on defence – all pointed away from competing for this project. The fact that its return on investment was no better than other, less risky, projects finalized the discussion – a decision diametrically contrary to the one reached at the seminar, where it was rated a 'Must Win Contract', they noticed.[3]

The dogs   The strategy decided was: any loss-making profit centre was to be closed down or sold at once unless the divisional managing director thought he could turn it round within a year to a

ROCE of at least 18 per cent. Any dog making less than 18 per cent also had one year to reach that figure. This applied to all companies with less than £20m turnover, many of them in Mechanical Handling. That left one major profit centre – Steel.

Steel division   The ROCE of this division, now 10 per cent and falling fast, even in the optimistic view, is plainly in doubt. There are the following alternative strategies:

(1)   Close it all down over the next few years and sell the premises. Very approximately, the cost in cash would be zero – the cost of redundancies would amount to £12m and the sites would fetch £12m in a sale.

(2)   Convert and modernize the premises to manufacture for Defence or Electronics. The cost would be approximately £20m, a saving of £15m on constructing new factories for these divisions.

(3)   Sell the division to one of the three competitors so they could rationalize the excess world capacity. Woodcock's financial advisors thought £25m might be a realistic price – it is, after all, currently generating a profit of over £6m.

(4)   Buy a competitor and then rationalize the two businesses. The cost would be, say, £25m to buy, and the cost of rationalizing would again be zero (sale of assets equals cost of redundancies). It was highly questionable whether the Woodcock Group ought to try to juggle with such large units in an international arena.

(5)   Sell to a multinational conglomerate, of which there were several possible candidates, who might well have the resources to rationalize two or three companies, and with the possible demise of the fourth, end up with a world monopoly.

(6)   Spend perhaps £20m to place Steel Division in a position to undercut one targeted competitor (the German one) and force him out of business. But even this would still leave 25 per cent over-capacity in the world.

(7)   Spend £10m to improve ROCE to 12 per cent as proposed by the divisional managing director.

(8)   Form a cartel, suggest a merger, invite a bid. Over the past two decades all the chairmen of all the competitors have met frequently to discuss what to do about the industry. None have been, nor are presently, in the mood for co-operation

because to co-operate is to place their company in the position
of the bride, not the groom.
(9) Do nothing. The division was, after all, not making a loss and
it acted as a flywheel to stabilize group profits.

By mid-November the team had decided not to adopt alternatives
4, 6, 8 or 9. It then took one full meeting, and many calculations
and estimating, to decide to adopt alternative 7; spend £12m to lift
profits to £9m by the end of Year 2. The justification for this
expenditure was as follows:

(a) Their concern for the stability of the group's profits. The
flywheel effect was considered important, especially because
the stock market had noted this favourable feature of the
company's record in recent years compared to others in the
sector, and as noted before, Steel is contributing over £6m
profit.
(b) The return on this £12m investment was expected to be over
20 per cent – not bad, although not up to the hurdle rate of 25
per cent generally required in the group. The proposals were
very specific and had been confirmed by consulting engineers.
(c) The other divisions would not wish to use Steel's factory space
for at least another three years. It would take at least two
years to find a buyer for the sites and it would take at least one
year to find a buyer for the Steel Division. If one of the
competitors was interested in it, they would, it was felt, be
more interested if they observed that considerable funds were
being invested in it by the present owners. If the profits rose to
£9m this itself would enhance the selling price by substantially
more than the £12m they were proposing to spend.

In other words, the team decided to investigate several of the
alternative strategies listed above in further detail and meanwhile
to enhance the value of the division in case it had to be sold. The
expenditure would also act as an installment towards Alternative 6,
should this be considered a sensible route in two years' time.

There was another reason for delaying: If, in spite of their
efforts, Steel was really to be closed down, it was essential to
replace its flywheel effect with some new activity of comparable size
that was not related to the existing business areas – in effect, a
whole new division might be required. Deciding what this was to be

and how it was to be formed would take some time. As noted above, they currently had no idea what this should be – one of the most important conclusions of the exercise was that they did not know this, that group was not equipped to select and manage any sort of activity that was not within the boundaries of one of the current divisions.

At this point the group chief executive said:

I feel that we have reached the end of this particular exercise. We have made three major decisions. We feel we should expand much more rapidly than we had intended – a far-reaching and quite unexpected result. I had no idea, when we started this exercise, that we would come up with something as exciting as that. Then, we feel we should alter the balance of the group, partly to prevent it becoming a defence group, partly to steer it towards the future which looks like being an electronic one. Finally, we should put our house in order in respect of industrial relations, productivity, and so on. End of the discovery part of the exercise, in my view; cue for action.

But, as I have said, I want to draw you into a group board where we can do two things: (1) supervise the application of this corporate plan, and (2) start thinking, perhaps in a year's time when we have truly launched the actions for this plan, towards the next plan. By Year 3 or 4 we should be well on the way to Electronics overhauling Defence. OK, but then what? More electronics, a big acquisition, should we still be sticking to Europe then or will it be time to move into the USA? The last thing I want is to find ourselves on a plateau, like the one we are just getting off, because of any failure on our part to start thinking strategically about the issues that lie beyond the ones we have just identified. In other words, a company of our size needs to think much further ahead – ten years at least.

So I think we have gone as far as we need. We could go further now – a major acquisition, perhaps, or we could get an outside consultant to devise us a more aggressive stance – but I do not feel we are equipped to do any more, at present, than the set of strategies we have already decided.

There was full agreement round the table with this summary.
Summarizing the strategies that had been agreed:

Growth To adopt a much more ambitious growth target. To double the intended rate of expansion of Electronics and to a much lesser extent, and depending on project viability, Mechanical Handling. To expand Defence but not so it exceeded 50 per cent of profits by Year 5. To increase the group's gearing to 20 per cent subject to annual confirmation. To acquire a number of specialist companies in closely related fields.

Industrial relations To launch a long-term, systematic programme. The aim was to re-establish the *management* as the employees' most effective route to a better working life and, at the same time, to enlist their help to make a major improvement in quality and productivity (say 30 per cent by Year 3).

Group board structure More emphasis on group. The group chief executive and group finance director wished the divisional managing directors to play a much greater role in formulating group strategy and monitoring *group*, not just their own, results. If the Chairman approved, he wanted them on the group board, not only in their role as divisional managing directors but responsible for functions as well. A small, professional team of group advisers should be formed in a 'planning department' to search for new business areas (especially if Steel Division goes), to oversee NPD at group level, seek acquisition candidates, and so on. These six executives, with their strengthened advisory staff, should begin to think towards the next corporate plan in about a year's time.

Dogs Greater determination to deal with these. All dogs were to be turned round to yield at least Tmin ROCE (18 per cent) within a year or closed or sold. Any that seemed unlikely to achieve this would be closed or sold at once.

Steel One last try to lift it. £12m to be invested immediately as detailed by the divisional managing director to the team. If, within two years, it has not reached 12 per cent ROCE, or £9m profits, it should be sold or closed. Meanwhile, very careful study is required to find a buyer. If Steel exceeds these targets a further £8m might be available to target one competitor to reduce competition in the industry.

The team felt that the general direction of the group was now very clear and that they should concentrate on drawing up the executive actions needed to put it into effect and to design the monitoring system.

APPENDIX A

The Introductory Seminar

Purpose

The purpose of the seminar is to facilitate the launch of the corporate planning process into an organization. This is achieved by inviting all those who are likely to play a part in the process – normally the top three levels of the management hierarchy – to learn what it involves and how they may assist. This alone is enough to arouse their interest and co-operation but, as a further reinforcement, the seminar also invites them to move through the process for their organization just as if they were members of the planning team itself for the two days of the seminar.

It should be carefully explained to them that it will not be possible for them to attempt more than a mere shadow of a corporate plan compared with what the planning team must eventually achieve; nevertheless, the seminar is intended as a serious exercise which will, at the very least, provide some valuable strategic pointers for the team.

This seminar invariably produces an extremely positive response among the participants and results in a marked lift in morale. Because they will be given a very clear idea of what the exercise entails, and because they will identify many of the key issues, the planning team's task will be much reduced; for an organization employing a thousand people, for example, it could reduce the time to develop the corporate plan from nine months to six. Indeed, on some occasions strategies are identified with such assurance that they are put straight into effect the day after the seminar.

Participants

The seminar should be attended by the chief executive, the executive directors (effectively the planning team) and all senior managers who report directly to them – virtually the top three levels in the hierarchy.

Because they will be working in small discussion groups, the number of participants is limited to between nine and thirty people. (It has been found that three discussion groups each with three members is a practical minimum, while five groups of six members is the effective maximum.)

These discussion groups should be well spread in terms of their members' ages, skills, seniority, departmental duties and personalities. The chief executive should probably not take part in any discussion group while other members of the planning team almost certainly should.

Small companies are recommended to invite at least one outsider to provide a bulwark against bias – the fewer the participants the less opportunity there is for strongly held biases to be eliminated by peer pressure and the more valuable will be the views of an outsider.

Method

The seminar, best held residentially at a hotel not too close to head office, begins with the organizer (i.e. the chief executive, the planning assistant, or a consultant) describing what corporate planning is, how it is normally performed and what results it is intended to achieve. Then the participants break up into their discussion groups and move rapidly through all the stages of the corporate planning process, using the organization itself as their 'case study', so that everyone present may observe how the exercise will be conducted in their particular organization, what their roles may be and where any difficulties may lie. During these discussions many of the key factors which will influence the planning team in its choice of strategy will be identified.

Careful preparation is required by the Planning Assistant before this seminar can be mounted to ensure that everyone who attends will do so in a thoroughly constructive frame of mind and fully conversant with the aims of the seminar.

The seminar described here assumes a full two days of working sessions including the evening of the first day, after dinner, at a hotel. Many variations are possible for these timings, locations and sessions, of course, but it is difficult to compress these events much further.

Specimen programme

First day

0900   Introduction. The chief executive explains why it is appropriate to introduce corporate planning into the organization at this time.

0915   The organizer describes the purpose of corporate planning. He explains the first few stages in the process with examples.

1030   Break.

1045   The organizer completes his description of the process. He decribes examples of strategies to illustrate what the output of the exercise should be.

1230   Lunch.

The seminar now enters its second stage where the participants are divided into discussion groups to move through the corporate planning process using their own organization as a case study.

In larger companies it should be made clear to the participants that this is a demonstration exercise only and that, in real life, the process will take many months to complete. It should also be stressed, however, that it is certainly *not* a mere academic exercise, it is expected that some very important strategic factors will be identified during the group discussions – indeed, the intention is that this seminar will provide the planning team with an almost complete list of the strategic factors they will need to address in their corporate plan.

In smaller simpler organizations it may be possible to reach an almost complete set of draft strategies in this two-day period. It would then be necessary for the planning team merely to confirm and fill out the conclusions after the seminar.

1330   The First Discussion. Participants break into their dis-
            cussion groups to start the process by discussing the

	objectives and suitable targets for the organization over the next five years.
1430	They report back. Discussion in plenary session. (This First Discussion in some non-profit-making organizations may take several hours.)
1530	The Second Discussion. Participants attempt to make a long-term forecast for the organization.
1630	Report back. Discussion. Calculating the 'gaps'.
Evening	The Third Discussion, before and after dinner. The groups discuss strengths and weaknesses – usually the most important of all these discussions. Between two and four hours is normally required.

Second day

0900	Report back. Discussion.
1100	Fourth Discussion. The groups discuss threats and opportunities.
1300	Lunch
1400	Report back. Discussion.
1500	Further discussions:

(1) Some possible strategies – a brief discussion on possible alternative strategies. (Because this is the start of the corporate planning process, not the end, only rough ideas of possible strategies can be expected to emerge here.)

(2) The next steps – discussion to consider how the organization should continue the planning process from now on, including such topics as the future role of participants who are not members of the planning team itself.

Seminar ends.

Warnings

(1)   It should be noted that this seminar is intended to review *all* the major factors that the corporate plan should address – this includes not just products, finance, employees, political trends and possible recession, but also the management at all levels. Highly sensitive issues may be raised, therefore, especially in family

businesses and non-profit-making organizations, and top management should be aware of this feature. The organizer would be well advised to ensure a relaxed, humorous atmosphere to encourage a full discussion. The programme outlined above deliberately begins with corporate objectives and targets, continues with the rather technical forecasting stage and only then, when the discussion groups are used to working together on these less sensitive issues, are the participants invited to consider the much more controversial area of strengths and weaknesses.

(2) Furthermore all these key issues, whether sensitive or not, will be raised in a rather public arena – that is, in the presence of a large number of senior executives – and this may be interpreted by these executives as an undertaking to attend to any issues raised. Thus the seminar effectively commits the management to tackling these issues.

The organizer should be experienced in handling these sensitivities. This warning needs to be made to ensure that there is no misunderstanding over the nature of this exercise. It is, deliberately, highly participative and not all organizations are ready to make major decisions and discuss such issues in this very open environment.

Mistakes to Avoid

Providing one avoids certain key mistakes most corporate planning exercises will result in a set of strategies being identified with quite remarkable clarity. However, there are half a dozen errors which can wreck the process – any one of the errors listed below can virtually guarantee that the process will not result in a set of practical corporate strategies.

The errors are listed in the sequence in which the stages of the process ought to be tackled.

The nature of corporate planning

All other types of planning deal with parts or sections or departments of organization: budgets, market plans, cash flow plans, manpower plans, product plans, production plans, MRP, zero-based budgets – almost every management technique known to man does this. Corporate planning is concerned with that extremely thin layer of decisions which relate to issues affecting the corporate whole. There are, by definition, very few issues that can be included under this heading – as soon as one begins to spell out more than a very few strategies one inevitably drifts in to non-corporate areas, issues that concern parts or sections or departments of the organization as opposed to those relating to the corporate whole.

A corporate plan which contains more than, say, half a dozen strategic statements has almost certainly strayed beyond the bounds of corporate planning into one of these other non-corporate areas. Few completed corporate plans will exceed a dozen pages of which the strategies themselves will account for no more than a page or two.

A corporate plan which contains only statements relating to products, markets or customers is almost certainly not a corporate plan but a market plan. A corporate plan which contains a large number of figures is almost certainly not a corporate plan but a finance plan, a budget, a business plan or a cash-flow plan. Many of the really important issues facing most organization are non-quantifiable.

A corporate plan with a horizon of less than five years (except in small companies growing at very high rates) will almost always address operational issues rather than corporate issues and will therefore fail to yield a set of corporate strategies.

Corporate planning cannot be used to generate new product ideas although it certainly will define the boundaries within which a marketing department should generate them.

The process can be used by autocratic entrepreneurs but they will almost certainly not wish to use it. The process is designed to yield steady sensible strategies round which a team of managers may form a consensus – not at all the sort of thing that entrepreneurial autocrats are normally looking for.

To summarize, failure to understand that corporate planning is different to all these other types of planning will result in an exercise that fails to do the unique thing that corporate planning is designed to do: produce a set of *corporate* strategies which will address the half-dozen huge issues that the organization must get right if it is to prosper over the following few years.

Composition of the planning team

A basic principle of any modern corporate planning process is its reliance on the formulation of a consensus among the top executives. This is required not only to ensure that a wide range of ideas and opinions is offered up and tested before a set of strategies is finally selected but also to encourage strong commitment among these senior people to the application of the strategies into action plans.

Consequently, the formation of a planning team is considered an essential element in the process. Without such a team (a) the strategies may not be the best available, and (b) even more serious, the senior executives may not feel the necessary enthusiasm to put them into action. So crucial is this participative element in today's style of management that it virtually rules out the production of plans by anyone other than the top executives themselves.

The team must include the chief executive without whom the 'elephants' may not be identified and will certainly not be addressed and since addressing the elephants is the whole point of the corporate planning exercise the omission of the chief executive will prove fatal to the project. If the chief executive is not willing or able to lead the team it is a waste of everyone's time even to start. Better to keep to the other types of planning.

A team of fewer than three is not suitable (except in tiny companies where one member ought to be an outsider). A team of more than six, certainly more than eight, suggests that something is not right with the top management structure.

False corporate objectives

Corporate objective are quite distinct from all other types of objectives, missions, goals or aims. The corporate objective, or purpose, states for whom the organization is supposed to be working, what benefit it is intended to provide for them, and how much is satisfactory. It is especially important to get this definition right in the case of non-profit-making organizations.

Failure to identify who and what these are renders the organization vulnerable to 'corporate perversion' and precludes the use of modern standards of management – including corporate planning. The corporate planning exercise will fail to address the key issues if the corporate objectives have not been correctly identified.

The corporate objectives must be strategy-neutral. They should be something that the beneficiaries (and the managers) find attractive and of which society does not disapprove.

Fallacious targets

The adoption of more than one or two CPIs almost certainly means that the correct corporate objective has not been identified. The CPI must reflect the organization's success or failure *as a corporate whole*, not the efficiencies of its various parts.

Both Tmin and Tsat must be stated, that is, the level of performance which represents approaching failure or disgrace must be made explicit, as must also the level that represents modest success. Of the two, Tmin – not Tsat – is the most significant, especially for non-profit-making organizations.

Forecasts

Both Fpes and Fopt must be calculated. Failure to do so permits the forecaster to hide any bad news in his 'best guess' forecasts, the vulnerabilities of the organization to risk will be glossed over and the plan will be devoid of any element of risk control.

The 'no change in strategy' assumption is important. Neglect this and the forecaster will insert all kinds of untried but miraculous ideas which will cloak the true situation.

The errors in long-range forecasts are often the most important part of the forecast; without a statement of the errors, such as the range between Fpes and Fopt, it is useless. This is something even professional managers have not yet grasped because their executive horizons are normally rather short. Short-range forecasts do not normally display this problem.

The appraisals

Keep it simple. Limit the number of elephants to half a dozen each (strengths and weaknesses, threats and opportunities) otherwise the corporate planning exercise will become an operational planning exercise, in which the team will attempt to attend to every tiny detail and thus miss the whole purpose of corporate planning.

The more people involved in these appraisals the better. The knowledge and experience of the participants adds, their biases cancel.

Alternative strategies

Brilliant new ideas are certainly required, but ideas, however brilliant, that are irrelevant to the organization's strategic situation are useless. The team should not expect corporate planning to yield the same level of entrepreneurial innovation as a real entrepreneur, but it should assure the organization of highly satisfactory progress at less risk.

Evaluating the strategies

Check that the chosen strategies really do look like hitting Tsat. More important, check that they are robust against errors in the forecasts so that, if the forecasts are wrong, the strategies prevent the organization's performance falling below Tmin.

Action plans

If there is a reluctance among the senior executives to carry out the plan it suggests that they have not been adequately involved in the process. It may be possible to draw them in even at this late stage, to ensure their enthusiasm.

Monitoring

This is not just 'checking results'. It is asking, more or less continually, whether the team still has confidence that the strategies they have selected will actually take the organization to Tsat and not drop it below Tmin. For their confidence to be maintained not only do the organization's results and action plans have to be on target but there must not be any major unforeseen changes in the strengths and weaknesses or threats and opportunities.

APPENDIX C

Definitions of Terms Used

Corporate Conduct   Any action taken (or deliberately not taken) because it is felt to be morally, aesthetically, socially or personally desirable (or repugnant). Actions taken for this reason would be taken regardless of whether they increased or decreased the organization's ability to achieve its corporate purpose or even if they made it impossible; they are taken because they are the right thing to do. Conduct is largely independent of purpose; it is determined by the mores of the society in which the organization operates. (Conduct is also called ethos, social responsibilities, culture, code of ethics, standards of behaviour, social conscience, etc.) Many conduct statements may be quantified as targets at the Tmin and Tsat levels.

Corporate Description   A formal description of an organization which must include clear statements of the following features: (1) the intended beneficiaries, (2) the benefit they expect, (3) the amount of benefit they expect expressed as Tmin and Tsat using a corporate performance indicator, and (4) the conduct statements with the relevant targets.

Corporate Objective   Used in this book to mean Corporate Purpose. It is also, most confusingly, often used by others to mean Corporate Conduct and Corporate Strategy as well.

Corporate Performance Indicator   The units of measure of the success or failure of an organization, as a corporate whole, to provide the benefit for the intended beneficiaries. It must not be a mere amalgam, weighted or otherwise, of sectional efficiencies or 'performance indicators'. It must be verifiable. It must be capable of being set at the Tmin and Tsat levels. It must be comparable with other similar organizations.

Corporate Perversion Any 'objective' set by any interest group or pressure group, (often the managers themselves) which has the effect of perverting the assets of the organization for their own ends, or at any rate, not to the ends of the intended beneficiaries. Corporate perversion is often disguised as statements made on behalf of the organization (relating either to its objective, conduct or strategy), but which in fact emanates from a pressure group. Any action taken on behalf of an organization that neither contributes to its purpose nor to its ethos will be perverted.

Corporate Plan A set of statements describing the corporate purpose and corporate conduct for an organization together with the corporate strategies which have been designed to achieve the targets.

Corporate Planning A systematic process for deciding what are the half-dozen key decisions that an organization, seen as a corporate whole, *must* get right in order to prosper over the following few years. The process that leads to a corporate plan.

Corporate Purpose Corporate purpose is the reason why any organization was formed and why it exists today. An organization's corporate purpose is the justification for all its strategies, all its actions, indeed, everything it ever does in its entire life history (except actions related to conduct). It is the justification for its very existence, its *raison d'être*. It is the sole criterion by which one may judge whether an organization is successful or a failure. It is the ends as opposed to the means. An organization's corporate purpose is unalterable; if it is changed, the organization itself would have to be reconstituted as a new legal entity. A corporate objective must be strategy-neutral.

Corporate Strategies Strategic actions are taken because, and *only* because, the management believe this would improve the organization's ability to achieve its purpose or its standards of conduct. If they believed such actions would not help to achieve these they would not take them. Strategies are means, not ends. Their sole justification is their effect on achieving the purpose or conduct. A *corporate* strategy relates to actions that affect the organization as a corporate whole – as distinct from strategies which affect only parts or sections of it such as market strategies, manpower strategies, and so on.

Forecast   A forecast is someone's opinion of what will happen in the future. Most forecasts are quantified. All forecasts are liable to error, the longer the horizon of the forecast the greater the errors may be.

Fopt   Fopt is a forecast based on optimistic assumptions.

Fpes   Fpes is a forecast based on pessimistic assumptions.

Foo   A forecast which assumes that the future will be identical to the past. A projection.

Fo   A forecast which assumes that the organization's environment changes (i.e. the forecaster makes pessimistic or optimistic assumptions about it) but that the organization itself reacts only as it presently intends, without adopting any new strategy.

Fp   A forecast which assumes both that the environment changes and that the organization adopts a new strategy towards those changes.

Intended Beneficiary   The person or group of people for whose benefit the organization exists.

Monitoring   Continually testing one's confidence in one's current strategies. It is thus more than merely 'checking results'.

No Harm Principle   The moral concept that, while in pursuit of one's objectives, one should cause no significant harm to others. If harm is caused full compensation should be made.

Strategic Factors   Each strength, weakness, threat and opportunity is a strategic factor. So are targets, forecast, gaps and conduct statements. Everything that is considered to be of strategic importance, and which is to be an ingredient in the strategic decision, is a strategic factor.

Target A Target is a quantified statement of the corporate objective or corporate conduct. It identifies levels of performance which the organization would, or would not, like to see.

Tmin Tmin is a level of performance which the beneficiaries would regard as unsatisfactory to the point where they begin to consider changing the management or even closing down the organization.

Tsat Tsat is a level of performance which the beneficiaries would regard as encouraging to the point where they may begin to consider expanding the organization beyond its current activities and where they may consider granting performance awards to the management.

Total Strategic Situation All the strategic factors together. It describes the organization as it is currently constituted within its present and future environment.

Brief Outline of the Argenti System of Corporate Planning, and Protection Against Errors in Forecasts

Brief outline of the planning process

All planning systems consist of a process, or sequence of stages, which result in a plan. In the Argenti System there are ten stages as outlined below.

As will be seen, Stages 2 to 5 are data-collection stages; Stages 6, 7 and 8 are related to strategy formulation; the remaining stages represent executive actions to give effect to the strategic decisions and to monitor them.

Stage Number	Title	Purpose
Stage One	Preparation	To start the process and to select a planning assistant
Stage Two	Objectives and targets	To define the aims and ambitions for the company
Stage Three	Forecasts and gaps	To calculate the size of the strategic task
Stage Four	Strengths and weaknesses	To decide what the company is especially good at and bad at
Stage Five	Threats and opportunities	To identify what major changes the future may hold for the company

Stage Six	Alternative strategies	To list all the alternative strategies available to the company
Stage Seven	Selecting the strategies	To decide which set of strategies is the most suitable
Stage Eight	Evaluation	To determine whether this set is good enough
Stage Nine	Action plans	To draw up detailed plans and budgets
Stage Ten	Monitoring	Continuously study progress over the years

Note. Although the above shows it as a simple straight-through process there would in practice be iterations, eddies and whirls throughout.

Protection against errors in forecasts

The corporate planning process described in this book contains a number of features designed to fortify the resulting strategies against errors in long-range forecasts. Errors in long-range forecasts, it will be appreciated, are sometimes enormous – far larger than anything seen in short-term forecasts which most executives are used to handling. In the sequence in which they appear the counter-measures are:

Stage Three   Multiple forecasts. The process demands that *two* forecasts are made to draw attention to the range of errors. The aim is to expose the limits of possible events which the future may have in store so the planning team can design their strategies to handle their full extent.
Error checking. A large number of techniques for checking for errors in these forecast are given in Chapter 6.

Stage Four   Great emphasis is placed on the strengths and weaknesses analysis. This, and the design of the subsequent strategy forming process, ensures that organizations select strategies based on their strengths so that, if the forecast turns out wrong, the management has the capabilities to recognize and correct the problem.

Stage Five   The system requires the planners to state the probability of any given threat or opportunity actually taking place. This again draws attention to the errors in the forecast of threats and opportunities.

Stage Seven The whole philosophy of keeping the number of strategies to less than half a dozen is based on the belief that you simply cannot get more than a very few major decisions right because of the levels of uncertainty in the modern world.

The system recommends that the strategic factors are listed in a cruciform chart and that, if it cannot be reliably forecast, the same item should be listed as both a threat and an opportunity (as 'defence' is in the example in Chapter 12).

Stage Eight One key element in the evaluation stage are the questions, 'What could go wrong? What would happen then?' Others are, 'Is the strategy robust? If not, what?' These represent more tests for uncertainty.

Stage Nine Features such as the 'abort buttons' in the design of the action plans described in Chapter 11 are also designed to reduce the consequences of errors.

Stage Ten Most of the monitoring stage is designed to pick up trends and events that have not been forecast and to do so as early as possible. It includes the design for an early warning system.

Tern's Trucks Ltd – A Case Study

The student is invited to imagine he has been asked by Mr Shiner, the owner and chief executive of quite a substantial family business, to join the planning team to devise a set of strategies for a new subsidiary company, Tern's Trucks.

Background

One day in October last year Mr Shiner was working in his office when he received a call from an investment banker of his acquaintance. He informed him that a Mr Tern, founder and owner of Tern's Trucks Ltd, vehicle builders of Southtown, was looking for a buyer for his business so that he could retire (he was 75) and was Mr Shiner interested?

Quite by chance Mr Shiner had been talking to his brother earlier that month about their long-range business strategy. Their business, Shiners Ltd, had done extremely well in retailing, rental and leasing of TV and electrical goods over the past two decades and the profits from the many high street outlets they now had in the district were approaching £6m. However, they had agreed that, due to the government action to damp down the economy, all forms of rental and leasing were likely to be in decline for as long as two years and so things were going to be rather flat until some of the new generation of exciting new consumer products – computers, audio-visual recording, electronic cameras, communications, electronic household aids, etc. – began to appear and to come down in price. This, they thought, was unlikely to happen for two or three years. They then agreed that the right thing to do was to look for diversification into a less consumer-oriented business situated in the Southtown district.

Ambitious plans for the new subsidiary

It was not surprising, therefore, when, after careful study, Mr Shiner bought Tern's Trucks in January this year for £4m. Mr Tern promptly retired and Mr Shiner, with the aid of professional headhunters, appointed a Mr Jack Push as chief executive of Tern's. Jack Push was 33, a qualified mechanical engineer, had been with a firm of consulting production engineers for four years followed by six years in a very senior management position with a major engineering group.

By early this year Jack Push had drawn up a business plan for Mr Shiner's approval. Here are some extracts:

1.1 The mission for this subsidiary is profitable expansion over the next five years as a vehicle body manufacturer operating to financial objectives which compare with the best in the industry.

1.2 The performance taken as satisfactory is as follows:

Year	0	1	2	3	4
Sales £m	36.0	45.0	54.0	64.0	80.0
Profits £m	2.70	3.60	4.86	6.40	8.00
ROCE %	18.8	20.0	25.0	25.0	25.0
Margin %	7.5	8.0	9.0	10.0	10.0
Capital employed £m	14.4	17.8	19.4	25.6	32.0

(Year 0 is the current year which started on 1 January. All figures in Year 0 Pounds.)

1.5 The broad policy is to exploit the vehicle body market but opportunities in other engineering or associated markets will be exploited if found profitable and capable of integration.

1.7 In view of the need to increase exports the company will seek to establish itself an international image and reputation.

1.9 The broad marketing policy is to achieve the forecast sales by introducing more professional marketing methods, by more aggressive selling and by offering the market the optimum mix of product quality, price, delivery and after-sales services.

2.5 Recognizing that the home market is likely to remain largely static for some years our objective will be to attain one third of sales and contribution from overseas.

2.6 In the home municipal market the policy is to attain an increase in share from 12 per cent now to 33 per cent by Year 4 for our existing range of products and to broaden the range.

2.7 In the commercial sector the aim is to increase our share from 1 per cent to 3 per cent and to broaden the range.

3.6 The overall output of vehicles will rise from 400 to 750 in Year 4.

4.2 The company will manufacture more of the product than at present, will purchase more effectively to gain bulk discounts, and will lengthen production runs and increase batch sizes.

(These policy statements were backed up by several pages of figures showing direct and indirect costs, P & L, balance sheets, capex (capital expenditure is scheduled to be well over £2m this year and again in Year 1), employees, cash flow, etc.)

This document landed on Mr Shiner's desk in May this year. He eyed it without enthusiasm. For one thing, he did not believe the forecasts in 1.2 – not even for the current year let alone the others, especially when he recalled that sales last year were £30m and in the first four months of this year they had shown no increase at all.

Of course, he mused, the losses last year were probably due to old Mr Tern not investing in the business in recent years and beginning to lose his grip on it and Jack Push was now certainly making things hum – he had already recruited a marketing manager and had purchased a small vehicle upholstery business in accordance with policy statement 1.5 – but Mr Shiner couldn't see much improvement in the attributable loss figure so far for this year – the exceptionals would continue at last year's level for another two years at least.

Then a cool four million more capital investment for the next two years with maybe more cash injections after that? No. He decided he could not accept this plan. Very tactfully he asked Push to think again.

The plan rejected

This time he invites you to join Jack Push's planning team to develop a new plan. No doubt you will wish to tackle this in a methodical manner, so start with the corporate objectives. How should these be stated, what indicators should be used? Unusually, it looks as if the most important indicator in this case is the cash flows into and out of Shiners Ltd, the parent company. It is a strange fact, but quite true, that Mr Shiner had not until now made it clear to Jack Push what the situation here really was, namely that Shiners Ltd was happy to invest cash in Tern's for the next two years – up to a total of £2m, but no more – but that Tern's must then come up with a flow of cash by Year 2 or 3 in order to provide cash for the expansion they were expecting at Shiners Ltd.

Mr Shiner now explains to you and Mr Push that he would be prepared to invest in Tern's at the rate of £1m each year, in the expectation that Tern's would then be able to generate at least £1.4m earnings for Shiners for several years – a fair return, he suggests, on the total of £6m that Tern's would then have cost. What he wanted, then, was a cash flow picture as follows:

£m *Year*	0	1	2	3	4
Cash in to and out of Tern's	−5.0	−1.0	+1.4	+1.4	+1.4

Now the forecast. Even if Mr Push does nothing new the attributable losses are unlikely to go much above £700,000 because Tern's is a stable, well-established name in the industry – it ranks seventh in the home market – and many of its products sell steadily at moderate margins. This gives an idea of the size of the gap: there has to be a turnaround in earnings from a minus £700,000 to a positive £1,400,000 within two years. That is Tmin.

Tsat is almost anything that is better or quicker.

The SWOT analysis

Now turn to the internal and external appraisal. Remember, you are trying to find a set of strategies for Tern's as a subsidiary of Shiners.

The promised cash from the parent is obviously a 'strength'. So is the customer loyalty displayed by many local authorites for many of the Tern range of simple refuse collectors, sweepers, gully emptiers and road gritters. There has been a most enthusiastic response to the two new high technology products, both designed by Tom Strachan (Tern's development engineer), namely a motorway service vehicle and a waste disposal vehicle (which both sell for approximately £180,000 at good gross margins) which were launched three years ago. Mr Push, too, must be included among the assets of the company; he is an expert in value engineering, method study and CAD.

Among the weaknesses are the poor factory layout, the aged equipment, the old-fashioned methods, low productivity (even on the production line for the two new vehicles). Jack Push says that to modernize the entire factory would cost £8m; the line for the two new vehicles alone would eat up the whole £2m which Mr Shiner has allocated. The losses look like continuing unless something is done. In addition, Parrishes plc, a company of international status and one of their key competitors, is their sole supplier of chassis. On the other hand, to use two chassis means altering the design of all the bodies and, as it happens, Parrishes have never let them down.

The main threats come from the competition, including Parrishes and three other very large vehicle manufacturers, together with a dozen companies of similar size to Tern's. The variations in government expenditure from year to year is a constant worry. There is plainly a declining market in the UK for medium-sized, medium technology vehicles; the accent is now upon higher technology, better equipment, improved driver productivity (and comfort) and smarter mechanisms.

Vehicles, according to a recent survey, are going to be either very large, or very clever, or both. A forecast from a well-known consultant says that overall vehicles sales volume in units will be static in Europe for many years. An opportunity is provided by the huge demand for simple robust vehicles, such as some of Tern's products, in developing nations – but here the risks of non-payment due to political and economic discontinuities are daunting. Even the Government-backed Export Credit Guarantee is not always available for some of these nations.

Your task is to devise a sequenced set of strategies for Tern's designed to achieve Mr Shiner's Tmins or better.

The financial records

Figure E.1   Tern's Trucks Ltd

Year (Year 0 £s)	−5	−4	−3	−2	−1
Old Products units sold	348	340	379	374	347
Average selling price £	68392	71952	64484	63108	61792
Average gross margin £	25086	27882	25839	23123	18834
New Products units sold	0	0	10	24	51
Average selling price £	0	0	159648	156888	167948
Average gross margin £	0	0	35719	93419	88520
Sales £m	23.80	24.46	26.04	27.37	30.01
Trading Profit	1.96	1.94	2.06	1.90	1.38
Exceptional	0.00	0.00	0.00	0.52	0.72
Operating Profit	1.96	1.94	2.06	1.38	0.66
Interest	0.42	0.24	0.32	0.36	0.57
Profit before tax	1.54	1.70	1.74	1.02	0.09
Tax	0.58	0.76	0.88	0.32	0.60
Profit after tax	0.96	0.94	0.86	0.70	−0.51
Extraordinary	0.07	−0.50	−0.18	−0.52	−0.16
Attributable	1.03	0.44	0.68	0.18	−0.67
Dividends	0.34	0.42	0.44	0.44	0.18
Retained	0.69	0.02	0.24	−0.26	−0.85
Shareholders' Funds	6.56	8.14	7.78	7.26	6.72
Net borrowings	2.34	0.04	2.66	3.80	5.30
Funds Employed	9.22	8.58	10.88	11.48	12.34
Fixed	2.90	2.90	3.94	4.26	4.98
Net Current	6.32	5.68	6.92	7.22	7.36
Capital Employed	9.22	8.58	10.86	11.48	12.34
%					
Trading profit to sales	8.24	7.94	7.91	6.93	4.60
Return on av Cap Empld	22.80	21.80	21.17	12.34	5.54
Net borrow as % Cap Empld	25.38	0.47	24.45	33.10	42.95

Shiners Ltd

(Year 0 £s)					
Sales £m	21.18	25.76	29.28	33.60	40.96
Operating Profit	2.14	2.88	3.68	4.48	5.76
Retained Profit	0.99	1.70	1.98	2.27	1.76

Fixed Assets	10.69	14.11	14.74	17.50	19.81
Working Capital	5.54	5.26	5.01	4.82	4.26
Capital Employed	16.22	19.38	19.74	22.32	24.06
Shareholders Funds	14.78	16.58	19.15	17.38	19.66
Net borrowings	1.44	2.80	0.59	4.94	4.40
Sources of Capital	16.22	19.38	19.74	22.32	24.06
%					
Operating profit to sales	10.12	11.18	12.57	13.33	14.06
Op Profit as % Cap Empld	13.21	14.86	18.64	20.07	23.94
Net borrow as % Cap Emp	8.88	14.45	3.00	22.15	18.28

Tern's Trucks – One Possible Solution

Overall conclusion   What is required is not Mr Push's massively ambitious and capital intensive expansion of Tern's but a low-risk, low-capital, low-volume approach to the specific problems revealed. A possible sequenced set of strategies would be:

- **Strategy 1**   Spend virtually the entire £2m from Shiner Ltd on modernizing the production lines for two new vehicles and employ Mr Push's expertise to improve the layout, etc., in the rest of the factory. It is not unreasonable to expect these measures to contribute virtually the whole of the turnaround from a loss of £700,000 to a profit before tax of approaching £2m, equivalent to the £1.4m target earnings at their rate of tax, etc.
- **Strategy 2**   Exploit the two new products in UK and in developed nations, employing the new marketing director to keep selling prices high rather than going for high volume.
- **Strategy 3**   Instruct the marketing manager and Mr Strachan, the designer, to begin work on a new, medium-sized, high-value vehicle such as airport or aircraft servicing. But this project is not to incur significant expenditure until Year 3 – see below.
- **Strategy 4**   Do nothing about sales to developing nations. (Tern's cannot afford the risk of not getting paid. They have virtually no experience of exporting.) Do nothing about chassis. (Parrishes have not let them down recently, certainly not intentionally. The cost of modifying the design of all the bodies to fit two chassis would be substantial.)
- **Strategy 5**   No further strategic decisions are needed for two years so merely monitor progress. By Year 2 it should be clear whether these strategies have succeeded or not. If they have then it may be possible to go outside for capital to launch the new vehicle or modernize the rest of the factory or whatever. If not then sell Tern's, complete with its new product ready for launch, to provide the cashflow back into Shiners. It is highly questionable whether Shiner should have bought Tern's in the first place.

Further Possible Strategies

When you listed the alternative strategies for Tern's did you include these, in addition to the ones mentioned in the solution?

- Sell freehold on present factory and move to modern, leased factory to make the new products. Use the capital realized in this sale to finance new production equipment.
- Cut working capital.
- Become a vehicle design consulting company.
- Invite someone else (Parrishes?) to manufacture all or some products.
- Develop knock-down kits, agents, joint projects in the Third World.
- Develop a spares, repairs, refurbishment and retrofit business.
- A partial sale of the business.
- Hire a new managing director for Tern's, leave Push to do the engineering.
- Make chassis.
- Purchase chassis from a second supplier.
- Sell out to Parrishes.
- Invite Parrishes to help Tern's to export to Third World.
- Sell upholstery business.
- Use Shiner's leasing knowledge to lease vehicles to local authorities.
- Borrow several million pounds to modernize the entire factory.

Notes

1 What is Corporate Planning?

1. Why not? Whole blocks of flats, complete with waste disposal systems, access roads, laundry, tennis courts, crêches and janitors, are privately run. Why not a whole town?

2. I had just written these words when I heard about the planning methodology of a major London company. They do a *one-year* 'corporate plan' within the framework of a seven-year development plan. Both consist almost entirely of figures. It is a budget, in other words, within a business plan. This, believe it or not, is a highly professional organization with 7,000 employees. Surely no further proof of the confusion surrounding this topic is needed. We corporate planners have certainly caused bedlam and bewilderment around us!

3. A corporate plan is like a goose. Treat it right and it will lay you an endless series of golden eggs labelled 'market plan', 'product plan', 'finance plan', etc. But no one confuses a goose with its eggs – they could hardly be seen as part of the goose.

4. I recall the finance director of a major British company telling me how his chairman came into his office early one morning in a state of great excitement, banged his fist on the desk and exclaimed, 'Power tools, Jerry, power tools!' It had occurred to him the previous evening, watching a television programme, that this was the diversification his company should pursue. Neither the finance director, nor I, could for the life of us see the relevance to the company's business. Thank goodness not all decisions are made like this. Thank goodness some are – see below where I extol the virtues of entrepreneurial autocrats.

5. The company I am discussing here employed several thousand people. It is not just small companies who are dependent on only one customer, supplier or shareholder.

6. See the case of Fulmar Life Assurance. At the end of each chapter I display the relevant sector of this company's corporate plan so you can watch it building up the strategic decisions in Chapter 10. The case in Chapter 12 shows the same progression in even greater detail.

2 Who Should Do It?

1. The view from the chief executive's chair is quite different to anyone else's.

2. An organization based in the east of England had a considerable number of operations in Scotland, but knowing what a keen salmon fisherman the chairman was, none of his colleagues dared to question the economic value of these branches to the company. When I dared to do so I was treated to a long and cogent justification of these activities. I politely referred to the figures showing many of them making losses. 'Ah, but . . .' and off he went again. Nothing can shift a well entrenched autocrat – not friendly advice, not angry shareholders, not outside consultants, not even corporate planning. Autocrats and corporate planning do not mix. Two types of organization do, however, need autocratic management: very small young ones and failing companies in need of a strong man to turn them round. In these I see no role for corporate planning.

3. One of these was a components manufacturer whose management was obsessed by the fact that they were not a 'prime' manufacturer – they felt it was less prestigious to make little bits of vehicle engines rather than engines. By the end of the process the word 'prime' had disappeared completely in favour of three other, far more relevant, opportunities.

4. I particularly enjoyed seeing a recommendation to a very staid and aged textile company to diversify into hotels, leisure, electronics and fish farming. The justification for this advice, which came from a professor at a business school, was that a competitor had recently launched a most successful programme of diversification. The boss there was a young whizz-kid.

5. One of these other divisional managing directors also doubled as the group finance director and as such was responsible for the accounting systems of the group. There was no doubt whatever that he had fixed the system to show his own division in the best light and this had dimmed the performance of the others. One of the decisions in this corporate plan was to appoint a new finance director.

6. I have several times seen organizations decide that one strategic issue is too important to deal with in one exercise. In these cases the company (in one case) decided to put certain strategies into action first and then come back to the most difficult one immediately afterwards: in another, a non-profit-making organization decided to put several urgent strategies into action and then return for a thorough review of its corporate objective which it plainly had to revise fundamentally.

3   Corporate Objectives and Corporate Conduct

1.   Not always! One would think it is perfectly obvious that the moneys in a miners' pension fund should be invested for the enhancement of the pensions for ex-miners. A few years ago the National Union of Mineworkers attempted to argue in the courts that the Mineworkers' Pension Fund (of which they were a trustee) should invest disproportionately in 'energy stocks'. This was in fact a blatant perversion, as the courts recognized, designed to encourage investment, and hence employment, in the mining industry. While this might be an excellent investment policy for the *union* funds it would have been a misuse of the *pension* funds which should plainly be invested to improve pensions, not for creating jobs.

2.   Fraud, misappropriation, misfeasance would be included in my definition of perversion but these form only an insignificant part of what I am discussing.

3.   Whether the beneficiaries are members or employees of the organization (introvert organizations) or outside it (extrovert) is also a factor but, I suspect, a second-order one. Examples of the former are a club, a family business and a worker co-operative; a charity, a public company and a government are examples of the second.

4.   One chief executive I know was determined that his brother should play a full part in the direction of the (large, well-known) family business. 'Even if we go bust,' he told me, 'it is my duty to my family that he should be employed as a most senior director.' They went bust.

4   Objectives for Non-profit-making Organizations

1.   I do not even need, in support of my argument, to quote the old, old cliché: 'If you do not know where you are going, any road will do. And you will *still* not get there!'

2.   I know it does not sound like it, but I am *not* criticizing the performance of these organizations and certainly not their members. In case the point has been missed, I simply do not know whether to criticize them or not.

3.   These sorts of figures always remind me of the drunk who was looking for a coin under a lamp-post, there being no light where he had dropped it. Just because a figure is available or readily collectable does not mean we have to use it. I should not complain too loudly about NPOs doing this, however, since most companies still use 'turnover' as their key indicator when 'profit' is universally recognized as the right one. The wrong one is easy to calculate; the right one is a brute, as we

shall see in the next chapter. I assume this is another manifestation of the ubiquitous Murphy's Law.

4. Not to mention poor old British Leyland saddled with *three* impossible objectives as described earlier.

5. I know of one town management who, a few days after an election, were stunned to receive, from their new political masters, a 103-page diktat describing how they were to run the town for the next five years. This is not quite what I mean by strategy-neutral!

6. Pronounced 'tee min'.

7. I recently saw an aged non-profit-making organization in which the planning team was having great trouble defining its corporate objectives. It has now dawned on the general secretary (but no one else as yet) that the role ascribed to it in society by the Government nearly 60 years ago is no longer valid in the modern world. His problem now is how to – and whether to – discuss this conclusion with his planning team and the sponsoring government department.

5   Setting the Corporate Targets

1. Be careful of inflation here. Inflation was 5 per cent in this case so the 20 per cent ROCE was 'really' 15 per cent and growth was 'really' 6 per cent.

2. Usually they are not! While it is sometimes very difficult it is essential that they are made comparable – some huge decisions are going to be taken later, using these figures. I recall the case of an integrated forestry company in New Zealand in which the forests and the timber operation both appeared to be making losses and only the final stage – furniture – was profitable. It was all an illusion, however; having reviewed their transfer prices it turned out to be the other way round!

6   Forecasts and Gap Analysis

1. While I was working for an Italian wine company we needed to use a particular statistical forecasting technique. We invited one of the world's leaders in this field – a German professor – to assist. We could not understand why his technique kept showing a declining market for brandy. Everything we knew suggested it was going to go on rising at about the same rate as for Mercedes cars. We then discovered that he was not only a vegetarian but also harboured radical opinions on the consumption of alcohol.

2. One company made its forecasts which showed that, on present strategies, profits would remain at the current level for about five

years. Unfortunately, they had neglected to set themselves a target so no gap was calculated and the current strategies were left unchanged. As soon as they adopted my process the gap appeared and they started hunting around for something a little more ambitious! I mention this because most companies set targets but do not make the forecasts. This one did the opposite, which at least is original. You need both, I am afraid!

7 Strengths and Weaknesses Analysis

1. I do not mean to imply that they should necessarily compete with competitors. I do mean they should *compare* themselves with their competitors.
2. I have seen the corporate planning process act as the final straw that led to a request from his colleagues for the chief executive to resign. In one case they asked the chairman to act, which he did with suave efficiency. In another the two sons of a very aged and obstinate chairman took him to see the director of their bank, who happened to be a cousin. As the old man entered his office the director said, by prior arrangement of course, 'Good Heavens, Uncle George, I thought you had retired years ago.' Having sowed the seed he then very gently refused the loan until (1) George had been elevated to Honorary Life President of the company (thus safeguarding his status in the local community) and (2) the oldest son had been nominated as chief executive.

8 Threats and Opportunities

1. If I may add one economic comment of my own, I think some companies have not fully realized how wealthy we are in the developed nations. There are a million millionaires in the USA alone, that is, one in every couple of hundred Americans is a millionaire. The accumulation of equities, gold, land, property, and pension funds in the world is staggering and every year it grows by a further perceptible amount. The implication for each company is different, but for many it means that price is becoming less important, sometimes much less important, than quality, reliability, delivery, design, and other elements of added value. My experience suggests this has not yet sunk in with many managers.

10   Selecting the Strategies

1.   When working as a member of a client's planning team I often experience The Fog myself. I occasionally even wonder whether, this time, my system is going to let us down. The feeling of relief when The Fog dissipates and the strategies shine out clear and precise, is worthy of more than a footnote!
2.   Assuming a maximum of 200 people in each profit centre (beyond that size lies an increasing risk of encountering the problems we are trying to avoid) there may be a limit to the number of profit centres any group or umbrella organization could manage. If that means that few organizations exceeding, say, 200,000 employees could survive, so be it.

11   Evaluation, Action Plans and Monitoring

1.   The consultant remarked to the chief executive that these two errors threw severe doubts on the competence of the team in general and the production and finance directors in particular. This debacle, with the accompanying loss of confidence, was one of the reasons for the choice of strategies described below.

12   The Woodcock Group

1.   Even this lengthy description is itself a heavily abbreviated version of what really happened. All names, figures, locations and products have been disguised.
2.   The finance director certainly thought that this lack of finance knowledge was an elephant of major proportions. He wanted the whole culture of the group swung towards being a profit-driven organization, as the jargon had it. As will be seen, the non-financial members of the team became extremely profit-driven by the end of the exercise, as they all agreed.
3.   This was the second major difference with the conclusions of the seminar where 'ventures in USA' was also a major strategy.

Bibliography

Ansoff, Igor H., *Implanting Strategic Management* (Englewood Cliffs, NJ: Prentice-Hall, 1987).

Clifford, Donald K. and Cavanagh, Richard E., *The Winning Performance: How America's High Growth Mid-size Companies Succeed* (New York: Bantam Books, 1985).

Doz, Yves, *Strategic Management In Multinational Companies* (Oxford: Pergamon Press, 1986).

Fawn, John and Cox, Bernard, *Corporate Planning in Practice* (London: ICMA, 1986).

Freeman, Edward R., *Strategic Management – a Stakeholder Approach* (Marshfield, Mass: Pitman, 1984).

Gardner, James R., Rachlin, Robert and Sweeny, Allen, *Handbook of Strategic Planning* (New York: John Wiley, 1986).

Hax, Arnold C., *Readings on Strategic Management* (Cambridge, Mass: Ballinger, 1984).

Henderson, Bruce, *Logic of Business Strategy* (Cambridge, Mass: Ballinger, 1984).

Hrebiniak, L. G. and Joyce, W. F. *Implementing Strategy* (London: Collier Macmillan, 1984).

Hussey, David, *Corporate Planning Theory and Practice* Oxford: Pergamon Press, 1982).

Hussey, David, *Corporate Planning* (Gee BIM and ICA, 1985).

Johnson, Gerry and Scholes, Kevan, *Exploring Corporate Strategy* (Englewood Cliffs, NJ: Prentice-Hall, 1984).

Jones, Harry, *Preparing Company Plans. A Workbook* (Aldershot: Gower, 1983).

Lamb, R. B., *Competitive Strategic Management* (Englewood Cliffs, NJ: Prentice-Hall, 1984).

McNamee, Patrick B., *Tools and Techniques for Strategic Management* (Oxford: Pergamon Press, 1985).

Peters, Thomas J. and Waterman, Robert J., *In Search of Excellence. Lessons from America's Best Run Companies* (New York: Harper & Row, 1982).

Porter, Michael E., *Competitive Strategy: Techniques for Analyzing Industries and Competitors* (New York: Free Press, 1980).

Porter, Michael E., *Competitive Advantage* (New York: Free Press, 1985).

Power, Daniel J., *Strategic Management Skills* (Reading, Mass: Addison Wesley 1986).

Rowe, Alan J., Mason, Richard and Dickel, Karl E., *Strategic Management: A Methodological Approach* (Reading, Mass: Wesley 1985).

Sloma, Richard S., *No-Nonsense Planning* (London: Collier Macmillan, 1984).

Smith, John Grieve, *Strategic Planning in Nationalised Industries* (London: Macmillan, 1984).

Steiner, George A., *The New C E D* (New York: Macmillan, 1983).

Taylor, Bernard and Hussey, David, *The Realities of Planning* (Oxford: Pergamon Press, 1982).

Index